TAILGATE
TO HEAVEN

TAILGATE TO HEAVEN

A British NFL Fan Tackles America

Adam Goldstein

Potomac Books
Washington, D.C.

Library of Congress Cataloging-in-Publication Data
Goldstein, Adam.
  Tailgate to heaven : a British NFL fan tackles America / Adam Goldstein.
    p. cm.
  Includes bibliographical references.
  ISBN 978-1-59797-692-3 (hardcover : alk. paper)
  ISBN 978-1-59797-868-2 (electronic)
  1. Football—Social aspects—United States. 2. Tailgate parties—United States. 3. Football fans—United States—Social life and customs. 4. Goldstein, Adam—Travel. 5. Football fans—Great Britain—Anecdotes. I. Title.
  GV951.G65 2012
  796.332—dc23

                                                      2012016052

Printed in the United States of America on acid-free paper that meets the American National Standards Institute Z39-48 Standard.

Potomac Books
22841 Quicksilver Drive
Dulles, Virginia 20166

First Edition

10 9 8 7 6 5 4 3 2 1

For my loving and supportive parents, Sue and Harvey

Thanks for buying me that American football and supporting my NFL passion!

When I was a kid I told my parents that I would one day climb a mountain.

This is the story of that "climb."

CONTENTS

FOREWORD

During the course of my career covering the National Football League for British media organisations such as the BBC Sky Sports and NFLUK.com, I have often found myself in the United States.

I've been to America literally dozens of times to attend mini camps, training camps, regular-season games, playoff contests, and even Super Bowls.

On the occasions when time and covering great distances has been an issue, I have just about tolerated internal flights across the United States. When you're interviewing Bill Belichick in Boston on a Wednesday and have an appointment with the Tampa Bay Buccaneers head coach Raheem Morris the following day, you have little option but to hop on a plane.

My preferred choice of travel, however, is to jump in a car and enjoy a little NFL road trip, particularly during training camps or mini camps when I am taking in several teams in one go.

There is no greater feeling than carrying out a bunch of interviews with one team, getting behind the wheel, and then being on your own timetable as you head off to the next club. You're free to stop and start as you please, there is no seat-belt sign telling you to sit down, and you can sing along to the tunes coming from the radio without offending anyone around you.

I have done that kind of trip on several occasions—New York (Jets) to Baltimore to Washington to Philadelphia to New York (Giants) was one East Coast tour I conducted in the early summer of 2009.

A year before that, I started out in New York with the Jets; drove to Bethlehem, Pennsylvania, to attend training camp with the Philadelphia Eagles; and then enjoyed the most wonderful four-and-a-half-hour jaunt through the Catskill Mountains en route to Albany, New York, to catch up with the Giants.

As I sat eating at a roadside diner in the mountains as the sun began to set, I couldn't have cared less that it would have been quicker by plane. This was my way of travelling.

In the summer of 2006, I embarked on a mammoth driving adventure, starting off in Tampa, Florida, with a visit to the Buccaneers. Over the course of ten days, I drove from Tampa to Atlanta, Georgia, to Jackson, Mississippi, and on to Dallas, Texas.

I drove through rainstorms, tyre-melting heat, and thunder of biblical proportions, and none of that bothered me one little bit—I had a blast. Sure, I was dog tired at the end of every long day spent behind the wheel, but it was a lot of fun.

At the conclusion of that monster road trip, I wondered what it would be like to keep going—to cover as much of the United States as was humanly possible, taking in as many NFL teams and games as I could.

I have to admit it was nothing more than a fleeting thought and I soon returned to reality, heading off to the airport and catching my transatlantic flight back to England, family life, and the routines of work.

I never quite had the guts to undertake such an adventure, especially not without the comfort and security of a decent expense account, prearranged car rentals, and some of the nicest hotels you could wish to spend a night in.

But Adam Goldstein did have the passion, courage, and determination to live out a dream that many of us gridiron fans in Europe have secretly harboured over the years. One fan, one season, and forty games, including thirty-seven in the NFL, taking in thirty-six different stadiums.

It is quite a story and one that caught my attention in the United Kingdom. I have interviewed Adam for NFLUK.com, and we also had him on our NFL show on BBC Radio last season. What comes through first and foremost is that he has an undying passion for the NFL.

But what struck me more than anything else is that he is perfectly normal. The first time I met him I expected to be confronted with a complete madman—what else was I supposed to think of a man who quit a perfectly decent job in London, sold his house, and left his beautiful girlfriend behind in another continent?

Adam simply felt he had to live out his dream or spend a lifetime wondering "What if?" and it's hard to be critical of that thought process.

If you love road trips and the NFL, this book will be right up your alley. You'll laugh at the adventures detailed in the coming pages, and you will rejoice in the way Americans from sea to shining sea welcomed Adam into their ranks, particularly during the much-celebrated pre-game tailgate parties.

You might even cry—but only if you happen to catch sight of Adam's credit card bill.

Most of all, you will be impressed by one man's desire to risk everything and turn his back on what was a relatively normal and, dare I say it, run-of-the-mill life to live out a dream and do something truly amazing.

In these pages you will find Adam's remarkable story, and I'm sure you will enjoy reading it as much as I did.

Neil Reynolds
NFL presenter for Sky Sports,
writer for NFLUK.com, and author of *Pain Gang*

FOREWORD

The origins of tailgating are a matter of great debate. No, really. Among those that care, which according to some sources is an estimated 50 million party-loving Americans, this tradition of grilling before gridiron games goes back as far as the first intercollegiate football game between Rutgers and Princeton, circa 1869, which is a very long time ago for us Yanks.

It's probably one of the most common questions I get asked, right after the obligatory, "How do I get your job?" See, I'm a professional tailgater (one of a handful), and as somebody who has lived in this world of tailgating almost entirely for the past six years, I have come to have the distinction of being considered one of the foremost experts on the topic. It is such a narrow and specialized field of expertise that it's a little like being the foremost authority on something like . . . malt vinegar.

And for many, tailgating is something like malt vinegar. It's something they enjoy very much, and would certainly miss if it were no longer there, but something that they have never really given much thought to at all.

For these people, if you ask them why they tailgate, they would probably answer that they just "always have." Many will tell you a story about their father or grandfather bringing them out to their first tailgate, and talk about Sunday afternoons spent tossing a ball and eating burgers in a parking lot. Like that malt vinegar on the table in your favorite pub, tailgating has just always been there.

But tailgating has not always been like tailgating is today. It has grown, changed, and morphed from a simple beer or bite to eat before heading into the game, into a recreational pastime all its own.

I have a theory about why tailgating has taken on such an extreme transformation, and it stems from two basic factors: 1. Most tailgaters are men (current data from the first Tailgate Census projects that more than 75 percent of tailgaters are male) and 2. Generally, tailgaters are sports fans first. And, as sports fans they have a competitive nature that compels them to be better than the other guy. Put these two things together, throw in a dash of cross-town rivalry and a few pours of alcohol, and you've got the recipe for one of the biggest, baddest cases of keeping up with the Joneses ever seen.

Still, the mystery remains—why, in recent decades, has tailgating blown up in America with all the intensity of a hibachi grill left beneath an unattended car?

When I first met Adam "Jumbotron" Goldstein in person at Super Bowl LXIII in Tampa, having coached and encouraged him through his whole crazy questing season, I knew that he was the perfect person to answer this question. As a cultural "outsider," raised in the land of soccer and rugby, bangers and mash and warm beer, he had become enamored (like most American boys his age) of the Super Bowl–shuffling Chicago Bears.

He had put his life on hold and come to America on a mission to visit the entire NFL, and he came to experience what it meant to be an NFL fan of the home team (something he, as a Londoner, had never truly known).

The yang to my yin, while I was a fan of tailgating who unexpectedly fell in love with the bone-breaking brutality of football, Adam was a football fan swept off his feet by the warmth, generosity, and unexplainable hospitality of the strangers he met in a parking lot.

Throughout his travels, and in the pages of this book, Adam approaches the subject with the curiosity of an anthropologist and a comic's eye for the absurd, as he tries to make sense of—and make a case for—American football, and the world of tailgating.

Karen DiEugenio
author of *I Got Your Tailgate Party Right Here!*

PREFACE
My Team

Football is a team sport and I could not have done this trip without the help of my teammates.

The Team
Me. Quarterback. Think Peyton Manning of the Indianapolis Colts.
"On the football field. The mythology of the quarterbacks on their journey. There is nothing else like it in all of sports."[1] The quarterback (QB) is the offensive captain and the on-field master general and has been described as "one part gun-slinger, one part field general, who would control the action and become the main protagonist in the drama of the game."[2]

Peyton Manning organises his team, and famously changes the play with his many audibles to avoid angry linebackers. I organised my trip, changed my schedule with my own audibles, and avoided big hits too (but mine were the big trucks on the road).

My Dad, Harvey. Head Coach. Think Lovie Smith of the Chicago Bears.
"In the game of American football, the notion of coach as father figure was not created by accident." Sometimes I would listen to my Dad's coaching, and other times, like an arrogant young quarterback, I would stick to my guns.

My Mum, Susan. Watergirl. Think Katharyn Richt of the University of Georgia Bulldogs.
At home, my Mum would make sure my friends (the players) were well fed and refreshed. Katharyn Richt is wife of Mark Richt, the head coach of the University of Georgia's football team and is the team's "Watergirl."

Baz "The Biggler." Centre. Think Olin Kreutz, the former Chicago Bear and New Orleans Saint.

The Biggler created my website and was constantly supportive. The centre helps protect the QB at all times, and is often someone who is humble, efficient, and takes a lot of hits without ever complaining. Baz has all of those attributes.

Bertie "The Princess." Cheerleader.

My sister was always supportive. When I got burnt out, she kept me in high spirits by asking how "my year holiday" was going. Not once would she call it a "trip" or a footballing pilgrimage, grrrr.

Justin "The Ripper Shroader." Wide Receiver. Think Chad Ochocinco of the New England Patriots.

A QB needs a good "go-to" wide receiver, and I could always rely on Justin, a die-hard Miami Dolphins fan, to "make the catch" and help me out in any way. He always let me stay in his apartment in New York City, as well as store hundreds of my "Adam's Football Trip" t-shirts and merchandise there. Plus, he always got me lunch when I was in the city.

Neal. Tight End. Think Rob Gronkowski of the New England Patriots.

Neal is from Chicago but lives in Las Vegas and is a party animal. Neal joined me for three weeks in the second half of my trip, just as I was burning out. And like a Pro-Bowl tight end, he is multiskilled. Neal helped out with driving, taking photographs, filming, finding friends to stay with, and making sure we had a fun time.

Steph aka Stephalicious. Mascot. Think Jaxson de Ville of the Jacksonville Jaguars.

Steph is my beautiful and supportive girlfriend, whom I left behind in London for three quarters of the trip. Like a good mascot, she always cheered me up when times were rough, and came out for the last month of the trip.

Traci. Running Back. Think Larry Johnson of Kansas City Chiefs.

Traci lives in Chicago and is a huge Kansas City Chiefs fan. She always allowed me to stay in her apartment, even when she was not in town.

Mike B. Punter. Think Mike Scifres of the San Diego Chargers.
Mike B. lives in New York City, though he is not a football fan. Mike is the punter because punters do not even have to like football to do well in the NFL, but when they are on the field they need to be reliable—just like Mike B.

Mike P. Kicker. Think Rhys Lloyd of the New York Giants.
Like Rhys Lloyd, Mike is English and loves soccer. Mike is a lifelong West Ham Football Club fan, and always respected and protected my lust for the NFL, even when the rest of my schoolmates teased me for it. Mike used to play goalkeeper for our high school, and his booming kick would have made him an excellent NFL kicker. Now he lives in Los Angeles, where he put me up for several nights.

Hans. Wide Receiver. Think Lee Evans of the Baltimore Ravens.
Hans is from Buffalo but lives just outside Detroit. Lee Evans is a "deep threat" receiver, and when I was facing the prospect of spending my first Thanksgiving alone, Hans came to the rescue and allowed me to stay at his house for the holidays.

Izzy "The Dizzy." Left Tackle. Think Michael Oher of Baltimore Ravens.
The left tackle protects the QB from the blind side. Brooklyn-based Izzy is not an NFL fan, but more important she was always "protective" of me when others were not. She also survived a rather torrid drive to Foxborough (Massachusetts) and kept the QB calm in times of stress.

Jay "The Tailgate Guy" and Karen "The Blacktop Babe" DiEugenio.
Tailgaters.
Jay and Karen reside in Southern California, yet they have not stopped tailgating across America for six straight seasons. They helped me out in so many ways, even though I did not meet them until Super Bowl weekend. They prefer to be on the blacktop rather than the field, where they create the tastiest tailgate feast imaginable.

1
Why?

The biggest risk you can take is to take no risks.
—Anonymous

A re you mad?" my British seatmate asked. I was on board a flight from London to New York on September 1, 2008. I had just quit my job, sold my flat in London, and left my beautiful girlfriend at home, all in pursuit of my Ultimate Footballing Odyssey. In short, I wanted to see one live game at every NFL franchise during the 2008 regular season. I had planned to see a monumental 35 NFL games in 17 weeks, taking in 33 different stadiums, including games in Canada and London. My seatmate's face went from shock, to intrigue, to denial, then back to shock. "But . . . but *why?*" she asked. My usual answer to this question: "Well, why the hell not?" But I was on a transatlantic flight and I had time to kill.

My Dad had always gone to soccer games while growing up in East London. He supported Tottenham Hotspur and went to their stadium, White Hart Lane, weekly. My Dad watched games in "the good old days" before Britain's economic tailspin of the 1970s and '80s, which spilled onto the soccer terraces, exploding into violence and "soccer hooligan" mayhem. The "English were the world's leading producer of deranged fans,"[1] said Franklin Foer, who wrote *How Football Explains the World*.

In 1989, during this chaotic period, I was nine years old and my Dad took me to see my local team, the exotic-sounding Leyton Orient Football Club, a then fourth division team that played at Brisbane Road, only three miles from where I grew up in Redbridge, North East London/Essex. In the U.K., and most domestic soccer leagues around the world, teams are relegated and promoted from division to division each season, no matter how "Big" your club they can still be relegated. The three bottom teams get relegated each season and three from the division below get promoted. There are four professional divisions (92 clubs) in the English and Welsh league, and as of the 2011–2012 season Leyton Orient were in the third division. However, because of promotion, in theory a "pub team" could keep getting promoted all the way to the Premiership. There is also a nationwide knockout cup (the FA Cup) that can involve up to 762 clubs including the professional 92, whereby a team of amateurs can, and sometimes do, face professional teams and knock them out. This is known as giant-killing.

Two minutes before the final whistle at the Leyton Orient game, my Dad told us we were leaving the stadium. I was confused. The O's were winning and I had anticipated seeing the players celebrate on the field with the joyous fans. My Dad rushed me out of the stadium, along with the rest of the crowd. It just didn't make any sense. Were we under alien attack? Was there a fire? Was the building crumbling around us? Perhaps my Dad wanted us to avoid hitting the bottleneck of fans that were cramming up the exits, or perhaps was he trying to avoid stadium traffic?

We weaved outside and onto the street. I heard a booming sound, growing louder and louder, and closer. Two thousand people came charging down the residential street, hollering profanities, throwing bottles, and smashing in peoples' front gardens. This molten lava of anger spread out away from the volcanic stadium and I realised that I was in the hot midst of a football riot.

"But Dad," I bleated, as he rushed me to safety. "We *won* the game!" I was trying to rationalise the hooligan mentality. If the Orient had lost I could have semi-understood the fans being upset, but to have won and *then* smash in someone's front garden just seemed like madness.

I was confused. These were the fans that I had just spent 88 minutes with, cheering with, laughing with, and standing in the cold with. Now they were rampaging down the street, destroying anything in their path. "But *I support* Orient, Dad!" I continued to whimper. "*They* don't care who you support, those bastards!" My Dad rarely swears, so I knew things were bad.

We got through the door of my home, frazzled, but amazingly in one piece. "Did'ya have a good time?" my Mum asked. "I'll put the kettle on." I couldn't remember a single moment of the game—not a corner kick, a good pass, a free kick, or even the goals. The sheer power of the riot bulldozed any of the "good" out of my mind. I could only remember being scared for my life. I could not understand the need for such violence.

Before 1989 more than 100 people had died at the hands of soccer hooligans in England. Sadly, it wasn't until the Hillsborough disaster in April 1989 that the British government addressed the problem. In that horrific game, Liverpool fans, who were in the standing-only section known as the pen, were grossly overcrowded. On that day, 765 fans were injured and 96 were crushed to death as they were pressed up against the metal cage that was designed to stop the "hooligans" from invading the pitch. In the 20 years since that disaster, a lot has changed in the English soccer world, (even Leyton Orient have moved up a division!). The standing terraces were abolished and hooliganism for the most part has started to decrease.

As a child, I did not want to be a part of this unhinged, barbaric culture. Luckily, Channel 4, then the "alternative" network, had begun beaming American football into British living rooms on Sunday nights.

The National Football League was already a mainstream sport in America, but in the United Kingdom it was new and exciting. Channel 4's chief executive, Jeremy Isaacs remarked that American football "appealed to us both as a fierce new addition to British sport and as an exotic spectacle."[2] I noticed that often, after scoring, the NFL player would spontaneously burst into a dance or a small medley with his friends. Pretty girls with pom-poms performed back flips and choreographed dance routines on the sidelines. The Chicago Bears had a song and dance recorded for their Super Bowl XX appearance, their famous "Super Bowl Shuffle." It seemed so unlike the violent spectacle I had experienced at Leyton Orient.

I didn't even know what the NFL initials stood for, but I sat glued to the telly every Sunday. On January 26, 1986, three years before my jarring first live soccer game, William "The Refrigerator" Perry and all of his 382 pounds rolled into the end zone for a touchdown, as the Chicago Bears beat the New England Patriots on Super Bowl Sunday. In literally three years, the estimated NFL audience went from 750,000 viewers in the United Kingdom to over three million. I was a five-year-old then, and had never seen humans dressed like gladiators colliding into each other, play after play, and then springing up like they were averse to pain.

The same year the Bears stampeded to their Super Bowl victory, Liverpool FC fans were involved in a stampede that caused 39 deaths. As a result of the tragedy, all British soccer teams were banned from the European competitions for five years, but could continue with their domestic league and cup competitions, and because of its tainted name, British soccer was hardly shown on TV. They did, however, show Italian soccer. The FA Cup was shown but live league (premiership) matches were not shown until 1990 when cable (Sky) bought the rights. Soccer teams enter several competitions each year: the domestic league and two domestic cups. If a team either wins a cup or comes high in the league, they then qualify to play mid-week matches in the European league (Champions League and Europa League) the following season. Because of the disaster in Liverpool British teams were not allowed to play in the midweek European games, regardless if they had qualified or not. John Bromley, the head of sport for the more mainstream network channel ITV at the time, said that without British soccer on TV "suddenly 'The Refrigerator,' William Perry, was a bigger name than Gary Lineker, Chicago Bears better known than Arsenal amongst the kids. Football made a big mistake—you must never go off the box."[3]

My favourite player was running back Walter "Sweetness" Payton, who played all of his thirteen seasons for the Chicago Bears between 1975 and 1987, only missing one game in his celebrated career, which was in his rookie year and this decision was down to his assistant coach—pretty impressive considering the average NFL career lasts just a handful of years. He may not have been the fastest running back, but he made up for it with heart, tenacity, hard work, and determination. He could run, throw, catch, and block, and is often hailed as the greatest NFL player. He even received a standing ovation when he played an away game against the Bears' fierce rivals, the Green Bay Packers.

Sweetness could dance gleefully around defenders, jump over them, stiff-arm them to the ground, or simply run right over them. Players and fans alike could not predict his runs. Payton was the star of the Bears (and the NFL) for many years while they were an awful team. In his autobiography, *Never Die Easy*, he said that his style "didn't come from athletics. It came from playing a childhood game."[4] He played with a sense of fun that only a "childhood game" could emit. "They paid me to play football," Payton said, "but I would have played for nothing because I had fun."[5] I remember once seeing Payton literally somersault over a defender to score a touchdown. A five-year-old child can easily connect with fun, no matter how far away it is, or what country it comes from. Fun is fun. Rioting clearly isn't. And that's how I became a Bears fan.

Passionate football fan and writer Michael Tunison, who wrote *The Football Fan's Manifesto*, said that "picking a team, is the most important decision of your life" and he says this needs to be done by "your eighth birthday."[6] So I was already slightly ahead of the game by picking the Bears when I was five years old. The fact that I could "pick" any NFL team was incredibly freeing because in soccer one is more or less born into a fan base, either based on location, family tradition, politics, or sometimes religion.

I was lucky enough to pick a team that I later would discover had such wonderful fans. Payton himself said that he couldn't "imagine a city in the league where the fans and the team are as linked as they are in Chicago. . . . Chicago is a Bears town."[7] In Payton's autobiography, Mike "Da Coach" Ditka, Payton's head coach when the 1985 Bears won the Super Bowl, drew comparisons between Payton and another Chicago sporting legend, Michael Jordan. Ditka felt that although Jordan was "revered, Payton was loved. . . . Jordan never made the same connection with the fans, [because] Jordan is almost like a god."[8]

Former Kansas City Chiefs player and now English professor Michael Oriard said the Bears "captured the public fancy, as a paradoxical collection of hip-hop throwbacks."[9] They had plenty of larger than life characters. The huge rookie, William "The Refrigerator" Perry; the quarterback, Jim McMahon, famed for his funky '80s headbands and wrap-around sunglasses; the bright-eyed, hard-hitting linebacker, Mike Singletary; and of course the elusive Walter Payton—all under the guidance of Ditka, the gum-popping, sunglass-wearing, ex-Bear with the slicked-back hair and famous moustache. This team was "fun to watch and had so much personality and character,"[10] said Walter's wife, Connie Payton, and I couldn't have agreed with her more.

Watching the game was as if Marvel comics had come to life in my lounge and its heroes were playing sports instead of saving the world. After scoring, these huge muscular men in full body gladiatorial armour would then dance. It was surreal, yet magic. In honour of Michael Jackson, in July 2009 NFL.com listed its top ten list of post-touchdown dance moves: the squirrel, the chicken, the sack, the Pom Poms, the Beyoncé, the dirty bird, Cincinnati Bengals running back Ickey Woods's creation the "Ickey Shuffle," the funky chicken, and the Riverdance, but the winner was Donovan McNabb's "Moonwalk."

Many players have staged fun celebrations that have polarised fans. Some, like myself, love them, while others see it as disrespectful. Players can get fined for "excessive showboating." Former wide receiver Terrell Owens has had several contentious celebrations: He took a pen out of his shoe to sign a ball for a fan, once grabbed pom-poms from a cheerleader to dance, used the ball as a pillow to sleep on, and controversially spiked the ball on the Dallas Cowboys' sacred midfield star.

Meanwhile, New England Patriots and former Bengal's flashy wide receiver Chad Johnson, who officially changed his last name to Ochocinco in 2008 ("Ochocinco" is the number 85, his jersey number, in Spanish), is unsurprisingly never one to be outdone. After scoring, he has dropped down on one knee and mock proposed to a cheerleader, used the end-zone pylon as a golf putter, performed CPR on the ball, and put on a yellow Hall of Fame jacket saying "Future H.o.F 20??" Johnson and Owens (who both played for the Cincinnati Bengals in 2010), however, were both outfoxed by former wide receiver Joe Horn, who hid a cell phone in the padding of the goalposts to make a post-touchdown mobile call.

In 2005, the league outlawed the use of props in celebrations and demanded that players stay on their feet, which at the very least promotes dancing—perhaps the NFL sees game-day Sundays as a place to audition or rehearse for the show *Dancing with the Stars*, which has featured current or ex-NFL players in 10 of its 14 seasons. Emmitt Smith, Hines Ward, and Donald Driver have all won, while Jerry Rice, Jason Taylor, and Warren Sapp have all been runners-up. Despite Chad Ochocinco's fine dancing in the end zone, he only got to fourth position in the show. Players now have seven seconds to celebrate but this must be done "tastefully" or they risk a "showboating" fine.

Payton, however, left his fancy footwork on the field, saying that he "never appreciated the guys that would do little jigs in the end zone."[11] For him, football "was about playing the game, [and] not drawing attention to yourself." Although I can respect that, I and many other NFL fans still love fun and creative celebrations.

When I was in primary school, I wanted to imitate the dancing NFL players and I enjoyed nothing more than throwing and catching the pigskin and then performing my own post-touchdown dance moves. But although the rest of the country had been hit with NFL fever, I was struggling to find other kids my age willing to play American football, and my dancing skills were put on hold.

The day after my ninth birthday, I confidently strutted up to school with the bright new American football my parents bought me, equipped with John Elway's signature. But I got teased for bringing in a "funny-shaped" ball. The other kids laughed at me, kicked my ball, and got annoyed with its unpredictable bounce. They didn't know or care for John Elway, and carried on blasting soccer balls at each other as hard as they could.

Like any good Dad, mine took a keen interest in his son's passion, and in 1990 he got us tickets for the pre-season game between the New Orleans Saints and the Oakland Raiders at Wembley Stadium. My Dad had spent the week leading up to the game doing his homework and tried explaining to me the rules of the game using bottles of ketchup and mustard. The rules didn't settle in, but I still loved the spectacle of the sport without knowing fully what was happening on the field. All I knew is that to score you have to get the ball into the opponent's end zone (and to be honest that's all you really need to know).

My Dad and I opted to root for the Saints. The Raiders' famous pirate image scared me a little, and my Dad really likes the jazz music from New Orleans. My Dad bought me a Saints hat, t-shirt, pennant, and a game-day programme. I had never seen a pennant before and thought just how "American" that small triangular piece of felt was.

When we first sat down we were surrounded by Oakland Raiders fans, who had a much bigger fan base than the Saints did in London. At the time I had not even heard of the New Orleans Saints but shops had been selling Raiders hats and jackets in London for some years, partly because they are iconically menacing. I looked around and only saw silver and black. I thought we had sat in the wrong section. Why would my Dad do this to me? Why had he gone to the trouble of studying the rules of the game and then get us tickets in the Raiders section?

This made me nervous because at soccer matches the fans supporting different teams have to sit apart from each other, and not just by a row or two, but in clearly delineated sections, sometimes separated by police guards and wire fencing. As recently as May 2010, after winning the game, even the away team York FC *players* had to retreat into their own fan section to hide from the onslaught of missiles from the home Luton FC fans, who had blocked the tunnel that lead to the players' dressing rooms. In that same week, the stadium security in Philadelphia seemed more prepared as a 17-year-old Phillies fan ran onto the field and controversially got stunned by a Taser gun.

Writer Clay Travis spent the 2006 season going to see a home football game at every college in the South Eastern Conference (SEC) where home and away fans sit in separate sections. Yet he was shocked to discover at Alabama's stadium, that the student section is "separated from the regular fans by a chain-link fence. This makes zero sense."[12] In the U.K. a fence would be shocking not because of its existence, but that it would not be a big enough barrier between fans.

At Wembley, I felt embarrassed and very small in that sea of black and silver. Where was the Saints section? The brim of my spiffy new Saints baseball cap was still flat and the gold of the fleur-de-lis Saints logo made me stand out like a cheesy tourist in a rough area. I felt left out.

Yet, my despair at Wembley amongst the Raiders fans started to evaporate. Come kickoff time, the few Saints fans in my section cheered. Surprisingly, the Raiders fans did not retaliate by striking them with an elbow or spitting on them. They just stayed quiet until it was their time to cheer. My confidence grew and I was soon shouting and cheering for the players. I realised why there were no fences or police separating the fans. There was no "us and them," we were all together as NFL fans, just rooting for different teams. Some wore black and gold for the Saints, plenty wore black and silver for the Raiders, while the rest wore jerseys of other NFL teams that were not even playing. I was as happy as a boy could be.

Starting in 1986 and continuing for seven years, the NFL brought two teams to London for a pre-season exhibition game each summer. The first game was a sell-out. By 1990, attendances did dip, but still 61,722 fans attended in 1990, which is an immense crowd for a 10-year-old to experience, especially when I thought I was the only Brit who was an American football fan. It's just a shame none of these fans went to my school.

"Did'ya have a good time?" my Mum asked when we got home. "I'll put the kettle on." It was so much more than a sport. There were fireworks, cheerleaders, mascots, and big players with huge shoulder pads and helmets running full speed into one another, yet there was grace, agility, and skill, as well as power and strength. It was un-human, outlandish, brash, and colourful—and I loved it.

I didn't think two sets of fans could actually sit together, side by side, wear their teams' colours, and be passionate and vocal without swearing, cursing, or striking the opposing fans right next to them. This "integrated fandemonium" was an epiphany.

"Did'ya have a good time?" my Mum asked again. I had fallen asleep in the car on the way back from Wembley. My Dad and I had lost our old Ford Cortina in the car park. We had both sworn we parked it on grass. We waited until *every* car in the car park had gone. With a warm hot dog in our hands dripping with mustard, ketchup, and onions, we finally found the car on concrete.

I tried to answer my Mother, but my throat was sore from screaming, my body was shattered from the adrenaline, and my eyes were tired from spending two hours looking for the car in the dark. There was no riot after the game, but my body felt like it had been in one . . . in a good way. With the little energy I had left in my young body, I blurted out the events of the day: Walking up to the famous twin towers of Wembley, the roar of the crowd when the players came out, the fireworks at the start of the game, the wondrous halftime show, the touchdowns, the touchdown celebrations, the cheerleaders (though I didn't speak too much about them as I was still only 10 and discussing girls in front of my Mum weirded me out a little), the crazy Raiders fans, and the food.

"So, who won then?" she asked. "Ummm . . ." I didn't actually know who won. Did it even matter? Would my day have changed? At this point I realised that American football is not about the results, it is not about the players wearing funny helmets and knocking seven bells out of each other, it is not about the actual sport on the field or whether you know the rules or not, it is simply about having *fun*. Doesn't every 10-year-old want to have fun? In fact doesn't *everyone*, no matter what the age, want to have *fun*? The famous NFL commentator John Madden said that "not only did the Bears have fun—they made football fun for the whole country. William [The Refrigerator] Perry in the backfield was like everybody's hero."[13] I don't remember anyone asking me if I had "fun" after seeing any kind of sport in the U.K. At soccer games, apart from avoiding hooligans, the game's end result determined whether or not I was happy (win), angry and/or upset (loss), or indifferent and frustrated (tie). I remember the intensity and passion, but fun? It's hard to say. Even ex-president George H. W. Bush highlighted the connection between fun and American sports: "When you get to be old that doesn't mean you have to stop having fun. It's why . . . I love to root at all these ball games."[14]

That 1990 Saints-Raiders game was just a pre-season exhibition matchup. If the same game were played in Oakland during the regular season, could I still sit amongst the Raider nation as a fan of the opposing team and enjoy the game? Can home and away fans even sit together in America? Are there riots in the stands at NFL games? Do NFL fans have a disdain for other people's front gardens? I wanted answers.

Ten years later in 2000, I was at college in Toronto, Canada, which is a mere football's throw from Buffalo—okay, fine, it's a couple of hours' drive. My friend booked us tickets to the Buffalo Bills football game through a company that takes you on a coach from downtown Toronto to the game in Buffalo and back, which included the game-day ticket. The kickoff was at 1 p.m. The coach left at 6:45 a.m.

The coach was packed with Canadian Bills fans and volumes of alcohol. It burped into drive, and we made our way to Buffalo. I was really excited to be going to my first-ever regular-season NFL game. The Bills were hosting their divisional rivals, the New York Jets, giving the game an extra intensity. We got to Ralph Wilson Stadium at 9:15 a.m. and the car park was already nearly full, even though it was four hours before kickoff.

In 1996 I went to see a West Ham United FC game (a Premiership soccer team in East London) with my old school friend, Mike P. Back then we walked from the tube station to the stadium and saw many of the houses near the West Ham stadium boarded up with temporary wood to prevent any would-be hooligans from smashing up their windows or stealing their garden gnomes. I remember discussing with Mike that we felt sorry for those families who have to endure the torment of living so close to a soccer stadium and having to go through such a ritual every game day, which can be twice a week, for up to 10 months.

By contrast, the streets near the Bills' stadium are strikingly different. The owners of each house also go through a design-changing ritual for their houses, but instead of hiding and protecting their homes, they dress them up. Every house on the wide road was a homage to the Buffalo Bills. They didn't board up their front gardens to deter hooligans but welcomed people on their properties by grilling food, selling their parking spaces in their front gardens, or showing off their Bills paraphernalia, including banners and flags that spanned right across their front gardens and their rooftops.

The coach honked its horn at each house, and we got waved on through to the coach parking section. Once there, we began drinking. The driver got out a small BBQ and grilled us up some hot dogs. I was, without knowing it, "tailgating." I was not used to drinking beer so early on a Sunday morning and felt a little tipsy. There were several other coaches surrounding us doing the same thing, and everyone was in good spirits. One woman was so excited she climbed on top of our coach and took her top off, completely exposing herself. Normally this kind of behaviour is not always a good advertisement for a family sporting event, but this woman was showing unrivalled commitment to her team. Not only was it 14 degrees Fahrenheit (-10 degrees Celsius to us Brits) outside, but she (or if she hadn't done it, a lucky Bills fan did) had painted Bills logos across her naked breasts. I definitely didn't see that kind of fan loyalty at the Leyton Orient game.

I joined in on some throwing and catching in the car park and came to realise I couldn't do either very well; I blame my parents for sending me to a primary school with no NFL fans. At the time I thought we had arrived at the game way too early. I had assumed that only the fans coming in on buses were biding time, as this was four hours before kickoff. I had no clue I was part of a much larger, and more powerful, tailgate culture—and it took me another six years to figure that out.

Fast forward to October 2006. Mike P. had moved from East London to Los Angeles, swapping his beloved West Ham United team for the Los Angeles Galaxy. David Beckham, also from East London, followed suit and signed with the Galaxy some years later. In October 2006, Mike was getting married in L.A. I was flying out there to be an usher in his wedding party, along with my friend Paul, when I noticed that the Chicago Bears were playing in Arizona the Monday night after the wedding.

Paul wasn't too sure about going to see the game, but I convinced him to come with me. Throughout my life in the U.K., I have always tried to show people just what a good time an NFL game is and the reaction is often the same: "Ahh it's rugby for pussies," "It's too stop starty," "What they gotta wear those bleedin' helmets for," and so on.

Trying to convince your friends in the school playground is hard enough, but convincing an adult to try something new is very difficult. Paul loves some of the finer things in life, and so he agreed to come with me if we stayed in a five-star hotel in Arizona. He works in the travel business and got us a good deal on the flights, the hotel, and somehow managed to get us two tickets for the game.

The Arizona Cardinals were showing off their swanky new stadium, the University of Phoenix Stadium in Glendale, built specifically to host the Super Bowl the following year. There was some traffic but the free parking was a nice surprise.

I wondered just how many other NFL stadiums have free parking. (Answer: not many!) We got to our seats with about 10 minutes to go before kickoff—just in time to see the Cardinals run out to a lovely fireworks display.

Wherever I go in the world, I usually sport some kind of visual Bears merchandise—be it a hat, t-shirt, wristband, or if I happen to be an usher at a wedding, some Bears underwear. Most of the time when I am in the States, an American usually asks, "Why do you support the Bears?" but before I can answer, they spit out, "The Bears SUUUUCK!" I then take a long breath in through my nose, stare at them, and unleash my answer with the same gusto as a blitzing linebacker: "Because they are my team! Regardless if they suck or not! A true fan sticks by the team no matter what." They either back off or simply repeat, "But they still suck." Grrrr. I knew I wasn't a "fair-weather fan," someone who only gets behind his or her team once they start winning. (Although for years I thought this was a fan who only goes to games in the warm weather.) Or even worse, a "bandwagon fan," who hops between good teams. Tunison describes the latter as "parasites in search of victory, needing only a host team to attach themselves to in order to suck all authenticity from the fan base."[15]

In 2006 the Bears were having an alarmingly good season, winning their first five games. Wearing my Bears hat after the wedding, I got many a "Go Bears," "Da Bearz," or the strange sounding, "Bear Down" (*Bear Down. Chicago Bears* is the fight song of the Bears) from passers-by. My Bears were no longer the laughing stock of the league, and it felt good. The press was calling them "America's team." The Bears quarterback, Rex Grossman, had finally recovered from his injuries and had played solidly all season. Add to that a rock-hard defense and a sprinkling of magic from rookie sensation kickoff and punt returner Devin Hester, and the Bears were a Super Bowl–calibre football team.

The Cardinals, however, were having a miserable season, and although it would have been nice to see the Bears win, I did want to see a bit of a challenge. I wasn't expecting to see so many fans of the opposing team, but plenty of Bears fans came out of the woodwork for the big game.

Just like in 1990, I was rooting for my team while being surrounded by opposing fans. There were several Bears fans in my section, but there was absolutely no conflict. On the very first play Grossman "unleashed his dragon" and fired the ball 40 yards to the galloping receiver, a chap named Bernard Berrian. Berrian didn't quite have the legs to make the catch and the ball hit the grass. Sadly, this kick-started Rex Grossman towards his downward spiral into his infamous Jekyll-and-Hyde-like inconsistency riddled season and career.

At halftime the Cardinals were winning 0-20 (in the NFL the home team's score is last). Paul was happy enough because in spite of being dragged out there he was rooting for the Cardinals and began teasing me about the score. None of the real Cardinal fans, however, teased the Bears fans in our section. That is not to say there was no atmosphere; on the contrary, it was electric.

By the fourth quarter the Bears were down 10-23 with an offense that had only mustered a feeble 38 rushing yards and 148 passing yards all night, and they certainly didn't look like they would be able to make a comeback. Grossman had thrown for ten touchdowns and only three interceptions in the first five games of the season, but in this game I witnessed him throw his fourth interception of the night. This last one was returned for a Cardinals touchdown. I and the other 63,339 fans thought it was game over. *I lost faith.*

I left the stadium with five minutes left on the clock. While outside on the concourse, I heard a series of noises. Apparently the touchdown the Cardinals had just scored was reversed because the defender who had intercepted the ball had been tackled and was ruled down by contact (prior to scoring the touchdown), and the Bears had miraculously just scored a touchdown themselves. Brian Urlacher, our beast of a linebacker, had torn the ball away from a Cardinals player, leaving the ball bouncing on the turf. Bears cornerback, Charles "Peanut" Tillman, picked up the fumbled ball and ran it in to the end zone for 40 yards. I raced back inside and could see that the score was now 17-23 Cardinals, with minutes to go. The Bears then lined up an onside kick.

In American football the team that just scores has to then kick the ball to their opponents. Most of the time it is a deep long ball, so their opponents have a long way to go to get a touchdown. However, when there is little time left and the scoring team is still losing, like the Bears here, they sometimes opt for what is called an onside kick. This is a short bobbling kick. The risk is that if the opponents get to the ball first, they then have possession of the ball and they can drain the clock and win, as well as only having a short distance to go to get a touchdown or field goal. The reward is that if the kicking team gets to the ball first (usually they don't), they keep possession and only have about 50 yards from their opposing end zone to score. It's a high-risk, high-reward strategy and usually done when the losing team is desperate and there is little time left. Unless you are New

Orleans Saints head coach Sean Payton. Then you shock everyone by calling an onside kick as the first play of the second half in Super Bowl XLIV. Their opponents, the Colts, were not ready for it (in fact neither was the camera crew). The Saints won the ball and went on to the win the game, in what many describe as the "gutsiest" call in Super Bowl history.

The Bear's onside kick backfired and the Cardinals gained possession of the ball with a short distance to the Bear's end zone. For the second time I walked to the car park. My tail was between my legs as I was upset with the score but still loving the fact I got to see an NFL game live, even if my beloved Bears were losing and needed a miracle to win.

In the far depths of the car park, I heard someone crying out the angelic chant, "The Bears have scored, the Bears have scored." Okay, this particular angel was an overweight drunk, skipping around and waving his Bears hat, but his message was heavenly.

"Have they got a TV on the back of their truck?" Paul asked in reference to a group of fans in the car park. They were animated, jumping up and down around some garden chairs that surrounded a truck and a tent that had a bluish hue emitting from it. I couldn't believe my eyes. Were they actually watching the game on a TV when the stadium was right behind us? I knew something extraordinary must have happened but I wasn't allowed back in the stadium. So I tucked my camera under my arm like a football, I sprinted past cars and drunken fans back to *my* goal line. Hester had just returned a punt 83 yards for a touchdown for the Bears, and I made it to the tailgate just in time for the replay. The Bears were now winning 24-23.

The Cardinals had one last possession and came storming down the field. With seconds to go they lined up a 20-yard field goal, which is an easy distance. Their kicker, a gentleman named Neil Rackers, had not missed kicking a field goal all season long.

We all watched the screen intently. There was no sound from the stadium. Thwack! I felt a blow to my back. A fellow Bears fan from behind chopped me in delight as we saw the ball go wide on the TV and miss entering the goalpost. "The Bears have won, the Bears have won, the Bears have won!" That night I learnt a valuable lesson. I'm not going to lose faith in my Bears again!

It was at this point that the idea for my trip began to dig its cleats into my mind. The fans in and out of the stadium were as welcoming and friendly as the fans had been back in 1990. I was an away fan, but this time at a huge Monday night game. The fine Cardinals fans in the car park had let *me* watch *my* team beat *their* team, in highly dramatic fashion, on *their* TV. I was the enemy, wasn't I? But they let me celebrate without getting angry. Then something odd happened— something that I would never have expected, because it simply would never happen in Britain: they fired up their grill. My cynical mind had not prepared me for what these Cardinals fans were planning. They began to cook.

"So you don't want to rally and create carnage around the streets of Glendale, Arizona, then?" I asked. "Nope. This is how we do things over here," the Cardinals fan said, as he handed me a hot dog. They told us we could not leave without trying their food and gourmet snacks. I had lots of questions: Why were they being so good to us? How was it possible that we were welcomed with such open arms? Is it common to bring a television and a grill to a stadium car park and not even go into the stadium? What kind of people allows away fans to watch the game with them, even when their home team is losing? Who, instead of starting a riot and beating people up, decides on having a "cookout" for two strangers whom they have never met before and will probably never see again? What is the name for this wonderfully delightful breed of human being?

Tailgaters!

". . . So on this trip I hope to find tailgaters at every NFL franchise," I told my neighbour on the plane. "I want to see what it is like to be a fan from every franchise, check out all the stadiums, see some great football, get more people into the sport, meet the great fans, and have one hell of a road trip!"

She had that look of shock on her face again: "Did you say *road* trip? You're *driving*? You *are* mad!"

2

From Soccer to Rugby to American Football: A Short, Personal History

"Soccer" is a word that started in the English public school system—bizarrely, as an abbreviation for Association Football—so you can blame the posh English kids for that one.[1]

In 1869 two American colleges, Rutgers and Princeton, not only played the first intercollegiate American football game but also spawned the first tailgate, as fans cooked for themselves outside. In his book *How Football Explains America*, NFL sportswriter Sal Paolantonio says that playing this "old world game of football was really an amalgam of soccer and rugby,"[2] called the Boston Game. In essence it was simply kicking and scrimmaging, much like my soccer games on the primary school playground. In 1876 four colleges formed an Intercollegiate Football Association. According to Paolantonio, these colleges wanted to make "the game more competitive and appealing," and one way to do this was to add more scoring than soccer, which he feels is "ninety minutes of whatever and then maybe one goal scored by accident."[3] In 1882, football forefather Walter Camp created the concept of the first down (the play stops when the ball carrier is tackled), and "it was like somebody flipped a light switch."[4] The attacking team had three attempts (downs) to advance the ball five yards and if they failed, the opponent would get the ball back. Paolantonio firmly believed this was a way of making the game more "American" by making it clearly different from rugby. America was a new country without the history of Europe, and they wanted their own game. He feels that "the creation of the first down simply mirrored the nation's quest for territory,"[5] as this is "something American players and spectators could embrace. Capture territory. Hold it. Advance."[6]

In 1905 the game was brutal and had 18 fatalities, so Walter Camp changed the first down goal to ten yards, then later changed it to four downs to improve player safety. A year later he introduced the all-important forward pass rule. For many years in American football throwing the ball forward was not fashionable and was seen more as a desperation tactic. It became more popular in the 1930s when the football became smaller and easier to throw. This helped create a T formation taking the quarterback away from the scrimmage, and it "brought a greater element of strategy and grace to the game. . . . The T helped to civilize the game further because it put an even greater emphasis on skill and speed over raw strength . . . [which] encouraged the sort of spectacular action and dense strategy that was rarely combined in any sport,"[7] wrote Michael MacCambridge in his historic book about the NFL, *America's Game*.

I have already expressed my disdain for the lack of cohesion in primary school playground soccer; thankfully, when I went to secondary school (7th grade), soccer was a little more organised. My small high school year (class of 63 students) had four soccer teams per grade. I was picked as a substitute for the year 7 A-team (which is the best team; the D-team is the worst) purely because of my height. I was tall and skinny like Peter Crouch, the six-foot-seven English soccer player. The teachers felt that because I was towering over others I could— or rather, should—score with my head.

In one of my first games, we travelled by coach with our A-team and the A-team from the year above (8th graders) to play another school. Three of the older players came down sick and couldn't play, leaving them with just ten men. Both managers (one was the economics teacher, the other a history teacher) got into an argument. Everyone on my team wanted to be picked for the year above as it would be such a huge honour. I must have been the only one who didn't want to play. I had little to no lust for the spherical ball game, and I was not good enough for my own A-team, let alone for the more elite team.

"Goldstein, you're playing for the year above." Shit! Everyone on the bus groaned. The managers put me up front where I could do as little damage to my own team as possible. After 87 minutes we were losing 2-1 in a cup game. In the game's dying moments one of our players took a shot. I had done nothing worthwhile all game but that shot ricocheted off the goalkeeper straight into my path. I didn't have time to steady the ball, so I just toe poked it first time from 12 yards out. The speed of the shot surprised me, the goalkeeper, and the rest of my temporary teammates as it flew into the back of the net. Goooaalll!

My name was mentioned in assembly, and the headmaster made particular attention that I was playing for the year above. I was proud, yes, but too embarrassed to tell anyone it was a fluke. Because of that goal I ended up starting nearly every game that year for the year 7's A-team. I didn't score another goal that season.

Every year after, I kept getting dropped down into the lower teams until I was captain of the D-team, which is where I belonged in the first place, yet the teachers still went on about *that* goal. Soccer was just never going to be my sport. It was time to move on and find another sport.

Seeing as I couldn't find an American football team, the next best thing had to be rugby, especially when the chief executive of the Rugby Players Association, Damian Hopley, said that "we need to compare ourselves with the NFL. That is the sport we are morphing in to."[8]

Our eccentric, rugby-mad Scottish science teacher finally got his wish to coach a rugby union team, which was made up of mainly bigger kids, teenage psychopaths, and people like me . . . kids who were shite at soccer. I thought I would be the next Walter "Sweetness" Payton on the rugby pitch. Granted, I was tall, but I was skinny, had no pace, couldn't tackle, and possessed no strength or natural aggression. Because of my height I was put in as a "flanker" which is amongst the forwards and played mainly by masochists.

In NFL terms as a flanker I was playing the role of an offensive lineman on offense and a defensive tackle on defense. There is a reason you never see a defensive lineman weighing 120 pounds in the NFL!

There are fifteen players on a rugby union team. The eight forwards are usually the bigger lads and do most of the tackling, rucking, and mauling. They form the "scrum," a tight huddle that pushes against the opposing huddle. The backs are normally quicker, do the kicking, and score most of the tries (touchdowns). Playing on defense on an American football team is like playing as a forward, you are part of a team within a team, whereas the backs in rugby are similar to players on an NFL offense, they have the "glory positions," they score most of the points, because they are usually quicker, nimbler, and good at passing.

For those that want to give rugby union a try, there are a couple things to know:

- Ruck: This is when someone gets tackled to the ground; the forwards from both teams then lock horns over the tackled player and try to push each other back to get access to the ball. When this happened to me I thought I was going to be crushed to death so I scrambled for dear life.
- Maul: This is when you are stopped by a defender but you do not go to ground. Instead you turn your back, your teammates then come along and slam into you as hard as they can to force you back; meanwhile your opponents are doing the same to you from the other side. When this happened to me I thought my body was going to be crushed, but I couldn't scramble for dear life, because I was stuck.

Personally I would have liked to have tried Rugby League Football, which is a breakaway from rugby union. It became a professional sport in the late nineteenth century as opposed to union which became professional in 1995. The 13-a-side league format is more similar to American football because it is uses a "six tackles (downs) and goal line" rule, similar to American football's "four downs and ten yard" rule. In Rugby League, after the tackle, the ball is rolled back to a teammate, and the game continues quickly, plus more importantly for me, there are no rucks and mauls in Rugby League. Sadly, Rugby League is mainly played in Northern England or Australasia, and when I was a 14-year-old going to school just outside London the North may as well have been in Australasia, so I had to settle for Union.

Football is a game for gentlemen, played by hooligans,
while Rugby is a game for hooligans played by gentlemen.
—Anonymous

This famous statement still rings true in many cases in the U.K., as rugby union is played more in private schools while soccer has always had its roots in the working classes. At rugby matches opposing fans can sit together and get along fine—not so in soccer. Rugby and American football fields may well be filled with carnage during the game but it turns 180 degrees after the final whistle. Keith Webster, a columnist for NFLUK.com, points out that it has often been said that contact is the most stimulating essence of American football and the exhilaration of being involved in that sort of contest (just as in rugby) is what drives people to play it. In both sports, the intensity of competition brings a satisfaction at the end of the game that makes you realise you really were involved in something. It is the very reason why in both sports, at the final whistle, players shake hands and embrace those from the other side with genuine feeling because they understand what the man opposite had to go through, win or lose.[9]

We only played four rugby games before our school banned the sport. We were so used to being a soccer school, we didn't know the rules of rugby, and none of us were sure what was legal physically and what wasn't—stamping, yes (stamping is usually something that one does when "stamping" out a fire, but here on the rugby field it's something the ref will turn a blind eye to); clothes lining, apparently not (clothes lining is usually something that one does in North American professional wrestling, when you fling your arm out horizontally to knock down the oncoming opponent, but here on the rugby field, the ref will not turn a blind eye to this and eject you from the game). Confused? Me too!

In both rugby codes you must go over the end-zone line and touch the ball down on the ground to score. Hence the term "touchdown" in American football, but in rugby it is known as a try. The "conversion" in rugby is like the "point after kick" in American football, but it gets two points, and is always kicked from 22 yards, but in line with where the rugby ball was touched down for the try. If a player scores under the posts, it will be an easier and more direct kick for the kicker. Scoring a try in the corner will give the kicker a much tighter angle. You can also score penalty kicks or drop kicks (like a field goal).

In our third rugby game we got our arses kicked and lost 75-5 to a team of savages who clearly saw the sport as an excuse to have a complete punch up. I believe they even had a bet amongst their team to see who could come away with an opposing player's ear. "You were lucky to get five," said my Dad, after.

In this game their nifty but large back, think a powerhouse running back like Brandon Jacobs, came near me and I made my way closer to make the tackle. I had missed him previously as he was quite fast. In an earlier ruck, I had attempted to get the ball back and fortunately moved just in time before his fist could connect with my head. His choice of running weaponry was that he kept his elbows high and caught people in the face with them, or if the would-be tacklers went low, then he would knee them in the face. This unhinged menace clearly had a thing for messing up faces.

I got close to my sadistic opponent but I knew I didn't have the upper body strength to bring him down with a high tackle, and I didn't want to go low and get kicked in the head so I allowed him to get level with me. I then, rather cheekily, stuck my foot out and tripped him up. I thought it was fair. Not the bravest of things to do, but it stopped him running and he tumbled to the floor. In fact I was quite pleased with myself. Our teacher, however, wasn't and stopped the game immediately, awarding the other team a penalty. He then shouted at me relentlessly for "dangerous play and unsportsmanlike conduct" and "not playing the game in the right spirit." Perhaps if I had punched him, stamped on his ear, eyegouged him (a popular rugby tactic), called his mother a whore, and then briefly urinated on him before gleefully skipping off with the ball, I might have got more credit from my teacher. It was all too confusing. Oddly enough, in 2010, a New York Jets strength and conditioning coach tripped a sprinting Dolphins player who was running down the sidelines. The coach was chastised and suspended until the end of the season.

Our fourth and final game was against the school where one of my closest friends, the mild-mannered "Biggler" went, who thirteen years later built the website for my football trip. He too was not good at soccer, yet he cared way less about sports than I do. As a 14-year-old, Baz was one of those kids who was already shaving his beard daily. At five-foot-nine and weighing in at nearly 200 pounds, with a huge trunk (he'll be happy I used that word), he was blessed with natural muscle and bulk, and he could well have had a career as a prop forward in rugby. He was thrown into the game much against his will purely because of his size.

I actually had my best game that day and made three tackles, but zero eye gouges, stamps, and punches. During a ruck, the ball bobbled out. Our teacher told us forwards two things: If we ever get our hands on the ball, then we should never pass it; "leave all the passing to the backs," he demanded. He was worried that we would throw what he called a "hospital pass." Which is a pass that floats up high in the air, so when your teammate finally gets the ball, an opponent has enough time to slam him to the ground, likely taking him to the hospital. Our teacher/coach's other demand was that a forward should always fall onto any fumbled ball and wait for cavalry to arrive, as opposed to picking it up and running for glory. This is because forwards are usually large and slow and are likely to be tackled before getting a try; best to protect the ball under a ruck and get stamped to death. You don't see many linemen in the NFL picking up a fumbled ball and running with it, because they too are usually told the same thing.

For my teammates and myself, we were confused most of the time and had no appreciation for tactics or teamwork. The games lacked cogency, and it was one human pyramid after another. So when I saw the bobbling ball just yards from the try line, I decided to ignore my teacher's tactics. A galloping Walter Payton flashed into my mind. I bent forward and picked up the live ball. I hit my first stride towards glory with the ball nestled under my arm, when a huge tree-like forearm came flying across my chest much like in the style of American wrestling and the ball bounced out of my arms onto the ground. "Did someone just *chop* me?" (It was a "chop," because I didn't go to ground, had I have done it would then have been a clothes-line manoeuvre.) This is ridiculous! I could understand it if someone wanted to trip me, but seriously, who chops people? I looked up. It was Baz with his massive arm standing in front of me.

"Baz!" I shouted, rather surprised at my friend. I was not shocked that he chopped me because in the rucks and mauls you never know who is who, as everyone ends up caked in mud, but I was shocked that he seemed to care enough about the game to stop his opponent, who just happened to be me. Years later I found out he didn't care for the sport at all, he just wanted to chop people. I think he watched too much pro-wrestling as a kid and I was just in the wrong place at the wrong time.

"Oh shit, sorry," Baz tried to tell me once he realised he had just chopped one of his closest friends, his voice muffled by his gum shield, our only form of protection in the game. He realised that his action had knocked the ball to the ground; he felt guilty for stopping me from scoring, even though it would be against his team, so he squatted his large frame over the ball and suddenly spread his arms wide, backing himself up into his own team like he was protecting them from a bomb. I'm not sure what his coach or the 17 parents that showed up must have thought. I saw the nice gesture and picked the ball up for the second time, but Baz couldn't hold off his *own* teammates for long enough and I got smothered.

In 1995, not long after this game of teenage carnage, rugby union finally became a professional sport. Ed Smith, the former England cricketer and current sportswriter, in his book *What Sport Tells Us About Life*, wrote that "the odd flurry of punches amongst the forwards was considered all part of the sport's rough and tumble. In the melee, who could be sure who did what? Best to 'let the game flow', as it was 'all part of the game'. But in today's rugby, fewer punches go unpunished. Rugby, though no longer amateur, is a cleaner sport."[10]

Unlike most sports, American football is not an easy game to just pick up and play. Even if you have players that know the rules, you need a lot of equipment, such as helmets and pads, not to mention a place to play. I have many American friends who love the sport and have never had the pleasure of "kitting up" (putting on the shoulder pads and the mystical football helmet). Paolantonio notes that football players from early on were well respected much like soldiers, cowboys, and later movie stars. He says that the famous U.S. Army general Douglas MacArthur "was the first to reward his football stars with special privileges. They were given elite status."[11] At some high schools, writer H. G. Bissinger discovered that girls from the school's "spirit squad" are assigned one player for the season, bringing their players home-baked goods, dressing up the player's locker, and even making "a large sign for her player that [sits] in his front yard and stays there for the entire season as a notice to the community he played football"[12] for his school, as he mentions in his book *Friday Night Lights*. I didn't get squat for playing for the year above's A-team, even after my glorious goal!

Oriard wrote that the great Green Bay coach Vince Lombardi "called football 'a game for madmen' that required hate but was also somehow a higher calling."[13]

You also need the perfect-sized pitch (turf) for American football. Nick Richards highlights in his book *Touchdown UK* that this was a problem even for the famous Wembley stadium, when it hosted the American Bowls in the '90s, as they had to add "an Astroturf strip to make it 120 yards."[14] Apart from school and college, players will only find a few amateur American football divisions. Other than the NFL, pro football includes the indoor Arena Football League (AFL) and the United Football League (UFL). The Canadians, with their slightly different rules and larger balls and pitches, have the Canadian Football League (CFL), while women can play in the Lingerie Football League, the LFL (a wet dream for male football fans, where women in lingerie play 7-on-7 indoor football). There was also NFL Europe and the XFL, but they both folded. For many pro football fans, there is only one league—the NFL. Just as in boxing, many fans have never played but just watch.

In the 1980s when the NFL was getting big in the U.K., American football teams started to pop up all over the place, and many even managed to secure sponsorship. Now there are over 40 British American Football League senior teams, and more than 70 at the university level, as well as youth and flag teams. College players in the United States play for their NFL careers (and to get laid, in my opinion), whereas college players in the United Kingdom are playing for fun (and also to get laid, I think).

The NFL in the late '80s created an image that their players are "larger than life," much like superheroes for young boys and girls. The pads and the helmet added to that image, making them look like modern-day warriors from another world, ready for battle. NFL Films took a more cinematic approach to filming the games, with low angles, tight close-ups, and powerful narration, and thus "amplifying football's epic or mythic power."[15]

After high school I studied for one year at the University of Wales, Aberystwyth. Despite being a proud rugby nation, this Welsh University actually had an American football team. I couldn't believe it. I signed up instantly and didn't even think that I might get hurt playing. They were called Tarranau, which is Welsh for lightning, and they were rather desperate for players. My only requirement to make the squad was that I drank beer. (I'm not a big drinker, but admitting that meant ruining my chances of playing for them and thereby squandering my chances to get scouted by the Bears.) I said yes to the beer and I was snapped up too quickly for me to even comprehend. For years I only knew of football through the portal of TV and Madden video games. Within days of signing up for Aber, paying my game fees, signing waivers, and getting initiated with alcohol-related games, I was staring at *my own* pads and helmet. It felt amazing. Fine, they were borrowed from the team, but they were mine for the season.

To play football in American high schools and colleges you have to succumb to grueling tryouts and show a ruthless commitment to your team at all costs, as suggested in cheesy American movies where the players all seem to be angry and shout a lot. Not so for my footballing career. In Wales, I just had to be able to drink.

I rather arrogantly thought I was the only one in the U.K. with any American football knowledge. That was until I met Richard, a third-year student who was our head coach; his football knowledge put me to shame. Not only did he know the professional stats and history but he also knew about developing players, systems, technique, and tactics. He now coaches at an American college.

College teams in the United States get massive sponsorship, TV money, and some can even fill a stadium with over 100,000 fans each week. There are 11 college football stadiums that have a higher capacity than the largest NFL stadium. We had to "pay to play" and only 15 fans showed up for our season opener—three people less than our whole squad.

I was moved from wide receiver to cornerback and my whole understanding of the game erupted. As a kid, or a Madden game player, I had always focused on the attacking offensive players, especially those who took the glory such as the wide receiver, the running back, and of course the quarterback. I wasn't blessed with much aggression but at Aber I became the starting right-side cornerback. We all got nicknames—mine was "Stretch" like the rubber Stretch Armstrong toy. A nickname helped me get closer to NFL fame. Bryant Gumbel, the host of the HBO series *Real Sports with Bryant Gumbel*, said that "in a league that covers every guys' face and discourages individuality, nicknames may not help players gain fame, but it sure helps fans remember them."[16]

After training, we all drank vast amounts of alcohol from a brandy glass the size of a beach ball, as our tactical training was in a pub and we were separated into defense and offense on and off the practice field. It was like having two separate teams. Sure, most of our linemen played both sides, but our defensive team was a unit that went out drinking together. Likewise, in a game, the defense are not usually the star players, but they all move together as one team on the field. The offense is often a culmination of "star" players looking for their own stats and touchdown scores. Even though I was one of the weakest players, being part of the defense made me feel much more part of a "team" than ever before.

In the changing room before the season opener, I was in magic land, pinching myself over the fact that I had pads and a helmet—and that I was finally "kitting up." Because of the rarity of the sport, our whole team felt like we were all making history with every pass, run, and tackle. Perhaps not NFL history but with every play we were at least taking strides in expanding the sport in the United Kingdom.

So there I stood, freezing cold, 19 years old, on the wet Welsh gridiron, dreaming this was my ticket to the NFL. Two minutes later, things changed dramatically. The opposing running back came straight for me. I went low, but as he was leading with his helmet, he dropped his shoulder, and ran right through me. *Crack!* An electric pulse went down my spine and I blacked out for a moment. The helmet-to-helmet collision had knocked me to the ground. My teammates picked me up and slapped my helmet, which made my head ring like a church bell on a Sunday morning: "Don't worry, you'll get him on the next play."

I quickly realised two things. First, getting spanked to the ground isn't actually quite as much fun as it looks on TV, and second, it was highly unlikely that I would ever make it playing for the Bears and should start thinking of other career options.

Even though I wasn't very good, no one on my team was looking to get rid of me. In fact, that whole season, all of my teammates were incredibly supportive. Maybe it's because there is so much stopping and starting again in American football that it is easy to eradicate your previous mistakes and start over with each play. My teammates nurtured me, which was a new experience for me in sport.

Because of the padding and the helmet, people went in with far more gusto than they would have in rugby. I'm not saying there aren't big hits in rugby because there are, but because of the padding you can really throw your body in there. Unlike in rugby, NFL defenders rarely "wrap up" and many football players literally fly through the air to make a big "hit." The helmet is at times used as a weapon as much at it is for protection, which the league is trying to eradicate. Playing an actual game with the full pads and helmet was alarmingly difficult. I found it hard to use my peripheral vision, and my shoulder pads wouldn't allow me to lift my arms much above my shoulders.

Very few teams that I faced playing for Aber had good quarterbacks, which meant they ran the ball most of the time. Since I was by far the skinniest on my team, the running backs were sent on sweep patterns right towards me. I couldn't always bring them down on my own, so in reality I ended up just hugging them for a while like glue, until the cavalry arrived.

After one season at Aber with a record of 1-6-1, my boyhood idolization of the NFL came to a slow end. I didn't want it to happen. The Internet came into the world, and I was not fooled by NFL propaganda like I was when I was younger. As a kid I didn't even believe that NFL stars went to college, high school, or even had parents. I thought they were from a different planet entirely, the same sporting planet that Michael Jordan, Pelé, and Muhammad Ali all came from. By playing the game, I soon began to realise that NFL players were no longer "super humans" with flawless characters (apart from Walter Payton, of course) despite flipping over defenders, making leaping catches, and playing through broken bones; they are simply incredibly gifted athletes who work extremely hard. My youthful idolization changed into respect.

The 1993 film *Rudy*, which is based on a true story, is about how one young man fought adversity to play for Notre Dame football team. If someone makes a "great play" in football, it is often coined as being a Rudy moment. My "Rudy" moment (my one and only I might add) came in my second game at Aber. I was marking or "covering" a nippy and somewhat arrogant receiver. He came bursting out of his blocks and beat me running deep down the field, something Coach Richard told me I should never let happen. Luckily, instead of the ball going over my head to the now open receiver, their quarterback didn't have the arm power to get it over my six-foot-two frame.

Don't drop the ball, don't drop the ball, don't drop the ball. I held my hands out and clasped the cold hard leather, which made my hands sting in the frigid British winter. I tucked the ball under my right arm and ran down the sidelines. All I could see was the end zone. To my left my teammate called for me to pitch the football back to him so that he could score. He could see what I could not: a huge man running at full speed towards with me with manic eyes. *Bang*! I got hit from the side and went flying out of bounds. I didn't score a touchdown, but we did soon after and I felt great as the momentum swung back our way. That quarterback never threw the ball my way after that—the double-edged sword every great cornerback faces.

In the pub after every game, the real competition was making sure that we beat the opposition at a "boat race," a relay drinking game, similar to America's flip cup game. After the boat race, Coach Richard dished out the awards: best play, best player, and so on. The "orange" award went to the player who made the worst play or the biggest fool of himself. If you received an orange award, you had to take your shirt off in the packed pub and have a cut orange squashed onto your head and body. Although the orange has a zesty appeal and can feel quite refreshing, the acid from the fruit burns into the cuts and scratches one would have received from the game.

My "orange" moment came against our divisional rival, Warwick. I was on the field covering their wide receiver on their punt. It was my job to block the receiver so he couldn't tackle our punt returner. Though the ball didn't go as deep as intended, I looked up and the ball was spinning vertically, falling right to me. I had flashes of returning the punt for a touchdown, like Deion "Prime Time" Sanders. Then I looked straight ahead at the opposing team, thundering towards me. I could see the breath snorting out of the grills in their helmets, like snarling horses. My teammates were making hand signals to get out of the way, because the ball was still ours if I did not touch it, and they could see I was about to get killed. So at the last moment I sidestepped it. The ball hit the ground three yards from me, phew. But then it took an almost impossible bounce and hit me on the shin, thus making the ball live for the opposition. A Warwick player pounced on the ball and recovered it. I knew I would be getting the orange for that one straightaway.

In my twenties I finally discovered the wonders of flag football. It may sound a little prissy, but tough-as-nails Carolina Panthers star receiver Steve Smith broke his arm in a flag football game during preseason in 2010. There is no hitting (you pull the flag from someone's belt to tackle). Other than the flags, cones, and a ball, you don't really need anything else. I found a group in London called the Texas Exes (University of Texas alum living in London). Every Saturday we simply pick teams and play. Sometimes it is as low as 3-on-3, and others as high as 10-on-10, but it is a lot of fun, and quite a few women have come out to play too. We play a "four downs and halfway or goal" system and there is no kicking the ball. Twice we have hired enough helmets and pads to form a team and flown over to Copenhagen to play against a local "kitted" team (a team that plays with helmets and pads as opposed to a flag team), called the Copenhagen Towers. I really enjoy playing flag football much more than the kitted version, because everyone plays both sides and you are involved in practically every play. Plus, you all get to be creative and design your own plays in the huddle. Whereas with all the gear, it really becomes much more about power and strength.

Stephen Fry, the quintessential Englishman and comedic actor, took in one American football game on his driving tour across America in 2007–2008. He attended the famous college rivalry competition between Alabama and Auburn and had trouble understanding the game, saying "Gridiron football leaves me entirely cold, with it's stop-start spasms, preposterous armour and tedious playbook tactics."[17] Hopefully Mr. Fry is reading.

The "armour" is there to protect the players, which helps make the game better for the spectator, as fans want to see players play at their very best. Granted, with all their padding and helmets the players are hard to recognise. Each player becomes a number, which can create de-individualization but it adds to the "team" aspect while also creating a mystique. The NFL football helmet is also a great "logo." The Los Angeles Rams were the first team to put their emblem on the helmet. Their rams horn logo "was a work of modern art on the side of a football helmet,"[18] says MacCambridge, and it inspired the rest of the teams to do the same, apart from Cleveland, who have the only plain (solid-coloured) helmet in the league. The Pittsburgh Steelers are the only team that has their logo displayed on the right side of the helmet only.

And so to Fry's so-called stop-start spasms: First, American sports are *all* stop-starty and filled with advertisements—it is inherent in their sports culture. Basketball and ice hockey are both very fast games, but both have several time-outs and stoppages, and baseball, much like cricket, is a staccato sport, all of which are good for TV commercials, which in turn gives the teams and players lots of money.

During a "stop" in the NFL, both teams can make various substitutions and bring in specialized players for a particular play. Think about David Beckham coming on and off the field just for his trademark free kicks and corners—that wouldn't be so bad.

Huddle up

Some Brits with reference to the NFL have often asked me, "What have they gotta have a bleedin' mother's meeting every twenty seconds for?" For the most part, after every tackle the players on the field come together and discuss the next play in "the huddle." Paolantonio calls it "a sanctuary in the middle of a maelstrom. A place to take stock, make a new plan, and make a promise: to believe in that new plan and deliver it."[19]

Initially, the huddle came about because of a deaf quarterback in 1892 who wanted to conceal his sign language from the other team. Before then plays were simply called on the line of scrimmage, though now it is a trademark of the game. A chap named Amos Alonzo Stagg, who was the head coach at the University of Chicago, "viewed the huddle as a vital aspect of helping to teach sportsmanship . . . a kind of religious congregation on the field,"[20] says Paolantonio. This is great for the players, like myself, who enjoy a breather, and also for creating plays and discussing strategy, but for the fans who are not into the tactical side of the game it could admittedly slow the game down.

The stops, however, are essential at making the football action better. Paolantonio wrote that Stagg recognised "the commercial appeal of the American game of football would grow with more and more scoring, and that meant more touchdowns could be generated by a wide open game. . . . The use of the huddle allowed Stagg and his contemporaries to become more experimental and detailed in their design of passing offences."[21] American football fans accept the fact that the stoppages are for the greater good of the game. If you do get bored, there is plenty to see during a "stop" at a live game, such as the cheerleaders, mascots, and jumbotrons, and if you are at home the networks provide lots of action replays.

Also, without the stops the players would burn out incredibly quickly, because every play is so full-on. When I play flag, our game lasts around three hours. If it weren't for the stops and the huddles, we would burn out after 20 minutes.

Granted some people do find the game a little long, but then again a test match in cricket is played all day for five days, and usually ends up in a tie. Rich Eisen, the smooth anchor of the NFL show *Total Access* on the NFL network (a station dedicated to the NFL 24/7), wrote that the NFL does not actually want "to lengthen the time of the game." It is "something the Membership hates. They want NFL games to move briskly."[22]

And so on to the "tactics." Most people only see the brutality of the sport, and of course many are drawn in because of that, but under the surface it is a very complex sport and has often been described as a giant game of chess with 300-pound men. In fact, back in 1892 Harvard's football team, "lined up in a return formation drawn up by a military strategist, chess champion and team supporter,"[23] explains Ryan McGee, a sports journalist for *ESPN* magazine.

The first-down rule, the forward pass, and the ongoing substitutions have taken the sport away from its brutal roots and into something far more strategic, and I am a firm believer that in football, the "system" a coach uses is just as important as the physical skills of the individual players. In soccer one man like Cristiano Ronaldo can score three goals in minutes and single-handedly win the game. Although the NFL has its stars, it is the system that is often just as important. A quarterback like Brett Favre may have a great arm and accuracy, but if he has no offensive line to protect him, he won't have time to throw, and if his receivers can't catch or don't follow their routes, then his skills become redundant. In the '80s the NFL really boomed, thanks in part to the offensive "genius" of Bill Walsh, then the head coach of the San Francisco 49ers, who popularized the "West Coast" offense, a system that uses short sharp passes. Michael Lewis, author of *The Blind Side*, wrote that it is "designed to compensate for a weak-armed quarterback."[24] Oriard said that this system "was more sophisticated and complex than any offensive scheme before it, and it made football more than ever a coaches' game of system and strategy."[25]

Many people said that Joe Montana was too weak and too small to play in the NFL. In the West Coast offense system, Montana flourished, became the face of the NFL, and possibly the greatest quarterback ever to play the game, as Walsh's 49ers won three Super Bowls in a decade, putting them amongst the best teams of all time.

In football *because* of the stoppages, strategy is admired and created before and after each play. Fans, like myself and my friend Justin, continually try to predict what the offensive and defensive play will be before the snap. Because soccer is "free-flowing" for the most part, the better 11 soccer players will beat the other 11 soccer players. If strategy were so important in soccer they wouldn't put the two managers right next to each other on the sideline, so they could hear their opponents hollering out instructions. In the NFL the head coaches have secret signs and often call plays with their mouth behind a large card so their opposition cannot read their lips!

In football, organisation and tactics can often make the actual lesser-skilled or lesser-powerful team victorious, especially for coaches like Walsh, where Lewis said the "the system is the star." This makes the NFL fascinating because on "any given Sunday" any NFL team can beat any other NFL team. The league is unpredictable (unless you are a Browns fan, then I wouldn't hold my breath). In Britain from the 1992–1993 to the 2008–2009 seasons, Manchester Utd won 11 of the 17 Premiership titles, and when they didn't win, they finished second (yawn); only three other teams have won it in that time (double yawn); and from 2003 to 2009 the so-called big four (Liverpool, Manchester United, Chelsea FC, and Arsenal) have all finished in the top four each season (triple yawn). That is the equivalent of seeing the same four teams in an AFC and NFC championship game for seven straight seasons. In those same 17 years, only two teams outside the top four mentioned above have won the FA Cup. In comparison with the NFL, in those 17 NFL seasons (1992–1993 to 2008–2009) there have been 11 different Super Bowl winners. The New England Patriots and Dallas Cowboys have won the most during that time span with three each, proving the unpredictability of every NFL season.

The other major factor is the "Collective Bargaining Agreement" (CBA), which MacCambridge describes as the "league's socialist financial structure" with "the league sharing [its] revenue while in the greatest capitalist society on earth."[26] Oriard calls this "capitalistic socialism on which the NFL had thrived since the first national television contract in 1962."[27]

Pete Rozelle, the NFL's commissioner from 1960 until 1989, assisted in the creation of this socialist model, where he felt "that clubs' individual interests were best served by sharing, not competing. Short-term sacrifice would pay long-term dividends. Sharing television revenue meant rough parity and financial stability throughout the league. . . . [Viewers] would have to be fans of the league, not just the New York Giants or Los Angeles Rams."[28]

Rozelle "wanted to define the NFL as a single entity with 28 partners, instead of 28 separate interests,"[29] and it certainly worked for me. I am a fan of the sport, the league, and every team, and I don't think I'm the only one. I would watch any NFL team play against each other given half the chance. Even though I'm a soccer fan who follows Tottenham, I rarely tune in to watch any other soccer teams.

Oriard points out that the "the Super Bowl extended the philosophy behind the national TV contract, which marketed the entire league, not individual teams."[30]

The CBA was created to give teams equality so that the league can survive. The TV revenues from all games get split across the teams. The weakest teams get the first-round draft pick of college players, the teams finishing strongest face strong teams the following year, (in two games) the revenues from the gate (though not the club-level tickets) also get split across the league. This way the league is only as strong as its weakest link. If a team does not get good TV ratings or put bums on seats (as in sell tickets, not to put actual homeless people in the stadiums!), then those teams may have to move because they are letting the rest of the NFL down. Teams also have to adhere to a salary cap and are only allowed 53 active players in their game-day squads. This stops rich owners from simply "buying the title," and puts more emphasis on strategy and training. This all means that many teams stay in the hunt for the playoffs until late on, making the league competitive every weekend, for every season.

Many other leagues have teams playing each other at least twice a season. Premiership fans, for example, can take for granted that they will see every team come and visit them every season. The fact that not every team plays each other in the NFL season means that fans watch over the rotating schedule hoping to see certain stars that might come to their town that year.

With my trip, I was able to see the whole spectrum of NFL stars and systems.

3

The Trip's Creation

Jay DiEugenio said in *Tailgater Monthly* magazine that seeing an away game can be "a mini-vacation while catching a game in an amazing city,"[1] and that is exactly what those Bears fans did at the game I attended in 2006. "Go Bears," chirped our air hostess on the way back to Chicago from Arizona the day after the game. Paul and I coincidentally boarded a connecting flight in Chicago before flying back home to London. The whole plane was filled with Chicago fans all greeting each other with "Go Bears" and heartfelt high-fives. We were all complete strangers but were spiritually connected by that amazing Bears comeback. With my Bears hat on I felt instantly accepted and at home.

Everyone discussed their favourite play of the game. I felt green with envy that I couldn't really talk about the game because I was so embarrassed for walking out. "You missed the ending?" gasped my neighbour with way too much volume. I tried to hush him, and play like it was our dirty little secret. "Puh . . . Puh . . . Please don't tell the rest of the guys." The whispers whizzed down the small plane like a Rex Grossman pass, fast but inaccurate, and my fellow Bears fans turned and stared at me with pity.

When I was walking off the plane many fans shook their heads, telling me that I missed "the best comeback in Monday Night Football history." Some tried to tell me about the key plays I missed, but of course I had seen them over and over again on television.

I had learnt some valuable lessons: don't leave before the end of a game and always be ready for a high-five. That's when I really started to think about what each team, and each set of fans would really be like. To make it "fair," the trip would have to encompass all the NFL teams, in their home cities during one regular season. That's 32 teams in 17 weeks.

Like many ideas, it started off as a pipe dream. I wanted to get a sponsor of some kind, but after sending off plenty of proposals, nothing materialised, and people seemed quite reticent about handing over tens of thousands of dollars for my dream trip. Suddenly it looked more possible when Baz, my sister, and I, who all co-owned an apartment in Canary Wharf, London, put our flat up for sale.

Three-time Super Bowl winning running back (and season three *Dancing with the Stars* winner), Emmitt Smith explained to Rich Eisen how to get from dream to goal: "My high school coach always told the team that it's only a dream until you write it down—*then* it becomes a goal."[2]

Coming Up With the Schedule

NFL teams play most of their games on Sunday afternoons, either at 1 p.m. or 4 p.m. (EST) for the duration of the regular season, which lasts 17 weeks, starting in September. One game every Sunday is played at night with an 8:15 p.m. kickoff time, and there is also one Monday night game per week between weeks 1 and 16. (Two Monday night games are featured in the first week.) There is one Saturday night game in week 16, as well as one Thursday night game each week from weeks 10 through 16 (three games are played on Thanksgiving Day). The current Super Bowl champions host the Thursday night NFL season kickoff, and the night games are nationally televised. As of the 2012 season, the NFL put in Thursday night football from week 1 all the way to week 16. So for those of you who may want to see all NFL teams play at home in one season, now it is much easier to do so.

In the United Kingdom all of the networks are national and you can also "pay" for certain channels and packages. So if a soccer game is on terrestrial TV, then the whole nation will see it. If it is on a paid channel, it is still national but only aired in homes that pay for that service. Not so in America. Being on "national" television in America is a big deal and is very good for NFL teams, because the whole country can watch, which potentially can create more fans.

In the United Kingdom, Premiership Saturday soccer matches that kickoff at 3 p.m. are not shown live on television. Highlights are shown later, and often the bigger teams (the big four) find themselves on Sky Sports (paid TV) live coverage on Sundays. Because these games often involve the big four clubs, the games are already a sell out, so being on TV does not take the fans out of the stadium. Then in time those clubs get larger fan bases because they are on TV more often. The danger with airing smaller clubs that do not sell out means that some fans would rather watch the game on TV than pay high-priced game tickets, and sometimes I have seen games on TV with many empty seats, which doesn't look good for the fans at home or help the atmosphere in the now half-empty stadium. In effect, the distance between the big and small clubs becomes greater.

Since 1973 American NFL fans are able to watch their "local" team on their "local" network, only if the fixture has "sold out" 72 hours before the game. If not then that matchup will be "blacked out" to homes that lie within a 75-mile radius of the stadium. This ensures that TV does not take fans away from the stadium. When teams play in "prime time" on national TV, it becomes a big deal. They are not blacked out and the whole nation is watching live.

The NFL tries to show the matchups that would be good for those who are "neutral." Therefore, high-profile teams often get the nationally televised games. And yet the 2006 Arizona Cardinals team I saw was not very good and had only a mediocre fan base, so why did they host a Monday Night Football (MNF) game? Because of their fancy new University of Phoenix Stadium. Allen St. John, author of *The Billion Dollar Game*, explains that this stadium was "the first one ever built to host the Super Bowl."[3] This MNF game was a dress rehearsal for when the city would host Super Bowl XLII the following season, when the unbeaten New England Patriots were surprised by the dogmatic New York Giants. That game came down to the wire and was voted game of the decade by NFL.com—a pretty good investment on the part of Glendale, Arizona.

In the U.K., sales tax (which, as of January 2010, stood at a whopping 20 percent) all gets put together into one national pot, which the politicians then decide how to divide. So the tax collected in car parks in Newcastle might end up going to a different city entirely, whereas in the United States, sales tax stays within that state or county, for the local politicians to spend.

So having prime time games means the fan base will increase and get wider. Out of town fans and tourists will then go to those games and spend extra money in that city. America is so physically large, and so many teams are far from each other, away fans would have to fly to Glendale, Arizona, thus spending money on hotels, restaurants, and car rental, boosting the local economy throughout the season. You can travel from one corner of England to the other in a day's drive or a train ride. Away team soccer fans tend to see the game and then simply go home afterwards. In 2008 the two Premiership teams furthest from each other were Newcastle and Portsmouth, which are 350 miles apart. With a 3 p.m. kickoff and soccer lasting just under two hours in real time a Newcastle fan could go to Portsmouth, see a game and be back home that night.

A city that builds a new stadium for a Super Bowl can often pressure local infrastructure to improve quickly. For example, Detroit needed a facelift and got one when they hosted Super Bowl XL in 2006. Allen St. John said that if "you go from the airport today to downtown Detroit, I defy you to find a pothole."[4]

The Bidwell family, who owns the Arizona Cardinals, barely attracted a 65 percent capacity at Sun Devil Stadium, their previous ageing arena, which they shared with Arizona State University, yet they wanted a fancy new stadium. The final cost for the new stadium was $445 million. Between 2003 and 2005, 68 out of the 756 NFL regular-season games were not sold out. The Raiders and the Cardinals made up for 60 percent of those 68 non-sold-out games.

As Oriard states in his book, during Paul Tagliabue's 17-year tenure (1989–2006) as the NFL commissioner, three quarters of the NFL teams built, renovated, or made contracts for new stadiums, as he believed that "stadium economics are changing dramatically and the entertainment marketplace is rapidly being restructured,"[5] as the NFL moved into "entertainment" as an industry. In 1994 the NFL hired former co-president of MTV Sara Levinson to promote the game to new fans as she became the president of NFL Properties.

In 1989 the brash new Dallas Cowboys owner Jerry Jones found a loophole where he realised that the income from club seats and luxury suites does not go back into the NFL, so he replaced ordinary seats with luxury seats at Texas Stadium and added something called "Personal Seat licences." The stadium's income went from $700,000 in 1992 to $30 million in 1993.

One could see why the Bidwells really wanted a new and luxurious stadium. The Cardinals themselves provided a one-off payment of $85 million. Allen St. John said that after two rounds of voting, the good folks of Arizona added "an increase in taxes on hotel rooms and rental cars, costs to be borne largely by out-of-towners"[6] to pay for the rest of the stadium. (*Ahhh, the genius of state-based sales tax!*)

St. John discovered an Arizona resident who, although she hated the Bidwell family, wanted "the stadium to do well because if the stadium does well, the area does well."[7] St. John continues that in the Arizona desert "you needn't be a marketing expert to understand that air-conditioned comfort could be a key to attracting new fans."[8] The Bidwells went further than just cooling the place. They wanted the ultimate in fan comfort, and by February 2006 the stadium was named by *Business Week* as "one of the ten most impressive sports facilities in the world,"[9] which I discovered in the Cardinals game-day programme.

The metallic outer shell of the structure resembles a rounded barrel cactus, and I was really impressed by the retractable roof and field—that's right, a retractable field! One of the end zones actually peels open, and the turf itself rolls out of the stadium in just 60 minutes to then grow outdoors in the Arizona sun. The stadium is so impressive I urge you to go even if you are not a Cardinal's fan or even a football fan.

To help me with my trip I went to the NFL directly. They have a U.K. subsidiary called the NFLUK. It turns out their headquarters is in London. I had a meeting with their PR guy, a chap named David Tossell, who has published several sports books. This was soon after the NFL's first regular-season game played outside North America—when the New York Giants played the Miami Dolphins in London. The Dolphins sacrificed a league home game by playing at the new Wembley stadium in October 2007, 25 years after the first "American Bowl."

For that 2007 game I was excited to see a "real" NFL game in London and returned the favour to my Dad by taking him to the game. It was a true celebration of the sport with every NFL jersey on display. Nick Richards explains in his book that NFLUK managing director Alistair Kirkwood called this a "Rainbow Coalition," showing the "world just how far the game had come in the United Kingdom."[10] Within 72 hours of tickets going on sale, the NFLUK had over half a million requests.

During the week building up to the game, the league paraded a 60-foot robot (animatron) of the then Miami Dolphins star player, Jason Taylor (*Dancing with the Stars* sixth-season runner up), around London. The animatron made its way all the way to Wembley for the game. NFLUK ran a competition: whoever took the best picture of the J. T. animatron would win a Jason Taylor–signed Miami Dolphins jersey. I put several pictures into the competition and won, which I took as a good omen for the trip.

Tossell told me that the London game went so well that it was highly likely there would be another game in London in the 2008 schedule, around week 8.

This was perfect timing, as I could only stay in the United States for up to 90 days without a work visa. That way I could come back to London and still get to see a game. I could have "a mini-vacation while catching a game in an amazing city"—my hometown. The 32 teams plus the London game then made it a 33 NFL-game trip in 17 weeks.

In April 2008 I spent a week in New York City with Steph, staying with my friend Justin. All across New York there were posters on the lampposts advertising the upcoming NFL draft to be held at Radio City Music Hall. On the last night of my trip the NFL announced the 2008 schedule. This was the moment I had been waiting months for, as I prayed for a "good" schedule, where Sunday games were hopefully physically close to Monday night games. If the schedule were too difficult, then I would have to wait another year.

I snapped 17 digital pictures—one picture for each week of the schedule—from Justin's laptop of the 2008 schedule and boarded our night flight back to London. While everyone else was asleep, I dedicated myself to the study of the weekly matchups. Unfortunately, I did not have a city-to-city map to know the mileage difference between the cities.

My challenge was to create a schedule that took into consideration the Sunday afternoon games, the big night games, the possible last-minute rescheduling, and the Monday night games, all while traversing 3,000 miles of America in a rental.

I decided that I could drive up to a thousand miles between a Sunday and a Monday night game, assuming the Sunday game was an early kickoff. I plucked that 1,000-mile figure from thin air, because I honestly did not know how tiring that much driving would be. The most I had ever driven in a day was 200 miles.

I initially used my wobbly knowledge of America to predict the routes. From Monday to Sunday I figured I could drive from any stadium to any other stadium in the country regardless of how many times I would have to drive coast to coast.

I was frantically drawing maps and coming up with possibilities. The green glow from the camera was giving me a headache but I kept going, determined to figure out the route. I was getting excited about the matchups and so many of the divisional rivalries.

"What's this?" I stammered, waking up my neighbours. "Is this an extra cheeky international game in week 14 . . . in Toronto?" Tossell hadn't told me about this game between the Dolphins and the Bills, who sacrificed a home game for the event. A regular-season game in Toronto was a must see.

Two clicks of the camera later I clocked yet another surprise. The Bears were hosting a Monday night game *and* a Thursday night game. If there were any team I should see at home twice, it had to be the Bears. On Monday, they would play their bitter rivals the Green Bay Packers—the oldest rivalry in the league. Steph stirred in her sleep as I was muttering "Go Bears" and giving myself practice high-fives. "So have you done the schedule yet," she murmured. "Not quite, but now I will be seeing 35 games instead of 33!" She shook her head and went back to sleep.

Several teams in the 2008 season hosted two and sometimes three prime time games, which meant the final route was so tight that I had to squeeze in a flight for the Toronto game and another for the Dallas game. I could not afford to miss any Sunday games. Some teams in the Northeast are very close to one another, but it was not possible to see two games in one day. (*See appendix A for my original route schedule.*)

The NFL schedule gets programmed the day after the Super Bowl. The league tries to avoid teams playing three road games consecutively and they decide when to give the teams a bye (a break in the schedule where teams don't play a game), along with factoring in weather and the prime time games. NFL schedule czar Howard Katz oversees this schedule and says that "all of the teams want to avoid schedules with horrific travel arrangements . . . some of our clubs love to play in primetime games, and ask for more. Some don't like primetime games and ask for fewer. We take those into consideration but try to do what is best for the league."[11]

I knew I wanted to "drive America." Cars are certainly the tailgaters' choice of vehicle, plus I would get to see more of the country, and it would be easier not to have to rely on bus, train, and flight schedules. Witty British writer Dave Gorman wrote *Unchained America*, where he embarked on an epic journey: "Go to America. Buy a car. Drive from one coast to the other. Whilst doing so, try not to spend any money in chain businesses. Sell the car. Go home. . . . What could possibly go wrong?"[12]

I tinkered with buying a car, but I played things safe and decided to rent a car (several actually) in advance via a U.K. travel firm. The only downside to this system was that I had to return the car from where it came, which wasn't terrible because the season started in New York City and all of my flights from the U.K. were to New York City.

Sure, I'll Squeeze in a Charity Run!

In July 2008 I got in touch with the Walter Payton Cancer Trust to see if there was anything my trip could do for this charity. Payton had died of a rare liver disease in November 1999. He was only 45 years old. The Walter Payton Cancer trust plans an annual charity run in Chicago. The race is 16,726 yards, the total number of yards that Payton rushed in his illustrious career.

"So how much is that . . . in miles?" I asked Carrie, the event's organiser. "Nearly 10 miles . . . so I'll put you down then." Ummmm, I don't even run for the bus.

I feel that if someone runs five miles a day by the end of the week they should be 35 miles away (my Dad, circa 1967). At high school I was so unmotivated by cross-country I cheated twice and nearly got suspended in my third year for refusing to run and for threatening to take my case to the European court under the child abuse law.

The charity race was scheduled for the Saturday of week 2 when the Bears were playing away, the same weekend where I would have driven across the country to see the Seahawks and then flown to see the Cowboys the next day. It was looking like a tough weekend.

After week 11, the NFL has what is called a "flexible" schedule. This basically means that any 1 p.m. Sunday game can be moved into a Sunday night slot, causing me quite the headache. If there is a mouth-watering 1 p.m. matchup, the TV networks will "bump" the game to Sunday night with only one week of warning. This did worry me with a few matchups as it meant that I might not then have enough time to get to the Monday night games. But as there was nothing I could do about that, I just hoped those some teams were to have a poor season.

With the schedule I had created, I would see the Dolphins and Steelers four times, both once at home and three times away. I would see my Bears three times, twice at home and once away when they played at the Indianapolis Colts, a rematch of Super Bowl XL in 2006, which the Colts won.

Favre

A few months prior to the trip Brett Favre retired from the NFL, having started an amazing 262 consecutive regular-season games, a league record for a non-special-teams player. At age 38, he decided it was time to hang up his cleats, even though he had played pretty well the year before for the Green Bay Packers.

Despite the fact that the Packers are the Bears' oldest rival, Favre was one of my favourite players. He is pure football and has played through broken ribs and other injuries. Like Payton and Ditka, he is featured as one of "pro football's fifty toughest players" catalogued by Neil Reynolds in his book, *Pain Gang*. Favre still has the hardest throw in the league and is simply brilliant to watch. Like Walter Payton, Favre hails from Mississippi and also loves the game. Favre explains, "I like to have fun too, I think the fans enjoy that."[13]

I was a little annoyed that the year I decided to do my trip Favre decided to retire. The Green Bay Packers were going to do a special ceremony to retire his number 4 jersey on their season opener, my third game of the trip. I found an e-mail address for Brett somewhere online. I told him that he was one of my favourite players (despite being a Bears fan) and that he should come back out of retirement to play again, just so I could see him play.

Despite his tears during his retirement speech, Favre had two weeks to digest my e-mail, at which point he decided to continue playing football. I don't want to take ALL the credit for his sudden change of mind, as I'm sure the millions of dollars may have had something to do with it and the fact he still loves playing the game. But by now the Packers had already started training with their second-string quarterback Aaron Rodgers, so Favre signed with the New York Jets. I looked at my schedule, and I was happy that now I would see Favre play twice.

And So I Interviewed My Parents

So with just days before leaving for my trip I decided to interview my Mum and Dad, good old Sue and Harvey, also known as Coach and Watergirl.

Me: Okay, Mum and Dad, am I crazy for doing this trip or what?

Mum: Yes, but I don't blame you for trying to fulfill one of your dreams . . . but you are crazy.

Dad: Absolutely.

Me: Or was it that you brought me up to be crazy?

Mum: A bit of both.

Dad: I thought I brought you up normal, but it was your Mother that brought you up crazy.

Me: Do you think I will make it to all thirty-five games?

Mum: You might.

Dad: You might not. [Thanks, Dad.]

Me: Do you think I will have enough money to go to the playoffs and the Super Bowl?

Mum: Nope.

Dad: You definitely need some sponsorship, please don't ask your father!

Me: So what else should I have done with the money from selling the apartment instead of this trip?

Mum: Bought another flat, or given your girlfriend a nice diamond ring! [Does my Mother really expect me to spend $50K on an engagement ring?]

Dad: Wine, women, and song and whatever is left over you should waste.

Me: You guys gonna come to any of the games?

Mum: If I can afford it.

Dad: The London game.

Me: Who do you fancy for the Super Bowl?

Mum: Chicago Bears. [I think that's the only NFL team my Mum knows.]

Dad: Jacksonville Jaguars. [He got that very wrong.]

Me: When I was following the NFL as a kid, did you ever think I might do anything as erratic or as genius as this?

Mum: Not as erratic.

Dad: Genius! Certainly not.

Me: Why have you not stopped me, hahaha!

Mum: You have got your own mind.

Dad: You have been advised to be stopped.

Me: What do you think are going to be my challenges?

Mum: Getting to the games on time and all that driving.

Dad: The distances, the change in the weather and you may get a jiffy tummy [upset stomach].

Me: See ya in eight weeks for the London game and some good home-cooked food!

Both Steph and I knew that the trip would be a strain on our relationship since I would be away so long. I would be having the trip of a lifetime while she would be at home working, and I knew it would not be easy for her. Steph's ex had once taken her to a soccer game in Watford, and although it was not in the bad times of hooliganism, fans at soccer games can still be pretty raw and even quite sexist. She told me that her experience going to soccer games was "just a bunch of yobs shouting 'the referee's a wanker' at any given opportunity."

Originally she could not understand my trip, thinking that soccer in the U.K. must be the same as football in the U.S. I was willing for her to come along, and it would not have been that much more expensive, but if you are not into American football going to see 35 games is a pretty big leap. Steph told me, "You are crazy, but at least you are driven and motivated enough to actually go ahead and do it."

I was convinced that as soon as she got out to the States and experienced a live NFL game, and especially the tailgating, she would understand my passion. I knew she would enjoy herself at a game even if she didn't like the sport.

Back in 2006 for Super Bowl XL, the Bears had matched up against the mighty Indianapolis Colts. I was dressed up to the max in Bears gear, and I even managed to persuade Steph to don a Bears t-shirt and bandanna for the game. "Watch Hester" I exclaimed, but Steph was already asleep on the couch when Devin Hester caught the opening kickoff amongst the flurry of flashbulbs. He fearlessly raced towards and through the oncoming Colts.

"It's Hester, trying to work it back to the middle . . .," cried the commentator. Hester had dodged two tackles and got to the Bears 20-yard line. All the blood in my body rushed to my head. ". . . he gets past the first wave, and here he goes!" Hester flew past the halfway mark and my heart was racing. "It's Hester inside the 30. Hester's going to take it all the way for a touchdown!" With the world watching, Hester propelled himself into a star and was coined the most exciting player in NFL. "Touchdoowwwn!!" I was up on my feet, screaming and running around the apartment like I had just won the Super Bowl myself. My sister, Baz, and the neighbours thought I was under some kind of attack but I didn't care because it was 10 seconds of pure greatness. It was the first time any player has ever scored on the opening kickoff of a Super Bowl and my Bears were looking at their second Super Bowl trophy. It was one of the best pieces of sporting achievements I have ever witnessed—the greatest 10 seconds of Bears football since their Super Bowl win in 1986.

Steph mildly lifted her head.

Although I explained to her just how amazing that play was, she was still unconvinced. So I moved the furniture around and got myself a football. I set up the furniture like they were the blockers and clumsy Colts players and reenacted that touchdown in the living room. She was still unfazed, and I was unable to sell her on the sport, but I knew that the tailgating and the overall atmosphere of a live game would thrill her.

I had known Steph for only six months when I first thought of the trip. Yet it wasn't until December of that year that we started going out. Of course I didn't tell her on our first date that I was planning a 17-week road trip to the States, happily blowing my way through $70,000. Not sure I would have got a second date, had I said that.

When Baz, my sister, and I sold our flat in November 2007, it afforded me the money for the trip and a few months to plan. Bertie and Baz maturely put their money into other abodes, while I cleverly invested all my money into the NFL, losing all of it and more on the trip.

Steph agreed to come to the London game with me, and then to fly out for the last few games. I was hoping that if by the end of the trip I could make an NFL fan out of Steph then I could do that for others . . . potentially.

David Tossell had told me that he had never heard of anyone going to this many football games in one season before. A stadium-sized floodlit bulb went off in my head. Perhaps my adventure could set a world record. What a lovely bonus that would be. I fired off some questions to the folks at the Guinness Book of World Records. Ten months later and with only 10 days to go before the trip, Guinness finally called me back telling me that a chap named Peter Baroody had already done it! WHAT?! Peter Baroody of Alexandria, Virginia, watched a complete NFL match at 32 NFL franchises taking in all 31 NFL stadiums in just 107 days, in 2002.

AARGHHH!

Guinness coined him the "Ultimate NFL fan." "That's okay," I told Guinness, still hopeful I still might have a record "breaking" trip on my hands as I proudly added, "I'm going to go to *35* NFL games, in *three* different countries in *33* different stadiums." But she took the wind right out of my football by explaining that the only way I could "break" Baroody's record would be by going to see games at all 32 franchises in *under* 107 days, which would mean 15 NFL weeks. Despite a 17th week in the NFL season, bloody Baroody just had to go and see all 32 teams in 16 weeks. The swine! He also had the luck of the stadiums, where his Monday and Thursday games were close to his Sunday games, and twice he had the pleasure of hitting two games on the same Sunday! I wasn't blessed with a schedule like that.

Could I see 32 franchises in 15 weeks? Two hours of juggling the schedule later, I had discovered the only way I could do it would be to sacrifice the London and Toronto games. Those two international games were really important for me in my quest to find the "NFL culture." And they were more important to me than breaking a world record. Oh well. It was a nice thought while it lasted.

Like any good football player, I needed a game plan and training. The trip's schedule was hard enough but on top of that, figuring out the travel, flights, my friends' work schedules, and places for me to stay was very tricky. Football is a highly planned out sport, where every "play" has been rehearsed and tested in training, and where every athlete plays his role for the greater good of the team. Michael Lewis said that "an NFL football field is a tightly strung economy. Everything on it comes at a price. Take away from one place and you give to another."[14]

Though even with a strict game plan, I still knew as the team's QB I would have to call "audibles." This is when the QB decides to change the play at the line of scrimmage just before the ball is "snapped." I knew things could go wrong or new opportunities might arise so I would have to change my route and adapt accordingly.

It was late May 2008, when I started getting e-mails from blog sites and online radio stations to interview me about the trip. Baz had worked hard on my website, AdamsFootballTrip.com, and my adventure was starting to percolate through the virtual world. I had originally planned to buy a grill and do my own tailgating at every stadium, until a Saints blogger named Dave Cariello of Canal-StreetChronicles.com interviewed me. Within a matter of weeks I had been sent several wonderful game-day menus from Saints' tailgaters who insisted on hosting me at their parties in week 12. I ditched my grilling idea instantly.

I knew that I could not just turn up at tailgate parties empty-handed, but I knew that being on the road I could not bring drinks and food. So I decided to print up hundreds of t-shirts. I knew that Americans love a good free t-shirt. My old college friend from Toronto, Jeremy, prints t-shirts. So I had him make up shirts with my website on the front and my 35-game schedule printed on the back.

In August 2008, just weeks before the trip, I spent my last two weeks at work before leaving on a high because I was in Chicago on a 17-day international trip with the senior youth drama group that I tutor; they were studying improvisation in Chicago at the world-famous Second City. As I was in Chicago, I got in touch with the Bears, mentioning that I was about to do my trip and that I'd love to see the stadium if possible while in town. Cary Dohman, who has one of the best jobs in the world, being the media relations assistant for the Chicago Bears, offered me a media pass for the upcoming "Family Day" training camp at Soldier Field, which would allow me to be on the sidelines during the camp. I couldn't believe it.

Although going to Chicago was supposed to be a theatre trip for the young people, I had persuaded them to visit Soldier Field with me for the Bears "Family Day" training camp on what was a scorcher of a day.

Although I had lived in Chicago during the summer in 2002, this was actually my first time *in* Soldier Field, because in 2002 they played in Champaign, Illinois, while Soldier Field was being renovated. The historic Bears stadium is now a mixture of ancient Greco-Roman design, featuring Greek-style columns on the outside, with the look of an alien space ship plonked inside, since renovations required that the new stadium bowl rise above and hang over the columns. Thankfully the drama group decided they wanted to see the training camp (I think they were all just being nice to me and were happy to sit out in the sun), and we all went to the fan zone on the grass outside Soldier Field. Just as it was time to go inside, they went through the normal gates to their seats in the nosebleeds, while I went to the media entrance with my heart racing, and goose bumps all over my body.

Dohman walked me through the stadium all the way to the field. I was so overwhelmed that I was nearly in tears. I pretended that the 25,000 screaming fans were cheering for me. I was mesmerized and dwarfed by the surrounding stands. I was told that I had to dress "professionally," which was harder than I thought, because I really wanted to throw on my Bears jersey and scream like the rest of the fans. I put on a shirt and wore my smartest, least shabby jeans. I was sweating in the heat, and when I looked around, I saw that the other "media" members were all in sensibly dressed in khaki shorts and polo shirts. I didn't know that was "professional" attire.

I was standing right next to a huge inflated Bear head when the players started racing out onto the field from the Bear's mouth through an abundance of smoke and fireworks, one by one. My favourite Bear, Mike Brown, was called and I cheered, but then I realised I was supposed to be "professional" and not a "fan." Urlacher got a big cheer, but the biggest cheer of all was left to the most exciting man in football at the time—Devin Hester. Players went through their training drills—catching, kicking, and passing, but no tackling. When Devin Hester returned a "practice" kickoff back to the end zone, it really excited the fans; even though he was up against zero defenders, it was hoped that he would do this in the real upcoming games.

The magical night finally came to an end and I was slightly unsure what to do. The reporters and journalists swarmed rookie running back Matt Forte. The lights went off and the fireworks started to pop. I got a text that our drama students had become bored about two hours prior and left to grab some food and see a late-night show. Apparently they were not as excited as me to see players just go through training drills.

At the end of the night, some of the players were still signing shirts and balls, and I really wanted to get them to sign anything I had, but I had to hold back because I was there as a "professional." Once the players went into the locker room, I wandered down the tunnel, not sure exactly where to go or what to do next.

I wandered by where all the players park, and oohed at the huge cars. Outside the locker room was a table with hundreds of fried chicken boxes, with what Americans call biscuits, but we Brits call scones. Why on earth would they be giving out fast food to the athletes? And why would anyone have scones with fried chicken? Athletes under such high pressure surely don't eat junk food? Then again, I thought, maybe all this fried chicken might have had something to do with the Bears not making the playoffs twenty weeks later.

Our star defensive tackle at the time, Tommie Harris, who had just signed a massive multimillion-dollar contract, picked up some chicken and walked to his car. He then mused for a moment and came back towards the locker room. I thought he might have wanted to talk to me as he was looking my way. He nodded to the staff member at the table, and another chicken box was placed in his mighty paw. It made me giggle to see that someone worth over $40 million would come back to get an extra free box of chicken.

Once I got home, a couple weeks later, my Mum was elated. "You're in the newspaper, my boy is in the newspaper!" she screamed as she saw a picture of me outside Soldier Field from that night. I had only done one interview for a newspaper before the trip and it was for the *Jewish Chronicle*. My Mum was immensely proud at seeing her son pictured in the holy grail of papers. To have her child do something good enough to get in the *J.C.* is every Jewish mother's fantasy, though she still wasn't too happy I was about to spank all my money on football.

Just days before setting off to New York City, I was interviewed on Britain's biggest sports radio, TalkSPORT. The two presenters were more impressed by the sheer audacity of the trip, as opposed to actually being excited about "American football." They felt the game was slow and boring, and one of them had even been to mecca itself: The Super Bowl. Sadly he felt rather limp about the whole sport. I'm not sure if they wanted me to pack my idea in then and there and go to every Premiership team instead, or maybe they felt let down that a British guy like me is more into an American sport than one created on my home soil.

Karl Baumann, the NFL producer for Sky Sports, which airs the Sunday and Thursday games live to Sky subscribers, was willing to do a piece on my trip when I came back for the London game. I told him I was interested in the tailgaters and the fans as much as the sport itself. "Hmmm," Karl mused, "but isn't the guy in Green Bay eating a hot dog the same guy as the guy drinking a beer in Buffalo?" "I hope not," I said, "otherwise I don't have a trip!"

The tailgaters *had* to be different with different stories, different foods, from different backgrounds with different paths bringing them to the tailgate. Rich Eisen wrote in Ray Lampe's *NFL's Game Day Cookbook* that "every football town has its own flavor (or flava depending on the city)" leading "to mass confectionary confusion,"[15] and I couldn't wait to try them all!

Another thing I wanted to find was the "ridiculous merchandise" from each team. Over the years I have collected quite the mountainful, but this time I wanted something from each game, as well as to unearth some of the more ridiculous items.

Two of my prized pieces of Chicago Bears merchandise are my two bobbleheads of Brian Urlacher and Anthony Thomas, which Traci gave me when I lived in Chicago in 2002. They were the first bobbleheads I had ever seen and were only available at McDonald's for $5 a piece.

At the end of that summer McDonald's recalled these products because they had too much dangerous lead paint on the players' faces. That week in McDonald's there was a sign saying "WANTED" and a picture of the two illegal mini football players, like they were outlaws in the Wild West. There was no way I was going to give them back, they are much more infamous now that they are dangerous, but only if you lick them.

My Dad has always taught me to buy the game-day programmes for any sporting event, and I have thus far not let him down. Some teams give out game-day programmes for free, others you need to buy, plus some teams also give out freebies to all their fans entering the stadium. Eisen says that even the professionals in the game love the free stuff. "If it's free it's me. We'd step over our own mothers for a bag of SWAG . . . which for the uninitiated stands for Stuff We All Get. Trust me. Anyone who denies that is full of it."[16]

I discovered "SWAG" in 2007 at the London NFL pre-game week-long hoopla while following the Jason Taylor Animatron. Dolphins goodies were being handed out by the Miami Dolphins cheerleaders, including a fetching Dolphins foam finger. For me the foam finger is the classic All American sports merchandise, it is ridiculous yet somewhat cool at the same time. At the game at Wembley a few days later, my Dad and I bought a programme and a match day commemorative scarf. Scarves are the British sporting merchandise equivalent of the foam finger, but obviously less ridiculous and slightly more practical. For this scarf, there was the Dolphins Logo on one end and the Giants on the other, and it was frankly ugly as sin, but I just had to buy it. We were all given a free Dolphins towel (the size of a beer mat), but *everyone* was asking me about where I got the Dolphin foam finger . . . I felt so proud!

I also wanted to discover Americana in the sport. For Webster the NFL had "created an excitement and an atmosphere [that] I had never experienced in British sport. It wasn't necessarily better or even more exciting. It was just different and it was the American-ness that made it so."[17] Americana, or what I call the "hoopla," are the parts of the game-day experience that do not involve the athletes but everything else the franchise adds—from cheerleaders to wacky mascots, jumbotrons, and giveaways. No one does hoopla like the Americans and no single sport in the world has as much of it as American football.

Eisen says that if you "add up the total running time of only actual plays during an average three-hour NFL game, it might when strung together, yield a mere 10 to 12 minutes of activity,"[18] which means that the rest of the 2 hours and 48 minutes is filled with pure Americana. Some teams obviously have more hoopla than others and use it in different ways. Yes, it makes the game go quicker, especially as there are so many stops, but it is more than that, it is a fun, creative way of appreciating the fans. If you are in the stands and you find yourself not salivating over the prospect of a possible play-action pass as the players are in the huddle, then the hoopla is for you. Don't worry, it doesn't make you less of a fan, the NFL is there to support both types of fans.

Some cynics would argue that if the game were so good, then NFL teams would not need such hoopla to entertain the fans. Though teams recognise that the game is long and that there are stoppages, and use this time to advertise in humorous ways. The eight-home-games-a-year also gives each game a "celebratory experience," and that comes through in the hoopla.

Like the NFL itself, the hoopla, for the most part, was born out of college football. In 1946, Paul Brown was hired as the Cleveland Browns' first coach. He had started off with the Ohio State Buckeyes (Ohio State University) where his success came from "his ability to elicit a community-wide dedication to the game," says MacCambridge, who points out that the college game has a "frenzied school spirit" where "the football team [is] at the absolute center of the school's social whirl."[19] Brown tried to bring that kind of community-wide dedication and hoopla to the professional league.

For the Cleveland Browns' AAFC season opener in 1946 (before it was known as the NFL), Brown lead his team out to a marching band consisting of 120 people, 30 marching majorettes, $10,000 worth of fireworks, and ballerinas. The team's mascot led an orchestra, two French chefs carved meat in the press box and a car was even given away to a fan as a prize—all before the ball was even snapped! That's a whole lot of hoopla! And I was hoping to see plenty more on the trip.

My trip goals:

- Find tailgaters at every game.
- Try to see every game from kickoff to the final whistle.
- Buy something from each franchise. The more ridiculous the better.
- Root for the home team.
- Not die driving thousands of miles on the "other" side of the road.

4

First Quarter

*Kickoff. As the action begins I feel like a kid ripping
through the wrapping paper of a present. Each NFL game
represents a different present for me.*
—Bob Papa[1]

A couple of days before flying to New York City, I kept waking up in the middle of the night. At first I thought it was because I was afraid to fail . . . what if I missed one game? What if it became one big waste of money? It's not like it was a bit of short change going on the trip. It was all the money I had—$70,000. I was going to blast through this cash in a matter of months just to see some football games. Until I started having these anxiety dreams, I never actually thought of the ridiculousness of the whole trip—I don't even like driving much in London and I just signed myself up to drive over 30,000 miles! What was I thinking?

Once I had said good-bye to my parents and my sister at Heathrow, it was time to say good-bye to Steph. We cried in each other's arms and I felt instant relief. I was nervous because I was about to embark on my mission while being in a committed relationship. Previously, my single life had allowed me to just pick up and go whenever I fancied. Prior to Steph, I wasn't used to thinking of someone else. I needed that hug. I began to feel that she would actually be there when I got back.

The ever-so-honest former Bronco and All-Pro defensive back, John Lynch, also suffered from pre-game nerves. As mentioned in Rich Eisen's book *Total Access*, Lynch's wife wrote him a note on the day of his first professional game:

"I know you are probably very nervous right now. Stop—take a deep breath and think how lucky you are. You are about to begin a great journey. You are getting an opportunity to live out your dream and you are so ready for this."[2] Before every game, Lynch's wife would write similar notes. Steph said the same thing to me at the airport, almost verbatim and continued to send me similar supportive messages via modern-day letters (the SMS text) before every game. Steph's support had exactly the same soothing effect on me as I'm sure it did on Mr. Lynch. Ahhhhh.

I spent the next few days in New York City at Justin's place, where the first batch of my "Adams Football Trip" t-shirts had been sent. He took me to a college bar, where he introduced me to a tailgating/college drinking game called Beer Pong, which involves throwing ping-pong balls into red "party" cups on a table that are a third filled with beer. Neither of us were any good, but it was sweet enough that Justin thought I needed to get in some training before tailgating.

The day before the 2008 NFL kickoff I met with two hard-core Miami Dolphins fans, "the 2 Michelles." Although they both live in New York City, they went to every Dolphins away game in 2007. It must have been a tough year seeing the Dolphins lose every single one of those games, but they stayed positive.[3]

The 2 Michelles go by "Tall" and "Short," and it didn't take a genius to see who was who when they interviewed me on camera at Short Michelle's apartment building. I told the Michelles that I would be rooting for the home teams, though there was a clash of interest in my second game, when my Bears played away in Indianapolis. The girls told me that I should go as an "away" fan and then compare that experience with being a home fan at other games, which was food for thought.

The 2 Michelles told me countless stories of the crazy fans they met, how they were treated as away fans, sometimes badly, but on the whole pretty well, and the players that they had met. When they talked of meeting Dolphin icons like Dan Marino, you could see the kid in their souls bubbling with joy and enthusiasm. I felt honored that these great fans had featured me on their first video blog of the season. Looking back through the interview I already looked shattered, and I hadn't even seen a game or begun driving.

They asked me about Stephalicious, a name they loved. They wanted to meet her and invite her to be a Dolphins fan, or just a football fan in general. The first half of the trip meant I was going to be away from Steph for eight weeks, the longest by far we had been apart. People at home had told Steph that she was a fool for staying with me while I was away. Plenty of guys had told me what a keeper she must be, and of course I agreed, but it wasn't going to be easy. The 2 Michelles understood my dilemma, and maybe it was because they are such football fans that they got it. They were the first women I had met who didn't think I was an asshole for leaving Steph behind for football. I just had to hope the first eight weeks were not too much of a strain.

Game 1. NFL Week 1, Washington Redskins at New York Giants, Giants Stadium

Final Score: 7-16. Home-win record: 1-0. Capacity: 80,242. Attendance: 79,742. Ticket face value: $80—I paid $88 via StubHub. Picture on my ticket: David Tyree's Super Bowl "Helmet Catch." Mascot: None. Merchandise: Giants foam finger. Local dish: Pizza, and sausage and peppers.

David Tossell had previously told me he *could* get me tickets for every game, but he wasn't going to. Not because he was mean, but he felt the challenge of the trip would be how I would go about getting tickets. In the United Kingdom, scalping is very much illegal, and for most Premiership soccer teams you either need to be a member of the club or have something called "a ticket buying history" just to get game-day tickets.

I knew that for teams like Green Bay, there is a long waiting list to be a season ticket holder, and the tickets are passed down from generation to generation. With this in mind, I impulsively bought a lot of tickets from Ticketmaster when some of the franchises released some of their tickets on "general sale" in the summer. By the time I had left for the trip I had secured tickets to 20 of the planned 35 games via Ticketmaster, though for the first three games I did not have a ticket.

Not having a ticket meant that I went straight to the ticket agency site Stub-Hub. Here people can sell their own tickets to the game at any price they wish, using StubHub's licenced website. StubHub adds its own charges and makes a healthy profit. StubHub had tickets for the game, but the ticket pickup location was "a short drive from Giants stadium." Well how far a short drive is anyone's guess, as Americans consider driving a few hours quite run of the mill. It turns out the pickup spot was three miles from the stadium. This was a bit problematic, however, because I had just booked Justin and myself on a "booze" bus arranged by a bar in Manhattan called the Blind Pig. For 40 bucks they drive you to the game, feed you up on beer and dodgy pre-mixed Bloody Marys and drive you back, but sadly they do not provide tickets.

The day before the NFL kickoff, StubHub told me that there was no way of getting the tickets sent anywhere else even though they have an office in Manhattan, the exact place where those who are "selling" tickets have to go to drop them off. Giants Stadium is about a 40-minute drive outside Manhattan, and it isn't even in the state of New York, but in New Jersey. "Sir, you are buying from the seller, not us," the StubHub man on the phone told me. "We are just the agency. We only have one pickup place." I felt like crying.

The Blind Pig employee laughed on the phone, like I knew he would, when I asked him if they could drop me off at the StubHub ticket pickup before driving me three miles further down to the game. So I marched into the StubHub shop front in Times Square, ready for battle.

At the counter I asked them what *actual* physical tickets they had in the building for the Giants game, but they were not allowed to give me that information. At a StubHub shop you cannot "buy" over the counter. You have to log in on one of their computers and pay for the tickets online. From what I could gather the counter is really only for staff to keep saying "We do not sell tickets, use the computer" over and over and over.

It was also too late for StubHub to send me the tickets. A StubHub staff member named Howie saw my disdain for their ridiculous system and told me to log in and find seats in my price range and give him the StubHub code. He then would look out back to see if those tickets were in the office.

Two hours later we were no further, and he finally cracked, telling me that ALL of the tickets come into his office on game day before they go on a van to be deposited three miles from Giants stadium. If I could get to StubHub before noon the following day he would put my tickets to one side. I felt like I had "beaten the system!"

The next morning was NFL kickoff day and I couldn't have been more excited. I got to StubHub anxious but was instantly relieved when the tickets were placed in my hand. Justin and I then hopped onto The Blind Pig booze bus, ready for my first official tailgate party of the trip. Beer and premixed Bloody Marys were passed around in red plastic cups.

In my years of watching American movies I have come to the conclusion that nothing symbolizes an "American Party" more than the presence of red plastic cups. In all those college films people drink from these glorious receptacles. So you can imagine my pleasure when I was handed my first red plastic cup. These cups are robust, they have a "grip lip" handy for the game "flip cup," and the grooves on the side are perfect for measuring and are used in games like beer pong. The trip had given me a starring role in my very own American party movie.

The irony is that the red cups are there to conceal its contents to the public, though by "concealing" the alcohol with a bright, garish, flashy red cup, you are blatantly advertising that you are actually drinking alcohol. A beige cup might be subtler.

We don't have these cups in the U.K., which surprised my new American friends. "So what do you guys drink out of?" "Err, actual glasses, or the bottles they came in." In the U.K. we are allowed to drink alcohol publicly. This shocked the Americans and they reacted like we Brits have lost all sense of moral coding.

Then they were surprised to hear that we are *not* allowed to barbeque in public. Every council is different in the U.K. but on the whole you can't do it, and certainly not on open-flame grills. Australia has the right idea. Their councils actually put up coin-based grills and set them up in parks and near beaches.

The bus trickled its way to the Meadowlands, but it only got us there just in time to make the new earlier kickoff time of 7 p.m., changed because of the U.S. presidential candidates who were speaking in NYC that night. I wondered if such speeches were really important enough to alter the time of an NFL kickoff? (Four years later, to kickstart the NFL 2012 season the Super Bowl–winning Giants, who beat the Patriots again, had to move their NFL kickoff game to a Wednesday night, again because of presidential speeches . . . unbelievable!)

Unfortunately, we had missed the real tailgating, but the bus ride experience created a great feeling of fandom because it was like we were all going to an away game together.

My seat was high up on the upper deck, and surprisingly there was little crowd noise. Considering we were watching the so-called World Champions (the Giants had miraculously beaten the New England Patriots, via the now famous David Tyree "helmet catch" as captured on my game-day ticket. The Patriots went undefeated during the 2007 season, until the Super Bowl XLII game), this game itself was not that great, and because we got there right at kickoff, I had missed the pre-game ceremony that included a gigantic blow-up 60-foot-tall Vince Lombardi (Super Bowl) trophy. And there was little hoopla throughout the game, maybe they kept it for all the pre-game festivities. There were no cheerleaders to watch, as the Giants are one of six NFL teams that do not have cheerleaders.

Rudy moment (aka the best play of the game—like my one and only interception when playing for Aber): Eli Manning, the Giants' quarterback, faked a pass and then ran a bootleg into the end zone for the Giants' only touchdown of the game.

Orange play of the game (aka the worst play of the game—like my muffed punt return that got me an orange squeezed over my naked torso in a packed pub): Eli Manning again. He was moving around trying to avoid the sack. Instead of throwing the ball away he threw a wobbly pass that landed easily in the arms of a Redskin.

Extreme fan: A man near me with a shaved head had his skull painted like a Giants helmet.

After the game I briefly saw some fans having a post-tailgate drink outside their minivan painted with Giants logos. There was too little time to really digest any true tailgating—the bus was waiting for us, and it was late and on a "school night"—but at least I got my red cup and a home win, and that was a start.

Two days later, it was a Saturday afternoon, and Justin came with me to pick up my first rental car. Of course, they didn't actually have the car I ordered for two hours, which put me behind schedule. We packed up the car in the pouring rain, and I was crapping myself knowing that I was about to drive on my own to Indianapolis, some 700 miles away. I was in the busiest city in the world, on the "wrong side of the road" with rain coming down with such velocity that my wipers couldn't keep up. I simply drove into a blur. "Good luck!" Justin shouted as I nervously pulled away, avoiding kamikaze cab drivers.

After driving 330 miles in the rain, it was getting dark and I was getting tired. For some reason this stretch of the American highway had no streetlights, and no cats' eye road markers. So I hugged the only lane that had a prominent white line. This was the fast lane, and because I was too scared to go fast, I left a trail of angry drivers behind me. I was clutching the wheel and my nerves were shot to pieces.

I saw a sign for a hotel and pulled off the motorway, where I was faced with a dual carriageway (a main road where there are two lanes of traffic on both sides) going across me. I could see the hotel to my right, but it was on the other side of the road and about a hundred yards away, but there was a raised median between the double lanes. Turning right would take me towards the hotel but then past it as I would be on the opposite side of the road. Turning left would simply take me away from the hotel. I was confused—how was anyone taking this exit supposed to drive *into* this hotel?

It was 2 a.m. and I waited a whole 10 minutes to see if any cars would go past and thus educate me on the American roads, but no cars came. I couldn't sit there all night—I had to do something. Finally, I bit my lip and drove across the midpoint of the road and turned right. I hit the accelerator thinking I might well be driving on "the wrong side of the road." The hotel was close and all I needed to do was go a little further and duck left into the hotel.

That's when I saw not one but two pairs of oncoming headlights in the distance. There was no "might" about it, I was *definitely* on the wrong side of the road facing oncoming traffic! Going up against one car might have been okay, but facing two on a two-lane road meant trouble. They were both going quick. Do I risk it and accelerate very quickly to then duck into the hotel? It was far too dangerous. I panicked, flashed my lights, screeched to a stop, put my head into my hands, and prepared myself for a head-to-head collision. Sometimes a quarterback has no other choices, and simply has to take the sack from the oncoming blitzing linebackers. Time stood still and I firmly believed this was going to be the end of my trip, and frankly the end of my life.

The two trucks (trucks! I wouldn't have stood a chance in my Chevy Cobalt) screeched to a halt and stopped just mere inches before me. The two drivers shouted at me but calmed when they saw the tears of fright on my face. Then I bleated to them, "I'm so sorry, I'm from England! I just really need to get in that hotel and can't figure out how to get in there . . ." Thankfully one of the drivers saw my desperation and guided me on to the right side of the road, where we drove level with the hotel where there was an opening in the median to turn left into the car park, which I hadn't seen due to the lack of lights. I thanked him, got into my bed, and thanked God I didn't die.

Like Mr. Gorman, I wanted to go chain-free as much as possible and seek out the delights of independent America, but I buckled on day two. The big neon signs of Walmart suckered me in and I got plenty of snacks for the road ahead.

Because of my previous night's brush with death I also bought a GPS. I named him Gippy, and he became my new best friend.

Sunday meant it was a game day and I didn't want to miss another tailgate. The delay I experienced at the rental car pickup and the rain had put me behind schedule. The Cobalt's accelerator was very sensitive and I kept going over the speed limit and then having to brake. With just one hundred miles to go until Indianapolis, I got pulled over. The blue lights flashed me and I pulled into a rest stop. I was actually incredibly scared. I never use the word "sir" to the police or anyone at home and haven't used it since I was in high school, but when in Rome, right? I was all, "Yes sir, no sir, three bags full sir!" I was speeding, and I told the policeman that I was getting used to the car while on a journey to every NFL team. He said he had to check out my U.K. driver's licence and he asked me to go with him into the police car.

As pissed off as I was for getting caught (though it did teach me a lesson) and having to pay a fine, I was actually excited to sit in the back of an American police car. It was like I was in the movies. I felt like an infamous criminal, but he didn't oblige in turning the sirens on. I wanted to ask him if he could slam me onto the car and call me a "motherf**ker," like in the movies, but I didn't think he would see the funny side.

Game 2. NFL Week 1, Chicago Bears at Indianapolis Colts, Lucas Oil Stadium

Final Score: 29-13. Home-win record: 1-1. Capacity: 63,000. Attendance: 66,822. Ticket face value: $64—I paid $115 via StubHub. Picture on my ticket: Colts and Bears logos. Mascot: "Blue," a horse-like figure. Merchandise: Colts coffee mug and magazine about Lucas Oil Stadium. Local dish: Fried or breaded pork tenderloin.

I got to Lucas Oil Stadium about 45 minutes before kickoff. I could smell the home-cooked BBQ as I passed several Colts fans' RVs parked on any space they could find. Since Lucas Oil is a stadium located right in the downtown area, there is not a lot of stadium parking.

I parked next to an RV with Bears fans, although they were not spilling with much brotherly love. I was expecting them to be pleased to see a Bears fan on the road, especially one from London, but they mocked the idea of the trip a little. Sure, they still offered me beer and a hot dog—they are Americans, after all.

In the U.K., away fans often arrive together on coaches or trains resulting in an "away team bond." There are physical barriers between both sets of fans— usually gates or police on horseback outside the stadium. These barriers can actually be a catalyst for the aggression between the sets of fans. The further you push or hide fans away from each other the harder it is for humanization.

It is much the same inside soccer stadiums, as away fans have their own sections, so there is zero interaction between the away and home fan. Chuck Culpepper is an American sports writer who followed Portsmouth FC for a whole football season and he was "surprised to realize" that in the U.K., the away fans had their "own segregated concession stand and segregated toilets."[4] The home-away segregation demonizes the other fans by making a clear "us and them" culture. I have found this strange. I don't go on vacation to Spain to then spend my whole trip in a British-themed pub—although I know plenty of soccer fans who do just this. Away fans even have to purchase their away tickets from their own club.

Because there is home-and-away fan integration at NFL games, these Bear fans at Lucas Oil did not feel the urge to protect me from the home Colts fans, as there was nothing to protect me from.

Because I had to pick up my StubHub ticket from a nearby hotel and the crowd was already heading in, I didn't meet any local tailgaters. Two games down and tailgating-wise, it wasn't looking good. I needed to start getting to games not just an hour before kickoff but at least three hours before, if not more.

It was the Colts' first regular-season game in their swanky new stadium— which probably drove up the StubHub price—a rematch of the 2006 Super Bowl, and I was happy paying a little extra to see my beloved Bears.

Lucas Oil Stadium is magnificent. It looks like a massive rectangular warehouse from the outside—rustic, industrial, yet modern and sleek. In the stunning atriums, planes and racing cars hung from the air, with black-and-white chequered flags dotted about. There was also a section for racing car arcade machines. At the south gate there is a huge Colts football helmet that holds six large plasma screens in its facemask. There is also a huge Colts player that hangs horizontally from the ceiling as the fans enter the stadium.

I walked up a not-so-steep ramp to the top, which took me about 20 minutes. Sadly when I did get to my spot I was in a section directly under the commentary box, so a huge slab of concrete was above me. When people stood up, I could not see anything. Luckily there were TVs attached to the concrete plinth. But who wants to pay all this money for a ticket to watch the game on TV? I may as well have watched it outside with the "TV tailgaters."

During the pre-game show the Colts offensive players were introduced one by one. They ran out of an inflated temporary tunnel, into an aisle made up of their other teammates and cheerleaders. All the smoke and fog made it look like an alien space ship had just landed. Fireworks and flames were pumped out as each starting player was called, with Peyton Manning getting the biggest cheer of them all.

One would think that the smoke could possibly hinder the players. They have to stand there in the tunnel for quite some time breathing it in. Yet, Minnesota Vikings defensive end Jared Allen told the NFL network that "fog machines are cool, no matter what." Smoke can give players an edge, as it really pumps them and the fans up for the game.

Clay Travis has grown up going to games and is now desensitized by some of the hoopla. He asks, "Hasn't the dry-ice trend been going on for long enough? Is anyone impressed by this?"[5] Well, Mr. Travis, I still very am impressed and long may it continue.

Watching the game on my own gave me the impetus to mingle and interact with the fans around me. There were a lot of Bears fans around me, which was not helping me root for the Colts (since they were the home team), but the Colts fans were not being chatty at all. Culpepper discovered that English fans "don't chat during matches."[6] I thought this might be the same in the NFL—until I moved to the Bud Light zone, the open platform area in the stadium above the north end zone. Here I met an amicable local family of three brothers and their father. These guys were more than happy telling me about the history of the Colts, their fancy new stadium, and how the city came alive once they drafted Peyton Manning.

I watched the remainder of the game from there. I discovered that some fans buy the cheapest tickets and then stand in the Bud Light zone or other "social" areas. Behind me was a huge glass wall, facing downtown Indianapolis. The 88-foot glass panels can actually lift up in four minutes, opening up the entire glass wall. The roof can also be fully opened, which only takes 10 minutes to complete. I later discovered that there are a whopping 1,176 plasma TVs inside this stadium, and in many of the suites, each seat has a built-in personal TV, like on the head-rests of an aeroplane.

In all the U.K. major stadiums fans have to be seated, so you can see the emancipation I felt for being "allowed" to stand and watch the game, especially since my seat was under a concrete slab.

Lucas Oil Stadium has the second-smallest capacity in the league of 63,000, though it is expandable for events like the Super Bowl where 70,000 can fit. Tonight's attendance was 66,822. Initially I thought they had expanded the venue, but later on I discovered that teams do not count "standing room tickets" for their official capacity but do count them for their attendance.

The Bears surprised everyone and actually won the game. And only then did all the Bears fans in the stadium get together. They did so by huddling around our winning team, clamouring for autographs, while the defeated home team trundled off. Suddenly, behind us on the concourse, a stage appeared with lights, cameras, and action. A table with four suited men appeared from nowhere and discussed the game. Since this was a Sunday night "prime time" game, us fans were allowed to watch this live feed of the NBC sports analysts on their post-game wrap-up, we were even allowed to cheer behind the pundits and were not pushed out of the stadium.

Rudy moment: I couldn't cheer against my team any longer, and I went crazy when our rookie running back Matt Forte broke through the Colts' secondary from the 50-yard line like a galloping thoroughbred to score a remarkable touchdown. I threw my Colts coffee mug to the floor. I felt totally safe rooting for the Bears even though I was surrounded by Colts fans.

Orange play of the game: Colts head coach Tony Dungy or Peyton Manning (as he often calls plays) called an obvious run play. While backed up on their 1-yard line, the Colts got smothered by the Bears, easily giving the latter two points for a safety.

Extreme fan: "Horse Shoe Warrior." He had on blue-and-white face paint, a Colts baseball cap with a stuffed toy horse on top, shoulder pads, a Colts jersey, football pants, and white sticks coming out of his shoulders. He attends every Colts home game, even though he lives in Nevada.

Over the years some Americans have been shocked to find out that I enjoy the NFL, because they felt it is a game watched and played by "dumb jocks," attacking the players and fans alike. Perhaps they can't see beyond the fact that it is a contact sport, but I have always seen football as a superbly intelligent game.

Fortune magazine in 1964 said that "in a time of mass education, [football] is an educated man's game."[7] In fact, Steph had said that she hoped "that the NFL fans are intelligent, rather than just a bunch of yobs shouting profanities."

The fans I met at this game were intelligent, welcoming, and passionate about their team. Those who have called me and other followers "dumb jocks" have expressed to me that "extreme fans," the ones who wear face paint and dress elaborately are even more "dumb." Horse Shoe Warrior was the first "extreme fan" I got to meet on the trip, and he was anything but dumb. Dedication does not equal stupidity, and it is the *fans* who make the sport so special.

Some years prior, Warren St. John followed the Alabama University football team around for a season in an RV. He discovered that researchers in 1993 highlighted that "the average GPA for the hardcore fan was 2.55, compared with 2.46 for the nonfan. Unresolved, is whether watching sports makes you smarter, or whether smart people are drawn to sports; but you might want to think twice next time you assume you're someone's intellectual better just because he's wearing face paint and screaming like a maniac."[8]

Not only are the fans smart, but the players are too with "play books so thick . . . it really does take a certain genius to succeed in the NFL,"[9] explains Rich Eisen. The players also need to pass the "Wonderlic," a test consisting of 50 questions designed to be "a short term measure of cognitive ability." A score of 20 out of the 50 is considered average intelligence, and most NFL players get about that. The NFL has made the Wonderlic test famous, and it is even featured in the new Madden video games, by asking the gamer a series of questions.

Of course NFL teams want players with the best skills, but that's all pointless if the player does not have the smarts to play what is a very complex sport. In soccer, if you can kick the ball the way they want you to, you're pretty much in. Legendary NFL coach Bill Parcells said that "success in football starts with the same thing you use to succeed in anything in life: your head."[10]

Game 3. NFL Week 1, Minnesota Vikings at Green Bay Packers, Lambeau Field

Final Score: 19-24. Home-win record: 2-1. Capacity: 72, 992. Attendance: 71,004. Ticket face value: $72—I paid $115 via StubHub. Picture on my ticket: Brett Favre smiling. Mascot: None. Merchandise: A foam cheese head, plus a free white G-Force towel. Local dish: Bratwurst, wild game, and, of course, cheese.

It has been a few years since I have been to a soccer game in England, but I still remember seeing the faceless fluorescent jackets of police on horseback. I remember the putrid smell of the horse droppings down the middle of the sectioned-off residential streets, the depressing grey temporary railings making sure everyone walks the same way, as if they were lab rats. It made me feel like a criminal and I hadn't even done anything wrong. Going to a soccer game felt post-apocalyptic, tribal, pugilistic, and war-like. It was as if everyone was stuck in a futurist dictatorship regime. Walk this way, walk that way, walk this way. Home fans in one section and away fans in another, shouting at each other.

Rather refreshingly, Green Bay—otherwise known as Titletown (thanks to the record number of championships the team has won)—is the very antithesis of all that.

Driving down Lambeau Avenue is quite the sight. To my left were rows of houses, several of which were heavily decked out in Packers gear, from inflatable Packers players to huge banners and flags.

I noticed a billboard advertising Brett Favre's restaurant, and then saw the glory that is Lambeau Field, named after the team's founder, Curly Lambeau. This stadium is nicknamed "The Frozen Tundra" because of the famous cold battles that have taken place here. I drove past the Vince Lombardi Museum adjacent to the stadium. Vince Lombardi was the Packers head coach when they won the first two Super Bowls. Now the trophy is named after him. The museum had a whopping Super Bowl replica trophy outside. Paolantonio calls Lambeau Field "the national Cathedral of American Football, "[11] and I could see why. When I got out of the car, the air felt just right for football.

Just to put things into perspective, New York has the largest population of any American city and they have two NFL teams, although they share a stadium and it is situated in New Jersey. Indianapolis is a medium-sized city of 750,000, while Green Bay is the smallest NFL city, with only a population of 100,000, but it probably is the one that has the biggest heart. Their stadium seats nearly 73,000. I don't think there is anywhere in the world that has such a close ratio between the city population and their stadium capacity. This place felt instantly like a football town and I loved it.

Before I had set off for the trip, I was interviewed by the *Green Bay Press Gazette*, and unbeknownst to me they printed the article that game-day morning. "Hey, you're the guy going to all the games, I saw you in the paper!" a man with a foam wedge of cheese on his head shouted at me. I was surprised, and then with more people recognising me I suddenly I felt like *I* was their star player. I was worried the article may have mentioned that I was a Bears fan, and that I might get attacked. It turns out they did mention that I was a Bears fan, but the Packers fans didn't care.

I was supposed to meet an English Packers fan named Dan at Fuzzy Thurston's by the Resch Center at the Packers tailgate. I know quite a bit about football, or so I thought, but I did not know who or what Fuzzy Thurston's was other than thinking it was a kickass name . . . surely it was a bar, right? Nope, Fuzzy Thurston had won several championships with the Packers back in the day. When Fuzzy's assistant told him about my trip, he honestly was gob smacked and was happy to pose for a picture with me.

As I walked around it dawned on me that there were no police on horses, or the stench of horse manure, but instead a sweet aroma of meat on a BBQ. There were no depressing grey railings separating "us" from "them." Instead there was a magical and utopic sea of green and yellow (Green Bay's colours), with a splattering of Viking purple mixed in. We were all one group, all tailgating. This historic rivalry between the Packers and the Vikings was not celebrated with a huge fight, but with a 50,000-person cookout. Now that's how you kick off a sporting sensation.

This is when I noticed that tailgating is what really turns an NFL game day into something much more of an all-day event for the whole community and not just the football fans. Culpepper believes that the pre-game meetings at a pub before a soccer game "usually beats the hell out of the game itself . . . during the pregame the "game" still maintains all magical possibilities."[12] For me, however, a tailgate party beats the hell out of a meeting at a pub, and not just because of the freedom of creating one's own mini party, but because not all tailgaters care about the game—many care simply about the tailgate.

As I was introduced from party to party, many tailgaters had actual buses dedicated to their teams as walk-in shrines, with their whole area boasting unrivalled "fan dedication," yet they didn't bring up the upcoming game—the words "party," "fun," "food," and "good times" were on everyone's lips, not whether their team would "win, lose, or tie."

In the midst of the tailgate, I saw an ambulance decked out in Packers gear, with its own outdoor beer tray. The owners took to me instantly. These older-generation fans were warm and welcoming and wanted to give me plenty of food and beer. Asking them too many questions would make the tailgaters feel like guinea pigs, so my notebook went into my back pocket and I simply enjoyed the party atmosphere.

There were plenty of Packers fans who were out tailgating with their rivals, and there was no hostility between them. Guilt came over me, because I was drinking beer from a Packers fan. I felt so bad that I had to come clean and tell them that I support their greatest rival. Like a discovered spy in foreign territory, I expected to be stripped naked and tied to the goalposts for the duration of the game, or at the very least be shown *some* hostility, maybe even a little bit of mockery? *I* was the old enemy for crying out loud . . . Or was I? Yet being a Bears fan was all water off a duck's back for these fans. They knew I would be supporting the green and yellow that day, and they didn't even ask me to take my hidden Bears sweatband or my Bears underwear off. The Packers tailgaters only wanted to do one thing: make me feel welcome and show me a good time—not because I was from London, and certainly not because I was Bears fan, but because I am an NFL fan.

I feel the "socialism" in the NFL (thanks to the collective bargaining agreement) creates an equality between the franchises where *every* team is as important as the next. This inclusivity and respect pours right down to the fans. We may support different teams, but we all support the NFL.

Clay Travis wrote that "if you aren't willing to welcome fans who are just like yourself, only clad in different colors, then there's something wrong with your fandom."[13] If only that message could have travelled to the U.K. in the '80s.

These Packers fans have two objectives: for their team to win, which they can't control, and to be hospitable, which they can.

Later I was stopped by a Vikings fan with several Packers fans in his huddle. "Do you want some?" he hollered at me. These four words took me by surprise especially in the way that it was said. In the U.K. this is a line used by drunken hooligans to instigate a fight. At Lambeau Field, this phrase meant: you cannot leave this tailgate without trying one of the local famous brats (bratwurst). He didn't just throw a hot dog in a bun—oh no sir, this was an art. He took care placing on chopped onions, mustard, and relish like he was a master of food feng shui. He added chips (crisps for U.K. readers) and the local world famous Green Bay cheese . . . simply wonderful. It was the best hot dog I have ever eaten and he called it the "everything." I never knew junk food could be so flavourful and gourmet. A regular hot dog will never taste the same again.

The vibe around Lambeau was very friendly, a slight contrast to the night before at Indianapolis, when some Colts and Bears fans had a couple of obnoxious comments for me such as: "Dude you know football here is *different*, right?" Yes, of course I bloody know! "So you *like* football? As in *our* football, *real* football?" No, I can't bloody stand it! In fact I hate it so much that my psychiatrist told me to spend all my money and leave my girlfriend in London, while I nearly kill myself driving 30,000 miles to see 35-plus games all in the name of getting over my fear of the sport. *Idiot!* Granted, I did realise that by doing something as extreme as this trip I couldn't expect everyone to be as warm and fuzzy as the Packers fans.

If you're ever feeling down or depressed and not sure what the best pickup might be, just head to a tailgate in Green Bay. The people were the friendliest I have met in my life, and the fans here love their football. But equally they love meeting new people.

For three games in a row, I used the now trusty method of buying my tickets through StubHub. This ticket had a picture of Brett Favre on it, which I assume had been printed before he decided to come back and play for another team. Still, his U-turn on his retirement took the StubHub price down from $300 to $115. Cheers, Brett.

Just outside the Lambeau Field atrium a cameraman and his reporter asked me if he could "borrow my ticket." I was not sure exactly what he meant by borrow. I hope he wasn't going to borrow it for the length of the game and then give it back to me afterwards. "Well, can I get on camera?" (just three games in and already I had turned into an "American" fan) I asked. He nodded and then showed *my* game-day ticket to the world, while I was somewhere in the background, bobbing up and down like *one of those* fans.

He gave me my ticket back and I entered the newly refurbished Packers atrium, which was stunning and surprisingly modern. There is an actual Green Bay fan hall of fame that honours great Packers fans, the first NFL team to do such a thing.

There was a hustle and bustle on the concourse. The Packers fans love signs and posters so much that there is a booth with white cards and pens for fans to use and make their own signs to hold up in the stands. Brilliant!

The fans were flying around like blood cells in a vein furiously swarming around a body, joining other cells and breaking away without a thought or hesitation. I was dizzy, not knowing where to go. Everyone else knew exactly where they were going and were doing it at rapid speeds. They didn't even have to look at the signs; it was as if they all lived there.

When I saw daylight through the tunnel to the stands I was hit by a wall of green and yellow. The sheer oval bowl of Lambeau felt instantly historic, like a football shrine. Gold-and-green-bead necklaces glistened like sparkles in the snow, and there were, of course, foam Cheeseheads sitting atop many a fan's noggin. The national anthem started, and everyone had timed their runs through the stadium to the food stands and then to their seats at exactly the same time. It was as if the 71,004 of us had all rehearsed this "play" over and over, just like a football team. There was not a soul left at the concession stands come kickoff time. These fans were ready for football!

I found my seat, which wasn't actually a seat but a number on a metal bench. The entire stadium does not have seats as it is all bleachers and then I realised why they were selling so many Packers cushions.

I sat between a Green Bay fan and one of the few Vikings fans present. In front of me, a fan wore a t-shirt that quoted ex-Packers head coach Mike Holmgren. It read, "Football is about kicking someone's ass. Football is about physically pounding the opponent." There was little "ass kicking" in the stands as I noticed the average age of the fans within a football throw must have been 75.

There was nonstop talk about the Favre situation. I had seen some fans with Favre's New York Jets jersey on and a few fans near me thought that some fans out in Green Bay had become bigger Favre fans than of Green Bay itself.

After spending so much time at the tailgate I had eaten up most of my camera's memory card, so by halftime I had to scroll back and delete a few of the blurry shots of the day to make some room for pictures later. As I nonchalantly scrolled back through pictures, I suddenly saw a shocking sight on my three-inch colour screen. It was a stark naked, flaccid penis. How the hell were there numerous pictures of said member on my camera? My cheeks went red with embarrassment, because the folks behind me could see the images in full clarity. Just prior to looking at my pictures I had actually turned to them to tell them "what a wonderful time I had at the tailgate." What must they have thought I was up to?

After some neat detective work I discovered the culprit. It was the away Vikings fan who demanded I eat his great brats at his tailgate. I had put my camera around his neck and asked him to take some pictures of all us. Thirty of the pictures were great shots of tailgating and such; however, for the other twenty he decided that it would be a good idea to snap his, or perhaps his friend's, bits and pieces. I was really angry and confused because he was so friendly but also such a prick, pun intended. It took me quite a while to see the funny side.

During the game the Packers fans walked around far less and really concentrated on the game, compared with the Colts fans. I later heard the myth that several Packers fans wear adult diapers so that they don't have to go to the bathroom and miss any action, despite the many stoppages during the game, which would allow for a toilet break.

Rudy moment: Although Packers QB Aaron Rodgers was the player of the game and he enjoyed his first "Lambeau leap" into the home crowd, the individual Rudy moment goes to his teammate Will Blackmon for slicing through the Vikings defense and returning a majestic punt 76 yards to score and bring the house down.

Orange play of the game: Tarvaris Jackson, the Vikings QB, never looked confident and with a chance to win the game threw an interception.

Extreme fan: British Packers fan Dan. After taking me around Titletown after the game, where there were Packers-themed bars everywhere you looked, Dan told me he was going to five home Packers games that season yet lives in Stoke in the U.K.—and he does this every year. He will soon have his own Packers season tickets even though he will be commuting to every home game from Britain!

After the game, once back in the car, Gippy's digital road diagram calmed me as I ventured west. The next day I drove through the Medora National Park in North Dakota and at night I stopped off in Columbus, Montana, and stayed at the silly-sounding Git's (Big Sky) Motel. I hit the local bar, the Sports Hut. The waitress was a San Diego Chargers fan, the local drinker, a Packers fan, because he likes the fact that they are the NFL's only publicly owned team in which fans can buy shares (maximum 200 each); apparently all the teams used to do this but it is only the Packers that continue the tradition. There are over 360,000 Packer shareholders, though these are not now shares in the "common" sense. Finally, the cook was a hard-core Rams fan. He likes their helmets, as they were the first team to have funky designs on them when he was growing up.

This was a great example of what I was looking for on the trip: Three people in one place, all fans of different teams, for all different reasons. The Packers fan looked at my schedule on my t-shirt and took me through America's food land-scape, explaining to me exactly what regional food I must sample at each location. He was getting more excited with every city and none more so than when he ran his finger over New Orleans and told me of the glory of Southern cooking.

Coming from England I thought America was *all* chains and fast food. Eric Schlosser, author of *Fast Food Nation*, said that "in 1970, Americans spent about $6 billion on fast food; in 2001, they spent more than $110 billion."[14] Hence why I thought I didn't know that America takes such pride in its regional food. Gorman did find Mom and Pop stores in his book, but he became more focused on independent hotels and gas stations. With this news of regional delights I was excited to peel back the lid and explore an underlying America, just like Gorman, where "I would find the real America, an America of substance."[15]

I continued to drive west through Montana and Yellowstone National Park. It was like something out of a cowboy film, with real ranches, dusty roads, strange-looking animals (mostly roadkill), and, of course, tumbleweed. Unlike the other highways, which were all saturated with chain hotels and gas stations, this high-way was very much the opposite—it simply was great countryside and beautiful mountains.

I took off into a dirt track as Gippy guided me to an independent gas station (perhaps he was in cahoots with Mr. Gorman?). The forest terrain opened up and I saw a cute log cabin with an old man, chewing on a yard of corn, sitting outside on the porch on a rocking chair. How wonderfully American, I thought. He told me the gas station there was expensive since this was an RV park, and he directed me to a multinational gas chain. So much for the independents looking after each other.

I was getting a little annoyed that Gippy was an inconsistent navigator. He would find a gas station or a hotel several miles away, but he could not see the five or so that we passed to get there.

On Friday I arrived in Seattle, having driven across the United States in a matter of days. It was around this time that I first connected with Karen Di-Eugenio.

In 2005, Karen and her husband, Jay, had a vision: to create a tailgating cook-book that "would be different from other tailgating books because this would be about the tailgaters."[16] Karen and Jay home-schooled their three sons on the road, taking them to every NFC tailgate (16 teams) in the regular season, in their search for the "blacktop's best" recipe. By 2008 they were into their fourth year of tailgating across the land and had created the biggest tailgate party showdown of the year at the 2007–2008 Super Bowl in Arizona, called Super Gate.

Karen provided me with the names and e-mails of some great tailgaters for my next few games. I had missed a couple of tailgates already, so having someone to aim for on game day was a good idea.

But before I could indulge in any true tailgating, it was time for the Walter Payton run. The night that I arrived in Seattle, I flew to Chicago, but because of bad weather in Chicago, my flight was delayed, and only then did I figure out that the charity run the next morning was actually not in downtown Chicago, but in Arlington bloody Heights, some 30 miles outside the city. Granted it was close to the airport, but I was staying with Traci, who lives in the city near Wrigley Field, where the Bears used to play from 1921 to 1970. It is also the current home of the Chicago Cubs baseball team.

I shared a taxi with a Bears fan to Traci's apartment, and he was so impressed with my trip that he paid for the ride. The race was scheduled to start before the mainline trains to Arlington Heights were running. So after getting a taxi, a replacement bus, a subway, and then another taxi, I made it to registration just in time. I got into the school hall and saw around 800 people all in their professional running gear, sweatbands, lycra, day glow, the lot. I was in my jeans and a t-shirt. Everyone was doing a group stretch or leaning against each other, and psyching each other up. They had their watches synced and they were all fiddling with their, socks, shirts, shoes, anything . . . they just couldn't stand still.

There was no changing room and a lady told me that "most people drive here, so they arrive ready," so I had to get undressed in front of everyone. "So let me get this straight?" I retorted. "All these people drive here, to then run?" She nodded, not catching any whiff of irony.

The race started and rather surprisingly everyone actually started to run. This threw me off my game plan. As it was a "charity" run and not an Olympic event, I was planning to walk it and I thought everyone else would be doing the same, though of course I was going to sprint at the end, for a good photo finish.

With everyone running, I felt embarrassed. My tactics had to change. I couldn't finish behind the 90-year-olds who were jogging the whole way. I *had* to run. For me the race became a "run, walk, run, walk" run, not the leisurely stroll that I had in mind. The weather got worse and I was soaked by the first mile. In the end I finished the 9.6-mile race in 1:49, not too bad, considering I was out of shape, did not practice, warm up, or even stretch.

On the train ride back into the city, two young guys spotted my hat and gave me a "Go Bears" salute so I sat by them. It turns out they play college football for a junior college in Illinois. They enlightened me with their stories, which opened up the long debate as to whether college players should get paid or not. Both young men appreciated their football scholarships, which cover their education, but they were not allowed to get jobs, even if they did have the time, so they were still stuck with paying for living costs. Both were studying criminal justice in order to be policemen if they do not make it into the NFL. Although they play at a small college their team still attracts crowds higher than some Premiership teams.

Although colleges make millions of dollars without paying their players, paying the players is simply not allowed by the NCAA rules, because they insist on keeping college football a strictly "amateur" game. College football becomes a footballing harvest for NFL teams to pick from. Players pursue a degree but they are also doing their "apprenticeships" in football. If college players were paid, the danger is that the players may pull out of their studies completely and just play for money. If that player then gets injured, he would therefore not have a degree or education to fall back on. Players cannot bypass college and head straight for the pros, like in other sports, which I think is a good thing.

Clay Travis says that "when a high school athlete chooses to play for your school [college], you bequeath him your allegiance for life."[17] College players for the most part choose which college they decide to play for, which the college fans naturally appreciate. But once they enter the draft, they get picked by NFL teams and have little say initially where they wish to play their football. In essence they really work for the NFL as opposed to working for individual teams. This is similar to why I always watch England play; the players do it for the love of representing their country. Naturally you cannot trade players at international. You have to root for whomever you have, similar to college football where players rarely move from college to college. It is the same argument as when Rugby Union became professional. Many people preferred it as an amateur sport because they felt people played it for the love of the game, as opposed to making it about money and a career.

When I got back into the city I was intrigued by this college football talk so I went to a bar and watched college football all day. A lot of college fans around me felt that the NFL has become polluted with money, and in this amateur version you see the players play with more passion, because they play for the love of the game or even simply just the love of their college. These college football fans feel many pro players are always on the lookout for a larger contract or a team that will pay them more.

Money will inevitably change the goal posts in any field. If someone "paid" me to do this wonder trip, would *I* have worked so hard on it? Would I really have risked my relationship on it? Of course I would not have turned down such an opportunity, it would be my dream job, but that is what it would have become, "a job" and that certainly would have taken some of the romance out of it.

With free agency in the NFL, many players move from team to team, whereas college players tend to play for their one college, throughout. College football, like Premiership soccer teams, has come from an institution. College football can only pick from its enrolled students, while many soccer teams originally came from teams made up from workers. Arsenal, for example, started as a group of workers at the Woolwich armaments; five years later they turned professional, whereas pro football was "created."

The college fans around me felt there is a stronger relationship between the college player, the college, and the fans in comparison with the NFL player, his team, and his fans. When the NFL introduces the players on TV, each player states his name, position, and then what college he played for, not where he was born or raised.

Clay Travis supports this by saying "no matter what he does for the rest of his life Peyton Manning is, eternally, in the mind of Southerners, a Tennessee Vol."[18]

In the morning, I flew back to Seattle for the Seahawks game. That's when I realised that every muscle in my lower half felt like it had been ripped to pieces, and I gingerly hobbled on and off the plane.

This was my second delayed flight in just two days and I was happy that I had decided to keep most of my travel arrangements on the ground. I was frustrated that I would be missing yet another tailgate. Luckily, I sat next to Ray, who is a season ticket holder for the University of Oregon football team (the unintimidating sounding "Ducks"), and we discussed football during the entire flight. Ray travels to all the Ducks' home and away games. In his back garden he has a concrete-shaped Oregon "O" which can be seen from a plane. Oddly he also has season tickets for their rival team, the University of Washington Huskies, which he sells. His favourite Ducks player of the last few years is running back Jonathan Stewart, who was drafted by the Carolina Panthers in 2008. Ray does not support any NFL team, yet while Stewart is a Panther, he will be a Panthers fan. If Stewart goes to another NFL team, he will then support that team, which I thought was odd but later discovered was quite common, especially for diehard college fans.

I mentioned to Ray about the two college players I had met the day before who wanted to get jobs but were not allowed or did not have the time, because of football. Ray felt sports scholarships are great because it means those who cannot normally afford college fees, can now get an education. He felt particularly bad for the college players who are "walk-ons"—students who earn a place on the team once they are already enrolled in college. Walk-ons play football and work just as hard as those with a scholarship, yet they still have to pay for their education and also have no time to work elsewhere.

Ray felt that the millions of dollars colleges earn from their football programmes is a good thing because it pays for the institutions' other sports programmes.

Game 4. NFL Week 2, San Francisco 49ers at Seattle Seahawks, Qwest Field

Final Score: 33-30 (OT). Home-win record: 2-2. Capacity: 67,000. Attendance: 67,951. Ticket face value: $115—I paid $115 via Ticketmaster. Picture on my ticket: Plain text on opaque West field logo. Mascot: "Blitz," a large blue muscular bird. Merchandise: Seahawks flag. Local dish: Coffee, salmon, and seafood.

We landed at 12:40, just 20 minutes before kickoff. Outside Qwest Field all I could hear was the roar from the crowd. I went to Will Call to pick up my ticket that I had bought in the summer via Ticketmaster. Sadly this was a crappy-looking "Ticketmaster" ticket, which meant there was just text on a plain background, with an opaque Qwest Field logo. Buying via Ticketmaster meant I wasn't able to get great-looking, colourful tickets like I had previously via StubHub. The line up at Will Call meant I missed the kickoff, which was annoying. In the summer I had bought tickets for this game from Ticketmaster. I made a rookie mistake with my tickets. When booking, I foolishly opted for the "printing at home" method. I thought I was being smart, since Will Call is always so busy, and I didn't have a U.S. address for the tickets to be sent to, but finding a printer on the road was tricky. I should have actually printed them at home and brought them with. Like I say, a rookie mistake. But thankfully this time Will Call folk printed my ticket.

The Seahawk fans were cheering so loudly that it made the hair on my neck stand up. In Seattle this is what they are famous for. I got to my seat with ease, on the 35-yard line in the lower section, about five rows back—perfect.

These fans made a heck of roar, one that made the hairs on my ears jump off. Interactive theatre pioneer Augusto Boal believes that "spectator is a bad word."[19] He inspires his audience to take on a role that he calls "Spect-actors." Fans have often been described as passive, because they are not the ones out there on the football field. However, the fans (Spect-actors) in the NFL have a huge role to play. Not only do the fans all get together at the tailgate for one mighty cookoff, but it is their vocal work that can actually help their team win. They have to be smart about not just what to cheer, but when to cheer it. When the home team's offense is on the field the fans go strangely quiet. I noticed the jumbotrons display "Quiet! Offense at work," which I initially found to be very strange, coming from a soccer culture, where the crowds chant throughout the game.

In the NFL, the QB needs to hear the plays from his coach via the speaker in his helmet. The players around him then need to hear him if he calls any audibles (changing plays at the scrimmage line). The home fans are thus quiet on offense, but naturally erupt once the team makes a great play. They then go quiet again before the next snap. When their defense struts onto the field, however, the crowd makes a racket to quell the opposing team's QB's ability to hear his coach and to hinder other offensive players from hearing the audibles.

When the home team's defense faces third-down situations is when the crowd really makes a lot of noise. Here in Seattle the booming sound of Seahawks fans has been measured down on the field at a level of 112 decibels—that's 18 decibels less than a Boeing 747 at takeoff. In fact, in 2006 the Giants team investigated Qwest Field to see if the Seahawks were actually pumping noise into the stadium themselves.

Most of the noise was coming from the Hawk's Nest section, a narrow metal triangular stand behind one of the end zones. The team could have built more seats and have more fans in this section, but they opted instead to have a smaller narrow stand so that the non–Hawk's Nest fans can get a great view of the downtown Seattle skyline.

Most NFL teams have a "fight chant" that they break out after a home team touchdown, yet the Seahawks do not have one, and probably do not need one. These home fans really worked hard and disrupted the 49ers offense, whose players ended up making several false starts because of the noise. In fact more away teams make this error at this stadium than any other in the league.

I was just four games into the schedule, and I had already noticed that most of the time the teams just have a few chants: [Enter other team's name] and then "sucks," or "Go [Enter your team name]" or the imaginative "D-Fense," in which two fans hold up a wooden "D" and a white picket fence.

At soccer games in the U.K., fans make up new chants for each game. This impressed Chuck Culpepper, as he explained, "the very idea you could just start up a brand new chant based on events you've just witnessed—*brand new!* —then have that chant infiltrate your section . . . just boggles the American mind."[20]

All around the stadium I noticed the number 12 on boards and ticker messages. In fact many fans had 12 on their jerseys and FAN on the back. The fans here are so loud that they are known collectively as the Twelfth man. The Seahawks even retired that number, so no Seahawks player can ever wear the number 12. The "twelfth man" was originally coined at Texas A&M University, because the "Aggie" fans were so loud that it made their opponents feel like they were playing against twelve men.

Here I also saw my first truly impressive halftime show. A whole stage was brought out, on which the band Alice in Chains performed. Later on I saw an actual pick-up truck hoisted on a wooden plinth high above the concessions, which I thought was a strange place to park.

Rudy moment: 49ers linebacker Patrick Willis intercepted the ball and returned it for a TD, which turned the tide of the game.

Orange play of the game: Seahawks QB Matt Hasselbeck threw back-to-back interceptions that brought the 49ers back in the game and silenced the crowd.

Extreme fan: I spotted plenty on the jumbotrons but not too many around me. Mr. Mohawk wins because he had a giant, bright green Mohawk haircut and was the loudest cheering fan around me, which is an impressive title amongst these fans.

After the game I popped into the Hawk's Nest, a bar that is more or less attached to the stadium, where I met two fellow Brits. By 8 p.m. most places, including several bars, were closing and most of the fans had left. The Seahawks had lost, but even right after the game, I had no clue where 60,000 people went. Qwest Field is a downtown stadium, and I couldn't fathom just how quick the area had dispersed. In London, it can take over an hour to leave the Wembley area after a football game.

I took an ambling walk back to the stadium when I spotted something glorious: A monster RV owned by an older chap named Jerry—a mad Seahawks fan known to veteran Hawkers as "Hawk Father." He was out there with a guy named Mike, who runs the fan site seahawkers.org. Jerry's RV, the "Seahawk Express," has airbrushed pictures of two Seahawks players on the sides and the whole bus was decorated so professionally that I actually thought this was an official team bus.

Jerry invited me to join him for jelly vodkas and beers. I spent two hours talking with him about the Seahawks and what it means to be a fan. The night sky came upon us, and if I had closed my eyes I would have thought I was at a campfire with two uncles. Instead, I was in a downtown car park, sitting on garden chairs in the mellowing light with glorious Qwest Field behind us.

Jerry, who must be in his sixties, is all about meeting fans from other teams. He takes immense pride in his bus as well as in his collection of souvenir drinking cups that he has collected from every NFL team. He insists that everyone drink from their own team cup. He also collects Seahawk mini helmets, and wants every player to have ever played for the Seahawks to sign the new logo helmet *and* the old logo helmet. Jerry has been following the Seahawks for years and knows all the extreme fans. He told me that although I was a "rookie" he still respected the scale of my trip.

Jerry arrives four to five hours before kickoff and sets up the TV, satellite dish, the food and the drinks, and his RV that is open and free for anyone who wants to hang. Each game day he spends over $200 including parking the RV for the day, and that's before he even buys a ticket.

Jerry parks his RV in a specific spot each week, in a "social area of the parking lot" so he can greet "all the fans; home and away." He told me that in other areas of the car park some home fans mock and jeer the away fans. Jerry, however, takes a different stance. He loves the away fans and respects them for coming to see a ball game in his stadium. If someone is willing to come all the way to Qwest Field to watch his football team, he is so appreciative he invites them to come by his tailgate, supplies them with food and drink galore, and invites them back the following year.

Game 5. NFL Week 2, Philadelphia Eagles at Dallas Cowboys, Texas Stadium

Final Score: 37-41. Home-win record: 3-2. Capacity: 65,675. Attendance: 63,472. Ticket face value: $60—I paid $65 via StubHub. Picture on my ticket: E-ticket. Mascot: "Rowdy," an all-American-looking cowboy. Merchandise: Cowboys beer koozie. Local dish: Chicken fried steak, beef ribs.

My flight to Dallas from Seattle was at 5 a.m., though to save money instead of booking a room I just stayed up all night in the lobby of the hotel where I was going to keep my car parked for a few days. I flew into Dallas without any sleep at all and my body was still stiff from the Walter Payton run. The plane flew over Texas stadium, and I could see the famous hole in the roof, which is similar in structure to a soccer stadium at home, with the fans covered. The Cowboys fan next to me told me the roof is there so that God can watch His/Her favourite team play. I replied to my neighbour that Leyton Orient also has a hole just like that, and I'm pretty sure that the Orient are not one of God's favourite teams. He shot me a confused look back. Out of the opposite window we could see where they were building the new Cowboys' stadium for the following season—the past Cowboys on the left and the future Cowboys on my right.

Once we landed I picked up a hire car from a chap named Rusty, who wore a classic cowboy shirt, tight denim shorts, and a greasy ponytail. I made my way to downtown Dallas some 10 miles from Texas Stadium to pick up my StubHub ticket. *Man, these StubHub people don't make it easy.* The lady at the counter handed me over a piece of paper. I looked down, and it was a printed electronic ticket from Ticketmaster. Some chap had sold his e-ticket via StubHub. I was a bit miffed, because I thought StubHub would only sell "hard tickets," and here I was with practically a parent-like note from Ticketmaster, saying "please let this person into the stadium today, since he has worked really hard this term!" I get the impression that only season ticket holders get the fancy pictures on their tickets.

I then drove to my hotel, which was across the highway from Texas Stadium. The hotel manager restrained me from walking to the stadium, as there was nowhere safe to cross the 12-lane interstate. I was already getting sick of driving and I wanted to walk. To get to the stadium I had to get a taxi, which drove me three miles down to the next junction and back—madness.

The taxi dropped me right by the "Talking Trash, Tailgate Bash" party. This was the first tailgate crew that Karen hooked me up with. This party had spent four years on the waiting list for their Cowboys season tickets. Then when they got them they had to spend an additional $4,000 just on a personal seat licence (PSL) to actually *buy* the tickets. (It is one of Jerry Jones's money-making loopholes outside of the CBA.) Tunison calls this one-time cost an "ever infuriating phenomenon."[21] More teams are using PSLs, especially when they open up new stadiums. The franchises make money on the PSL price, while the ticket price on top of that goes back into the league to then be spread across the 32 franchises. For the Cowboys' new stadium, which opened in 2009, the PSL prices were from $2,000 to $150,000!

Despite paying the large PSL cost, this "Tailking Trash, Tailgate Bash" crew do not actually go inside the stadium. Instead, they sell their game-day tickets so they can afford to pay for their tailgating setup. From an English perspective, this is simply nuts. Apparently the Cowboys will not take away their licence even if they knew they were selling their season tickets to friends and family, as long as they still get their money.

This crew buys up four parking spaces, one of which they use to erect a portable toilet. They also boast a flat-screen TV, satellite dish, and a decent-sized grill, and like the Hawk Father, they pick their parking spot wisely and get to the stadium many hours before kickoff just to secure it. They park right by a pedestrian road near the stadium, so they can see the many fans pass by, giving and receiving many a high-five from their Cowboy tribesmen, or dishing out a little ribbing to the away fans.

They welcomed me with open arms, a cold beer, and a hot and delicious "chili dawg." I was already pumped for the game, but they got me even more excited as they dished out the "trash talking" to Eagles fans. "Green isn't a good color in Dallas . . . Eagles don't fly in Dallas!" It was unbeknownst to me at the time, but the Eagles seem to be a team that most other teams like to hate. The Talking Trash guys told me the Eagles have some nasty fans, especially if you go to the Eagles stadium as an away fan.

With all their historic star players, power-hungry owner, and Super Bowl wins, this oft-called "America's Team's" stadium looked bleak and grey from the outside. I don't want to sound snobby or ungrateful, but it was a long way from the impressive stadiums I had seen on the trip up till this point. This was no way as impressive as Lambeau, Lucas Oil, and Qwest, or so I thought. From the outside I could see why they were going to knock it down at the end of the season. Lambeau was built in 1957 but was redeveloped in 2003, yet they kept the historic bowl intact. Texas Stadium, built in 1971, was the fifth eldest in the league at the time, which is old by NFL standards and just looked tired. It was no longer the jewel in the NFL stadium crown like it was in the '70s. It's not that it was bad per se, but it just didn't have the wow factor of the others.

This was the last-ever MNF game in this venue, and I could sense something special was going to happen.

I got to my seat, which was high up behind the end zone. My opinion of the grey drab exterior changed in an instant, because the energy inside crackled with all the excitement of a MNF game. The steepness made me feel like I was on the inside of a cauldron. It was dark, claustrophobic, and powerful.

Initially I did not think it would be a good seat, but being so high up you can really see each play develop. The fact that the game was one of the best games ever made it more than worth it.

A chap named James sat next to me. His neighbourhood in Houston was without power due to a hurricane that passed through the week or so before, so he thought the best thing to do was to drive two hours to Dallas to see this game. It turned out to be a great decision, not only for him but for me as well because he was my personal commentator for the evening. He talked me through every player, the player's history, and skill. By the end of the game I knew what brand of pyjamas the Cowboys roster wear!

The game was nonstop action, and I don't remember sitting down at all. I got so many high-fives that my hands pulsated. Although it was not as loud as Qwest Field, it was still plenty loud and very intense.

Rudy moment: With eight TDs in this game it was hard to pick out one play. Perhaps Terrell Owens's 72-yard catch for a TD against his old club, or Felix Jones' 98-yard TD kickoff return. Though I gave it to Donovan McNabb for juking away from blitzers before he made an unorthodox spontaneous underarm throw to his receiver when everyone in the stadium thought he was sacked.

Orange play of the game: Tony Romo's fumble in his own end zone giving the Eagles a TD would normally easily win the Orange award, but then along came Eagles rookie receiver, DeSean Jackson. He burst through the Cowboys defense, skipping towards the end zone with the ball. He did a post TD celebratory dance. Rather foolishly, he had actually dropped the ball on the 1-yard line in order to do his showboating boogie. Now I'm all for spontaneous dancing, but make sure you run that ball *into* the end zone first! Ah, the double-edged sword of a national televised game on MNF. What a plonker!

Extreme fan: I only found one. He was wearing a Cowboys jersey, a very large Cowboy hat and blue-and-white face paint.

The next day I woke up pinching myself that I had seen such an immense game. I had previously received an e-mail from Clarence Carter at ESPN Dallas radio (103.3 FM KESN) asking me if I would like to be on one of their shows that day. As I woke up I called Clarence and I was pinching myself again, because he said, "Michael Irvin really wants you to come by the studio." I nearly dropped the phone in surprise. "Sorry, what was that? Did you say Michael *Irvin*? *The* Michael Irvin?" The Michael Irvin who won three Super Bowl rings with the Dallas Cowboys and is in the Pro Football Hall of Fame? "Yeah, Michael Irvin and Kevin Kiley," Clarence replied. "They are the hosts . . . you know, 'The Michael Irvin Show.'" Clarence may as well have just said "duh." I was ecstatic and rather taken aback that Irvin, the legend, wanted to meet *me*. Clarence told me to be there at 11:40 a.m. Not a problem, I thought, as I looked at the clock in the hotel. I had plenty of time.

Once I checked out of the hotel and looked at the clock on the car, it said 11:20 a.m.! Shit. Damn that hotel alarm clock. I was going to be late for Michael and Kevin. In the rush I broke off one of the arms of my eyeglasses. Gippy didn't like the digits for the zip code I entered. He found Lamar Street, but I needed East Lamar. I figured I would head for Lamar and then ask someone from there. Everyone must know where Mike and Kevin work, right?

Gippy was making me a far worse driver because I was concentrating so much on him and his pesky ways. In the past few days he had said things like, "Go 5/8s of a mile." Well, what the hell is 5/8s of a mile? Or he'd say, "Stay left and turn right." How do I do that? But since being in Dallas I think Gippy got pissed off because he suddenly went quiet. I had thrown the instructions away in

Wisconsin so I couldn't figure out how to turn his volume back up. I was driving frantically with my glasses falling off my face, racing around the city looking for a street that he couldn't find while having my ear as close to him as possible.

The phone rang. It was Clarence telling me they could not wait any longer, and we had three minutes until we went live. I pulled over, and I was actually *on* Lamar Street. Surely that's the same as East Lamar, I thought. The door number that Clarence had given me was right where I had parked. Because I was in such a panic I did not think it was strange that the door I was parked at was that of a humble residential building. I sprinted up the perfectly mowed lawn and rang the doorbell. A small Asian child answered.

"Hi there, I'm here to record an interview with Michael Irvin." She looked up at me a little confused and then ran to get her Dad. That's when I realised I really needed *East* Lamar, not just Lamar. Though I couldn't just run off, that would look pretty crazy, plus there was still the slim possibility that ESPN beams their shows out from the basement of this fine abode.

"Hi there, I'm here to do a radio interview with Michael Irvin?" My voice was far less convincing this time, and I must have looked ridiculous to this older gentleman as he looked at me with utter confusion. Soon three more members of the family were in the hallway staring at me. "E-S-P-N," I stated clearly. "Are you recording ESPN radio with Michael Irvin here?" Blank faces just looked back at me. "Okay," I added, rather embarrassed. "Looks like I have the wrong . . . er, house, sorry!" I raced off into the car, called ESPN and did the interview over the phone with the small Asian family watching me through their window.

Michael had a good laugh at me down the phone: "You told your honey, I'm outta here, you told the banker to give me all m'ah money, I'm going to take this most important trip, all over the place, watch all football games, then you walked into the store and said gimme the cheapest system." Fair point, Michael, though it wasn't Gippy's fault, I had told him that the city was Dallas instead of Arlington (rookie mistake).

Michael and Kevin told me that I needed to save some money because when I got back home to Stephalicious, she would not stick around if I were broke and had no apartment. "Perhaps a shallow woman would leave me, but real love is stronger than that. Steph has been really supportive and we love each other very much. She is proud that I am following my dream and I am proud that she is supporting me" is what I wanted to say, and I only really thought of that after the interview was finished (typical!). I was caught off guard with the personal question, and I felt uneasy about being so open about my relationship. I thought they were going to talk about football more. I told them I had similar aims to that of an NFL player—that I wanted to continue into the playoffs, the Pro Bowl, and the Super Bowl.

After the interview, Clarence told me that Mike and Kevin still wanted me to swing by the studio to meet them. Gippy finally figured it out, and I got into the studio while the guys were still on the air. I was put in a small booth where I could watch the show. My sight, however, was blurry as I had taken my glasses off. I couldn't be talking to ex-NFL stars with only one arm on my glasses—they would think I was a moron.

Michael Irvin was beaming, and nearly crushed my hand with his handshake. He was huge, much bigger than I thought for a wide receiver. Kevin too was very friendly. Michael asked me if in the short time since coming off the air, anyone had donated any money to my cause. I felt like pointing out the fact that he has three Super Bowl rings and perhaps he might have a spare few thousand dollars, but I didn't have the bottle.

I gave Michael a trip t-shirt, and he beamed like a child and jumped right out of his seat. He ran his finger over the fixtures checking out all the games, pointing out which matchups would be good games. He said "awesome," over and over. It was a real pleasure to see that ex-NFL players still get so excited about the sport.

I then rushed back to the airport and flew back to Seattle to pick up my car to begin my drive south down the coast. I got a call from Karen. After two hours of talking on the phone, I was feeling refreshed, confident, and inspired. I realised this woman was going to be responsible for turning my dream trip from being a limp hot dog on a camping grill to a full-scale Super Bowl tailgate party.

Karen interviewed me for her article in *Tailgater Monthly* magazine, where she was the editor in chief at that time. This magazine gets published once every two months and is written by tailgaters for tailgaters. I listened intently to the advice she gave. The trip was already becoming slightly blurred. The media wanted to talk to me about my experiences thus far because I was supposedly an "extreme fan," yet I was trying to find the extreme fans myself. I wanted to be the interviewer, not the interviewee.

Karen became my road trip mentor. She had been through the many travelling foibles that I had already come across and was always answering my e-mails with advice, words of wisdom, and information on where to find the best tailgates.

After the phone interview, I headed south, and while I was looking for gas, Gippy pointed me to a station in Twin Falls, Oregon. The place was amazing, and not only that, it also had a Best Buy. I knew Gippy wanted his voice back, and rather embarrassingly I had to ask the store staff if they could show me how to get the volume back up (they thought I was a bit of a plonker, and I certainly felt like one when the man just tapped the screen twice, and all was fixed). I could have hit the road quickly after filling up, but Twin Falls was far too beautiful not to explore. I was pretty pleased that Gippy was taking me to some great views.

While driving south through Oregon, I had a telephone blog radio interview one evening at 6:30 p.m. I found a gas station and pulled in. I turned off the engine, and a pretty 20-year-old blonde girl popped out of nowhere as I opened my door. "How much?" she asked with the enthusiasm of youth. I had to recheck that I was at a gas station and not frequenting the early shift at a red light district.

"Um, what are your services?" I tried to come up with a line that did not have a sexual subtext, but it was impossible. "How much do you want me to put in?" she asked innocently, not picking up on any sexual innuendo, while I giggled to myself. It felt weird having someone else fill up the car. Oregon is one of two states where it is illegal to fill up one's own car with gas. Here "professional pumpers" have to do it for you.

I tried to make the call to the radio station for the interview, but my phone kept saying "call failed." In the end I asked the girl at the gas station if I could borrow her phone for ten minutes. I told her I would pay her for the call, but she insisted she had free minutes anyway. Lee from the radio show had previously told me that when I call in, he would put me on first because he knew of my manic schedule. He picked up and muttered something about me holding on. I could hear the radio show going on, through the earpiece. After thirty minutes I was still on the phone, apologising to the girl profusely. After 45 minutes I heard someone on the phone calling out, "514, we have a caller from 514 . . . 514, you there?" I had no clue what they were on about, but seeing as I had been on the phone so long I politely said, "Er, hello? It's Adam from London?" Lee had not realised it was me on the phone all this time because he was expecting a call from my mobile, which had a Chicago number, hence he had me speak last. I left the gas station staff with plenty of my trip t-shirts as payment for using their phone.

The next night I saw a sign for Roberta's Cove Hotel. This made me laugh because that is my sister's name, so I had to stay there. It turns out Roberta's Cove was dirty and cheap, which my sister didn't appreciate.

The next day I passed through a town called Mesquite en route to Vegas, where even the supermarkets had slot machines. In Vegas, I was going to see my friends Neal and Roberta; Roberta was in town spending the last night on her holiday there with a friend.

When I initially thought of the trip I had Neal in mind as the perfect companion. Neal is a Bears fan and was born and raised in Chicago. When he was 18, he followed the band Phish around for one whole summer, taking in over 60 shows. He is a good road trip guy, doesn't mind long driving, is laid back, and likes football, so it was perfect.

But sadly a few months before the trip he got something called a "job." *Asshole!* So we planned that I was going to take the trip solo, yet he was going to join me on a mini trip to the Oakland and Arizona home games, as well as allowing me to stay with him whenever I would be passing through Vegas.

With strict instructions from our mother, Roberta took me out that night for dinner, but because my diet had consisted of mostly snacks on the road, cheese puffs and beef jerky during the week, and then monster tailgate food on game days, my stomach had shrunk and I couldn't even eat a full meal.

Roberta brought some goodies for me from home, including a touching letter from Steph, with a CD of pictures from her graduation that I had missed because of the NFL kickoff. I wasn't too bothered about turning up for my university graduation, and rather selfishly I assumed that others felt the same. I looked through Steph's pictures, with her proud face in her graduation gown. I really felt bad that I had projected my own cynicism of higher education onto her experience. Her degree clearly meant a lot to her, and I felt ugly that I was not there to share something that was very important to her.

Just before getting back on the road, Neal gave me a road map of the United States, something I probably should have bought at the start of the trip. I kept it hidden from Gippy, because I didn't want to hurt his feelings. On the back of the map was an invaluable U.S. city-to-city road matrix telling me just how far in miles each city was from each other.

Game 6. NFL Week 3, Detroit Lions at San Francisco 49ers, Candlestick/Monster Park

Final Score: 13-31. Home-win record: 4-2. Capacity: 69,843. Attendance: 67,249. Ticket face value: $115— I paid $115 via Ticketmaster. Picture on *my ticket: E-ticket. Mascot: "Sourdough Sam," a caricature of a 49er, a prospecter from the 1849 California Gold Rush. Merchandise: 49er beanie. Local dish: Dungeness crab and clam chowder in a sourdough bread bowl.*

I arrived at Monster Park at 9:30 a.m. for a 1 p.m. kickoff, and the first thing I noticed was the sweet smell. A lot of people were already cooking (and drinking), and the tailgaters must have been using some kind of honey sauce. I saw an actual 16-seater dining table, with wine glasses and silver cutlery laid out by someone's truck. The juxtaposition took me by surprise and I just had to introduce myself. Mike is an older man who runs this tailgate party and creates this fancy shindig at every game. He takes honor in having the finest tasting tailgate. He cooks chateaubriand, and has fine wine and cheese and other gourmet foods that were way too posh for me. This is the kind of tailgate I would send my Mum to!

Karen's hookup was a party called Club 49 run by a chap named Alex Chavez, who had "SF or FU" on the back of his 49ers jersey. The club probably had exactly 49 people around its two tents, which boasted a full bar and bar stools, and of course flat screen TVs. I had already become desensitized by the TVs and satellites, but dining tables with silver cutlery and a full bar with stools took me by surprise.

In front of the tents at Club 49 was a great spread filling up three foldout picnic tables. It was enough food for around a hundred people and I was told to simply dig in. One of the members told me they all bring something each week, and they take turns as chef for the day. This day was an Italian theme and for the following week, because the Patriots were in town, would be New England chowders and such.

I was introduced to the whole Club49.org family, and several times they would stop the music and announce over the PA for everyone to do a shot. Fifty people would rush over even if they did not know any of the Club 49 members. Everyone hunched into the tents, and they all promptly found themselves with a shot glass, filled with liquor. I have no clue what liquor it was, but each time I knocked it back it burnt my esophagus. I wondered if the burning was a sign of a high-quality drink or not.

About an hour before kickoff the Club 49 bar was broken down and the air was let out of their blow-up 49er balloon, as this is a group who do go inside the stadium to watch the game. It takes organisation and dedication to set up a tailgate of this magnitude so early and then pack it all away before kickoff.

I had bought two tickets at $115 each, via Ticketmaster, but I couldn't even sell the second ticket to a scalper, who laughed at me when he saw the section my tickets were in. It didn't help that it was a printed e-mail ticket, which looked crappy (though I did manage to print them off the night before at the hotel so I didn't need to spend a long time at Will Call).

Despite being right on the 50-yard line, I was all the way at the top, on the highest possible row, and there were a few empty seats around me. It was a nice view, though—I could see the glorious mountains in the background.

I noticed many of the security staff were wearing black undereye strips, like many players wear. When the Lions made a mistake, a "wa wa wa" sound, like in cartoons, came over the PA, much to the dismay of the Lions players. There was a British couple in front of me who were on their honeymoon and they gave me my "game face": two black undereye strip stickers. A few Lions fans came and sat by me in the first quarter, but they lasted just the one 49ers TD before they got up and left.

Things started well, but as it soon became a one-sided game, the atmosphere diminished somewhat as the home team began pounding the Lions.

Rudy moment: The 49ers performed a delightful reverse trick play, which saw the ball get handed off from the QB to a wide receiver, who then laid it up for another wide receiver going the opposite direction. This really got the crowd going. I saw my second streaker of the trip, but this one got pinned down before making it across the whole field. This game Rudy though actually goes to the 49ers fans. When it was fourth-and-one, their team was on the Lions' 1-yard line and winning easily. They lined up to try for a field goal, but the crowd started to boo. The 49ers listened to their fans and, realising the people wanted their money's worth, brought the offense back on, went for it, and got the touchdown.

Orange play of the game: The whole of the Lions D-Line. They couldn't get close to making a sack or a tackle all day.

Extreme fan: At the tailgate I saw a gentleman in his late sixties, who had hundreds of 49ers pin badges attached to his huge red felt top. He also had hundreds of red beads around his neck and was holding a battery-powered blender. He was blending bright red margaritas, and then handing them out to fans in a fresh supply of paper cups. I did wonder if he was allowed to take the blender into the stadium.

Game 7. NFL Week 3, New York Jets at San Diego Chargers, Qualcomm Stadium

Final Score: 29-48. Home-win record: 5-2. Capacity: 71,500. Attendance: 68,922. Ticket face value: $98—I paid $98 via the box office. Picture on my ticket: Text on collage of opaque Charger players. Mascot: "Boltman," a muscle-man character with a lightning bolt for a head. Merchandise: Chargers foam finger shaped like a lightning bolt. Local dish: Carne asada burrito and chorizo-and-egg breakfast burrito.

Mike P. and I arrived at the Qualcomm Stadium—otherwise known as "The Q"— car park, and it was jampacked. This was the third oldest stadium in the league at the time, and although it was built in 1967, it still looked great. I particularly liked that there was a flag flying from all 32 NFL teams around the stadium roof.

As I was parking, I noticed that many people rather cheekily had put tents and BBQs up on neighbouring spaces, either to save the space for their friends, or simply because their huge BBQ and TVs needed that much room. While driving through the busy tailgate, I noticed people were cooking and throwing footballs in the narrow aisles. I felt like I was driving through a carnival down the streets of Spain. When I finally found a spot it was not a case of simple reverse parking— I had to gently caress the car into the space, not wanting to knock down any-one's tent.

Two San Diego cheerleaders came around the tailgate selling their calendars, the money for which was going to charity. This was my first meeting with any NFL cheerleaders on the trip. When I originally told Steph I was going to do this trip, she rather jokingly said to me, "So what are you going to do? Go out there and try to shag all the cheerleaders?" I hadn't actually thought of such a sordid trip myself (*well, of course I had*). When I saw these two cheerleaders up close, I was starting to think it could be a good project for a single man to attempt.

The Bolt Talk tailgating crew, led by Charger Ray Chan, had found me through the web. There was enough of his crew to make up a whole football squad, and they all rushed towards me, hugging me like I was a long lost son returning from war. The eldest member of the group and resident musician (he was playing a trumpet) thanked me for coming to see their tailgate and his team.

I felt like a fish with several lines attached to me—everyone wanted a bite. Karen's tailgating hookup, Dog Nut Dan, came racing over and told me where to meet him as well as a British Chargers fan. Luckily everyone I was supposed to meet were all near each other. The Bolt Talk crew wanted us to eat, drink, and take plenty of pictures.

When I finally got to Dog Nut Dan he was packing away his BBQ and tailgate, though he did save us a couple of his famous Dog Nut Dan nuts! They were jalapeños wrapped in bacon and they packed a punch. These bad boys were hot! Even Mike P., who was always the first of my friends to be able to digest a hot vindaloo back home, struggled with these. Dan told me he had won one of Jay and Karen's tailgating cookoffs with this specialty.

Until this point, I thought tailgating was all very inclusive in its nature and that it was all about "sharing." The competitive part of the day, I thought, was left to the players on the field. But America has a hungry lust for the competition drug. When Jay and Karen went from tailgate to tailgate at each franchise, they decided that whoever had the best-tasting food would win a grill. Dog Nut Dan and his powerful mouth-kicking nuts won, and he was so proud showing me his winning grill that he had just used for his hot nuts. Dan wanted us to get there earlier because we had missed his other fiery delicacies, which might have been a good thing.

Local Chargers tailgater Dave Lamm, who runs tailgatingideas.com, is a "traditionalist" when it comes to his definition of tailgating: for him, tailgating "is a group of people sharing food, drink, playing games, and socializing prior to an vent in the parking area within walking distance of the venue." He says it is "all about hospitality and the sharing of food and fun." Much like the Hawk Father, he "personally welcomes in any and all fans of any team to my tailgate." Dave adds, "I am a San Diego Chargers fan but I do not care what team you are a fan of." He continues that "in a day and age where people keep to themselves all too often, the tailgating experience breaks down those barriers. Tailgating brings people together."[22] Likewise, Karen believes that tailgating "fills a need," where tailgaters will "pass a fork to a total stranger to offer them a bite." She explains that such community and openness, "is just what we, as a country are hungry for." She adds that she is "not a sports fan . . . but a fan of the fans and the food of course."

The Chargers PR team sold me two tickets directly, right behind the goal line on the lower bowl where the atmosphere was great. I was pinching myself that I finally got to see Favre play. It was like a dream come true and being so low down, I was right in the thick of the atmosphere. When Favre threw down field, it was like he was looking right at me. Sure I couldn't see the plays develop, but that's what the jumbotrons are for.

Mike P. was over the moon because we sat next to two American West Ham fans. Throughout the game someone wearing a Packers hat was holding a sign that read, "nEver Seen favre Play until Now" (spelling ESPN down the side). So I then held up my sign about my trip. We then got hit with a few ice cubes. Although I was annoyed that someone threw ice at me (or rather my sign), I was more disgruntled that it hit the lady next to me. This was the first time I felt any sort of negativity about my trip, but maybe those fans just throw ice at anyone with a sign?

In front of us was a friendly married couple who was rooting for the Jets. They later e-mailed me to tell me they had an awful time leaving the Q. They told me the Charger fans had spat at them and had verbally abused the woman. I was rather shocked, because I really didn't think this sort of thing happened at an NFL game.

The game started fast with the Jets intercepting and scoring a touchdown early. The Chargers came right back in it with some nifty offense of their own and by halftime the Chargers were winning by quite the margin. The game got exciting towards the end when the Jets recovered an onside kick and they were just two TDs behind, but they left it too late. The crowd remained cheering throughout as the Chargers stormed the Jets for their first win of the season. I didn't get to see any dancing from rookie Chargers running back, Mike Tolbert, who told an NFL reporter, "I've always loved dancing . . . if I make a big play I'm going to dance,"[23] so we were left to see dancing from the cheerleaders, which isn't a bad thing, probably a better thing in fact.

Rudy moment: San Diego's Antonio Cromartie intercepted Favre by plucking the ball out of the receiver's hands and then ran it back for a TD.

Orange play of the game: Mr. Favre involved again. For his second interception he threw the ball way over his receiver and straight into the arms of a Charger.

Extreme fan: We didn't see too many extreme fans here. We did see two fans dressed as Batman and Robin, but it was the girl who showed me her Charger bolt tattoo on the back of her neck that won the award.

After an impressive home win, many people were still tailgating after the game, as it was only 9 p.m. local time. We found Dan and he told me that he too loves

Favre but come game time he wants to see him get sacked, and, boy, did Brett take a few big hits that night.

The Chargers were to host the Oakland Raiders the following week. Dan, like many others, warned me about the Raiders fans. When they visited a few years back, Dan told us they sent "fear around the parking lot . . . they dress up and look intimidating." That might have been the year when infamous U.K. soccer hooligan (and Chelsea FC fan) Alan Garrison lived in the States and decided to support the Raiders. Franklin Foer wrote that "at a game in San Diego he [Garrison] organized Raiders fans to make 'a run' through the parking lot, throwing punches and asserting dominance over the home crowd that stood turning hot dogs on their portable grills." Garrison explained to Foer that "we tried to teach them [Raiders fans] how to behave like proper hooligans," he said, and the Chargers fans "didn't know what hit them."[24]

Mike P. was buzzing after the game. He had been to a game before but never took in this much tailgating. Being British, he had never even thought about going to a game three hours early. Mike P. had lived in L.A. for a few years so he knew American generosity, but even he was taken aback by the abundance of the tailgate.

After three weeks on the road, driving 5,000 miles, seeing seven football games, taking in five flights, and a 10-mile charity run, I was starting to burn out. I had initially planned on driving back across to New York for the next game, but like an ageing sports star (let's say Brett Favre), my body was telling me to stop.

I took a time-out and called an audible and decided to relax in L.A. at Mike's for a few more days, to then drive only as far as Denver where I would fly to NYC for the Jets game.

Just a matter of hours after making this decision, the San Diego Chargers staff asked me if I would like a free tour of the stadium, something they do not normally do during the football season. "Would LaDainian Tomlinson be joining us per chance?" I asked Linda, the PR lady. My answer was met with laughter and then a straight "nope." I was over the moon to add a stadium tour to the trip, something I hadn't even thought about doing.

A couple of days later I was back in San Diego where I met Betsy from the Chargers' ticketing department, and she took me on a wonderful tour, showing me all the different views, private boxes, commentary box, and media suite at

Qualcomm. Betsy was a great host answering all of my questions, and Linda took time out of her day to show me some websites where I could find cheaper hotels along my journey.

After the tour I drove to Denver and began to notice a hell of a lot of road kill—coyotes, porcupines, foxes, beavers. Late one night when it was dark, I accidently hit something. I heard an unholy crunch. It was something very large— so large that it brought the car off its wheels and I was airborne for a split second. I screamed at Gippy to quickly find me a hotel. I got to my room, jumped under the covers, and hoped I had imagined the whole thing.

With the road map I could see where Gippy was taking me. Before then I had never questioned his mischievous path and simply followed his guidance without really knowing which way I was heading. So when Gippy wasn't looking, I sneakily looked at the map (I felt oddly guilty for doing so) and noticed that we were going to drive right through Vegas. So I stayed with Neal again, and we went out to a pool party, which was a good way to end the first quarter of the trip.

5

Second Quarter

Game 8. NFL Week 4, Arizona Cardinals at New York Jets, Giants Stadium
Final Score: 35-56. Home-win record: 6-2. Capacity: 80,242. Attendance: 78,222. Ticket face value: $75—I paid $50 via Craigslist. Picture on my ticket: Linebacker David Harris. Mascot: None. Merchandise: Favre pennant. Local Food: Hot dog.

I flew into NYC and this time travelled without Justin on the Blind Pig booze bus to Giants Stadium, which they share with the Jets. Because of the headache I had with StubHub before, I decided to use Craigslist. This is not actually a ticketing site but an "anything goes" site: you can find everything from roommates to a second-hand vacuum cleaner, oh, and hopefully tickets to your local NFL game. You e-mail the person and figure things out yourself. The risk is that someone might mess you about, you have no knowledge that the tickets are legitimate, and most people want to sell pairs of tickets not singles. After 12 e-mails I finally got a ticket the day before the game.

We got to the stadium around 11:30 a.m. for a 1 p.m. kickoff. My new friends from the bus told me to look out for an extreme fan called Fireman Ed who orchestrates the Jets cheers.

Three of the guys from the bus took me under their wing and to their master, I mean their chef, via quick lefts and rights, weaving me between cars and RVs, while giving and receiving an abundance of high-fives as we passed through the masses. It was just like the famous scene in *Goodfellas* where the gangsters go through the kitchen to get to the cabaret.

George was our tailgating host, and even before he knew my name, he placed beer in my left hand and a plate full of honey barbecued chicken and pasta in the other. It was drizzling rain the whole time but this did not stop the tailgaters, who just carried on drinking and grilling in the mist.

Sadly, I did not have any t-shirts to give to George, but he was proud enough that his three friends thought of *his* tailgate to bring me to. George then began pouring vodka into sandwich bags and handing them to his guests. The ritual is that every time the Jets score a touchdown you have to take a sip of vodka.

I would have thought this kind of thing would happen at Premiership grounds where they cut off selling alcohol after halftime and you are not allowed to take alcohol to your seats. Webster feels that the alcohol policy in NFL stadiums is tricky because "beer companies put a lot of money into football and a lot of that is for the right to sell in the stadium. It would be difficult for the league to put a total block on in-stadium sales or on advertising, especially as beer or any other alcohol is perfectly safe when used moderately and responsibly."[1] I later found out that in the 2009 season the New York Jets banned the sale of alcohol for their last regular-season game. It was a prime time night game, with playoff implications at stake. Knowing some of these Jets tailgaters, it probably wouldn't have bothered them because of their vodka-in-a-bag system. But the danger is that if more and more people do this, you could have even more trouble and the security staff will have to be more vigilant, frustrating the fans entering the stadiums.

I said my good-byes and made my way to the stadium. I had been to the Meadowlands twice before, but only for Giants games. This Jets vibe was very different—more electric, more rustic, and the people were all in a party mood despite the rain. I saw several kitted-out Jets buses, plenty of which already had Favre's name on them. There were even fans wearing Packers cheese heads and Packers Favre jerseys out of respect for the great man. I even spotted one fan with a Packers cheese head that had been sprayed green with a Jets logo on it.

I sat high up behind one of the end zones. The rain came down during the entire game, and after the first quarter there was no score. The game was all sloppy play with fumbles galore, an interception, and a blocked field goal. Despite this, the crowd was certainly louder than the Giants fans on kickoff day. Could it have been the Favre factor?

The Jets, in their old school throwback jerseys, put up an amazing 34 points in the second quarter alone. After the break it was the other ageing QB, Kurt Warner's, time to shine. He and the Cardinals scored 21 unanswered points in the third. Favre wouldn't let a 34-point lead slip away. He plucked away at the Cardinals secondary and secured the win with three more TDs in the fourth. I can now tell my grandchildren, "I was there when Favre threw for six TDs."

Throughout the game, four guys in their twenties sat behind me. They were loud and perhaps a little colourful with their language, but they were getting the crowd into the game, smacking everyone with high-fives.

There were two women a few rows down with their husbands. The women began making out with each other every time the Jets scored. To the delight of the guys behind me and the ladies' husbands it was a very high-scoring game. The guys took to the ladies more so than the game, jeering them with, "Holler for a dolla, do something strange for some change." More Favre TDs became more female-on-female action. Two shows for the price of one.

Rudy moment: With a whopping 12 TDs there were lots of great plays, but for me, it was Favre's magic on his second TD pass. The Jets were facing fourth-and-one on Arizona's 40-yard line. Everyone was expecting a QB sneak or a run play to get that yard, and play things safe. Everyone except Favre and his receiver, to whom he uncorked a perfect deep pass to for yet another TD. The sheer audacity of the play at that time speaks volumes about the kind of player Favre is.

Orange play of the game: Any one of Warner's four fumbles or three interceptions.

Extreme fan: Captain Jet—see later in chapter. Sadly, I couldn't find Fireman Ed but I did see him on the jumbotron.

After the game fans were still tailgating, many of them carrying on with the party and watching the later games in the lots. My Blind Pig crew said I had 30 minutes before the bus left back to NYC, which gave me just enough time to whizz around, looking for more tailgaters. I found a string of Jets buses still furiously cooking away.

First I encountered a man who owned a "short" bus. Of all the wonderful Jets gear inside, his prize possession was his trophy cutting board, proudly fixed on his door with "2005 tailgate champion. New York Jets" engraved on it.

I found another tailgater who presented his whole lounge in front of his bus, consisting of two recliner chairs and a leather couch, carpeting, and a tall standing lamp, all in front of a big old box TV, which made the car park feel homey.

I then found famed super Jets fan "Captain Jet." He wore a plastic aeroplane on his head, a green cape, a foam shield with his name on it, yellow aviator glasses, and green soccer shin pads on his arms. It sounds like a bad Halloween costume, which would be socially acceptable if worn by a nine-year-old, except that this chap was probably over 60. His huge tailgate was still going strong out of a fully fledged Jets-themed school bus and he was definitely the extreme fan of the game.

Captain Jet told me that he is a member of PFUFA (Pro Football's Ultimate Fan Association), but with all the shenanigans of the post-game tailgate, I didn't have a chance to ask what that meant. Captain Jet kept giving me fish balls and insisted I take more food home with me. I was starting to get the impression that perhaps my Mum had called up every tailgater in the land, worried that her skinny son was not eating well enough.

I got back to Justin's apartment just in time for the Sunday night game between the Bears and the Eagles. As I entered the apartment, Justin was shouting at the screen because the Bears were failing to move the ball. I was confused because this game had no bearing on the outcome of Justin's favourite team, the Dolphins. During a timely break he calmed his nerves and showed me something called the spread. This innocuous-looking white piece of paper had the day's matchups alongside various numbers.

Justin plays the "spread" with about 40 guys from his work, and it is a rather genius betting system. All of the guys put five bucks into a kitty each week and pick the outcome of all the games using predicted handicaps, which come officially from the legal gambling world in Vegas. Justin backed the Bears, so for him to score a "spread" point it meant either the Bears had to win or, if they lost, they would have to lose by three points or less, because the Eagles were the favoured team and the Vegas bookies felt they would just win so the handicap was three and a half points. If the Eagles won by four points or more, then Justin wouldn't get a point and all the people backing the Eagles would. Most NFL fans could correctly predict the outcome of most games, but with the handicap it makes each matchup a trickier thing to get right as many times.

I looked down on the paper. Justin had picked a whopping 9 correct out of 11 fixtures on the day. "Come on Orton!" Justin shouted again at my QB. "I need you to help me go 10 for 12!" Whoever gets the most correct each week wins half of the weekly pot (around $100), while the other half of the pot each week builds up for the overall season winner, around $1,700.

The spread is without a doubt gambling, but because gambling is illegal in most states, underground fans have created clever ways to bet. Because the spread is not traditional gambling in the sense that Justin was not putting money on one game with odds coming from a bookie, it felt less illegal. It is more creative, more fun, and much more like fantasy football, which is legal, even when it costs to play and gives cash prizes. It only then dawned on me that NFL stadiums do not have betting concessions. Go to any professional sports team in the U.K., and you will probably find betting stands. Even several Premiership teams are sponsored by gambling websites, showing just how accepted gambling is in the U.K., which might be why we don't have such creative gambling games, like the spread. We have fantasy football but it is nowhere near the size or scale of NFL fantasy football.

With Kyle Orton repeatedly allowing the Eagles to get back into the game, it really frustrated me as a Bears fan and Justin as a spread player. Thankfully the Bears battled on for a win, taking Justin to 10 points with one just fixture left—the big Monday night game in Pittsburgh against the Ravens that we were both going to go see.

Game 9. NFL Week 4, Baltimore Ravens at Pittsburgh Steelers, Heinz Field

Final Score: 20-23 (OT). Home-win record: 7-2. Capacity: 65,050. Attendance: 64,038. Ticket face value: $65—I paid $100 via StubHub. Picture on my ticket: Text over Steelers watermark. Mascot: "Steely McBeam," a big-chinned caricature wearing Pittsburgh dungarees and a black hard hat. Merchandise: Steelers baseball cap, "Terrible Towel," and Steeler napkins. Local dish: Primanti Bros. Sandwiches and pierogies.

Justin and I hired a car for one night to get us to Pittsburgh and back. I hadn't used Gippy in a while and he must have got really pissed off me, because his directions getting out of Manhattan were a joke. We gave ourselves enough time to have at least one to two hours of tailgating, assuming we could avoid traffic and find a parking spot. Gippy was having a bad day and became allergic to Pittsburgh. He got us into a right mess around the three bridges of the Steel City. We only had enough time to park up and hustle past the busy bars to make kickoff in time.

The Steelers-Ravens game is a massive rivalry, with two of the best defenses in the league. I queued up to get my game face on, quite literally, as I paid a man $5 to spray "Steelers" onto my face. This is a team that has little in terms of hoopla. But who needs hoopla when you have this much passion for your team. The home players do not run out through smoke and the Steelers have no cheerleaders. Like the city, the team is pure blue collar.

We watched the kickoff from the great steel ramps that lead to our high seats behind the end zone, facing the huge Heinz jumbotron, equipped with massive red ketchup bottles. Because of the Heinz connection and the fact the Steelers play in yellow, this stadium is also known as the Mustard Palace. Next to the jumbotron there were no seats, just two massive windows of empty space like at Qwest Field.

Like at Lucas Oil, many Steelers fans stood watching the game in an array of areas. The several steel ramps in each corner of the stadium were populated with fans who brought large flags to drape over the railings, and of course they furiously spun their famous yellow Terrible Towels, which made the stadium look like it was under some kind of yellow pulsating wave.

The crescendo of noise just before kickoff was deafening. The ball flew into the air, and a Baltimore player caught it and ran towards the Steelers defense who were in their throwback uniforms. The whole stadium then heard an almighty crunch that made the steel frame beneath me shudder, and everyone around sucked air through their teeth and grimaced, before high-fiving one another. The poor Raven player was taken out of the game on the very first play. Welcome to Steeler Football, where they hit hard!

The second quarter picked up for the Ravens, as they led 13-3 at the half. My neighbour told me that a gentleman a few seats down was wearing a Super Bowl ring from the 2005–2006 season. Without hesitating I introduced myself, and there the Super Bowl ring was on his finger in all its beauty. It turns out the man was the head electrician for the Steelers when they had won the Super Bowl. I couldn't believe that franchises give out rings for the staff too. "Sign me up for the concession stands!" I shouted, but it turns out they do not give out the diamond-encrusted rings willy-nilly. This chap was in his retiring year, and he had been working for the Steelers for decades when the team had won the Super

Bowl. During his tenure he was given two free season tickets. Now that he is retired he has to pay for the tickets, and guess who he gets them from? From the current electrician.

After the break a different Steelers team came out to play and they began moving the ball better. The Steelers fans woke back up and began jumping on the floor, which actually shook beneath me.

With five minutes to go, the Steelers were up 13-20. The Steelers were favoured to win and their spread was at 7.5, but Justin had backed the Ravens, meaning that if the Ravens win or if the Steelers won by less than eight points Justin would win another spread point.

The night became a double narrative for me. I wanted the home team to win, but I was also rooting for Justin. Although he would have got his point with a Ravens win, he didn't want to cheer too much for them as we sat amongst some of the louder members of Steeler Nation. His involvement was self-centred as he has no affinities with either team, but by gambling on the game he got far more into it. He became torn when the Steelers were playing well because he wanted a home win, but just a small one. At some moments he wanted the Ravens to score to close the scoring gap, but he couldn't show the home fans that.

The Ravens scored a TD taking the game into overtime. Although the home field groaned, Justin was happy because it meant the Steelers could only win by a maximum six points. We then sneaked down to the lower section where there were now some empty seats.

Rudy moment: When Ravens QB Joe Flacco saw the Steelers' D breathing down his neck, he scrambled 30 yards sideways all the way to the sideline and back to the middle to make a long pass.

Orange play of the game: The Steelers rookie running back Rashard Mendenhall had been bad-mouthing the Ravens before the game and early on got hit very hard by Ray Lewis. Mendenhall broke his shoulder in the collision and was knocked out for the season!

Extreme fan: While I waited to get my face painted, there were two brothers in front of me getting over half their faces painted. They were both soccer fans as well as Steelers fans. One supports Chelsea and the other, Manchester Utd. Their high-spirited energy got me really pumped for the game.

For some games on the trip I was struggling to get behind (or root for) the home teams which I had not followed much in the past. I had no problem appreciating the skill of the players, the atmosphere, and having a wonderful time, but when I watch the Bears my heart beats wildly with every play. I didn't have the same emotional connection to some of the other teams. In the U.K. a "neutral" fan like myself might "have a flutter" on the game to "get more into it." Filling my emotional fandom void with a different feeling of victory. The thinking is that while it's not my team, I still get the buzz of "winning" by correctly predicting the outcome, and a cash prize is always nice too. Sky, the cable network that beams out the Premiership, and the NFL both have their own betting engines and their clever motto is, "It matters more when there's money on it." Though I knew I didn't want to bet on the home games, because I have seen enough Martin Scorsese films to not even dip my toes in the murky depths of illegal gambling in the United States, I was, however, intrigued by the thought of playing the spread. I was not sure if it was legal or not. It just felt like fantasy football.

Paolantonio says that "for the longest time, the NFL kept fantasy football at arm's length. The thinking: that fantasy play was dumbing down the game's appeal and legacy. . . . It was a way to legally gamble."[2] Now the NFL fully embraces fantasy football, with over 27 million people playing every season. Everyone kept asking me who was in *my* fantasy team. But I didn't play fantasy football on the trip—I was already inside one huge footballing fantasy.

In fantasy football, one picks various players from several teams, which didn't appeal to me because I wanted to root for the home team wherever I went and didn't want a clash of interest. So this spread system was perfect. The following week I joined Justin's pool, and my Dad and I have played it every season since. Newspapers print the Vegas spread weekly, yet to stay safe they include a disclaimer that states these "odds are for recreational purposes only." Every week I made sure I backed the Bears despite the spread numbers and always picked the home team I was seeing that weekend. In addition to showing me this game, Justin also showed me the wonders of cruise control. At last I was safe from the highway patrol.

Game 10. NFL Week 5, Tampa Bay Buccaneers at Denver Broncos, Invesco Field at Mile High Stadium

Final Score: 13-16. Home-win record: 8-2. Capacity: 76,125. Attendance: 75,480. Ticket face value: $77—I paid $50 via Craigslist. Picture on my ticket: Broncos Hall of Famer Gary Zimmerman. Mascot: "Miles," a cari-

cature wild white horse with an orange mane. In addition, the stadium
boasted a real white horse named Thunder. Merchandise: Broncos beer
koozie. Local dish: Rocky Mountain oysters.

I flew into Denver and picked up my dusty yet trusty Cobalt from the trip's first quarter, which had been living in the Denver airport for about a week. I then made my way (using cruise control) to Mile High Stadium. I parked up next to a school bus that had been decked out in Broncos gear. I introduced myself to Derek, who showed me around the great bus that he owns with his parents and wife. Inside the bus the back door said, "Raiders Suck," and the inside was littered with Denver players' autographs. This crew call themselves the "Mile High Dukesters," and they once won "Denver Tailgaters of the Game."

They invited me to their weekly game called "Left, Right, Center." Not the most creative of names, but it was fun and costs $3 to play. Thirty of us sat around two Broncos carpeted mats, each with three single-dollar bills tucked under the mats. The first person rolls three dice. On the dice there is either a dot, an L, an R, or a C. Each die represents one of your dollar bills. So if you roll a dot, that dollar bill stays put. L means you slide one of your dollar bills to the player to your left. R means you slide one of your bills to the right. And C means you throw your bill into the middle, which then becomes the winning pot.

I didn't quite understand the game at first but it was fun. I finished in third place, but there are no prizes for third.

I thanked the group for their hospitality. They had given me snacks, beer, and two Broncos koozies, which wrap around a beer can to keep your beverage cold. Before leaving I gave them a bunch of t-shirts, and I was chuffed that they put them on straight away and wore them at the game.

I made my way closer to the stadium when I noticed there was an official tailgate party in a huge tent that cost $8 to get in, but it was already 12:30 p.m. and I wanted to meet the other tailgaters who Karen had told me to visit, so I sadly gave it a miss. I went over to Bronco Billy's tailgate in section C, where I was given even more great food. I found a tailgate group in this section that had a huge BBQ grill on a wooden manmade hut that they pull every week to the stadium. It was the biggest grill I have ever seen.

I then walked past the live band and waited by the Bronco statue–water feature at the front of the stadium. This statue-water feature consists of five broncos, one mare, and one colt, and was designed in Italy. They are 1 ½ times life-sized and are depicted running uphill in an alpine mountain setting. The waterfall is slightly heated so that in the winter, the steam rises. I also noticed that on top of the stadium sits a 1,600-pound, 27-foot-tall white bronco standing on its hind legs.

I purchased tickets via Craigslist from a lovely man named Bob. He was so impressed with my venture that he sold me his spare ticket for $50 when the face was $77. I was really looking forward to seeing the game with him because he was a really proud fan. Throughout the game Bob talked me through the players, the history of the team, and the differences between this stadium and the old Mile High Stadium. Bob was so knowledgeable that he should charge people a fee to sit next to him.

Our seats were behind the goal line in the second tier. The stadium has a curved wave on the top that is very unique and easy to spot from a distance. Being up a "mile high" the air was predictably thin, and I found myself losing my breath. This is why away teams struggle to win here because they are not used to altitude.

During the pre-game a real white horse named Thunder galloped across the pitch with an American flag just before the national anthem was sung, and instead of a halftime show, there was a ceremony where former Bronco Gary Zimmerman was applauded, as he was rewarded with a place in the Pro Football Hall of Fame.

After the home team scored in Denver, I heard a huge boom. I felt a rush of heat on the left part of my face. I looked up, and behind the bronco that sits on top of the stadium, flames were erupting and flying out. The flames really caught me off guard. I had expected fireworks, but not actual fire.

It was a defense-heavy game with both offenses struggling to get a first down. The fans never booed the Buccaneers QB, ex-Bronco Brian Griese, which surprised me. Seven years after leaving Manchester Utd., fan favourite and ex-captain of England, David Beckham, returned to play against his old team; he got cheered during the introductions, but every time he kicked the ball he still got booed.

When a Bucs pass fell incomplete, the Broncos fans yelled "In-Com-Plete" really loud—a simple but effective chant. Despite the 6-6 halftime score, the Broncos fans stayed positive and got much louder. Like in Pittsburgh, the Denver floor began to shake from the stomping. We could all feel a touchdown coming.

Broncos QB Jay Cutler pulled his arm back and zipped a 10-yard pass to Brandon Stokley for a touchdown, making the stadium erupt.

In the third quarter a huge black cloud appeared from nowhere, and the heavens opened up. I got sunburnt in the first half, and just when I was about to get drenched in the second, Bob got out two Denver Bronco anoraks. These weren't those crappy one-time-wear ponchos. This was a real jacket that he brought for me in case it rained. What a nice man! We looked like lifelong buddies in our matching coats.

Rudy moment: It would have been Jay Cutler's TD pass, but I saw a Broncos fan who used the jumbotron to propose to his girlfriend. I wondered if Steph would find that romantic.

Orange play of the game: When the Bucs made a hash of their onside kick and kicked a long bouncing ball.

Extreme fan: I witnessed many extreme fans on this occasion. Barrel Man had been one of the first extreme fans in the NFL. He used to go to Broncos games dressed only in a wooden barrel for over thirty years. The Broncos even gave him a Super Bowl ring in 1998. Sadly, he was too ill to come to this game and passed away the following year. I did spot Orangeman who had dyed his beard orange, plus he had an orange afro, glasses, and makeup. He looked like a giant ole Oompa Loompa. Another man was wearing an all-orange dinner suit, with matching orange top hat and cummerbund, but his blue sunglasses were his Achilles' heel. The winners were two guys who call themselves the Mile High Monster. They were dressed completely head to toe in blood orange pom-pom material—with their bright orange face paint, they looked ridiculous and amazing.

Playing the spread got me more involved with this game and the other games around the league too. In the first four weeks I was only ever conscious about the team I was watching and the teams in the NFC north division. But now because of the spread, every matchup became fascinating.

I only got five picks right in my first week. Justin teased me because *I* was supposed to be the extreme NFL fan and yet I got so many wrong. I couldn't go to all these games and then get beaten by my friend. This was a battle. As the NFL wasn't taking over my life enough, I now had to get the spread right—and I needed help. So I bought NFL magazines, trawled the Internet for injury information, trying to get some inkling to the outcome of ALL the games. My NFL experience was exploding all over again.

After the Denver game I headed north. The next night I watched a great MNF game on TV in a motel. The Saints somehow lost to the Vikings, in what was a very bizarre game. It already felt strange that I wasn't there, as I had been to the first four MNF games of the season.

The next night I stayed in Chicago with Traci. It was late on a Wednesday night when Jeff, Traci's then-boyfriend, told me that every Thursday in Chicago the great Mike Ditka makes an appearance on ESPN radio, airing a show from one of his two restaurants, both appropriately named Ditka's. One of his establishments is in downtown Chicago, while the other is in Oak Brook Terrace, some 25 miles from Traci's apartment.

"Da Coach" is how he is referred to by Chicagoans who often pronounce the "th" parts in words as "da." Ditka talks on the "Waddle and Silvy Show," hosted by Tom Waddle and Marc Silverman, and joins them from 11 a.m. to midday. Gippy got me to the Oak Brook restaurant in good time, and I sat at the table at 9 a.m.

Silvy was not there due to it being Yom Kippur, the holiest day in the Jewish calendar, when one of such faith is supposed to fast for 25 hours. Silvy was at synagogue, which is where as a Jew I was also supposed to be, but as an international Bears fan, I was in exactly the right location.

Many people had brought Bears helmets and mini balls for Da Coach to sign, but I was going to get him to sign one of my trip t-shirts. Ditka walked in with a manly swagger. He is tough yet surprisingly humorous, down to earth, and larger than life. In *Pain Gang*, Neil Reynolds described him as a player "who stood for no funny business from the opposition,"[3] and that sense of respect was very present. I was really excited and my heart skipped a beat when I saw him. His moustache is now grey, but he wore his trademark sunglasses and still looked every bit as iconic as he has over the years.

Ditka's menu was a meat lover's paradise, and I ordered the only thing that I thought I could eat at 10 a.m.—the nachos. When they arrived they were topped with pulled pork. As tasty as they were, I really could not eat much of the pulled pork so early, especially on the holiest day in the Jewish calendar.

During the commercial break Ditka signed my t-shirt and I got a picture with the great man. I felt like a child again. I told him about my trip and gave him a shirt. He was shocked at first and then said, "Good for you . . . Good luck." I was thrilled that I had his support, considering he was one of the reasons I am so into football. With my shaking hand (the hand that touched Ditka), I texted Steph telling her that I just met Ditka the legend. She replied, "What is a Ditka? That is one letter away from diktat." Steph wasn't actually born when the Bears won the Super Bowl in 1986 so I had to forgive her naiveté. My text back was simply, "Ditka! It will be the name of our first child!" She didn't respond.

After midday Ditka trundled out of his own restaurant and I raced back to Traci's. Eating pork on the holiest day of the Jewish year came back to kick me (quite literally) in the ass, as I suffered just what my Dad had predicted: "A jiffy tummy."

Two days later I headed north to Minnesota, and the leaves had started to change colour. I pulled off for lunch and got back in the car to head back onto the highway. By this time I was getting used to Gippy's habits, but on this day he was particularly eager in telling me to go left back onto the highway. "Go left now!" he screamed at me. Because of the slight uphill, and poor signage (there was a wonky arrow pointing to the left), I couldn't see the correct left turn up ahead. I took his orders and swung the car left down the ramp to the highway. It felt wrong, but Gippy didn't say anything like, "You're driving the wrong way down the highway!" or "In five-eighths of a mile, you will die!" After 50 yards I had that strange feeling again—that I was on the wrong side of the road. I pulled onto the hard shoulder and waited for cars, so I could make sure. After 20 seconds two cars came towards me and then slowed down, no doubt wondering why my car was on the shoulder facing oncoming traffic. I threw Gippy into the boot for a few days and planned the rest of the route with the map. I wondered why he was trying to kill me—maybe it was God punishing me for eating the pork nachos on Yom Kippur?

It was nearing 7 p.m. and it began to get dark. Then it got a little rainy. Then a humongous lightning bolt lit up the sky. I had never seen an actual lightning bolt before. It first went horizontal, and it looked awesome, but then the next bolt came down, right near me, then another, then another, and then another. Amazement and wonder quickly turned into fear and anxiety. I was getting scared. I was not sure how far away the bolts were, but they must have been close. I was only 30 miles from Minneapolis, the city where the Vikings play, so I just bit my lip and kept driving. Finally I made it through the storm and got to my hotel, which I picked because it was in walking distance to the stadium.

The hotel had an odd mock medieval theme to it, almost Tudor in its design, with a big fireplace, large old leather chairs, and exposed wooden beams, and the receptionist was able to print off my e-ticket, which was handy. It was a Saturday night so I strolled down to First Avenue, where the concierge told me I would find some nightlife.

I found an Irish pub. That's right, I came all the way from London to Minnesota and settled for dinner at an Irish pub. I ordered what I thought was a meat and ale pie, a traditional pub dish back home, but it turned out to be more of a soup, with some baked pastry on top. It looked strange. No wonder us Brits get a bad name in the States for our food—this thing looked awful!

Karen had told me about a chap named Hans, whom she also had interviewed for *Tailgater Monthly.* She told me that, like myself, Hans was on a quest to go see a live football game at every NFL stadium in the United States, but he was planning on doing it across four football seasons. He named his project "Quest for 31."

I got a call from Hans, and I rushed over to his hotel to meet him and his two friends. Karen had noticed that my Vikings game was the only time our paths would cross, and she put us in contact. We got on like a house on fire and bar hopped into the night. Hans is a Bills fan, and much like me he is a fan of the NFL in general. Hans spends the whole weekend on his "quest" in each city, which means he can really absorb the local culture. Like me he supports each home team, wherever he goes. Unlike me, however, Hans buys a home jersey for each team and often gets really dressed up like a super fan—I wore my "Adam's Football Trip" t-shirts, my Bears wristband, and some other items from the home team to each game. Hans also has his own car, aptly named the Quest Mobile.

Game 11. NFL Week 6, Detroit Lions at Minnesota Vikings, Hubert H. Humphrey Metrodome

Final Score: 10-12. Home-win record: 9-2. Capacity: 64,111. Attendance: 62,867. Ticket face value: $87—I paid $87 via Ticketmaster. Picture on my ticket: E-ticket. Mascots: "Viktor," a traditional caricature mascot who has horns attached to his football helmet, and "Ragnar," the league's only "real" human mascot—a bearded, long-haired man who wears animal hide. Merchandise: A purple-and-white jester hat. Local dish: Chili and beef.

A few days prior to the Vikings game I called their PR staff and jabbered on at them about my trip. The nice man on the phone then put my name down for a pre-game media pass. He then shocked me by actually apologising for not being able to do more for me, when he had already been so nice. I suddenly began liking the "Vikes" a whole lot more, which was new for me because they are the Bears divisional rivals.

I was at the Vikings tailgate very early, despite suffering a hangover thanks to Hans. I was so early that even the fanzone hadn't opened up properly. I came by a huge truck that had lots of NFL logos on it. It was a small TV studio hosting a nationwide fan competition. The NFL was looking for fans to talk about how much they love the NFL and to tell great fan stories to the world. If you won, you got tickets to the Super Bowl. The door then swung open, and Super Viking Syd Davy stepped out. Syd Davy has often been described as the NFL's number-one fan, and goes by the nickname "100% Cheese Free." Syd is famous for being the fan that used to catch ex-Vikings player, Randy Moss, after Moss scored a touchdown and leapt into the crowd.

Syd invited me to his tailgate but I had already made plans to visit Karen's hookup, the Battle Wagon. The four wagoneers—Terry, Doug, T. J., and Michael—clubbed together in 1998 to make the ultimate Viking tailgating vehicle. They transformed a truck into a Viking haven. They decked out the inside like an actual lounge, with a nice cozy armchair, an actual fireplace, and, of course, a flat screen to watch the game. Hans introduced to me some other tailgaters who call themselves Purple Pride. Their head chef was cooking up Hans's brats, though soon after, Hans and his friends left on a quest to find some Viking horns. The tailgaters next to the Purple Pride got wind of my trip and insisted I have a bowl of their wonderful beef stew. Here I noticed some tailgaters who were sitting on the roof of their van hanging out on deckchairs, enjoying the view. You could never get away with that in England.

I saw a huge gorilla wearing a Vikings jersey and horns riding on the back of a tricycle. An older man was cycling on the front and I can only assume someone else was in the gorilla outfit at the back. Together they just cycled around the tailgate. I was dumbfounded to see such a thing. It was frankly ridiculous, but I loved the fact that no one else seemed fazed by it.

The Vikings staff had told me I could get my pre-game sideline media pass one hour before kickoff, but 30 minutes before kickoff I would have to then go and find my seat. I took my bag with my camera and long lens and headed to the media window. I was nervous, thinking this was surely too good to be true. I felt so professional, so adult. They didn't even ask to see my real game ticket.

Once inside the Metrodome I made my way down the stairs to the field. There were lots of other fans down there too, but I had never been in a stadium so early before and I didn't even know the players did pre-game warm ups for the crowds to see.

Jared Allen, the Vikings new sack-making machine, came strolling over, signing autographs. I spotted him instantly, not because of his large frame or his friendly smile but his famed "Wisconsin-waterfall" hairstyle that is the stuff of mockery. But when you see him chopping quarterbacks in two with ease, one thinks twice about mocking his haircut. I made my way to the front, and everyone had their pens out. I told Jared about my trip, asking him to sign my shirt. His head sprung up from the footballs. He looked at me and said, "That's a great idea" and signed my t-shirt straight away. Perfecto!

Then I met Ragnar. It turns out he is the official mascot of the Vikings and the only mascot in the league that is a real person, as opposed to "actors" dressing up in a costume.

It was soon time to go and find my seat. In hindsight I probably did not need a game-day ticket after all, as I could have found an empty seat in the upper deck somewhere, because once I was in, I was in. Though with 30 minutes still before kickoff, I decided to pop back to the tailgate and find Hans.

Leaving the stadium was a rookie mistake. The Battle Wagon members told me I could not go into the stadium with my camera bag, even though I had just come out of the stadium with it, and it had a Metrodome security pass tag on it. I didn't have enough time to walk back to my hotel, so I left my larger lenses and video camera with the tailgaters, hoping they wouldn't steal it or, like the Packers fan, put anything too inappropriate on there.

I found Hans and his friends, and we walked into the stadium together, just as we saw a couple of cheerleaders parading around the tailgate on their official golf cart. Lucky thing those Battle Wagoneers were looking after my bag, because I saw several people with bags get turned away.

I got my e-ticket out, and it clearly said at the top, "Guns and Weapons prohibited." I had seen plenty of dressed-up Vikings at the tailgate harbouring an assortment of medieval weapons. I wondered how they were all going to get in? The seat from my pathetic-looking e-mail ticket was high up on the 20-yard line. It was a good view, but the game wasn't great though my seat was actually next to yet another honeymooning couple, this time from Denmark. Going to football games on one's honeymoon was starting to look like quite an idea. The Vikings are so called because of the large amount of Scandinavians living in the area, and Skol Vikings is their fight song.

The crowd was getting into it, but with little to cheer about it became harder for them as the game wore on. Adrian Peterson did rush for over 100 yards, but the game was tiring. Only when the Lions scored a touchdown did the Vikings pick themselves up, and it was the ex-Bear, Bernard Berrian, who caught a long pass for a touchdown. The crowd got loud . . . finally.[4]

The Vikings really had a lot of hoopla and fan interaction throughout the game, especially with competitions and giveaways—or maybe I just noticed it more because it wasn't the greatest of games. Or perhaps it was because the Vikings play inside a dome that they were then able to do a lot more of this kind of stuff. They had a fan air guitar competition. Then later a woman tried to throw a football into the trunk of a car from 10 yards out. Later a number of mascots came on the field and played full tackle football against small children in full uniform and gear oddly named "Pop Warner." When the "Pop Warner" kids finally scored, they received the biggest cheer of the day.

Rudy moment: Bernard Berrian's long TD catch. Why couldn't he catch the same deep ball in 2006, when he was playing for the Bears?

Orange play of the game: Lion's QB Dan Orlovsky foolishly walked out of bounds in his own end zone, giving the Vikings literally a free safety. D'oh!

Extreme fan: There were plenty to choose from: G the Vike lives in England and yet is a Vikings season ticket holder; Syd Davy, aka 100% Cheese Free, is such a popular Super Fan that he is now featured on Madden video games. He travels to every home game even though he lives in Winnipeg, Manitoba, Canada. His attire is chain mail, a vest (no matter what the weather), a WWF style belt, yellow-and-purple face paint, and a helmet with horns and yellow pigtails. He also proudly has tattoos of every team logo where he has caught Randy Moss in the end zone. But the winner had to be Hans Steiniger for his Quest.

I left the game in the fourth quarter, because I had to drive 700 miles to Cleveland by the next night. Even if it is not a good game, I still hate having to leave a game early, because you never know what could happen. I headed back to the Battle Wagon, and thankfully my belongings were untouched. Here I watched the Vikings win the game on TV with minutes to spare. I was getting annoyed that the NFL teams are so far apart—in this case causing me to miss a dramatic comeback win.

With night falling and the cold kicking in, Doug, who owns the bus, proudly went to work faster than any Vikings offensive player that day and started up the real fireplace he had installed in his wagon.

I said my good-byes and headed southeast to Cleveland. I stopped for a Chinese buffet as my cheese puffs and beef jerky had run out. I cracked open my fortune cookie and it read, "As soon as you feel too old to do a thing, do it!" I e-mailed a picture of it to Steph.

Game 12. NFL Week 6, New York Giants at Cleveland Browns, Browns Stadium

Final Score: 14-35. Home-win record: 10-2. Capacity: 73,200. Attendance: 73,102. Ticket face value: $60—I paid $60, via the box office. Picture on my ticket: Text on opaque Browns collage. Mascots: Four dog caricatures—CB, Chomps, TD, and Trapper. Merchandise: I bought a foam Browns paw but was given lots more free goodies. Local dish: Steak and Great Lakes fish.

Browns super fan, Dog Pound Mike, told me that "tailgating and football are the same thing. It's like peanut butter and jelly—one doesn't work without the other." Excited about the Cleveland tailgate, I rushed to the famous "Muni lot," but the rest of the fans were already heading into the stadium and I felt like a salmon, swimming against the current. The spirit was high, and the Browns fans, whose mascot is a dog, were making plenty of dog noises. Muni lot is quite small, but this is where all the dressed-up cars and RVs park. This is where Jay DiEugenio claims the best tailgate in the whole of the NFL occurs when the Steelers come to town.

In the dark distance I saw a 38-foot-long dog made from an actual school bus. Next to the bus was a huge wooden shack like the one I saw in Denver. I walked up onto the deck to find their leader, and as I introduced myself a succulent steak was placed onto a plate and into my hands. Mark Fielder and Scott Nunnari run this tailgate, named the "Muni Lot Browns Backers."

Their bus was rammed full of people and it was an actual party. There was music, drinking, and dancing. There were lots of Browns trinkets, merchandise, and pictures of famous Browns players. The bus had been gutted. Down the centre aisle was a long breakfast bar that people were sitting next to on both sides, facing a huge flat-screen HD TV. Towards the back is where they had two pumps for beer, both hooked up to kegs. Actual working beer pumps on the bus! No wonder it was busy. This dog on wheels actually has a side leg that raises where the dog leaks water. Mark even has a look-alike fire hydrant to add to the image. At the back of the bus hangs a pair of massive furry dangling balls, outside, above the back door. From various points inside people can pull a lever that brings the furry balls down swiftly, resulting in the "tea bagging of any Pittsburgh fan."

Back at the wooden structure I got to talk to Mark as I finished off my wonderful steak. He had a friend there with a huge mane of curly hair, who had previously come back from a trip where he got on his Harley and rode across the whole country with his new girlfriend. I asked him how easy it was for him to just up sticks, and if his girlfriend was supportive: "Well it was an easy decision for her, I'm 45 and she is 24." Fair point. "It was our second date and she wanted to come, so she left her job and now she is moving in with me!" Hmmm, maybe this guy should have talked to Steph before I set off; perhaps he could have convinced her to come with me for the whole trip?

The party was still going strong right up until 8:15 p.m. I raced around the parking lot and took some more pictures before Mark told me that Joe Cahn was here in Muni lot.

"Joe Cahn is here? I thought he was doing NASCAR this year." "He is," Mark told me, "but he is here tonight." I had a tough decision—make the MNF kickoff or meet Joe Cahn?

Every culture or subculture has a guru, a mythical figurehead, a living legend—a Jedi master. For the tailgating world, it is Joe Cahn. I already knew that Joe Cahn doesn't actually go into the stadiums and was likely to leave before I got back after the game, so it was now or never.

I raced over to his huge granddaddy of an RV and introduced myself to the legend. I was actually nervous. Joe has been called a national treasure by many tailgaters, and it didn't take me long to understand why. Cahn has been tailgating nonstop since 1994. He is retired and lives permanently in his RV with his wife and cat, Sophie, and he runs his own site called tailgating.com. He has gone to over 500 football games and has driven over 500,000 miles. He even drove to every NFL stadium in one season back in 1994. There was no reason for me to be nervous because he was all ears when I told him what I was up to.

Joe invited me into his house (his monster RV that he calls the JoeMobile) where we sat and had a lovely chat over a nice cup of tea—only there was no tea, it just felt like there was. The self-appointed commissioner of tailgating, Joe walks around meeting everyone, making sure they are having a good time and eating well. With the kickoff looming this was the only time he was actually by his RV the whole night.

His bedroom closet was open, and bursting out was his NFL jersey collection. Joe has more than one jersey for each team and was wearing a Cleveland Browns jersey and a warm smile that night. His lounge area had NFL pennants from every NFL team. Those odd triangular pieces of merchandise took me back to my youth when I saw my first-ever game in 1990. I was impressed when Joe told me he was at that game too. He was also at the Bears game in Arizona in 2006 and the NFL 2008 season-opener just a few weeks before in New York. This man is everywhere!

Joe is a warm, humorous, welcoming man and has the wise manner of a grandfather. Not only was he interesting to listen to with his plethora of experience, but he was also interested in my passion for the sport and for tailgating. A rare trait: to be interesting and interested at the same time. Joe has to be one of the nicest people I have ever met. I was a complete stranger, and there I was in his house and in his bedroom checking out his collection of NFL jerseys.

When he crowned himself the "commissioner of tailgating" in 1996, everyone in the tailgating world accepted it, probably because no one else has tailgated so much or for so long. Joe explained to me he doesn't go inside the stadiums because he gets "too into the game." If he could have his own way "both teams would win."

Joe advised me to ask a lot of questions, talk to people, write down their names, and mainly to enjoy myself. "It is your trip, no one else's, so just go out and have fun." I gave him one of my t-shirts, and he in turn gave me a jar of the spices that he uses on his food at the tailgates. It had a picture of himself on the jar and proudly stated, "The Commissioner's Seasoning."

Like myself, Joe has made sacrifices for his tailgating journey. He started out as the head of a cooking school. He sold his house and his cooking school as he wanted to go on the road and cook for people with his "mom-and-pop home-cooking style," and he hasn't looked back since.

I was already having a blast going from game to game and wondered if I could live on the road for the rest of my life going from tailgate to tailgate, from football game to football game. I'm not sure Steph has the hunger for that yet, but maybe she will when she has her first bite of a tailgate?

For every mile that Joe travelled in 2005, Campbell's Chunky Soup donated one can of soup to the food banks of the Gulf Coast area, which was recovering from Hurricane Katrina where Joe had his cooking school. People constantly ask Joe where the best place to tailgate is and he always answers, "It is where you are at that moment." Joe has said that "tailgating is the last great American neighborhood and the new community social, where everyone is welcome, and no one goes hungry. The parking lot is a neighborhood where everyone is happy to see you, and everybody is there to share in the fun, food, and football."[5]

Joe also expressed to me that tailgating is like the "reception before a banquet." The mingling, the socializing, the excitement is often more fun than "the Banquet." Many tailgate parties have grown because they have simply befriended and joined the tailgate party next to them. A tailgate is a community of people that look after each other. I'm not sure a gathering or a flock of "picnickers" would "join" in the same way.

I mentioned to Joe that I had caught the tailgating bug and would love to be a tailgater myself one day. His advice: "No matter what food you have for a tailgate, just make sure you have more than what you need, so that you can share it with your neighbors. It is important to make sure your tailgate is about being social. Remember that the most important aspect of a tailgate is spending time with your friends. There is no single better ingredient to have at a tailgate than friendship; it makes all the food taste better."[6] Although I was upset that I missed the kickoff, most of the first quarter, and the pre-game hoopla, I was happy to have shared such quality time with Joe.

I said good-bye to Joe and rushed to Renia, who works for the Browns marketing department. She had found me a ticket, just hours before kickoff. Although she could not get me in the Dawg Pound, she got me right next to it. The "Dawg Pound" is behind one of the end zones, where all the extreme Browns fans sit, or rather stand and bark. This is considered one of the loudest and most passionate sections in all of football. The Dawg Pound members demanded their section be all bleachers and not seats when their team was reborn in 1999. The Cleveland Browns were actually sold in 1995 and became the Baltimore Ravens. The mighty Cleveland fans demanded the Browns' return, and so they did.

The Cleveland Browns were pretty happy about hosting the Super Bowl champs, the Giants, not only because it brings prestige to the city and the travelling fans spend money there, but the players always want to play against the best . . . and try to beat them.

I got close to my seat, and I could see all the extreme Brown fans barking in the pound. The score was already 7-3 in favour of the Giants, but the atmosphere was like a rabid pounding pulse. The Browns were driving down the field, and the stadium was loud and powerful between snaps. Something big was brewing, and within minutes the Browns had scored a touchdown from a Jamal Lewis run. The crowd in the Dawg Pound went literally barking mad. From then on it was nonstop Browns action all the way. Eli Manning and the Giants could not find their groove, and the Browns were stunning the world champions.

There was a couple with their young son sitting next to me. The father heard my English accent and began asking me plenty of soccer questions. He told me he is a soccer coach, plays in goal, and is an Aston Villa fan because the Browns owner also owns Aston Villa.

There was an enthusiastic fan named Josh in front of me who had a specific hand gesture to say, "Ref, pull the flag," which is very similar to that of the wa**ker gesture in the U.K. So in both countries the fans have the same gesture for the referee, only the American name for this gesture is more formal and polite.

At halftime, two fans behind me called out my name as they recognised me from that day's local Ohio paper, *The Plain Dealer*. They told me that at the front of the luxury box a few rows behind them was Eli Manning's wife, Abby Mc-Grew, who was sitting with none other than Cowboys legend (and the man who beat Walter Payton's all-time leading rushing yards record), Emmitt Smith. When I finally had the balls to go up to him and tell him about my trip and meeting his old teammate Michael Irvin, he had left to prepare for post-game interviews. I wanted to give my card with my trip website on to Abby, to pass onto Emmitt Smith or to her husband, Eli, or to basically anyone she knows who might be affiliated with the NFL, but I didn't. It would have opened the floodgates for every male fan in the stadium to give her their cards.

The game restarted and everything clicked for the Browns. The night was filled with passion, joy, and music. During the second half there seemed to be lots of sing-along songs; "Hang on Sloopy" was played, and everyone mimed out the letters of O-H-I-O with their arms.

I had been receiving texts all night from an unknown phone number about meeting up. After the game I met this mysterious person down by the sidelines. I looked around but all I could see was an older man with a tear in his eye. I asked him, "How long have you been a Browns fan?" "Thirty-five years," he replied.

"Oh wow, so how long have you been waiting for a win like tonight?" "Thirty-five years." That's when I heard someone call my name from the sidelines. The mysterious texter was a member of the Browns staff who was holding up a Cleveland Browns plastic bag, with plenty of Browns goodies for me, capping off a perfect night.

Rudy moment: With the score at 14-27, Browns cornerback Eric Wright caught an interception on his own 10-yard line and took it back for a TD, running past the bumbling Manning, which totally killed off the Giants.

Orange play: Manning's second interception was way off the mark and was easily plucked by a Browns defender.

Extreme fan: PFUFA member, "Bone Lady." She wore a Browns dress with the words "Bone up" and her headpiece was a large, brown, bonnet-style wig filled with pin badges. She makes her own costume and owns the "Bone Mobile," an orange station wagon filled with Browns bumper stickers and an eight-foot lighted bone on the roof.

After the game I made my way back to Muni lot. People in the streets were happy, and drivers were all honking their horns and doing the Dawg chant. I saw Scott as he was packing away his tailgate. He told me that one of his proudest moments "was winning the contest as the Browns' top tailgate vehicle," which he describes as his "Browns museum." He proudly told me that their "tailgate specializes in steak and shrimp. There are many other tailgaters that have much more exotic food, but we're pretty happy with ours . . . From August to January, our whole social life revolves around this team and we schedule everything around the games and associated events. The sacrifice is worth it for the friends that we've made. We start earlier, end later, consume more, create crazier vehicles, create better party/tailgate themes, and generally go all out all of the time for a team that hasn't produced a championship since 1964 or many winning seasons of late. We are the cream of the crop in fan support."

While Scott spent over an hour packing up his tailgate, he told me that "without the tailgate, the entire experience is based on the team. Tailgating gives us control over the party. I like to say that you can't control how your team performs, but you sure can control how hard you party." Despite the fact that my original plan and inspiration came from Monday Night Football, after seeing five MNF games I started to realise that the night games can be very difficult for the tailgaters. Scott pointed out that on Mondays, "the tailgate lot that we use is shared by workers on weekdays. It makes it a strange mix of cars and tailgaters. The game excitement is intense, though, and because of the post-work rush-hour traffic, Mondays games are a little rushed."

BROWNS STADIUM TOUR

This was my first audible call in the second quarter when the good staff of the Cleveland Browns took me on my second stadium tour of the trip. On this tour I was actually allowed to go down on the sidelines. My guide, Steve, filmed me as I raced down the field like a child with too much sugar in his blood, all the way to the end zone. I caught my breath for a second and then sprinted back towards the empty end zone. I imagined that I was a receiver sent on a deep route to the end zone. I could actually hear the echoes of the cheering crowd from the night before and the fans going wild in my mind. The Dawg Pound cheered me on, hoping, nay, praying that I would catch the ball and win the game. I looked over my shoulder. I saw the imaginary football whistling towards me. I opened my hands and reached out for the fizzing brown leather that I caressed down to earth. *Touchdown!*

After my celebratory dance, I returned the imaginary ball to Steve, sporting a wide smile on my face. "I can make you a copy of the film," I told him, "and you could show it to the head coach, just in case you guys need any more receivers." "It's okay," Steve replied. "I, er, think we are fine." Maybe he didn't like any of my dance moves? I really do need to work on those if I am going to play in the NFL and then win *Dancing with the Stars*.

Steve took much joy in pointing out to me the different TVs around the building, the size of them, weight, if they were HD or not, and how much they cost. I was already becoming aware that TV and football are inextricably linked. Paolantonio believes that "*Monday Night Football* helped pro football overtake baseball as America's most popular sport."[7] NFL Films continues to be at the cutting-edge, using more and more cameras and gimmicks to bring the TV fan closer to the action.

For many fans, such as TV tailgaters, they prefer the action on TV than in the stadiums. Tunison says that "with its overpriced beers, poor stadium sightlines, and heinous traffic, the dirty secret about NFL fandom needs to be defiantly put forward: that it's much better to watch the game on TV anyway."[8] And yet, despite television's wonders and impressive state-of-the-art tools, the NFL still continues to grow each year in average attendances.

The jumbotron, other than being a major tool for the franchises to show off (see the Dallas Cowboys' new stadium, with its 160-foot-long HD screen), is actually quite necessary for the game. At soccer stadiums, jumbotrons rarely show live replays in case the referee gets a call wrong and the fans start a riot, which nearly happened at the World Cup in 2010 when a replay showed a clear goal but the ref "didn't see it." Despite the technology, FIFA (the world's governing soccer body) does not allow referees to use technology in making their decisions. If the technology is there, they should use it! Like other sports, such as cricket and Rugby League, the NFL uses the TVs to get their calls right. NFL coaches are allowed to challenge the NFL officials. They use the TVs to determine whether or not a play was correct, which has enhanced the strategy in the game.

After each play, especially the really good ones, it is great to see an action replay. Because of the stoppages in the game, if you missed the play, you can catch it again on the screen. It's like a habit, you watch the play, it ends, you high-five people, then you turn your head to the jumbotron, watch it again and get another high-five.

Aside from replays and advertisements, the jumbotrons are also used for games, quizzes, important messages (such as the "Fan Code of Conduct"), information about players, their stats highlights of past games, the teams' work with local communities and charities, sideline interviews, fans from the tailgate, half-time shows, other scores from around the league, as well as powerful graphics for chants and cheers, and of course, wedding proposals.

In just a handful of games, I came to realise that NFL fans (or maybe it is just American fans in general?) love being "filmed for the jumbotron." As soon as fans see themselves on the jumbotron they become elated, even if their team is losing. It's as if for some the main motivation for going to the game is the chance to be on the jumbotron. Some teams filmed the fans with a "hug cam" and a "kiss cam," while others looked for the best dancing fan or the loudest fan. NFL players too like to get in on it and often check out the jumbotron to see a replay of themselves.

In the '60s, the NFL chose Sam Huff to be the first player to be "miked up." During a game a player had given Huff a late hit. After the game "the offender told Huff he was just trying to get on TV."[9]

Steve took me into the away team locker room, where I could hear still hear the crying echoes of the Giants players after their shocking loss the night before. We then went into several executive boxes, press boxes, and the famous Dawg Pound.

Steve then took me into the basement to show me the prison cells, where they keep any drunken yobs before the police come to pick them up. I couldn't believe that stadiums actually have cells. I was later told that the Philadelphia Eagles not only have cells in their stadium but a judge too. There were 21 arrests in the stadium the night before, which sounded like quite a lot considering I didn't even hear one swear word the whole night.

We discussed how frequent scalping is, because I was surprised to see sellers at every stadium, flagrantly selling tickets even in front of the police. With sites like StubHub, were the Browns not worried about who gets their hands on tickets?

Steve pointed out that although fans and ticket holders can sell their tickets, there is a consequence if things go badly. He told me the Browns work on a "three strikes and you're out" rule. If a fan is ejected, that gets one strike against his name. If a season ticket holding fan gives or sells a ticket to someone and that someone gets kicked out, then both the owner of the ticket and the user gets a strike against their names. Get three of those and season ticket holders forfeit their right to buy tickets again. The system is in place so that if you do sell/give your ticket away, then you had better trust that person.

I told Steve that in the U.K. our season tickets are done as a book, or at least they were when I was growing up. You keep the book of tickets for one season. Inside there are many stubs that have a number, say 1 to 100. Every time you go to a game, the team puts a number up that has not been used that season thus far. Let's say 34. So you take docket 34 out and hand that in. Pretty simple. That way you cannot just sell one game ticket, because until you get to the stadium and they open the doors, you will not know what game ticket number they will be using that day. If fans do give their book to someone, it better be someone they trust. I hear teams now use a swipe-card system, which is nicer to trees. The downside to both systems is that you do not get fancy ticket stubs that are your own "pieces of the game."

We then met up with Renia, whose birthday it was the night before. She was happy that I brought her Browns a win, so she gave me yet another goodie bag with even more Browns merchandise.

A few days later, I had a telephone interview on a Cincinnati radio show called "The Animal." I told the listeners that my home to away win record was 10-2. The presenter then told me that if I could bring their so-far-winless Bengals a win for my next game then they would give me a season ticket for the rest of the year! I was hoping that my decent home-win record could continue throughout the regular season and that teams would offer me tickets for their home games in the playoffs.

HALL OF FAME

In a garage on September 17, 1920, Pro Football was founded in Canton, Ohio. It consisted of 11 charter member teams, two of which are still in the league: the Chicago Bears, who were then called the Decatur Staleys, and the Arizona Cardinals, who were originally the Chicago Cardinals. Two local teams, the Canton Bulldogs and the Akron Professionals, have both disbanded, but Canton, where the Professional Football Hall of Fame is located, is an hour's drive from Cleveland. The hall is officially a museum and is not run by the NFL.

I was unsure just how much time I would spend at the hall. Like for Disneyland, is one day really enough? I turned off the highway down "George Halas Drive," and I got goose bumps all over my body. If Lambeau Field is the cathedral of the NFL, then this is its birthplace.

A small green gridiron by the parking lot lead to the museum, a round squat building with a retro '70s-style football-shaped rotunda poking out of the top. It's almost as if God had scored a touchdown and then spiked this massive ball right into the hall's roof.

I was welcomed with open arms by the friendly staff at the hall. Vice President Dave Motts introduced me around before letting me into the hall for free. Like an excited child I headed off straight into the great rotunda. I was too excited to follow the sign that actually said that the museum starts upstairs. I realised later that I had actually completed the tour from back to front.

Parts of the museum were fun and interactive, such as the football throwing challenge, like I had seen at numerous NFL fan zones. There was an impressive stand describing the 20 years of Monday Night Football, plus a series of televisions showing great historic moments. There is a movie theatre where they showed highlights of the Super Bowl–winning Steelers from the 2005–2006 season, interspersed with interviews including player and fan reactions. The deep gravel voice of the commentator and the powerful music actually brought a big, fat tear to my eye. Even thought the Steelers are not my team, I was moved.

There were numerous displays spanning historic moments from every generation, including Walter Payton's actual game boots, jerseys, and helmet. There was a display for the Patriots when they went 21 games without a loss but then lost to the Giants in the Super Bowl. They had a series of XBoxes hooked up to even more TVs to promote 20 years of John Madden's video game series.

When I was younger I thought John Madden was simply the face of the most popular NFL video game franchise, which was my staple football diet for many years. I later discovered that he is also the most famous NFL commentator. Like many commentators, he has seen hundreds of games and has visited every NFL stadium numerous times, but John is different, because like myself he "road trips from game to game" on a massive RV named the Madden Cruiser. He does this because he has a fear of flying. The bus is equipped like a modern apartment with leather couches, plasma TVs, and a full-on kitchen. It is worth $800,000. While on the road he had two drivers, and they lived full time on the bus all season long, every season.

John Madden was actually drafted to play for the Philadelphia Eagles but suffered a knee injury and never got to play professionally. In 1969 at just 32 years of age, he became one of the youngest people to ever coach an NFL team, taking over the reins of the Oakland Raiders. After coaching he took his "booming" style and passion for football into TV as a commentator, and that's when he became the figurehead for the famed football video games. In 2006 he was inducted into the Pro Football Hall of Fame.

The 2008 season was his last season as a commentator before retiring. After 28 years of touring the country, he decided to hang up his "commentary cleats." In his last few years he mainly covered the Sunday night games. While I was at the Vikings game just days before, John Madden had decided to not take in that Sunday night game in San Diego because of travel conflicts, breaking his 476th NFL weekend streak.

Following his commentary on the Super Bowl that season (February 2009) he retired at the age of 73 to spend more time with his family. His bombastic, energetic zeal could turn a somewhat flaccid game into something much more electric. The NFL's commissioner, Roger Goodell, said that John "had an incredible talent for explaining the game in an unpretentious way that made it more understandable and fun. . . . He was the ultimate football fan who also happened to be an extraordinarily talented coach and broadcaster. "[10] John and I had shared just one game on the trip and that was the Sunday night game in Indianapolis in week 1. I say share because we were in the same stadium at the same time.

Madden also loves the tailgate so much he put his name on his own tailgating cookbook, saying that "the more I look at this tailgating the more I realize that for some people it's as important as the game, maybe even more important."[11]

I then made my way through the Hall's Super Bowl Experience, which had some great items from each Super Bowl, including the actual Vince Lombardi trophy. There is a display consisting of one Super Bowl ring for each Super Bowl–winning team. I spotted the Bears' ring, which was actually one of the smallest, while the Ravens' ring was huge and had more than 200 diamonds in it.

I discovered a section dedicated to the NFL fans, called the Visa Hall of Fans. In January 1999, Visa sponsored this nation-wide project where 31 super fans, one for each NFL franchise at the time, were handpicked to be in the Pro Football Hall of Fame. Each fan became known as a Hall of Fame Fan, and every year more fans were added to the honourable list. Each NFL player spends a career trying to get into the Hall of Fame, and with this project the fans can be "enshrined" too, just like the pros. To apply, fans had to submitt essays explaining why they were super fans of their team. They were chosen not just on how many NFL games they had attended home and away, year after year, stadium after stadium, but how they "promote the fellowship of all fans, encourage sportsmanship and support charitable activities."[12]

Every year the group grew and grew with new fans proving their worth. In 2005, Visa ended its sponsorship and the selection process was stopped; however, in 2007 the Hall of Fame Fans wanted to continue the project themselves. They renamed themselves the Professional Football Ultimate Fan Association (PFUFA) and decided that current members would seek to find new members. Danny Dillman, whose alter ego is called Sergeant Colt, was the PFUFA president in 2008. He stated that "PFUFA is now searching the stadiums of the NFL to find more great fans!"[13]

Up until this point I had met two PFUFA members: Bone Lady and Captain Jet, but at that time those letters didn't mean much to me. Now the penny had dropped! In the hall was a big poster of Barrel Man, as he was in the first Hall of Fame Fans class. Sergeant Colt explained that "the standard we put on these fans is very high. In this manner, we handpick each one. Of the numerous possible draftees selected, only a few will be asked to join the organization. It is not necessary for possible draftees to dress up in costumes or outfits. Instead, we are looking for fans who passionately represent their team, *but* who will also respect another fan that passionately roots for another team. Each [PFUFA] member is encouraged to be *highly selective* in the fans that receive a Draft Card and that good character fans were sought."[14]

Once a fan receives a draft card, he or she then has to receive an 80 percent of the committee vote to be a PFUFA nominee (potential veteran). They are then invited to the PFUFA reunion that August at the Hall of Fame, during the same weekend when the NFL enshrines a number of ex-NFL players into the hall. If a PFUFA nominee then receives a further 80 percent vote that weekend, they become a full PFUFA member.

Joe Cahn, and Jay and Karen DiEugenio are all honorary members, while Hans received his draft card during the 2008 season. I suddenly had another aim: to be nominated with a draft card into this elite community of super NFL fans.

At the end of my journey through the museum (which, for everyone else who pays attention to signs, would have been at the starting point) was the majestic and breathtaking Hall of Fame itself. This is a low-lit, quiet room. Bronze busts of every player who has been enshrined into the Hall sit around the perimeter of the room. The sheer number of NFL stars looking back at me was both eerie and magical. The busts are so well done you can really recognise each one. It was even stranger when I saw both Mike Ditka and Michael Irvin's busts, because I had only just seen them in the flesh weeks before.

Five years after retiring, NFL players are eligible to be voted into the Hall of Fame. Some players are enshrined in their first year of eligibility, while other players just make it to the nomination stage year after year. John Madden told Roger Goodell on NFL.com that he believes that once all the lights in the hall are turned off, the busts talk to each other.

Back downstairs I spent hours in the gift shop, where they have an abundance of merchandise for every team. The cashier there felt the most ridiculous item was either the bright red Harley Davidson that had hundreds of Hall of Fame signatures on it, or the selection of team "foam heads." Personally I felt it was either the NFL-themed Christmas tree decorations, or the NFL team toothbrushes. Although I was on a budget, I still emerged from the shop a few hundred dollars lighter.

Dave Motts asked me to come back the following day, where they were going to give me full access to their actual archives, known as the bunker, which the public does not get to see. Dave had recommended that I stay in the hotel across the highway, as they do a good Hall of Fame discount. What I didn't know, until much later, was that this is the very hotel that the NFL workers and players actually stay in when they come for the Hall of Fame ceremony in August. I would have loved to know which NFL player had slept in my bed.

At 5 p.m. I was on another radio show in Cincinnati, the "Eddie and Tracey Show" on 700 WLW. They told me that when I arrive in Cincy I needed to try their famous three-way. "I've been trying to get a three way my whole life," I said. "We've heard that one before!" groaned the host . . . Apparently a three-way in Cincy is a type of chili. There is also four-way and a rather ambitious five-way!

Because the Bengals had lost their first six games, I figured I could find cheap tickets on StubHub, but the producer of the show, a lovely man named Russ, told me that he would give me his spare ticket. My first free ticket!

The next morning, I was back at the Hall excited to see the archives. I had texted Steph about going into the bunker, but her reply back was not quite as enthused. If she were out here, then she could have looked at all of the files that the Hall keeps on every NFL player to have ever played the game. She was definitely missing out.

As well as files, they also had tons of real game artefacts that were either being restored or that they just didn't have room for in their displays. There were old jerseys, shoulder pads, and classic throwback helmets. I found a copy of the Bears' first-ever game-day programme.

Dave gave me some great Hall of Fame goodies, such as a sports bag, a sweater, a t-shirt, and a poncho. I ran to my car to return the favour and gave their staff a handful of my football trip t-shirts.

Dave asked me what I was doing that night. I told him nonchalantly that I had been invited by Scott from the Muni lot Browns Backers to "party on his old school bus, a 36-foot-long dog on wheels." "Oh okay," Dave responded with a slight degree of confusion but then realised how I might attract some bizarre social excursions on this trip. "Well, how would you like to go to a high school football game my son is playing?" Hell, yes!

Dave and his colleagues made some calls and got me a press pass, because the game was actually sold out. That's right, a high school football game was a sell out, and it wasn't just a small stand but a 12,000-seater stadium. I couldn't believe it.

Game 13. GlenOak Eagles at the Hoover Vikings, North Canton, Ohio, Hoover High School Memorial Stadium Complex

Final Score: 10-14. Home-win record: 11-2. Capacity: 12,000. Attendance: Sold out. Ticket face value: Unknown—I got in for free. Picture on my ticket: No physical ticket, I was on a media pass list. Mascot: Hoover's mascot is a Viking and GlenOak's mascot is the golden eagle. Merchandise: A Hoover Viking t-shirt given to me by the principal.

Later that evening I was lost in downtown Canton, which is the most run-down and dilapidated downtown I have ever seen. It looks like something out of those budget movies you see on late-night TV. It was getting dark and I couldn't see a stadium anywhere, despite being told "it is easy to find." I didn't want to get out of the car and ask for help, for fear that my rental car would be stripped for parts within seconds. The people on the streets looked like they were either homeless or on drugs, or both.

I finally stopped at a small fried-chicken place to ask directions. The lady behind the counter and the lady in front of the counter kept asking me what the school's name was. I was embarrassed because I didn't know. All I knew was the address and that one team play in green and the other in orange.

I was half expecting both ladies to ask me something about my accent, because there can't be too many middle-class white boys from London who turn up at their chicken shack on a Friday night looking for high school football. But all they wanted to do was help me.

The chatty ladies spent the next 15 minutes looking through the yellow pages and phoning their friends to find out where the big high school games were being played that night, but to no avail.

Finally I got through to the high school's principal. He told me I needed to punch "North Canton" into my GPS, not "Canton." I was at the correct address of 525 7th street but in the wrong city. It seems like I didn't learn anything from my Dallas/ESPN error. One of the customers finished buying up her chicken and told me to trail (tailgate) her car as she escorted me all the way to the stadium, going out of her way by at least five miles.

I felt bad that just moments before I had made negative judgments about the good people of Canton, thinking the locals would only want to rob me instead of help me. My other regret was that I never got to buy any of that delicious-looking chicken.

Driving into North Canton, I could see the "Friday Night Lights" up ahead, and parking looked tricky. So I followed someone who I assumed was going to the game. Out of nowhere, he suddenly turned left off the road, up the high curb, over the pavement/sidewalk, and onto the grass where he suddenly parked. I rather nervously put my car next to his. "Err, can we park here?" I asked. "Sure," he replied, "I have been coming to games here for 20 years, never got a ticket." "Oh okay, so what about that 30-foot ditch in front of us?" "Oh, it will be fine!" So I left my car precariously teetering on the edge and raced to the stadium.

I met Anthony, the principal, by an actual ticket office, which had its own little hut and I was chuffed that I had my own media pass . . . for a high school game. It blew my mind!

Anthony escorted me through the gates to the running track that separated the supporters and the players on the field. A gust of wind picked up suddenly. I turned around, and there behind one of the end zones was a FOX TV helicopter about to land. The best we got at my high school soccer games would be if *all* of our Dads showed up.

I was introduced to two students at the school: Lauren and Brooke, both of whom were on the yearbook club taking pictures of the players. Both had huge lenses and great cameras, which they can "sign out like a library book." I wished I could have borrowed their equipment for the rest of my trip. After seeing the FOX TV helicopter land, I was by no means surprised by the 10 professional photographers and journalists on the sidelines.

I stood on the running track alongside the freezing cold cheerleaders, the school's marching band, and the school's sprit squad. I spotted some rather nutty supporters, who happened to be shirtless in the freezing cold. Anthony threw some of my trip t-shirts to the crowd, I guess so they would cover up, but they didn't. I really would have liked to shoot one of my t-shirts out of the firing guns that I saw at other stadiums. Because of my media pass I was given total access to any part of the grounds, including the commentary box.

The fans were segregated by the field—home fans on one side, away on the other—yet there was no north or south stand, just terraces along the sidelines. The crowd sat on cold metal bleachers, and many younger fans had brought cushions and blankets. There is no alcohol sold at high school and college games, and that helps to curb any possible drunken aggression. Anthony told me that he has never seen a fight here and that's when I noticed a distinct lack of police or security, which was impressive considering there were 12,000 fans there, double what you get a Leyton Orient game.

The quarters are shorter in high school football but the tackles are by no means less hard, and there were some crunching hits as both teams were moving the ball well. Peter King, in his much-loved weekly football column "Monday Morning Quarterback" for *Sports Illustrated*, often writes about his love and passion for high school sports, and I could now see why. This was magical stuff.

Halftime was upon us too quickly, and the home team Hoover Vikings were losing 10-7.

By this time I had seen a fair few decent halftime shows, but this one blew me away. The home band came onto the field and there were hundreds of students taking part. They played in perfect sync. The young lady at the front had a baton that she threw high into the air and caught while doing cartwheels and jumps . . . oh, and did I mention that the baton happened to be on fire?! I couldn't imagine school children in London throwing batons on fire into the night sky—the whole school would burn down in minutes.

It was "Senior Night," which meant this was the last home game for the seniors. For many of these teenagers this was the last time they would play, sing, and cheer on home soil. For many of those playing, it would also be their last in full kit, as many are unlikely to play at the college level.

Each member of the band then came forward to have their name called out, where they took a bow. It really was a touching experience, and I have never seen so many teenagers so proud of their high school.

When Walter Payton was a youth he played the drums in his high school band. He actually "concentrated on being in the school band" over football. His school "was so small that often football players would join the band at halftime and perform in their uniform."[15] The visiting GlenOak Eagles team brought with them around 6,000 of their own fans, including their own band and cheerleaders. The home fans applauded and cheered, and I didn't hear one "boo" the entire night.

Someone then explained to me just how the point system in this high school league works. If your team beats a team that then goes on to beat other teams, your team then gets extra points. GlenOak is a good team and they were tied in the division with Hoover. Hoover wants to beat GlenOak . . . naturally, but after that Hoover would actually want GlenOak to win the rest of their games, as Hoover gets points for every GlenOak win. If you beat a team that then loses games, you don't gain any extra points. Also if you beat a team late in the season and they have won a bunch of games already, you get those extra points too. It changes the whole notion of a rivalry and wanting to see your rival squander; this way you would want them to do well.

Anthony took me on a tour all around the stadium, introducing me to his staff, fans, players' parents, students, photographers, journalists, and radio commentators in the press box, which was a wooden hut at the top of the away section. Anthony told everyone that I was a journalist from London, writing for the *London Times*. I didn't want to correct him to mention that A) I was not a journalist but a crazed football fan, B) that I didn't actually work for the *London Times*, and C) that the *London Times* doesn't actually exist. There is *The Times*, a British national newspaper, owned by media mogul Rupert Murdoch, who happens to own FOX TV, Sky, and probably bought the helicopter sitting behind the end zone with his pocket change. I didn't want to lie to people, but I also didn't want to correct Anthony either.

Everyone was pretty happy to chat with me, either because I was English, or they thought that I was writing for a London newspaper. The real "journalists" however merely made a few grunts my way. Perhaps they knew I was an imposter?

After the game Anthony walked me into the locker room. The smell of sweat, mud, and adrenaline attached itself to the condensation on the tiles and the brown ceramic floors, and the slaps of winning high-fives echoed around the walls.

At the end of the evening I was in the principal's office—a statement that sounds wonderfully American. Anthony handed me plenty of Hoover Vikings t-shirts and I responded by giving him more of my football trip t-shirts. It was as if we were captains of two soccer teams at a cup final, where teams exchange flags with their team's crest on.

Anthony offered to drop me off at my car, but I couldn't tell him where I parked, other than that it was "on a grass patch somewhere," just like my Dad and I thought we had done back in 1990 at Wembley. It was hard to see the car in the darkness and I was worried that the wind from the helicopter may have blown it down into the ditch. Finally we found it, and I don't think Anthony was too impressed with my parking.

Just as I was saying my thanks he told me that he used to play football and that he was an "All-American." I didn't know what that meant at the time, and I thought it was rather an odd thing to say. I don't drop people off at their cars in England after discussing my soccer playing days to then finish off the conversation, with "I was an All-English . . . toodles." However, it turns out All-Americans are those nominated to be the best in their position in football for college players.

Rudy moment: After the game the lights went out. The home team's marching band then performed a "glow show" using glow sticks to play out for the fans. The defeated away fans and band stayed to watch and show their support. Then they marched the fans down the streets all the way back to the high school, still playing in perfect sync as they went. Now that's the way to end a football game.

Orange play of the game: My being late and missing so much of a magical night.

Extreme fan: The four teenage boys that stood in the front row with their shirts off and body paint on, despite the freezing conditions.

After the game I drove back to Cleveland to "party" on Scott's dog bus that he keeps in his huge front garden. Here I was able to see the bus in more detail as it was far less busy. Scott took great pleasure in showing me the pictures of the bus over the years and how they have added new bits and pieces.

I arrived late, when most people had either left or were drunk. One of these drunks decided to berate me for being English, telling me several times over that America beat England in the war. He suddenly got very aggressive, telling me he has the right to kick me out of "his" country because his forefathers apparently did the same to my ancestors. I was pretty intimidated. Thankfully the other members of the party backed me up. He wasn't happy about his friends going against him and they asked him to apologise.

The next day I was back at the Hall for my third day running, for a Halloween-themed day. Outside the Hall on the small grass gridiron I discovered a mini tailgate party, with food stalls, a petting zoo, and a huge inflatable football helmet, all organised by the Hall. All the staff and children were dressed up in fancy dress and I whizzed around the museum once more. The museum was now peppered with pumpkins, ghouls, and ghosts. It was a good thing I came back, because the Hall had yet another surprise for me. There was actually a college game taking place next door at the historic Fawcett Stadium, which was built in 1938. The Malone University Pioneers were playing the Walsh University Cavaliers.

The Hall gave me a ticket for the college game. I felt like Peyton Manning, firing off lots of audibles and scoring lot of TDs. I made my way to Fawcett Stadium, where the NFL holds its first pre-season game and where the Hall of Fame enshrinement ceremony takes place. The stadium has a capacity of just over 22,500, which means it is actually considered too small to be an official NFL stadium.

Game 14. Mid-States Football Association Conference (MSFA) college game, Walsh Cavaliers vs. Malone Pioneers, Fawcett Stadium

Final Score: 21-24. Home-win record: 12-2. Capacity: 22,375. Attendance: 3,000. Ticket face value: Unknown—I got the ticket for free. Picture on my ticket: Text on a card, it actually said "coupon." Mascot: Didn't see one. Merchandise: A soft small ball thrown at me by a cheerleader.

Both Malone and Walsh Universities play their home games at Fawcett Stadium, but this game was considered a "home" game for the Walsh Cavaliers. It was a very empty stadium, and my ticket was not specific to one seat, so I could sit wherever I liked, even in the away section (the other half of the stadium) if I wanted to. There wasn't much crowd noise, but both sets of cheerleaders tried their best to rally up the small crowd.

The only person I met here (and I had to look hard for someone to talk to) was a girl whose boyfriend was on the team. Sadly he never once made it onto the field, so we didn't have too much to cheer about.

The game itself was pretty good with Malone winning in the last minute with a great touchdown driving the whole length of the field. Still despite this not being one of the big college games that attracts over 100,000 fans, I was over the moon to see more football than I had bargained for.

Rudy moment: The last drive from the home team to win. They needed a TD to win. Their 80-yard drive was perfectly engineered to score and run out the clock.

Orange play of the game: When the cheerleaders formed a human pyramid, the girl on top fell off. Thankfully she was caught. Minutes later she was back on top, but fell off again.

Extreme fan: With hardly any fans at the game, I saw nothing "extreme."

Game 15. NFL Week 7, Pittsburgh Steelers at Cincinnati Bengals, Paul Brown Stadium

Final Score: 38-10. Home-win record: 12-3. Capacity: 65,535. Attendance: 65,860. Ticket face value: $70—I got the ticket for free. Picture on my ticket: Bengals and Steelers logo. Mascot: "Who Dey," a Bengal creature. Merchandise: "Jungle towel" and beads. Local dish: Cincinnati Chili, and Chili Mac (noodles with chili on top).

It's 7 a.m., freezing cold, and 30 themed busses were parked already, with more pouring into the Bengal lots. Grills and awnings were out, tents up, chairs laid out, TVs on, coffee, liquor, and breakfast all being prepared and consumed.

I headed to the famous Longworth Hall Lot, which is in front of a stunning 1904 huge long warehouse. One group here called their bus the Bengals Prison Van. They apologised to me that they were not in their usual game day attire of bright orange jumpsuits. Then I met a gentleman named Mike Sensel. He had heard about my trip from the radio and insisted I come down to check out his party. There were about 40 of his friends there. Mike introduced me to his daughter, Jen, who became my filmmaker for the next 30 minutes. This is where I played my first game of cornhole. I lost, and lost bad . . . 8-2. Apparently cornhole is a Cinci tailgating tradition.

After this embarrassing loss Mike introduced me to a sweet dice-based game popular at this tailgate called Shut the Box. Mike brought out a bright orange box the size of a laptop. Everyone threw in one dollar. It is a maths-dice-based game and the object is to get as little score as possible. I got a feeble 14, the winner had 3 and took mine and everyone else's dollar. More money lost gambling at the tailgate.

The next stop on my tailgate tour was to see the Bengal Bomb Squad. The Bengal Thing met me and introduced me to his friends and family. He was nominated for PFUFA that year, and he dresses like The Thing from the Fantastic Four comic book series, but with a Bengals shirt on and The Thing mask. He had several copies of that month's *Tailgater Monthly* magazine. I was chuffed to pieces to see Karen's double-spread article, titled "British Invasion,"[16] all about my trip. I was so proud to grace the glossy pages of one of the most widely read magazines on tailgating, even though I was still a "rookie." The Bengal Thing was also featured in the magazine, and we signed each other's copies.

His party then supplied me with my first "three-way," a hot dog with Cincinnati's famous chili topped with grated cheese. I took a big bite and thought it was a very nice experience indeed. Their secret ingredient: chocolate!

It was then time to move on to the "Home of the Mexican Happy Hour" tailgate party. They had specifically told me to be there for a "show" at midday. I couldn't believe five hours had flown by. I made my way to see Adam and his loud Bengal-based school bus. Before I knew it I had a sombrero on my head and was hoisted onto the roof of his bus.

Mexican music was being pumped out loud and clear and a large crowd began to gather. Was I supposed to have prepared a speech? After the music was done I was told to throw jelly vodka shots into the crowd (the shots were in little covered cups), and the crowd was going crazy. I stood back for a moment and thought to myself, *Just how on earth does a London guy end up in Cincinnati on a Sunday morning, standing on top of a Bengals-themed school bus throwing out jelly shots to hundreds of people?*

There were a lot of themed buses and vans in Cinci, more so than probably any other tailgate I had seen until that point. The vehicle of the day was the Cinci-themed hearse. I had seen NFL-themed ambulances, and an array of trucks, school buses, ice-cream-type vans, and SUVs but never a hearse. The sides were painted with orange and black Bengal stripes and they had a huge Bengal stuffed toy perched on top. At the back was a pullout grill, a shelf for food, and a built-in wall with a TV, car music player, and several speakers. It was a thing of beauty.

This was when I saw "paper bag fans," three fans walking around the tailgate with brown paper bags over their heads, because they were too embarrassed to be recognised, since the team had lost their first six games.

It wasn't long before kickoff so I rushed over to meet Russ, who gave me his extra ticket. Channel 12 was also there to interview me. The interview was really tough because every time a fan walked behind me, they would suddenly start to wave their arms and heads about saying all sorts of obnoxious and loud things. Once out of camera range, they would then snap back into being calm, diligent folk enjoying their stroll to the stadium. The camera lady was getting annoyed, and she rolled her eyes at these Jekyll and Hyde fans.

My seat was in section 128 of the stadium, which is in the lower level behind the end zone. This stadium is nicknamed the Jungle, but it wasn't intimidating for the away Steelers fans because thousands of them were peppered throughout. Russ was telling me that he used to have tickets on the opposite end zone on the upper level. The upper level, like with most NFL outdoor stadiums, has no roof for the fans. His former section never saw the sun and he told me that the wind from the river in the winter "would cut you in half." I was glad that he had up-graded.

During the game I noticed what I thought was another streaker, but it was actually a small child. He stopped on the field and then ran back to the sidelines. How strange. I saw him do the same thing later on. Then I realised he has the awesome pleasure of delivering the kicking tee for kickoffs. What a great job! In rugby someone brings on a mini mud pyramid to secure the ball on kickoffs. In the World Cup some years ago, England experimented with using a small remote-controlled truck to bring on the mud. It worked well until a French player stamped on the truck.

I noticed that Bengal helmets were carved into the back of each seat in the stadium, and tigerish cat noises were pumped through the PA system when the Bengals got a first down, which wasn't often. I was particularly surprised by the hot dog seller, who filled the stands with his booming operatic voice—his sales were helped by the fact that he was wearing a bright orange funny Mohawk wig in homage to Chad Ochocinco, who famously once sported a blonde Mohawk. The wig itself was available in the gift shop and was certainly the most ridiculous piece of Bengals merchandise on display. The vendor also works for the local baseball team, giving him cult status in Cinci. Word on the street is that he is the best vendor in the whole city.

At halftime the Bengals were only losing 10-7, and I was really hoping my home field luck would have helped them. In the second half, however, the Steel-ers came out blazing and crushed the Bengals, so no free Bengals season ticket for me.

Rudy moment: Chad Ochocinco's diving catch, which capped off a great drive for the Bengals, giving us all hope they could get their first win of the sea-son. I was, however, hoping for a slightly more creative celebration from number

85 than just a jumping hip bump with a teammate. Clay Travis is concerned because he feels that "this particularly bi-curious celebratory dance has taken over."[17]

Orange play of the game: It is was either the Bengals defense for not showing up in the second half at all, or the Bengals offensive line, which allowed their QB to be sacked seven times.

Extreme fan: One fan came to the game dressed like a Bengals mascot in full fur costume and large animal mask, but my fan of the day was the Bengal Thing.

Sadly I had to leave the game late in the fourth quarter to get a good start for my 900-mile drive to New England, where I had to be the following night to see the Pats.

Five hundred miles later I finally checked into a hotel. My phone rang late from an unidentified number and I heard the voice of an older man. He told me that he worked for the Bengals and that he was impressed with my trip. I was too excited to question why he was calling me so late on a Sunday evening. After 15 minutes of me practically jabbering on about myself, he then said, "Everyone here at the office is wondering if you are a homosexual." I thought this was an odd question to ask, but I didn't want to question the appropriateness, so I simply referred him to my site and told him about Steph and our relationship. A minute later I heard his voice crack into a muffled laugh. Damn that pesky Justin!

The next morning I called the Patriots ticket office on the off chance that they had tickets. They surprisingly had seats left, including "standing" tickets. As I was taking my friend Izzy, who isn't a football fan, to the game, I decided to splash the extra five bucks for two "seated tickets" for $60 a piece, a bargain.

Later that day I endured what was probably the worst drive on the entire trip: getting to Foxboro, Massachusetts. Izzy had intercepted me at a train station, but Gippy was not having a good time, as going through so many tolls confused him. Izzy was scared to death with my constant lane changing, my high level of panic, and constant missing of crucial exits and highways. The Patriots tailgaters had warned me of rush-hour traffic mixing with MNF game traffic, but I couldn't believe it was this bad. During the last hour alone we moved just 200 feet, which meant we had missed all of the pre-game tailgate.

The Patriots front office had told me to check out "Patriot Place," which includes a cinema, a nature trail, a hotel, a live music hall and sports educational centre, a hall of fame dedicated to the Patriots, and, of course, the stadium itself, but I missed all of that apart from the stadium.

Game 16. NFL Week 7, Denver Broncos at New England Patriots, Gillette Stadium

Final Score: 7-41. Home-win record: 13-3. Capacity: 68,756. Attendance: 68,756. Ticket face value: $60—I paid $60, via the box office. Picture on my ticket: Text on plain background. Mascot: "Pat Patriot," a caricature of someone from the American Revolution. Merchandise: A great Pats woolly hat with fold down ears. Local dish: Stuffed quahogs (clams).

Gillette Stadium, nicknamed the Razor, sits in the middle of a forest and is beautiful. There is a bridge between two of the stands, plus two huge mock fire towers, which have digital Patriots logos that look like blue flickering flames.

Once inside we kept going higher and higher until we were right at the very top. It was a shame that superstar Patriots QB Tom Brady was out for the season, but that didn't stop the Pats from crushing their opponents with ease.

At every NFL game I had been to at this point of the trip there was an abundance of national patriotism. The national anthem was sung every time (we Brits only do that for international games and cup finals) often followed by Air Force airplanes. Then later in the game members of the armed forces (Hometown Heroes) who have returned to American soil would be introduced. These brave men and women got an almighty applause every time. So naturally at the Patriots game I was expecting plenty of national pride. The Patriots captured the nation when they came from nowhere in 2001 to win their first Super Bowl, just months after the 9/11 terrorist attacks with their own Cinderella story: their quarterback, Tom Brady, a 199th draft pick, stepped in for the injured star Drew Bledsoe and made himself a household name. He has never looked back, gunning the Patriots to five Super Bowl appearances and two more Super Bowl rings.

Yet despite expecting plenty of "Patriotism," I was still a little surprised to see 12 old-school Patriots (dressed like they have just come from the American Revolution) standing behind each end zone, pointing their long rifles downfield and executing gun shots every time the Pats scored. To be honest, it looked like they were trying to assassinate the opposing 12 Patriots at the other end zone, or perhaps the away team.

I spoke to a local fan about this, and he told me that he loves the fake minute-men on the field. "Is it because you like lots of gunpowder and shooting?" I asked. "Well, they're dressed up and they protect the team and the stadium," he answered. "Hell, they are pure American, they protect the country," he continued. I couldn't exactly figure out how they protect the country, per se, but who was I to argue? Though I still wasn't sure why they were aiming their guns at each other.

This same man also had an alarming disdain for the Patriots mascot. "What the hell does the mascot do?" he angrily asked me. "I would knock his head off!" he added, raising his voice. I have never met anyone that actually dislikes a mascot. Personally I like the mascots, I think they are fun, work hard, and get kids into the sport.

We had missed a tailgater named Tony before the game, so at halftime when the Pats were up 0-20, we went downstairs where the crowd was louder to meet Tony and his wife, Erin. We all then stood on the concourse looking over the lower section for the remainder of the game, chatting away.

I couldn't imagine a hard-core soccer fan giving up watching the second half of his team to chat to an international fan on the concourse. I had come to realise that the stop-start nature of the NFL is perfect at making the game more social for the fans. We could chat to each other between plays. Of course Tony and Erin glanced over to the field or watched the live feed on the huge TV for the important plays.

Rudy moment: Syd Davy ("100% Cheese Free") from the Vikings, who had flown out to this game in the hopes that he would "catch" Randy Moss after a TD. For his second of three TDs I saw Moss on the jumbotron running to Syd. I told Tony that I knew Syd, and in a flash Tony gave me his lower ticket pass, as his seat was just three rows behind Syd's. I rushed down just as Moss had flung himself into Davy's huge arms. Syd and his wife recognised me instantly. The Patriots mascot came by and wanted to be lifted up too, so he was. Syd then joined us for the rest of the second half on the concourse. He told me he would have to add a tattoo of the Pats logo on his arm, to go alongside the other team logos where he has caught Randy Moss. So this is a split award for Moss, Tony, and Syd.

Orange play of the game: The Broncos' fumble was a comedy of errors as the unpredictable bounce kept dancing away from all of the players. The scene would fit well in a Buster Keaton movie.

Extreme fan: It really was Syd Davy, but I want home extreme fans for this segment. So it had to be the extreme Patriots fan who paid for Syd's flight, hotel, and game ticket for this game.

After the game, Izzy and I made our way to Tony and Erin's car, where they gave us some prawns (the Boston area is famed for its seafood). The weather had turned cold and there were a few impromptu fire pits going. I was gutted that I had missed the tailgate, especially as New England food is so famously good. I had started to notice there is a distinct lack of post-game tailgate when it is a night game and the car park's staff does not want people to stay too late.

Tony and Erin then offered Izzy and me to stay in their house that night, instead of us having to drive back to Manhattan. We had literally just met them that evening. We took them up on their kind offer and followed them deep into the forest. That's when we got a little scared as their home was in the middle of nowhere. I remained confident that although they were strangers, they are "tail-gaters" and therefore hopefully not murderers. As can be expected, Izzy, a female heading to a strange person's home in the woods, was a little nervous, but once we arrived, Tony and Erin welcomed us to their home, just like tailgaters across the land had welcomed me at their parties.

I was at the halfway mark and was feeling pretty good about the trip. Sure I had a few computer glitches, which meant I lost some pictures, and I had missed some tailgates, a couple kickoffs and the game endings, and overspent on hotels, but I had gone to every game and more. It was time to head home for a "bye week," and I was excited to see my family, my friends, and, of course, Steph.

6

Halftime (Bye Week)

Just before flying back for the London game I met up with the 2 Michelles. This time they had a gift for Steph—a signed copy of the *Female Fan's Guide to Pro Football* by Betsy Berne. I was really thankful that they got Steph such a nice present. Here I discovered that NFL franchises actually hold football clinics for women to teach them more about the game. The 2 Michelles would be excellent candidates to teach these classes.

At times in the first quarter of the trip, Steph had been unwell and had had numerous hospital checks. Of course I wanted to be there for her, and due to the international time differences it was difficult to speak to her regularly. I was so focused on the mammoth task of driving to the games, listening to as much sports radio as humanly possible, writing my blog, and finding tailgaters and tickets, that I had become selfish and obsessed with football. My brain just couldn't really handle anything outside of the trip, even my poor girlfriend.

I was nervous about going home. I knew I had been a "crappy" boyfriend in the last two months, and hopefully the 2 Michelles' gift would be a catalyst for Steph to get more into football and thus enjoy her time better when she came out. Of course, I also got her some non-football-themed gifts. I'm not a complete asshole.

The night before I flew back to London, a journalist from Britain's biggest-selling national newspaper, *The Sun* (owned by, guess who, Rupert Murdoch), interviewed me for 30 minutes. I mostly expressed my passion about the power of the tailgate culture, specifically because that is something not often explored in the British media about American football.

In the morning I landed in London without sleeping a wink on the overnight flight. I saw my parents, before rushing back into central London to meet Steph, where she had booked us a hotel for the night. The hotel that Steph got us was nice, but being in London, it was tiny and very expensive. The wi-fi was something like $10 per day, and parking (if I did want to park) was over $30 per day, plus the breakfast was over $25 each. I had gotten used to the luxury of Days Inn (!) with its free wi-fi, free parking, and free breakfast.

Steph opened the door to the room and she looked beautiful. She was smartly dressed, and I could sense she was nervous about seeing me. She had a stunning new short haircut. I was unshaven, unshowered, and wearing a crappy t-shirt. I felt pretty bad. She had made such an effort and I hadn't. I was in the doghouse.

We didn't actually have much time together, because I was told at the last minute that the *Sun* photographer was downstairs and wanted to do a photo shoot with me and two of the New Orleans Saints Cheerleaders, the Saintsations, to go alongside my interview. I didn't realise just how not fun that sounded for Steph. She was getting sick of me talking about football, and now I had come back for a few days so we could have some "us" time and had a photo shoot with cheerleaders. Okay fine, I didn't *have* to, but how many times in my life am I going to get an offer like that?

The two Saintsations, Randi and Chrissy, were friendly but quiet. I had heard that the NFL players are not allowed to date cheerleaders from their team, and if they did, then the cheerleaders would lose their jobs. Both girls were in college and with practice four times per week have little time for anything else. They arrive at each game four hours before kickoff and dance throughout the whole game.

At the park, an NFL game-day ball with the "International Series" logo on was placed in my arms for the photo shoot, but sadly no one wanted to go deep and play a little football. The photographer took a lot of pictures and, to be honest, was quite pushy. At one point he put us by a tree. A few minutes later he told us to move because the tree was in the way. "Well why the hell did you put us by the tree, then?" I muttered, slightly too quiet for him to hear, but the cheerleaders laughed. He didn't make the whole process very comfortable for any of us. If this is what the cheerleaders had been doing all week, then I would be pretty glum too.

For those that do not know about *The Sun* newspaper, it is a tabloid and is famous for publishing topless women on page 3. I know what you are thinking:

we Brits cannot have naked flames in a BBQ in public, but we can have naked breasts in our public newspaper—what a strange little country we are. Towards the end of the shoot, the photographer demanded that both cheerleaders kiss me on both cheeks. I told the girls they didn't get paid enough to kiss me, having just come off a night flight. I wasn't smelling my best—I wouldn't kiss me. I was lucky enough that Steph had given me some smooches just before.

Although the photographer took maybe a hundred shots, I knew the only shots we would see would be the ones printed in the paper. Steph was holding my camera to take shots when she was not involved. After we said our good-byes to the cheerleaders and headed back to the hotel, I scrolled through my camera. "Three shots, Steph! Why did you only take three shots—we were there 40 minutes?" She flashed me an unhappy glare. "Well, just *how* many pictures do you *need* of the cheerleaders?" I wanted to say a lot more than three, but I knew if I said that I would be further in the doghouse.

That night Steph and I ate at one our favourite Dim Sum restaurants where we had been on one of our first dates. Things were getting back on track for us, probably because I spoke very little about football.

The next morning, Steph rushed downstairs to get a copy of *The Sun*. The article, which was on page 27, was only one paragraph long, despite the 30-minute interview, with nothing about tailgating. As per *The Sun* it used a pun in its headline, "American Footbill," because my football trip was costing so much. Witty, right? It ended with a quote from me saying, "I'm living the dream."

It was Saturday, and Saturday is my day to play to flag football. Steph and I had previously argued over whether I was going to play football that day. My feelings were that the whole trip is about football, so why would I not play flag football that weekend? Her side of the coin was that we should spend time with each other away from football, because that is all she had heard come out of my mouth throughout the whole trip and probably for the three months leading up to it. What was more important to me: my football trip or my relationship?

To be honest, doing this trip while in a relationship had actually been very good . . . for the trip. It meant I was able to focus all my attention on football and the culture surrounding it. If I had been single, I may have got distracted on the odd occasion and perhaps tried out some chat-up lines in my British accent. The relationship helped the trip, but ironically the trip didn't help the relationship, at least not in the short term.

Oddly, many male fans in their twenties whom I had met at games were adamant that I must be receiving a lot of "action" (their words, not mine) from the opposite sex. "Ahh, thanks, is it because of my dashing good looks?" I would say sincerely and with an appreciative tone; they would then look slightly uncomfortable and say something about the "awesomeness" of my trip. I expressed to them that they probably knew very little women, if they think women are excited by a man who practically lives in a car and spends all of his money on football.

Steph was right. There was no need for me to play flag football. Instead I left my cleats at Dave's (the Saints fan from Canalstreetchronicles.com) hotel, and he played instead. As it turned out, however, our romantic day together still ended up being about the trip.

In the morning I had a radio interview with Vernon Kay, who hosts a national magazine show on BBC radio one every Saturday. Vernon used to play defensive back and now he plays free safety for local team the London Warriors, and for an extra bonus point he is also a Chicago Bears fan.

Vernon came out of his booth with a spring in his step and I entered the plush BBC soundproof room. Vern (I like to think we are on nickname terms already) explained the trip to his listeners. Things were going swimmingly, and I got to talk about the culture of tailgating and the extreme fans. Vernon then said, "Your girlfriend looks very . . .," he paused and mouthed something to me which I missed, and then said, ". . . off," which I didn't understand. "Off"? What does he mean by "off"? Has she gone off? Does she smell? I thought he was going to ask how could I leave such a woman behind in London for so long. This time I was prepared for such a question. But Vern was actually mouthing "pissed off" which I guess he is not allowed to say on the BBC airwaves.

"Oh right, no, it's just early in the morning," I replied back, once I twigged. It turns out Steph was not actually pissed off, but I'm not sure she suddenly wasn't too happy that Vern had just told the whole country that she looked grumpy. Nice one, Vern!

I asked him to come out and meet Steph and me at a Bears game in December, as a fun double date. He stumbled for an answer and then jokingly said that his wife (celeb Tess Daly) would not let him go!

Steph asked if we could have our picture with him, "or am I looking too pissed off?" she added in a friendly sarcastic way. Vernon laughed and we got the snap. I gave him a t-shirt so he knew the rest of the trip schedule just in case Tess was to let him come out and play.

In the afternoon we headed to Wembley. It was the day before the big game, and I was pleased to see lots of posters of the two teams on display all over the stadium and down Olympic Way (so called because the Olympics were held at Wembley Stadium in 1948).

We met up with the Sky Sports crew at the tube station. The cameraman was a perfectionist and took lots of shots of us walking out of the train station to the stadium. Bianca, the Sky Sports presenter, arrived, and she really knew her football. This was the first time both Steph and I had been interviewed together. Steph told Sky Sports she was really proud of me for doing this trip because I was following my dream, which warmed the cockles in my heart.

We popped into the Wembley gift shop, and I was happy to see they were selling merchandise from numerous NFL teams. I got myself a game-day pro-gramme for $15. I got my Dad a pen, and for my "ridiculous merchandise" I picked up another ugly commemorative scarf, with the Saints logo on one end and the Chargers on the other. Many NFL teams have copied the Steelers Terrible Towel and now have their own little towels. In British soccer, the team scarf is often lofted above one's head and stretched between both hands during a game.

That night Steph and I met up with a few friends, including Dave. He told me he had a great time playing flag football in my place. We met up at the 02 Dome where a Louisiana-style party was taking place as part of the build up before the game the next day. The famous New Orleans musician Dr. John played, and I was hoping the event would give people a taste for New Orleans culture.

There were people wearing several NFL jerseys. Dave spotted some Saints fans. He rushed over to them shouting, "Who Dat!" which is New Orleans' speak for "Go Bears." The two fans looked blankly back at him. They must have been English, hence they had no clue about the words "Who" and "Dat." Two guys then recognised me from *The Sun* article: "Mate, you're that nuttah going to all those American football games, right?" I was glad to see some people read *The Sun* beyond page 3 and as far as page 27. Hoping that the article might inspire them, I asked them if they were going to watch the game. "Nah, f**k that, I hate that American football! . . . Good luck though." Grrr.

Game 17. NFL Week 8, San Diego Chargers at New Orleans Saints, Wembley Stadium, London.

Final Score: 32-37. Home-win record: 14-3. Capacity: 86,000 (though 90,000 for soccer games). Attendance: 83,226. Ticket face value: £125—I paid $200 (approximately) via Ticketmaster. Picture on my ticket: Photo of Drew Brees, and it arrived in a fancy Wembley box. Mascot: for the Saints, "Gumbo," a dog and "Sir Saint," a caricature of a man with a big chin. Merchandise: Huge game-day programme and ugly International series scarf. Local London dish: Fish and chips.

On the morning of the game, Steph and I arrived at Wembley via the train at around 10 a.m., which is pretty early for a 5 p.m. kickoff, yet we still saw a fair few NFL jerseys. We had a TV interview with ITN. Many fans walked past the camera, and the interview was over relatively quickly partly because no one was stopping the shoot blurting out, "Chargers suck woo woo!" or flashing us their hairy stomachs!

We made our way to the tailgate section. It was barricaded, and you had to walk through security and ticket scanners to get through. NFLUK claimed it as the largest "tailgate party" in the NFL, which depends on your definition of a tailgate, but in my opinion this was a fan zone, and a great one, but not strictly a tailgate. One main difference between the two is that the teams or the venue organise the fan zone, while at a tailgate, tailgaters are free to arrange their own parties in and around the lots, and they do not have to have game-day tickets or in this case special tailgate tickets—or be body searched. Tunison says that the tailgate is "basically like college in a car park."[1] I think Tunison means the partying side of college. Though this fan zone (and more so for the 2009 season and beyond) was like the other yet less glamorous side of college: education. The stands and tents were great at educating the fans on the NFL rules and highlighting historic moments as well as highlighting New Orleans music and culture.

Often the tailgate and fan zones coexist in the same vicinity, and sometimes it is hard to know if it is a mad fan dressed up like a gorilla on a bicycle for the fun of it, or if the team is paying him to do so.

The area for the Wembley tailgate was on the concrete next to the stadium. Making a tailgate a ticketed affair does take away from the inclusivity of an actual tailgate. People across America travel for hours to tailgate at a game, and never have the intention to see the game on anything but the TV at their tailgate. Would I go to Tottenham High Street to watch the Spurs at a nearby pub? I don't think so.

In the 2007 London game, there was a huge jumbotron screen set up for people at the tailgate who did not have game-day tickets, who could be like their American counterparts and watch the game at the tailgate. You had to win tickets for this. In 2010 and beyond, the NFLUK made forward strides with their fourth annual tailgate party, which was open to anyone with a game-day ticket, as opposed to fans having to win tailgate tickets via a lottery beforehand.

As we got into the tailgate, we were greeted by performers on stilts throwing footballs. Steph told me she heard several people whispering, "Is that the crazy guy going to all the games?" I felt proud. Though, people in England are slightly more reserved and no high-fives came my way as impulsively as they did at American tailgates.

The beer and food tents kept some of the fans sheltered from the on-and-off rain. There were several inflatable activities for kids, such as kicking, throwing, catching, and a running back assault course. On the stage just in front of the arena, bands played Cajun music. Steph and I spotted some of the floats they were using on the parade, which included models of players from both teams, horses, and singers from New Orleans. The party was pumping, and despite the rain, people were buzzing around.

We took some pictures of the giant models of LaDainian Tomlinson and Reggie Bush, which were outside the merchandise tent. We then met Dave at the Bobby Moore statue. Moore was England's captain when we won the World Cup in 1966, our only World Cup to date. Wembley is the "Home of Football," and Bobby Moore stands over the crowd watching the fans as they enter his fortress.

Steph then pointed out a film crew. They had a cardboard cutout of their presenter, Mike Carlson, the highly knowledgeable American NFL pundit. I wasn't sure where the real Mike Carlson actually was, but the cutout was lifelike enough, and they took this fake Mike Carlson around the tailgate interviewing people about the game. Nat Coombs, then of Channel Five, interviewed me alongside the cardboard cutout of Mike Carlson.

For the London games there has been an "unofficial" tailgate party at a pub called the Green Man near the stadium, which was organised by Martin and Tom, who work for the Colchester Gladiators British American team. Tom wanted this tailgate "to promote the sport in the UK . . . a space where we could provide food and drink to fans from around the U.K. to gather, talk football and have fun before the game, by doing that we'd in turn be banging the drum for British American Football." Martin went on to tell me that although the NFL's official tailgate party was fun, he believes his tailgate is more like a real tailgate because it is less formal, where no ticket is needed and it is far more relaxed.

The pub cooked up plenty of food for people to buy. So if I were to be a real stickler, because you have to buy the food, then by some people's definition it is not a "real" tailgate. Martin had told me that in 2007 the police were against his idea because they were worried about having both home *and* away fans in the pub, which this pub does not allow for soccer games. Martin had to convince local parliamentary counsellors, obtain licences, and get security just so he could integrate the NFL fans. After a successful year in 2007 with no trouble, the Green Man and local community have welcomed all NFL fans to the pub for every international game at Wembley since.

Prior to the trip my flag football group thought it would be good if we all sat together for this game, so we booked up spots in club level, at £125 each (approximately $200). Dave from Canalstreetchronicles.com wanted to come and see his Saints at Wembley, but he didn't get tickets originally from the Saints. So we did a swap, I let him have my spare ticket in London as long as he gives me his spare ticket for the upcoming Saints MNF game against the Packers.

Steph, Dave, my Dad, and I entered the stadium through a fancy club entrance. I had seen the club level and luxury boxes at Qualcomm and the Browns Stadium on those stadium tours, but this was my first club ticket for a game. The club entrance was very calm as an escalator took us to our level. The indoor club-level concourse was quite plush, and there was a great view of London from the glass windows, which non-club-level concourses do not get to see.

There was a champagne room that served swanky food, but I noticed a distinct lack of televisions. I know the Americans go crazy for a flat screen but to have zero televisions is a bit silly, considering this is such a modern stadium. If you miss part of the game because you are deciding what kind of champagne and truffles to have, you should still be able to catch the action.

Our actual seats were not fantastic, on the corner by the end zone, but high so you could see the game unfold. I have to say, club level is highly overrated. There was still hot food in the club level, and my Dad and Steph grabbed an overpriced burger, though everywhere else at Wembley they had run out of hot food before halftime, for the second year running. A soccer game lasts just 90 minutes, and the crowd only usually gets a snack at halftime, usually a dire meat pie, and during the one stoppage. In the NFL, food and drink vendors come right to your section so fans can eat throughout the entire game.

For us Brits watching the game, we were probably all looking for "an American experience" and perhaps a New Orleans one to some degree, as they were the so-called "home" team. However, the American fans travelling to London probably wanted a taste of how the U.K. interprets the NFL. Sportswriter Ed Smith questions, "Does a sport really have a natural home?"[2] Well, of course America is the natural home of "American" football, but can it exist in other countries? Soccer can weave itself into the cultural landscapes of many countries and cultures, but the NFL isn't that transferable. Yes, American Football as a sport is played in several countries, but the whole NFL package, with its tailgating community, passion for family entertainment, overall hoopla, and national patriotism make it so American, that it would be hard for any other country to fully replicate.

The pre-game was as good as any that I had seen stateside and included both the British and American national anthems. However, the halftime show was somewhat limp. The New Orleans–style Mardi Gras floats went around the outside track of the field but not actually on the grass itself. In the following year I was shocked when there was no halftime show at all!

In 2007 the NFLUK used the jumbotrons to beam various questions to NFL players about London, which got some laughs. Though every fan did receive a free gift (a Dolphin mini towel in '07, and a "home" team flag every year after that), there were no other giveaways during the breaks and shockingly not one single t-shirt thrown to the crowd. Surely the t-shirt gun is the backbone of American sports. The cheerleaders tried their best to reignite the crowd at the break, but they had to share the turf with groundsmen who were focused on twisting and turning patches of the field.

I didn't want to burst Steph's bubble as I really wanted her to enjoy herself, but there was not half the hoopla that I had seen at American games. Yes, Steph loved the Saints mascot, which is oddly a big dog, and there was certainly far more fan experience than at a soccer game, but then again we just don't do hoopla like the Americans. It's not in our culture and some may agree that anything like that during the international games has either felt false or desperate.

Webster has debated this point in his columns on NFLUK.com, and he says that "if you are going to entertain the idea of playing games outside of America, then be prepared for a lack of American-ness. You only get real American-ness in America." And here lies the ambivalence. British fans are drawn to the game and Americana alike. Webster continues that Americana "is part of the appeal. British people wanted this experience to be as American as possible,"[3] but the Brits can't do Americana the same way (and why should they?). On the other side, why would American season ticket holders, who are giving up one home game for their team to play abroad, pay for international flights to see their home team in London, because in terms of hoopla they would receive a diluted version of what they are used to? The appeal would be experience and to see a new stadium, meet British and European NFL fans, and hopefully a win for their team.

Webster feels that this battle of Americanness "should not stop the two of us coexisting. International NFL games can showcase the best American sport to the world and showcase the world to American sport." Webster also experienced games in Germany during the NFL Europe seasons. Here the Germans blended their sporting experience with that of America, and Webster notes that because the "Germans never pandered to the American prototype for a football game. They did it with their own twist . . . [fans] loved those days out because it was American football with a German bite to it."[4]

So perhaps Britain needs to find ways to integrate its (positive) sporting culture with the American version. To be fair there was some of this. At all five international games there have been Mexican waves (the Wave) circling the stadium with up to seven rotations, and they had game-day scarves, even if they did look as ugly as sin. Personally I would like to see more original chants made up and used by U.K. NFL fans.[5]

Sadly, Wembley is not really built for American football games. The first few rows are very close to the action and are low down. So the NFLUK covered the first 10 rows or so with banners from each team. The cynic in me would say that's just a way of getting more sponsorship money, but then again a fan would have a hard time viewing the action from behind the NFL players standing on the sidelines.

The one good thing about the club level is that you can hang around for one hour after the game. The previous year's exit was nigh on terrible. My father and I were forced to go to the underground station by the pedestrian traffic pattern, even though we didn't want to go to the subway. The police told us it would not be safe to allow so many fans go wherever they want. Sure, that's fine with soccer fans, but NFL fans are different. For the five international games at Wembley there has not been a single arrest, and that's even with alcohol allowed on the terraces. Treat people like adults and they might just act like adults. Who would have thought?

Despite my cynical ramblings, the game was thankfully all action—just what the NFL and the U.K. fans were hoping for. It was a pure shootout. Dave was getting really into the game and he pumped my Dad, Steph, and me right up. For all of my comparisons with other games, come kickoff time it goes out the window to a certain extent, because for me and probably the other British NFL fans at Wembley, I was pinching myself for the second year running, seeing a live regular-season game in our country. With or without the tailgate or the hoopla, I would still be ecstatic to see a live NFL action in my country.

Rudy moment: Saints receiver, Lance Moore, caught a spectacular, high-leaping TD catch from a long pass. He then did a soccer dive on his knees but got a penalty for showboating. The crowd booed the referees and in this case rightly so.

Orange play of the game: Winning 30-37 and with 14 seconds to play, Drew Brees, the Saints QB, bizarrely ran backwards into his own end zone, eating away at the clock, but gave the Chargers a safety. This still gave the Chargers time for one last play with which they could have won. Brees used to play for the Chargers so maybe he was getting a little confused? In his memoir, Brees claimed that the London game was the highlight of his season that year. Hopefully as much of that is to do with helping the sport grow in the U.K. and not just because he beat his old team.

Extreme fan: I only saw one extreme fan in the stadium (the curse of sitting at club level) and that was Optimus Saint, whom I only spotted on the jumbotron, but there were plenty I saw at the tailgate. Here there were some English lads who were dressed up as Marvel super heroes, while others dressed as Mexican wrestlers. Several fans wore an array of NFL team helmets and jerseys over real shoulder pads. But despite all of that I'm going to be self indulgent and give the award to myself as the extreme fan of the day.

There was no post-game tailgate, just the usual hour-long queue getting to the tube station. When we got home we watched the ITN news report, which ended romantically with Steph and I having a big smooch with Wembley Stadium in the background, as the camera swept around us.

Two days later I was preparing for the second half of the trip, and my bank manager discovered that I was going to be $3,000 short! I really should have asked Michael Irvin for some financial help when I had the chance!

Knowing the second half was going to be colder, I packed some winter clothes and flew back to NYC, ready for some more football and a whole lot more driving.

7

Third Quarter:
The Adam and Neal Trip

Although the first half had gone well—very well—I still had to go out there and give 110 percent as I knew that the second half would be far more demanding. I had 21 games scheduled, plus from week 10 onwards there would be three games per week instead of just two.

After my halftime team talk, I called an audible at the start of the third. I booked flights from NYC to Tennessee, then to Washington, D.C., then to Las Vegas to pick up Neal, then flights to Oakland, Arizona, and then a flight back to New York to pick up my "second half" car where I would reignite the "road trip" from New York to Atlanta. This way I could avoid gas money and costly hotels by staying with Justin and Neal longer.

The Tennessee Titans game was a noon kickoff, and I planned to get into Nashville the night before. Unfortunately, the driver on the shuttle bus from Manhattan to JFK airport decided that passengers leaving *my* terminal would be dropped off last, which meant an extra 45-minute wait. I rushed with my backpack and my mum's large hold-all bag (I had broken her suitcase in the first half) to the Delta Air Lines counter. The woman there would not allow me on the plane as it was 45 minutes before takeoff and my hold-all was too big to bring on board as a carry-on. Sadly, there were no more planes that night to Nashville.

The only thing Delta could do was put me on the next morning's flight, getting me in to Nashville at 11 a.m. The other downside was that they wanted $900 for me to change my flight! Suddenly this cheaper audible was not looking good at all.

I really didn't know what to do. I called Steph and broke down crying in the airport. The trip was taking me over psychologically. I had put myself under

151

incredible pressure. I wanted to complete all 32 teams, and I would have kicked myself to miss one game because of a missed flight. Feeling sick, I called Expedia and paid for the new flight. I sulked on the subway ride back to Manhattan, where Mike B. picked me up and took me out to cheer me up, but I couldn't crack a smile, knowing I had just burnt $900 on the flight.

I should have done my research about Delta because I later discovered that a few years earlier Bengals running back, Corey Dillon, made the same mistake with this airline. In the end he arrived to training camp six hours late and was charged $5,000 by his team.

I was back at the Delta check-in counter early the next morning when Joanne, the Delta check-in lady, said, "Mr. Goldstein, I'm sorry but you are not on this flight. You are supposed to be in Nashville, already." I just couldn't take any more bad news. "I *know* I am supposed to be in Nashville, but I missed my flight," I nervously replied. "Oh . . .," she continued, while punching the crap out of the keyboard, followed by some rather negative "umms" and "ahhs." It turned out that Expedia did not put me on the flight, despite the fact that they gave me a Delta number and an Expedia reference number. My heart sank. After a long tirade with Expedia I was told I was not on the flight as my credit card was maxed out.

Joanne heard me yelling out expletives on the phone, and she began to laugh out loud when she discovered it cost me 900 bucks to change flights. "You could have changed it for 50 bucks!" Now she tells me! Why the hell did her managers *not* tell *me* this tidbit the night before? "Trudie, come over here," she motioned to her friend. No, no, please don't bring your friends over to laugh at me. "This guy missed his flight to Nashville and had to pay 900 bucks to change it!" Too late. I was the laughing stock of the Delta staff.

"This flight is not even half full!" she added. Yes, well thank you, Joanne, for making me feel a whole lot better! Joanne saw my dreams fade away as real tears rolled down my face. After 10 minutes of trying to figure something out, she did something miraculous. She took my passport, scanned it, punched the keyboard some more, and told me to "go to the gate and enjoy the game!" She had put me on for free! What an angel. The sense of relief was overwhelming, and she was instantly the proud owner of a football trip t-shirt.

The flight was scheduled to get me to Nashville hours before the game. But just when I thought my luck had turned back around, it hadn't. At the luggage carousel, after landing, my bags did not come out and I panicked like a lost child in a department store. I went to the Delta baggage office, and the laid-back, gum-popping woman at the desk muttered at me with poor diction, "Yeah, your bags are probably still in New York." What?! "Probably? Probably? What do you mean by probably? Where the hell is my stuff!" In a bored manner she lifted her head about an inch and said, "Not sure but give me your number and where y'all staying and we will call you. This happens aaaalllll tha' time." Note to self: never, ever fly Delta again! "Well I'm only here for a day, then I fly to Washington, D.C., tomorrow," I gasped in a panic. "So then we will fly your bags to Washington," she answered. "But then I am in Vegas . . . then Oakland, and then . . .," and before I could finish telling her the rest of my schedule she moved on to the next customer who was rather calm about her bags not being there, almost as if she never expected her bags to arrive in the first place. Damn Delta!

Game 18. NFL Week 9, Green Bay Packers at Tennessee Titans, LP Field

Final Score: 16-19 (OT). Home-win record: 15-3. Capacity: 68,798. Attendance: 69,143. Ticket: $70—I paid $70 via Ticketmaster. Picture on my ticket: E-Ticket. Mascot: "T-Rac," a sort of large gerbil. Merchandise: Red foam sword. Local dish: Southern chicken and burgers (traditional Southern comfort food).

I didn't have to time to check into my hotel or catch much of the tailgate, as I took a taxi straight to the stadium. The staff at LP Field would not allow me to bring in my backpack, even after I explained about my trip, so I needed somewhere to leave it. Tailgaters are a good breed of human, but could I trust a tailgater to keep my computer with every picture and video from the trip safe?

I saw a large tailgate with a big spread and a flat-screen TV. It was clear these were "TV tailgaters"—the kind who watch the game from the car park instead of going inside. These fine people said they would only look after my bag as long as I sat and ate their food with them. Their leader, known as Rabbit, was keeping the food warm for when the rest of their party came out after the game, so they could all watch the 4 p.m. games together. The tailgate group goes by the name of "Titans' Boro Tailgating," and these are just a few of the things I managed to sample from their menu: beer brats, steamed onion and peppers, chicken brats, fried oysters, fried catfish, slow-cooked pork and kraut, hamburger sliders, potato dish, hot German potato salad, and Old Milwaukee beer.

Once inside LP Field I looked straight up the many stairs, and there was just one vacant seat right at the very top between joining two sections on the 40-yard line. It was an alarmingly hot day and the stairs nearly killed me. Once at my seat I was afraid to jump up and down, because if I fell forward I would have tumbled all the way down the stairs.

LP Field is a beautiful open stadium—much like Heinz Field, and there are two wide concourses behind each end zone. The concession stands below the screens are made to look like "old school" beach huts, which either gives the stadium a homey feel, or just makes the place look like a huge public swimming pool. I really liked the setup.

Even though the lady and her husband next to me offered me some nachos, they were not that talkative. So I popped down to the smoking section at halftime, where a chap named Titan Tim introduced me to all of his friends and family and took me on a tour around the stadium. In the halftime show there was a huge map of America that stretched right across the whole field.

The Titans had not lost a single game in the season so far. The game went into overtime, and as the Titans went on to beat the Packers and win the game, I made my way downstairs to check out the huts on the concourse.

After the game the staff was really helpful in telling me where to stand if I wanted Titans player signatures. A few Titans players came by instead of heading straight for their cars, but sadly without their jersey numbers on, I couldn't recognise any of them.

Rudy moment: LenDale White's thundering 54-yard run crashing through the Packers defenders.

Orange play of the game: It was going to be the Titans QB Kerry Collins, for his high-looping hospital pass begging to be intercepted, but it quickly became three Packers defenders—all of whom got under the high ball and then proceeded to collide with one another, and thus none of them caught the ball.

Extreme fan: I met three girls who all had green paint on one half and yellow paint on the other half of their faces. I also saw a boy, about 10 years old, wearing just army shorts and the rest of his body and face were covered in green and yellow, with "Go Pack Go" across his chest. The fan-of-the-day award, however, goes to Titan Tim who had a "T" shaped out of his facial hair on his cheeks.

He has never missed a Titan home game and wore a Titan hard hat with plenty of player signatures on it. The Titans used to be the Houston Oilers. They moved to Tennessee in 1997 as the Oilers and then changed their name to the Titans in 1999.

After the game I made my way back to 'Boro tailgating where Rabbit and many more friends were enjoying the post-game food. Thankfully, my bag, which they nicknamed "car bomb," was still there. I enjoyed their tailgate post-game party, by eating more brats and potatoes. 'Boro Tailgating gave me a game-day t-shirt commemorating this 100th Titans game. I was finding that receiving free t-shirts was becoming an addictive pastime.

Rabbit told me that they often cook for up to 100 people. While I was in London the week before, the Titans played a MNF game and it was such a cold night that Rabbit had put up tents with heaters. Sixty people stayed in the tents that night to watch the game, as it was too cold for them in the stadium.

I said my good-byes and walked around beautiful downtown Nashville. I called Steph and apologised for my anger and panic the night before when I was stressed out at the airport. After a great game (a Packer's loss) and wonderful tailgate, I was in a far better mood. I passed the phone over to a local and Steph actually giggled at the sound of the local southern accents. She couldn't believe people actually talk like that. That's when I realised I had left a plastic bag at the tailgate containing my game-day programme and my Titans red foam sword. I rushed back to the car park, but by then it was dark and everyone was gone. Thankfully, Rabbit boxed up my lost items and sent them to me a few weeks later. Not only that, he also put in some large Titan plastic mugs in the package for me too.

That evening Delta delivered my luggage to my hotel and the next morning I was back at the Delta desk, hopping my next flight, slightly nervous and wondering if my luggage would be coming with me.

On the plane to NYC, where I was connecting to D.C., I sat in front of two Packers fans who were at the Titans game the day before. They told me just how excited they were to be tuning into that evening's MNF matchup between the Redskins and the Steelers. They explained the Redskins Election jinx: "During a presidential election weekend, if the Redskins win, then the current party stays in power. If the opposing team wins, then the challenging party wins the election."

This jinx has actually come true on 16 of the 17 last elections. The only time it didn't come true was for George W. Bush's first presidential campaign.

This jinx made me even more excited for that night's game, and I'm sure that Bears fan Barack Obama would be for one night rooting the Steelers. The decision of who would be the head of the free world rested on the outcome of this game. This was probably why it was so hard for me to get tickets.

I got off the plane in NYC and rushed to my connecting flight to D.C. There I saw my angel friend: Joanne from Delta. She recognised me and gave me a quick high-five and a shout of "good luck" as I rushed to my next plane. The flight to D.C. was delayed, but thankfully my bag was waiting for me this time.

The drive from the airport to the stadium was one hell of a pain in the ass. Having to cross so many lanes and so many interconnecting highways was a mind bend. There was no stadium parking for cash parkers, so I had to park three miles away at a temporary over-spill lot. The parking lot was full so I parked on a side street for 40 bucks! For 40 bucks I want to be parking my car in the locker room!

I made my way onto the free shuttle bus that took us to FedEx Field. The driver told us to get the "McCormick" bus on the way back. The bus was a good way to meet the local fans all wearing their Redskin colours. One woman was heavily pregnant, and she told me unless she was in labour that day she would not be missing a single home game all season. I thought that was a sign of being a hard-core fan. Then again, what kind of hard-core fan doesn't plan the timing of her procreation around the football off-season? Steph's birthday lies on January 8, which is right in the midst of the playoffs, and I don't think I will ever be able to fully forgive Steph's parents for such bad family planning!

Game 19. NFL Week 9, Pittsburgh Steelers at Washington Redskins, FedEx Field

Final Score: 23-6. Home-win record: 15-4. Capacity: 91,704. Attendance: 90,512. Ticket face value: $90—I paid $180 via a scalper. Picture on my ticket: Picture of Antwaan Randle El. Mascot: None. Merchandise: Maroon jester hat. Local dish: Oysters.

I was supposed to meet the tailgating group called the Extreme Skins in Lot 43, as well as Jay DiEugenio, who was tailgating with the surreal PFUFA fans, the Hogettes.

In the '80s the Redskins had a famous offensive line, nicknamed the Hogs. In 1983 Redskins fan Michael Torbett dressed up in his grandmother's dress to cheer her up. The image stuck and now he and a group of 15 friends make up the Hogettes. These men wear old ladies' dresses, football socks, floppy hats, sunglasses, plenty of beads and pin badges, pig noses, and they often smoke cigars and have beards. It looks very strange. They sit in a section of the stadium that they call the pig pen.

Sadly I could not find anyone I was looking for and was pissed off having to spend over an hour just frantically running around the car park looking for people.

FedEx Field is the NFL's largest stadium. (This was before Jerry Jones built the whopping new Cowboys stadium in 2009.) The Redskins have a season ticket waiting list that stretches over 10 years. The Redskins have never officially sold out the entire stadium, but the team has never had a game blacked out on local television because the franchise does not count premium club-level seating when calculating sell outs.

StubHub was coming in around the $180 mark the night before for a nosebleed seat. Not only was this the "election" game, but both teams had solid winning records. I decided to finally risk it and buy from a scalper. I knew the closer to kickoff, the cheaper the tickets would be, but I also wanted to get in there and see the players come out of the tunnels. I found a scalper, or rather he found me. I had seen handfuls of scalpers at every other stadium, some of whom use a sophisticated system to find would-be ticket buyers. They either hold up a sign or wear one around their necks, saying, "Got tickets? Need Tickets?" Some of the signs are just pieces of cardboard made up that day, though the long-term guys have had their signs laminated on brightly coloured paper and used eye-catching fonts.

I looked at the ticket the scalper offered me. He had a laminated sign on his neck that was dogeared at the edges, so he must be a real pro and not some newbie. I figured he was only showing me the best tickets he has and hiding his cheaper ones. He wanted cash only and he couldn't knock the price down even if I threw in some of my football trip t-shirts. He was also very reluctant in selling just the one ticket. In fact he tried to make me feel bad about it, like I was the one screwing him over. It was a mental boxing match. I walked away at the $200 mark, but in the end buckled under the pressure and handed over $180 cash for a ticket that had a face value of $90. This better be a damn good game, I thought to myself.

I was nervous if my ticket would actually be legitimate. Thankfully, the ticket scanner people let me through. I got to my seat and was surprised that it was actually pretty good. I was in the lower section on the corner of the end zone. Behind me sat Tony, Dexter, and Andre, who told me in great detail what I had missed at their tailgate: salmon, ribs, crab cakes, and a margarita machine.

They were Redskins fans, but on this night they said they would rather see a Redskin loss if it meant an Obama win. The atmosphere was politically charged, and at least a third of the stadium was Steelers fans. How did they all get *their* tickets?

I had seen an ESPN poster promoting this "election game," saying that the network would show the speeches from McCain and Obama at halftime. Naively, I actually thought Obama and McCain would be at the stadium doing their speeches. Come halftime I waited and waited but there was very little in terms of a halftime show. The speeches that the politicians were performing were only for the TV viewers at home. I felt duped and was pissed off. They didn't even show the speeches on the jumbotron.

There were actually more posters about voting for the pro bowl than for the presidential election. The Washington Redskins band did, however, take to the field at halftime. They are the oldest marching band in the league, and only a handful of NFL teams have marching bands.

In other stadiums, the staff moves up and down the aisles selling food and drink, but at FedEx Field they do this to sell merchandise too. Rich Eisen noticed that FedEx "may be the stadium most splattered with advertising."[1] And for some, this may feel like the team has sold out to mass corporations; yet for me, a Brit born in the '80s, there is something about American advertising that just seems so kitschy and accepted. I liked the large FedEx sign, much like I loved the massive Heinz ketchup bottles at Heinz Field.

The Redskins played yet another sluggish game, just as they had at my first game in New York. After a poor halftime show I really wanted to go and find that scalper and get a refund.

But the election jinx did come true. The Steelers beat the Redskins and Barack Obama became the 44th president of the United States.

Rudy moment: Steelers backup QB, Byron Leftwich, came on and set the game on fire. He had his true "Rudy moment" when his 50-yard pass was caught down field leading to a TD.

Me and my Dad outside the new Wembley stadium for
the first NFL regular-season game outside North America.
We busted out our Bears gear—but check out that great
Dolphins foam finger!

The view from
the apartment we
sold in order for
me to do the trip.

Before the trip, my flag football crew and I went to
Copenhagen to play a full kitted game, and here I am
in training wearing my Walter Payton jersey. Notice
my weedy arms—no wonder I never made it pro!

Titletown: Green Bay, Wisconsin. I had Baz make
up some signs last minute for me in the stands.

PFUFA fan "Captain Jet" and his tailgate bus.

Mile High Monsters outside Invesco Field, Denver.

Syd Davy, aka 100% Cheese Free.

An old man, a gorilla, and a tricycle, Vikings style.

Me and the only "human" mascot in the league, Ragnar, down on the Vikings sideline.

The Bone Lady's car, the Bone Mobile.

The mighty Joe Cahn proudly displaying his tailgating seasoning.

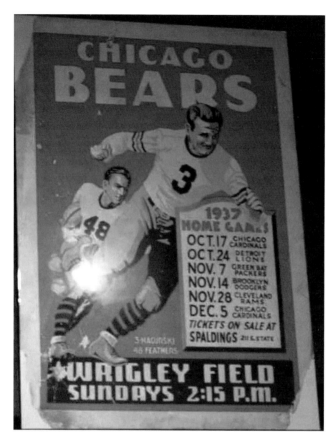

A sweet old-school Bears poster that I snapped a picture of while I was at the Pro Football Hall of Fame.

On top of the Mexican Happy Hour bus in Cincinnati.

Sitges Sack, a group of NFL fans from across the globe, sporting their wonderful homemade hats!

A big Kyle Vanden Bosch fan at LP Field, Tennessee. I liked those cute kiosks under the jumbotron.

Me with Kingsford Kirk
in Oakland. Don't look
into those eyes!

Raider Jerry putting
on my game face
with war paint, not
makeup!

This quote will forever be stitched into Arizona folklore.

The groom, hours after his wedding ceremony, in Arizona.

The Atlanta Falcons Bird Lady.

Chef Who Dat.

Extreme Lions fan who goes by the name Lion King.

NFL teams love to set new records. The Detroit Lions did in fact become the first team in NFL history to go 0-16.

I got lost a lot! In Charlotte, North Carolina.

Steph and me at the first Bears tailgate.

Steph is freezing cold in Kansas City.

Rocking out at the Bears MNF game, with two Bears claws and Staley, 'Da Hat.

At the "What the Buc?" Tailgate in Tampa Bay.

Steph and I clashed helmets at the Capital One Bowl Game in Orlando.

Extreme Raiders fans at the Super Gate II in Tampa Bay.

Extreme Raiders fans with great Packers fans at the Super Gate.

The 100-yard
shot stick at
Super Gate.

Jay DiEugenio and Kingsford Kirk prepare the pig for the
Super Bowl party snack.

Hangin' with the PFUFA crew just before the parade through
Canton in August 2009.

Who Dey, myself, and
Ram Man at the Pro
Football Hall of Fame
2009 enshrinement
weekend.

Me and the
London taxi that
Stephen Fry used,
in Chicago.

Orange play of the game: It would have gone to the Steelers for starting the game with an onside kick that didn't work, but ironically it went to the Redskins player who injured Roethlisberger, because that brought Leftwich on and he won them the game.

Extreme fan: I saw plenty of Steelers fans wearing "Joker" face paint, and although I couldn't find the Hogettes, I did find Chief Zee. He sat in the front wearing a white vest and a Red Native American Indian headdress, holding a pole with feathers and a mini Redskin helmet on top. He was one loud character who also happened to be wielding a 12-inch tomahawk! How did he get into a stadium with a weapon, while I got 20 questions about the length of the lens on my camera.

After the game I made my way through the car park. The temperature had gotten colder, and I swiftly zigzagged between fire pits and grills as I headed back to the shuttle buses. Rather fortunately, I finally found a welcoming tailgater. These young guys wanted to hear more about my story and wanted to give me food, beer, and high-fives. They even fired up the grill just for me. "We Redskins fans are the smartest NFL fans in the world," one chap told me. "You mean in America, because there are no NFL teams outside America," I retorted. He was confused so he just high-fived me.

This group made sure I got pictures of them, their bus, and a picture of their poster of Sean Taylor, the Redskins safety who was tragically murdered in his home the year before. In the 2008 season, every player in the league wore his number, 21, on their helmets. The Redskins also painted a large #21 on their field. The so-called hardest-hitting player in the NFL was posthumously voted into the Pro Bowl, and on the very first Redskins defensive play after his death, the Redskins lined up with 10 men on the field instead of the usual 11.

In my research after the trip I discovered there is an infamous Redskins tailgating party that is dividing opinion amongst tailgaters. They go by the name of the Dead Tree Crew (DTC). They openly admit to not welcoming the away fans. Their website is full of hate towards other teams; they even have a rap song out called "Hit a Muthaf***in' Eagle Fan," which they uploaded to YouTube. Dave Lamm of tailgatingideas.com interviewed their "leader," the self-proclaimed "Mayor of FedEx Field," who was unfazed by allegations of being territorial:

Lamm: Your critics say you and the DTC are a bit more adversarial toward opposing fans and create a hostile environment.

Mayor of FedEx Field: I don't think tailgating is defined by what you have to do. I don't have a rulebook on tailgating and I don't ever expect to see it. As for our theory on not letting any opposing fans in, we protect FedEx Field. We want Redskins fans to come. We don't want Philly fans, Ravens fans, Cowboys fans pushing their way into our stadium and taking it over, singing their songs and chanting their teams.[2]

Lamm is ambivalent about the DTC as he tells me the Mayor "is a big protector of tailgaters' rights and would be a great ally in the fight to keep parking lots open and to not have the NFL or other bodies limit and restrict how we can tailgate." The only irony is that for tailgaters like DTC who are passionate about their team and their tailgate, their ethos and their unruly and hedonistic drunken behaviour naturally scares off other home and away tailgaters, and in the end, the authorities may curb the freedom that tailgaters often have. The territorial, tribal, and pugilistic soccer hooligans had a similar effect. The hooligans ruined the experience for other fans, and now big soccer rivalries in the U.K. often start at noon instead of 3 p.m., giving the hooligans less drinking time.

In the 2008 season many franchises opened their tailgating lots later to curb people from drinking, but decreasing tailgating "hours" in the lots isn't necessarily going to help. People will find somewhere else to park, drink, and cook. By curbing people, in my opinion, they will either become angry or more frustrated, and thus binge drink even quicker.

Jay DiEugenio feels this curbing of tailgating hours is all part of a scheme "to pull tailgaters away from their lifestyle and force them into overblown, over-corporatized, pregame parties"[3] that are created by the NFL teams, like the ticketed tailgate tent that I saw at the Broncos.

Lamm tells me that "sometimes being a fan of a particular team can blind them (DTC or tailgaters like them) to the overall intent of what tailgating is all about. So when that love and passion for a particular team is so embedded into the person's psyche, they may view the parking lot as an extension of the playing field. If home field fans make it a very friendly experience for opposing fans, that may encourage more to come to future games and thus lessen the home field advantage." Personally, the DTC worries me slightly because their territorial ethos sounds like it could be inching closer to hooliganism.

Despite the DTC wishing to scare off away fans, they did not succeed in tonight's game, as there were more away fans here than I had seen anywhere else.

The shuttle bus headed back to the parking lot and was filled with cheering Steelers fans. A nice family from Pittsburgh told me the Steelers are such a good "travel" team because when the steel industry stopped in Pittsburgh, many of the fans had to move to other cities for jobs. They then brought up their relocated families as Steelers fans. They also told me the Steelers have more female fans than any other team. The fact that women are made so welcome at the NFL is a true testament to its wider appeal. By this point on the trip I had met several women in the stadiums who were more into football than their boyfriends or husbands, who were either sitting next to them, back outside at the tailgate, or simply at home. I thought back to the Pittsburgh home game I went to with Justin, and he was surprised by the amount of women at that game.

When I was on the British radio station TalkSPORT before the trip started, their presenters warned me ahead of time that NFL fans don't tend to travel to away games, resulting in a loss of atmosphere. They couldn't be more wrong— this was my 16th NFL game, and I had seen plenty of away fans at each game, but none more so than at this one. Because there are no actual away sections in NFL stadia, every ticket can be either a home or away ticket. Sure it is harder to spot the away fans because they are mixed in with the home fans, and when you know you are "mixed in," perhaps some people do not wear their "away" team colours, but they are still there.

In the U.K., it is the away club that sells the tickets to their away fans. So if I want to see the Spurs play at Manchester Utd., as a Spurs fan I would buy my away ticket from the Spurs and, for a big game like that, would probably have to enter an away ticket lottery. If a soccer stadium's away section is not sold out, then those seats go to waste; the home team is not usually allowed to sell those tickets to home fans, in case there are fights. Teams are not pressured to "sell out" like in the States because in the U.K. we do not have the TV "blackout rule."

Culpepper loves the U.K. system of dividing the fans, and he says that the "stadium segregation is an ingenious concept, galvanizing competing noise."[4] Yes, the upside of segregation is that sets of fans can chant as "one" as they root for their team and this certainly adds to the passion at a game, but it can, and does, spill into violence. Granted, integration is safer, but I admit it can lead to fan dilution. Many people love the "passion" of segregated fans, even if that means no cultural interaction, and a possible fight. Though for me, I'll take the slightly diluted atmosphere and no fight, thank you very much.

In tonight's game there was actually a small scuffle between two home fans who were both drunk. Webster suggests that "whatever extra security may cost, we can tell them from this end and our experiences with soccer that the costs are far greater if you let the problem develop."[5] Although the last thing I want to see at a game is hundreds of police and security like at soccer games, the DTC motto of "Get drunk or go home" doesn't help matters—but how do you really curb it?

The HBO network did a whole segment about alcohol consumption and anti-social behaviour at NFL games on their show, *Real Sports with Bryant Gumbel*, which aired just before the Super Bowl some weeks later after this Redskins game. They could have picked any hundreds of other tailgate parties that I discovered and they would have had a different piece, but they picked the Dead Tree Crew. The host, Bryant Gumbel, said that with regards to the drunken fans that "there is little that the NFL or the local authorities can do to stop it."[6] Taking away alcohol or providing more security just deals with the symptoms, neither is a cure. Like proud tailgaters, fans should be able to police themselves. Curbing tailgating hours and curbing alcohol hours will help but it may in fact create more of a binge drinking culture. Yes, the camera doesn't lie, but it also didn't show the 90 percent of other tailgaters who act responsibly. Most tailgaters appreciate the free reign they have in the lots and know it can be taken away at any point, so they party responsibly. Tailgaters like Joe Cahn, Dave Lamm, and the DiEugenios promote the maturity and responsibility at the tailgates on their websites.

Dave Lamm explained to me in an interview that "showing images of tailgaters sharing shish kabobs doesn't really have that shock value of belligerent fans throwing haymakers at halftime. . . . Today's media mentality of 'if it bleeds, it leads' tends to put a negative light on anything. When tailgaters demonstrate childish, obnoxious and boorish behavior that shocks people, the cameras will be there." Plenty of tailgaters were outraged that their name and pastime were being tainted.

And so back to the shuttle bus that left FedEx Field and headed to the car park. I had parked on the street overspill and not in the parking lot, and rather foolishly did not make a note of the particular street that I parked on. I saw no street, no street sign, no staff, no cones, and no signs that said "FedEx parking" that were there before. It was 1 a.m., and being alone in the dark streets of Landover, Maryland, where FedEx Field is did not bode well for me. I walked around looking for a clue. I kept popping the button on my key fob, but nothing. Could the rental car be stolen?

After forty minutes I found a policeman in a parked police car. Although he had finished his shift and was on his way home, he could tell I was out of my depth and told me to get in the car. We drove through a residential area, where the policeman made it clear that if I did park on these streets, then the car would definitely have been stolen. Lovely. We drove around for 45 minutes when finally I saw my car sitting lonely on the side of the road, just like at Wembley all those years ago.

The following morning I flew to Las Vegas. Two days later, Neal and I watched the Thursday night game between the Cleveland Browns and the Denver Broncos on television at his friend's place. To be honest we also watched a movie on the big screen, and he had the game on the "small" 32-inch TV but with no sound. I would never have thought to have two TVs in my lounge, and I couldn't figure out if this was classy or trashy. It was a great game, yet it felt wrong that I was not there, and more so because it had no sound. All I could hear was the movie. Surely this was blasphemous to the game. Had I have driven instead of flown across the country, I could have been at this game. I was kicking myself for flying. I wanted to apologise to the NFL Gods, because I strangely felt like I was letting the world of football down.

The next morning, I felt rather guilty, like I had cheated on the NFL with a movie. Luckily, we swiftly flew to San Francisco for our NFL doubleheader. We stayed with Neal's friends Jordana and Katie, who took us to an Ethiopian blues restaurant. I had eaten some odd things at tailgates, but at this place you eat the food with your hands by scooping up the meat and vegetables with a thin foamy bread that has a similar consistency and texture to that of rubber inner soles. I don't think I am really selling it too well by describing it that way, but sadly that is the best I can do. The food was tasty, but I didn't know what to do when the inner soles ran out (bad pun, I know) and there was no cutlery.

Game 20. NFL Week 10, Carolina Panthers at Oakland Raiders, Network Associates Coliseum

Final Score: 17-6. Home-win record: 15-5. Capacity: 63,026. Attendance: 47,888. Ticket face value: $150—I paid $150 via Ticketmaster. Picture on my ticket: E-ticket but I was given a cool "press box" ticket with the Raiders *logo and my name on it that I had to have strapped to my wrist. Mascot: None—there is no need for a mascot here, as so many of the fans are extreme. Merchandise: Raiders baseball cap. Local dish: Tri-tip steak, seafood, and beef.*

Many people had told me not to go to Oakland because the fans are so rough that "they will take your firstborn." The Raiders famously look scary but are they really? The day before the game, John Herrera, the PR chap at the Raiders, returned my call and told me he would be able to give me a pre-game sideline pass, like the Vikings had done. So much for the scary image. John was lovely.

On the morning of the game, Neal and I hopped in a taxi from San Francisco across the bay to Oakland. Looking to my right I could see the famous large metal cranes of the port of Oakland. Rumor has it that George Lucas was inspired by these and made very similar looking At-At Walkers in Star Wars. The Coliseum might be grey and old (built in 1964), but the sense of futuristic grimness hits you very quickly.

Raiders owner Al Davis (who sadly died in 2011) looks very much like Darth Sidious, and as we parked we saw extreme Raiders fan Darth Raider, dressed as the dark lord himself. The rest of the hundreds of extreme fans dressed from a post-apocalyptic world. There were fans everywhere with spikes coming out of their bodies, silver-and-black face paint, lots of chains, black leather, and anything else that symbolises a dark underworld.

Our aim was to find Kingsford Kirk and his barbecue party, as recommended by Karen. Getting to the other side of the cark park took a while because there were so many people to take pictures of. One tailgater brought an actual pig that was on a spit roast being turned, and he was just about to deep fry a whole turkey.

We finally found Kirk and his group, who go by the name of "Tailgaters BBQ Party," and what a party it is. They cook for well over a hundred people on their famous huge grill, named the GrillZilla. Their large section creates a horseshoe shape that welcomes in *all* fans, not just Raiders fans. They have one long Raiders-themed RV, plus a sleek, modern trailer that hosts a Raiders leather couch, a Raiders neon light, oddly a stripper pole, and on the outside a huge flat-screen TV. Don't worry, there is a TV on the inside too. Next to that was their other trailer, which is mainly their "kitchen" on wheels, stuffed full of tailgating equipment. The spice rack on the door reads, "Danger. Men Cooking."

Neal and I watched segments of the Bears game, and they were surprisingly up 7-0 to the unbeaten Titans. Kirk was surrounded by some more extreme Raiders fans wearing spike-ridden shoulder pads and black-and-silver face paint. Kirk himself was not wearing any extreme attire, apart from his blood red eyes. He looked like some kind of rabid animal. When someone is dressed in a cooking shirt and holding a spatula, one is not normally intimidated, but throw in some red eyes and it really does change a few things.

Kingsford Kirk and his team—Barbecue Bob, Uncle Stan the Barbecue Man, Rotisserie Ron, Marinade Marcus, Raider Ron, Toozak, Raider Jerry, The Violator, Sal the Dicing Daddio, and more, were all extremely passionate about welcoming everyone to their monster tailgate. The chefs wear their own black team chef jackets, with the Raiders logo and their names embroidered on the front. Ribs, tri-tip steak, teriyaki salmon, chicken, oysters, and hot dogs were all on the grill. I was introduced to extreme fans Raider Jerry and Toozak, both of whom gave me their football cards with their pictures on them. I soon became more at ease talking to people who had black-and-silver paint on their faces and spikes coming out of their bodies.

These larger-than-life fans picked at chips and wings, making the atmosphere feel like that of a "green room," where made-up performers relax before a show—only instead of a stage, these "performers" come to life inside the stadium.

Although the Raiders are famous for having "aggressive fans" or at least territorial fans, I can honestly say that everyone at Kirk's tailgate welcomed the away Panthers fans. Kirk said, "We're here to change your image of the Raider Nation," and they did just that.

That's when I heard someone from behind me shout out, "Oy! *Redbridge!*" in a booming, aggressive voice that can only be described as a soccer hooligan holler. I remembered that I had done an interview with *The Wanstead and Woodford Guardian*, my local newspaper, when I was in London the week before. The journalist had asked me, "So you are from Ilford then." Ilford is close to my home area of Redbridge. "Oh, I don't mix with those Ilford ilks!" I joked back. "So can I print that?" he asked. I didn't want to come across as snobby, but I said okay for a laugh. I didn't think it would come back to haunt me so far away.

With my height, it is rare that I physically have to look up at people, yet "Dodgy Dave" from Ilford towered over me and he had read *that* article. There I stood looking up at this Raiders fan who had made it all the way from Ilford, some

8,000 miles away. Perhaps it was no fluke—maybe he read the article, checked out my schedule, and flew out after me! "Oh shit!" I thought. Pissing off people from Ilford I can just about handle, but pissing off a Raiders fan in Oakland from Ilford was not a good situation.

Thankfully "Dodgy Dave" saw the funny side of the article and gave me a big hug. He was there with his friend Keith, who goes by the moniker "The Raider Crusader" and hails from Romford in Essex. These two actually met on the terraces at Leyton Orient many years ago and still go to games there. (What is it about Leyton Orient spawning so many NFL fans?) The Crusader Raider dresses up as St. George with chain mail, sword, and a shield with the St. George's crest. (He doesn't do this for soccer games.) I wondered if the Raiders' staff would really let him in the stadium with a sword? What on earth did the airport security folks think when he flew over?

U.K. flight people: Sir, you have chain mail, a sword, and a shield. Which exact medieval war will you be re-enacting?
Crusader Raider: No, no good Sir, I'm just going to be a spectator at one of America's finer pastimes: watching football.
U.K. flight people: Excuse me?
Crusader Raider: I am an Oakland Raiders fan.
U.K. flight people: Oh, tally ho then, old chap. Enjoy the game!

Like myself, Dave and Keith got into the sport when it used to be on Channel 4 back in the late '80s. They liked the colours and the Raiders' bad boy image, and these two fans make the pilgrimage at least once a year to see a Raiders game and have been doing so for over 30 years. Crusader Raider was the first Brit I had seen that really looked "extreme," and whose costume was up there with the best of the PFUFA bunch.

At Jay and Karen's Supergate, the season before, Kirk and his crew walked away as Grand Champions of the Black Top and I could see why. These guys had a huge setup. I knew they were the real deal when they had their own t-shirts saying, "I tailgated in Oakland with Tailgaters barbecue party."

Before leaving to find our other tailgaters, Raider Jerry put some black-and-silver war paint on me and my assimilation was starting. I did not have a lot of time left because I had a pre-game field pass (like at the Vikings), but we quickly made it to Raider Ran's tailgate. Everyone here introduced themselves with "Raider" as their first name. We ate some more food at Ran's tailgate and drank some kind of red alcoholic concoction. Both Neal and I reacted in disgust at the sheer potency of it, while our hosts cackled on.

"When I saw your post on the site," Raider Ran told me, "I said man, I don't invite the world because, you know otherwise we have a thousand people here, this is kinda family you know, a lot of people are welcome, but a lot of people don't understand and they just wanna come and eat." I did not want to seem ungrateful to any of my hosts, or be a tailgating "moocher" who, as Lamm explained, "is someone who wanders from tailgate party to tailgate party and takes advantage of the tailgating community's general hospitality and generosity."[7] "That's why I bring my trip t-shirts," I explained, and Raider Ran made me feel right at home. While hugging me he said, "Adam it's all good, this is family you know." I felt stupid for being so scared of the Raiders fans back in 1990 at Wembley, because here it was solely my passion for football that made these warm fans embrace me. Although other fans had accepted me, this was that much more of a surprise because so many people told me the Raiders would simply be after my blood.

Cory from the Raiders PR team then came over to collect me for the pre-game field pass, and I left Neal at the Ran's tailgate. Like myself, Cory is a Tottenham Hotspur supporter, which made for good chat while we were in the lift. Before I knew it I was actually down at the tunnel by the locker rooms. I saw the light at the end of the tunnel, and in my excitement I made a dash for it, as I saw the onlooking crowd, but Cory held me back because the Carolina Panthers were coming out of their locker room. If only I would have dressed in full Panther kit, they would never have known and I could have warmed up with the team, maybe even play a little and redeem myself for all my missed tackles at Aber. Once the whole Panthers team was in front of us, we followed them as they "click-clacked" their way into the Sunday sunshine down the tunnel. I might not have been dressed in NFL shoulder pads and helmet, but I felt like I was. Never did I ever think I would be marching out of the tunnel with an NFL team. The Raiders cheerleaders, called the Raiderettes, then followed us out. This was for the pre-game warm-ups, before the teams come out properly with all the fireworks, when the Raiderettes come out before the away team.

The Raiders have historically used shrewd tactics to beat their opponents. Former Rams running back Marshall Faulk said that "the Raiders are the only team in the league that makes the opposition run out on to the field through the *home team* cheerleader"[8] as a distraction tactic.

While the teams were warming up, John, Cary's boss, came by to meet me. He gave me a brand new Raiders baseball cap, which I wore for my "sideline" interview with former Raiderette Jeanette Thomson. Then I heard "Oy! Redbridge!" again. Both Dodgy Dave and Crusader Raider had also got field passes. I'm not sure the Raiders knew what they are doing allowing people from Ilford *and* Romford on the field—ha!

I had already bought two tickets from Ticketmaster in the summer for $150 each, as that was the only section Ticketmaster would give me. The Raiders, rather predictably, were not having a good season, although the Panthers were still in the hunt for the playoffs. The game was far from a sell out and the cheapest StubHub tickets were going for $15.

I made my way to my seat, which I only then realised was in club level, hence the hefty price tag. Once in club level, all that Raiders "festive menace" quickly disappeared. There were televisions everywhere and a Q-and-A was taking place with some former players. I even spotted a woman face down on a massage chair getting her back rubbed. Perhaps she did have a tough day at the tailgate, but seriously, a massage chair at a Raiders game!

I found Neal at the bar watching the end of the Bears game, which we lost. We got to our seats above the "Black Hole," which is the famous Raiders section similar to the "Dawg Pound," and like Cleveland, this was loud. The stadium had a fair amount of noise considering most of the upper deck was empty, as was our section. Sitting in club seats wasn't what I had in mind when coming to the Raiders back in 1990. Still I was shocked that some teams do not sell out even if they do "suck." There are only eight home games for the regular season, and when you can get tickets on StubHub for as little as $15, it seems ludicrous that more people were not at this game.

Rudy moment: Panthers running back DeAngelo Williams starting from his own 30-yard line, knocked one tackler off, spun off from another, and then shook off two more as he raced for a 69-yard TD that sealed their away win.

Orange play of the game: It was either the Raiders' fumbled kick return on the first play of the game, or any of the terrible four interceptions thrown by Panthers QB Jake Delhomme.

Extreme fan: Where do I start? Raider Jerry, Toozak, Destruction, Kingsford Kirk, Gorilla Rilla—who dresses in full gorilla costume—Big Tony, the Violator, Dodgy Dave, The Raider Crusader, and many more whose names I do not have. I'm giving this award to Raider Jerry, but The Raider Crusader comes in second.

There was little post-game tailgating for us because we had a plane to catch to Arizona. Although I had become acclimatized by wacky merchandise after going to so many games, it was here at the Oakland airport where I was honestly stunned . . . in a jewelry shop I found a mini Raider football helmet encrusted with diamonds. It was on sale for 12 grand. Surely Steph would rather a diamond-encrusted football helmet over a diamond ring, right?

While I was thinking about diamonds, Neal got talking to two ladies wearing Panthers jerseys. They told us they were at the game watching their boyfriends play. "What?! Your boyfriends? They played in the game?" I asked, half in disbelief and half amazed. Risalyn was wearing a DeAngelo Williams jersey and Laine was wearing a Maake Kemoeatu jersey. At first I did not believe them. They did have their jerseys signed by these two players, but I would have thought the wives and girlfriends travel with the team, but apparently not. I believed them once they showed me pictures of them with their boyfriends.

Excited about my trip, they told me we should stay in touch with them especially when I went to Carolina, or if I go back to Pittsburgh, because Maake's brother, Chris, plays for the Steelers.

Game 21. NFL Week 10, San Francisco 49ers at Arizona Cardinals, University of Phoenix Stadium

Final Score: 24-29. Home-win record: 16-5. Capacity: 63,400. Attendance: 64,519. Ticket face value: $76—I paid $76 via Ticketmaster. Picture on my ticket: E-ticket. Mascot: "Big Red," a big red cardinal. Merchandise: Six-can Cardinals cooler. Local dish: Southwest and Tex Mex.

Once we landed in Arizona we hired a car and spent Sunday night with one of Neal's friends, a chap named Sunny. The next day we headed out at noon towards Glendale for the Cardinal's Monday Night game. We parked for free, the only NFL stadium that has free parking. We first made our way to the statue of ex-Cardinals player Pat Tillman, who left the NFL to fight in the U.S. Army and who sadly died at the hands of friendly fire.

We then headed towards the back lot where the RVs were parked. As we passed through a grass field, we spotted a great-looking van with "Big Red Woody" (the name of the Cardinal's mascot) written on it. This tailgate team always cooks a scrumptuous feast that plays on the theme of the away team. Because of San Francisco's large Chinatown, this tailgate team opted for Chinese food today. They used their wit to incorporate current and ex-49ers players to describe their food—Singletary's "hit the shower" Wings, Joe Montana's "one time" wontons, and Jerry's "fried" Rice.

"You know I am the vice president of the team," I heard over my shoulder, and this certainly piqued my interest. I spun around, bubbling with questions. This man was none other than Michael Bidwill, son of Bill Bidwill, who does own the Cardinals. Sadly, even as vice president he could not do much for me in terms of letting me have a pre-game pass, access to the locker rooms, or a spot on the Cardinals roster, but he did offer us Chinese food and a tour of his amazing tailgate bus, which was great.

He and his family were very friendly and became intrigued by my trip. Other than his very classy Cardinal bus, the real clincher to his tailgate was that his Cardinal stadium seats were from inside the stadium.

We said our good-byes and inched closer to the official RV section when I heard what can only be described as a (British) "dirty Northern accent." A rotund man was cheering with his family at his tailgate. They were very friendly, and he has been living out here for 16 years. Many Northerners at home are a tough bunch and are very proud of their rugby roots. They often see the NFL as "rugby with pads," but he was all about enjoying his life in the desert, especially at American football games. He had bought his RV the year before and has fully embraced the tailgating culture. "Look at this place, the sun is shining; back in my home town I'd have me woolly socks on . . . we're cooking a turkey, buddy, deep frying a bloody turkey!" He was as amazed as I was. His American son began deep frying the bird while his American wife made sure we drank the local brew.

We then made our way to the "Cards' number one tailgate team," as recommended by Karen. This is a team of highly skilled chefs and party connoisseurs. Their captain, Dr. Randy Earick, who writes for *Tailgater Monthly* and goes by the name "Poonster" when on the black top, was accompanied by his two sons, T-Bag and the Shocker.

This trio was excited to see me, and they were cooking up a storm. Poonster had a great Cardinals truck with enough merchandise to compete with the Bidwell family. With names like Poonster, T-Bag, and Shocker, it was not surprising that this family took "pride" in creating a menu of a sexual nature. They chose to reflect San Francisco's famous gay community: "The return of our famous baby brokeback mountain ribs with taste me, taste me glaze, and give me 'a reach around' coleslaw." For "Libations" there was Cardinal Juice—a potent cocktail that came from a smoking red liquor fountain, Cardinal red heat Jell-O shots, and Big Red's testicle cherries, otherwise known as cherry bombs, where glacier cherries are left to soak in alcohol for many hours. They also had "Maul the opponent Margaritas," powered by a gasoline engine, and their Cardinal Koolaid victory fountain for the nonalcoholic drinkers, plus ice chests full of beer and sodas. Their baby back ribs were the best I have eaten in my life.

Poonster, T-Bag, and the Shocker always wear three new custom-made hats for each home game, which Poonster actually makes himself. Sadly, I had to leave to find another tailgater before they could show me what their hats would be for that evening's game. Fortunately, the following year I had the opportunity to swing by Poonster's house and check out his "hat room." The room is dedicated to the storing and the making of the said hats, which he has written about in *Tailgater Monthly*. His world "becomes a flurry of activity as soon as our schedule is announced . . . we change our hats depending upon league standings, seasonal holidays."[9]

The trio had originally used "pink furry hats" for their annual games against the 49ers, "but no one got it," explains Poonster. So now they use a white hard hat with two boxes of famed San Francisco's rice brand, "Rice-A-Roni," attached to them. Poonster is still waiting for every NFL franchise to come to Arizona so he can have a custom-made hat to wear against all the NFL teams. He believes his hats show that "we are forever Arizona Cardinals fans, and at the same time, poke a little good-natured smack [talk] at our opponents."[10]

Poonster doesn't just tailgate at Cardinals games but also at Cardinals charity events. Several local companies, one of which is a local strip club, sponsor his tailgate.

After I signed Randy's *Tailgater Monthly* magazine and he signed mine, it was time to go check out the fan zone. Mr. Bidwell came by and offered Neal and me a lift back on his Cardinal-themed golf cart. You know you are a "royal" tailgater when you have your own golf cart to zip around in.

In front of the stadium is a long, narrow, and perfectly kept lawn. At the top end the band was playing great rock songs of old. The grass was filled with tents and tailgate stands stretching right down the lawn. No one is allowed to park on the grass, so people have to park nearby and move their grills to the lawn. Tailgating on grass felt like a luxury. The sun was going down and the evening was starting to mellow.

I was kicking myself for missing all of this two years prior. Neal felt the vibe was somewhat similar to when he followed the band Phish across the country, cooking food at each concert as he went. With only eight home games, fans want to celebrate their team, especially as there are so few teams in the NFL across such a vast country. In the U.K. we take soccer much more for granted as we have 92 professional teams that all play more than 40 games per season, in a country roughly the same size as the state of Michigan. Plus we have our international games too.

We then spotted Chef Joe, and his massive grill, who has won several tailgate competitions. Even though I was stuffed from Poonster's great ribs, Chef Joe insisted we try his famous cheese jalapeños. He warned me of their hot potential, but I was feeling confident because my road snack of choice by then had moved up to the Flaming Hot version of cheese puffs. But even from just a mere nibble this caused a real flaming hot sensation in my mouth. My taste buds were literally *on fire*. Joe laughed and carried on with his cooking. The chili was too intense to be neutralized by the cheese inside, and my brow began to perspire and my face went bright red. Neal, like a trooper, tried it "all in one go." This little bad boy of cheese and fiery goodness brought my friend to tears.

We made our way to the stadium and I saw a wonderfully dressed couple. The man had on a groom's outfit with a Cardinals jersey under his tuxedo while sporting a Cardinal mask. His wife was wearing a red velvet ball gown and heels. It turns out it this was actually their wedding day. They had their wedding service that morning and were kicking off their honeymoon at this Monday Night Football game.

I asked the groom if he thought I could convince Steph on our wedding day to come to a football game. While he stayed quiet pondering the possibility, his bride excitedly said, "Yes! Tell your woman it's all for the NFL." Not sure that would work with Steph, but I will try.

Later that year in Arizona, Jay, Karen, and Poonster helped Hans with his undercover "game day proposal" to his now wife, Crystal. Hans wrote in his blog afterwards, "When the scoreboard message flashed and the Cardinals mascot was perched in our section, it set off an autonomous chain of events that culminated in a tearful acceptance (her tears, not mine) as we celebrated with 65,000 fans."[11] Neal and I noticed that someone had made a lovely custom-made sign out of carpet material that was left on grass; it read, "We are who we thought we were," which is in reference to the infamous 2006 Bears-Cardinals post-game press conference. After that game, the Cardinals head coach at the time, Dennis Green, went ballistic in his press conference, smacking the microphone because his team had lost the game when they were up 0-20. He kept repeating over and over in a crazed monologue saying that the "Bears are who we thought they were." Sports bloggers quoted this line over and over until it became part of Cardinals life.

Even though I had been to the stadium just once before, I felt like I had been there dozens of times. Our seats were high in the upper deck but we never made it to them. Neal, being a bit of a smooth dude, just walked past the security that lead to the lower section right behind the end zone, where there were somewhat better seats than the tickets in our pockets. The security just let us pass, and although it was a Monday Night Football game, there were a few spare seats around. Sadly, soccer stadiums are not built like this—you have to go to a specific stadium entrance (turnstiles) depending on where your ticket is. We managed to watch the first half in someone else's seat, before simply moving back a few rows for the second half. That's when I got a tap on my shoulder—it was the gentleman I was sitting behind when I was at the Chargers game with Mike P. What are the odds?

Rudy moment: The Cardinals goal-line stand to stop the 49ers from winning the game at the last minute. And a worthy runner-up would be the opening play where the Cardinals kick returner brought it back to the house for a TD.

Orange play of the game: While up 24-20, the 49ers had the ball with minutes to go. But they fumbled the ball on a snap, giving the Cardinals great field position, which allowed them to come back in the game.

Extreme fan: Poonster and his two sons, T-Bag and the Shocker.

After the game we drove to Tucson, where Neal has lots of friends. He insisted we head to the famous Congress Hotel to party because they had an '80s night theme. We spent a couple of days in Tucson at Neal's friend Aric's house relaxing before we drove back to Vegas. It was a beautiful drive that took us across the Hoover Dam and around the Grand Canyon. Neal's two brothers, David and Bryan, had just done a road trip themselves driving down from Chicago to Vegas. On a stretch of road in Colorado they had run out of gas with no stations within miles. At the start of the trip I was often worried about doing this. Justin told me there were gas stations everywhere, and I became more relaxed, but still I had come close a couple of times.

By this point, Neal was aware that a few things technically were not quite going fully to plan for me. My camcorder broke in Arizona; the servers that hosted my blog were making the site go slow and had also lost two weeks worth of e-mails from tailgaters; my compact camera stopped gaining focus; and I was frankly getting burnt out. Neal was caught up with football, or rather tailgate fever and proposed to join my trip to help me out—another audible if you will. We juggled some flights around so that Neal could be with me on the trip from my Bills game until Steph came out. This way we could share the driving, I would have someone to share the experience with, meet more people, and I would not have to live from motel to motel because Neal had several friends across the country we could stay with.

The next morning I was back on a flight from Vegas to NYC. I was shattered and wanted to catch some sleep, yet I was kept awake by two ladies behind me as they discussed their somewhat exuberant tales of Vegas nightlife. I'm not sure if Carmen and Nikki are models with questionable morals or if they are straight-up strippers or hookers, but either way their sordid stories kept everyone entertained.

Once I discovered that Carmen was a Raiders fan and Nikki a Cowboys fan and that they go to at least two NFL games a season, the conversation turned to nonstop football. I got some pretty angry looks from the other male passengers, who had been revelling in the ladies' unsavoury tales.

Only upon landing did I realise that the Patriots were hosting the Jets that night on Thursday night football. If I had booked an earlier flight I could have made the game. I was gutted because this was now the second game that I could have thrown in as an "extra game."

The next morning I was back at my original rental car place in NYC to pick up my second-half car, a PT Cruiser. Driving down to Atlanta, I noticed two particular things on the highway that repeated every 30 miles or so. First there were lots of adult stores. I had noticed these on several other highways, but here there was quite an abundance of them. The second type of popular stores along this highway was fireworks shops. I'm still trying to figure out the relationship.

Game 22. NFL Week 11, Denver Broncos at Atlanta Falcons, Georgia Dome

Final Score: 24-20. Home-win record: 16-6. Capacity: 71,228. Attendance: 64,644. Ticket face value: $108—I had paid $108 via Ticketmaster. Picture on my ticket: E-ticket. Mascot: "Freddie Falcon," a caricature falcon. Merchandise: Falcons woolly hat. Local dish: Fried food and chicken.

Oddly, I could not smell any meat grilling. With the parking lot and tailgates on a separate level, you either do the tailgate thing or the fan zone thing. I zipped through the fan zone, which was excellent, with lots of inflatables, colourful fans, free giveaways, and cheerleaders signing autographs. It was probably the best fan zone I had encountered.

I walked around the parking lots downstairs looking for the tailgating spot known as the Gulch, described as a huge "gangsta' rap video." I could not find it and could not see any themed buses like I had at other stadiums, and there seemed to be a real lack of atmosphere.

It is not like the Falcons were a terrible team either. They were sitting pretty with a 6-3 record and their rookie QB Matt Ryan had been playing well, filling the massive boots left by then jailbird, Michael Vick.

As per Karen's recommendation I did find the BirdWatchers, which is a tailgate party run by Tom and Diane Dunn. In 2005 they were picked by Campbell's Chunky Soup to represent the Falcons in their national NFL-wide tailgating promotion. The BirdWatchers tailgate out of their "Fanbulance." They introduced me to their friends who had a great-looking old American pick-up truck all decked out with Falcon logos as well as literally a truckload of food. Tom and Diane buy up parking spaces for the whole corner of the lot so that all of their friends can park and tailgate together.

Like other tailgaters' menus, theirs took inspiration from the away team Broncos players. There was Jay's veal cutler, Eddie's clams casino royal, Tatum Bell's nacho bags, Brandon Stockley's beans, Matt Prater's kicking chicken, Brandon Marshall's deli slices, and Denver omelettes. Tom had explained that after Michael Vick was sent to prison for dog fighting, the Falcons lost a lot of their supporters.

Ironically, before the Vick era the Falcons hardly sold out. When Vick arrived, tickets went through the roof and he became one of the most popular players in the league, because of his unorthodox QB style, preferring to run the ball rather than put it in the air. He may not have been the best QB in the game, but he was always exciting to watch.

The BirdWatchers let me check out their whole bus, which had airbrushed players on its side. Inside at the back, Tom and Diane have a birdcage, which that day imprisoned a Denver Broncos helmet. They have a helmet for each team. A large stuffed Falcon perches on top. For their Bears helmet, Tom has an actual game-day helmet Brian Urlacher himself had worn.

Tom told me that "without the tailgating, many fans would stay home and watch it on TV." NFL teams really need to embrace the tailgating culture, otherwise they could be left with half-empty stadiums. Many TV tailgaters had told me how they prefer watching the game on TV as opposed to in the stadium. With the commentary and action replay, it is fair to say, that if you want to study the game on the field then the TV version is for you. Tom showed me his perfect solution, his portable TV, which he takes with him into the game. It is the best of both worlds.

As we finished up tailgating, the Falcons Drumline, their marching band, came powering through the tailgate, all wearing Falcons jerseys with the number 28, and it was a nice way to end the tailgate before heading into the Georgia Dome.

My ticket was another impulse buy from Ticketmaster, and another club-level seat. I got to my section, #215, and only then did I start to realise that if the section begins with a two it is probably a club-level seat. At home, stadiums are not normally built with the same three-tiered system: lower, club, and upper.

The concourse on the club level was very nice. The food looked splendid and was served by chefs with big white hats. There were TVs everywhere and the carpet was very thick and plush. My seat was on the corner of the end zone and there were a few empty seats around.

At the merchandise stand, they were selling old Falcons jerseys for half price. Rather deadpan, I inquired about Vick jerseys. The seller didn't see the funny side and shot me an angry look.

The Drumline came onto the field before the players were announced, and once the game kicked off they moved to the far corner and pumped out a six-second drumbeat every time the Falcons moved the ball forward.

During the national anthem, I noticed there were sign-language signers, for the hard of hearing, which I had not seen at a game before. The home fans were particularly quiet, and the pedestrian atmosphere made me far more of aware of all the "hoopla." Because there was so much of it, such as giveaways and fan interaction, it did come across as slightly desperate, which was odd because the game was a decent one. The cheerleaders danced to hip-hop beats and were the best I had seen.

When Clay Travis came to the Georgia Dome in 2006 for an SEC bowl game, he wrote that he found the venue to be "very antiseptic and almost too formal for an SEC football game . . . the Georgia Dome just doesn't feel right to me. It's like showing up to a football game in a suit."[12]

Every time I got up to cheer or applaud, I was asked to sit down. I came to realise that I didn't like being in the club level—it's too much like being at a cricket game. Though at halftime the crowd got louder, because the Falcons introduced most of the members of the 1999 Falcons Super Bowl (losing) team. They had fireworks and player introductions just like they did for the start of this game. Every one of these players got a huge cheer, as opposed to the feeble support for the current players.

Rudy moment: Broncos wide receiver Brandon Marshall was sandwiched between two defenders, but used all of his strength and agility to come down with the ball, setting up the Broncos game-winning TD.

Orange play of the game: Atlanta QB Matt Ryan backpedaled and within the panic of a blitz threw a high pass off his back foot that was easily intercepted.

Extreme fan: The Preacher Man," a cheerful man who comes to every game, has a black-and-red opened-up umbrella, a tambourine, a long grey trenchcoat with Falcon logos all over it, and an Obama baseball hat. I thought it was bad luck to open an umbrella indoors, and even though he said otherwise, his team did lose.

After the game Tom and Diane invited me back to their tailgate, but I had to decline because I had a 900-mile drive to Buffalo for a game the next night.

On the next day, and only a few hours shy of Buffalo, I found myself driving through a blizzard. I was listening into sports radio shows, and on a particular Buffalo show there was the firm belief that the Bills game that night could be the first snow game of the season, and how the snow could be advantageous for the

Bills against the Browns. I phoned in and told them that it was snowing where I was, and that as a football fan, I think it would be great to see a game in the snow. They told me that although it wasn't yet snowing in Buffalo, I should prepare for the cold. Bad weather is not only good for the Bills team but also for the NFL. Oriard points out that TV networks want bad weather, "for the stunning shots of snowflakes floating gently down on embattled armies, of muddied warriors trudging to the line like Napoleon's forces before the gates of Moscow."[13]

I swung by Buffalo airport, picked up Neal, and we headed for the stadium hoping for snow.

Game 23. NFL Week 11, Cleveland Browns at Buffalo Bills, Ralph Wilson Stadium

Final Score: 29-27. Home-win record: 16-7. Capacity: 73,967. Attendance: 71,645. Ticket face value: $65—I paid $65 via Ticketmaster for my nose-bleed seat. I paid $70 for Neal's sideline ticket. Picture on ticket: E-ticket and text on plain background. Mascot: "Billy Buffalo," an eight-foot, bright blue buffalo. Merchandise: Bills woolly hat. Local dish: Buffalo chicken wings and beef on weck (a type of bread native to Buffalo).

We parked the car in someone's front garden by the stadium, yet only when I was too far away from the car did I kick myself for wishing for snow and not listening to the radio presenters, because by the time I entered the tailgate wearing just a hoodie, it was freezing, and the crowd was coming in as thick and fast as the snow. The atmosphere reminded me of the Patriots' Monday night game, with it being so busy, frantic, and cold. In one of the tailgate lots the Bills have installed a shower block so the tailgaters can arrive the night before and sleepover in the car park.

As we got to the tailgate lots, there were a bunch of people already cooking up a storm. I couldn't believe just how many fire pits I saw. We found a tailgate group whose own rock band was pumping out beats from a stage in their tent.

We only had one tailgate group to meet, the "Bills Backers" who tailgate with a man named Kenny and his famous car, "The Pinto Ron." Kenny had told me that he puts on a show at 8 p.m. We asked around if any one knew the Bills Backers and although people pointed us towards them, they all wanted to show off their own tailgate and buses. "Their tailgate is nothing like ours," Scott explained as he led us onto his bus called "Illegal Motion," where he presented me and Neal with plenty of shots. His tailgate caters for up to 600 people per game and is called the Conklin's Tailgate Bar and Grill. It was even featured on the pilot episode of the show *Tailgate Warriors* on the Food Network the following year.

We finally made it to the Bills Backers and Kenny's tailgate. And what a tailgate they have, though Karen warned me to not eat anything from them, because they cook their whole menu from old spare car parts and other old metal contraptions. It looked disgusting yet fascinating. Upon the bonnet of this old station wagon banger, aka the Pinto Ron, was a saw that fried bacon, an old rake used to grill sausages, old screwdrivers used as kebab sticks, a rusty WWII army helmet to heat up their wings, and an old steel ironing board to grill their pizza on, all fired up with briquettes. It looked unsanitary and bizarre, but I had to dig in.

We signed their guest book and took some quick snaps before they gave me their true Bills Backers initiation: Kenny poured alcohol into the holes of a bowling ball. I then had to drink from the ball, drop the ball on the ground, then pick it up (trickier than it sounds, especially when it is freezing cold out and there is alcohol all over the ball), and place it back on its plinth. Then I had to blow into a massive horn. The tailgate was rustic and a little grungy, but it had lots of character and it reminded me of one of the *Rocky* films.

Eight o'clock was nearing, but that was the same time I was supposed to meet Andy Major, the head of marketing for the Bills. We sadly had to miss Kenny's show, which I later found on YouTube (HBO even did a special on him). Every game day, Kenny takes most of his clothes off in the parking lot. His friends then get up on the roof of their bus with condiment guns. Kenny walks towards them with an ungarnished hamburger. He then stands there and gets completely and utterly drenched from head to toe with ketchup and mustard. Kenny's crew and tailgate has to be one of the most surreal parties on the NFL spectrum. Kenny is a quietly spoken bearded man, and for as much as I could see he does appear to have all his marbles.

We met Andy Major, and it was a real honour that on Monday Night Football he gave us a royal tour. We met with two Buffalo Bills cheerleaders (called the Buffalo Jills), then went behind the rock band stage and met some hard-core fans who go to the game with nothing but red-and-blue paint on their torsos. Then we met Vic Carucci, a top writer for the NFL. We also met with football legend Steve Tasker, who is a former Bills player (and rugby player) and is now a CBS analyst.

Andy was great at telling me about the history of the team and what it means to these fans to have a Monday night game. The fans here are hard core, especially the half-naked ones partying in the freezing cold.

Later Andy e-mailed me, saying that "as a fellow NFL fan, I am a bit envious of your trip but would have to bring my wife (also a big fan) with me—some day down the road!" This struck a chord with me because I was very envious of his job.

I had bought one ticket at face value in the summer, but Neal fancied watching this game, as he thought it would be warmer in the stadium than at the tailgate. At the last minute Andy got us the extra ticket.

Once inside the stadium we realised that our two tickets were very far away from each other. Mine was at the top in the nosebleeds section, while Neal's ticket was in the lower section. We decided to head up to the top where we hoped to find two available seats open. This was very difficult, which surprised me because it was so cold. The snow started coming down, and without boots, a scarf, long johns, or a jacket on, and just one pair of gloves between us, we were soon getting cold in the icy Buffalo wind. There were posters promoting their hard-core naked-torso fans, with the tag line, "It's not the same sitting at home."

Finally we found two seats. Neal and I soon noticed that when the Bills fans moved around, they raced around as quick as the players on the field. One particular large gentleman came pacing up three stairs at a time with a beer in each hand and his nachos wedged under his chin. In between plays all the action and speed was on the concourses and bleachers, where people made spin moves, sprints, and diving catches. Someone should film the Bills fans in their natural habitat, as they are really athletic.

I wanted to check out the lower bowl seats, so I left Neal to warm up on the concourse. The seat was on the 2nd row and right on the 50-yard line. I could have touched the players. It was much warmer down there and I felt bad for Neal, as he was getting frostbite somewhere higher up. Behind me were a group of Browns fans. They saw that I was freezing cold, and even though they saw my Bills hat, they insisted on giving me a lovely, warm back massage throughout the fourth quarter.

Rudy moment: Josh Cribbs, the electric Browns receiver came across on a reverse play, took the handoff, cut inside, dived, and went airborne backwards over a defender while another one was tackling him in mid-air. He held onto the ball for a gobsmacking TD.

Orange play of the game: Any of the Bills QB Trent Edwards's plays could have qualified—he threw three interceptions in the first quarter alone!

Extreme fan: It could well have been Kenny, but I missed his ketchup-and-mustard show. Or it could have been awarded to PFUFA member Scott, who grows a mohawk for football season and paints the Bills logo on each side of his skull, or any of the hard-core "naked-torso" fans that the Bills attract. But I'm going with the "Buffalo Bills Beadman." He was dressed in Bills face paint, wore hundreds of beads, a foam Bills hat, homemade Bills pants, and Bills shoes.

After the sad Bills home loss, Neal and I headed north to Toronto, Canada, where I was picking up the rest of my football trip t-shirts. My good friend in London, Amy, is from St. Catherine's, Ontario, Canada (which she calls the Shitty Kitty), a city that lies between Toronto and Buffalo, where her family owns a couple of hotels. After waking her up by calling her at 6 a.m. England time, she made some calls and got us a free hotel room for the night.

The next day, after picking up the t-shirts in Toronto, we headed to the States back through St. Catherine's. It's a lucky thing that Amy's family also owns a sports bar. Neal, a Chicago Cubs fan, was happy the bar was named Wrigley's Field. Here we got a free lunch, and the friendly bar maid, Kayla, gave us lots of NFL merchandise, including rubber beer mats, posters, and an NFL metal bin.

I had originally planned to then spend a few days in NYC before driving Justin and myself down to Miami for my next game, where he has family. Instead, we called another audible, this one heading us off to Pittsburgh. Neal's friend Gabe lives there and told us we could stay there for a few days. Laine, the lady we met in Oakland, whose boyfriend's brother plays for the Steelers, told us she could get us free tickets for the upcoming Thursday night game between the Steelers and the Bengals, so we spent a few days relaxing and bar hopping in Pittsburgh.

Gabe introduced us to pierogies, which are wrapped pancakes that you fry or grill and make for a lovely late-night snack. He also took us to the famous Pittsburgh sandwich place called Primanti Bros. When my sandwich arrived, I could see what made it so special. Many fine sandwich creators across the globe have only ever put the two delicacies of fries and coleslaw on the side, but not the Pittsburgh faithful—they put it *all* between the bread.

We made a shopping trip, buying plenty of warm winter clothes such as long johns, gloves, hats, scarves, and hand warmers because we didn't want to be caught short again, like we had in Buffalo.

Game 24. NFL Week 12, Cincinnati Bengals at Pittsburgh Steelers, Heinz Field

Final Score: 10-27. Home-win record: 17-7. Capacity: 65,050. Attendance: 59,854. Ticket face value: $85—I got the ticket for free. Photo on my ticket: Old-fashioned letter with the Steelers logo as a stamp, plus a black-and-white picture of the "Monongahela Incline." Merchandise: Steelers woolly hat.

It was 5 p.m. on a workday (Thursday), and the car park and surrounding bars were far more vacant than the Monday night game I had experienced with Justin at the beginning of the season. We spotted a black A-Team-style Steelers van. I knocked on the door to ask if we could take a picture, and a man named Dan opened the door; by sheer coincidence he was the tailgater that Karen had recommended and who I missed because of traffic in my previous visit to Pittsburgh.

Dan was with his friend and they were preparing some good, hearty food for us to stay warm. Dan told me he was cooking haggis especially for me. I actually had never tried haggis before and would never have thought that my first taste of it would be at a Pittsburgh tailgate. Dan said that they normally have up to 20 people in their party, but because of the cold weather, coupled with the fact that it was a Thursday night game and that the feeble Bengals were in town, it meant a smaller tailgate party for them.

Dan's friend told us he was inspired by my trip and that he really came out that night in the blistering cold just to cook for me. Dan's van is something of pure footballing beauty. Inside it is filled with ticket stubs, cards, posters, and an array of other Steelers merchandise. It all felt incredibly homey. Perhaps it was Dan's warm character or that there is something wonderful in a grown man still having so much passion for his team, just like he did when he was a kid. Or maybe it was the fact that his wife had personally handmade the curtains and the other decorations herself, all in black and yellow of course. Many of the other tailgates I had seen were on a large scale and elaborate, but these were just two guys kicking back in their van, taking in the world. They were Neal's favourite tailgaters. It felt calm and cozy, like the four of us were all together on a fishing trip. I have never actually been on a fishing trip, but if I do go I hope it would be like the tailgating experience I had that night in Pittsburgh.

Neal and I left Dan to make our rounds, checking out the fan zone and Dan told us that dinner was to be ready in one hour. As we walked around, one tailgate party in particular caught my eye. The party had a huge spread littered with food, at least 40 yards long. Some guys behind them were playing beer pong on an astro field beer pong table, and behind them was some contraption that was their pride and joy—a long pole with black-and-gold stripes protruding vertically from a table top. On top of the pole was a funnel. Coming off the pole at the bottom were eight tubes. This was an octopong. Basically, you pour beer down the funnel and eight people drink at the same time. I was beginning to think that Tunison was spot on with his description of a tailgate as "college in a car park."[14]

We got back to Dan's just in time for dinner. His van felt like home, and we ran back like school kids, making sure we were not late. Dan made American-style haggis, which was haggis (sheep offal) stuffed into the body of peppers. He cooked up some brats he had been marinating in beer and brown-sugared apples for over 10 hours, served with warmed potato salad.

A dinner date with Dan is not complete without his famous cherry bombs. They were almost exactly the same as Poonster's cherry bombs in Arizona, but mix in the sub-zero conditions and this fiery cherry bomb will warm you up pretty damn quickly!

We then went to the Will Call booth to pick up our tickets and the lady behind the counter passed us *four free* tickets. We thought it would just be two tickets. I called Laine to thank her, and she explained that we should not sell the two spare tickets because if that person decides to get drunk and be a nuisance, then Steelers guard Chris Kemoeatu could lose his rights for tickets in the future since these were his tickets.

"Let's get some hot chicks to go with us!" beamed Neal. I wasn't exactly sure where Neal thought where he would find two ladies who happened to be at a Pittsburgh tailgate on a freezing Thursday night and *not* already have tickets or even boyfriends with them. I'm pretty sure women don't come to tailgates this cold without game-day tickets—or do they?

Neal pushed out his chest like the leader of men about to do battle. "*I* will pick us up two hot chicks!" I did not want to dampen Neal's confidence, but there were far fewer women around tonight than there were back in September.

Still, Neal didn't even need to go to a nearby bar. While we were tailgating with Dan and other friendly Steelers fans, Neal suddenly spun around with two girls, one on each arm cooing. "Adam," he said proudly, "Danika and Tara are joining us at the game." Wow, this guy works fast. The two college sorority girls were at the tailgate raising money for a charity with two other girls, and none of them had planned on seeing the game. "Excuse me, ladies," I inquired, "this might be a bit of a personal question, but are you wearing long underwear?" They (and Neal) stared at me blankly, unsure if I was creepy or not. It turns out they were not sporting long johns (which is absolutely essential for a Pittsburgh game in December), and because they were unprepared, they were freezing cold during the game. I did warn them.

Our tickets were in the lower section about 12 rows back on the 40-yard line—perfect. The atmosphere was loud and the girls got right into the game, until the snow became too much for them to bear without wearing cold-weather clothing.

Rudy moment: Steelers guard Chris Kemoeatu got the award. Not just because he got us the free tickets, but because he protected Ben Roethlisberger, not allowing his QB to get sacked at all during the entire game.

Orange play of the game: Bengals wide receiver Chad Ochocinco was sent home before the game even started for missing a team practice earlier, and thus weakening his team. Plus, I was supposed to be on a radio station before the game, but once the hosts found out about Ochocinco's punishment, they wanted to discuss him and my story got bumped off. Thanks a bunch, Chad.

Extreme fan: A man wearing a black hard hat, on top of which sat a small van, the "Iron City Beer" logo on the side, an American flag, a beer can on the back, a Super Bowl pin, and a figurine of Troy Polamalu on the peak of the hat.

After the game, we offered our two new friends, Tara and Danika, a ride back to their dorms. Only once we got near the car did we remember that it was filled with our suitcases and boxes of t-shirts, meaning there was only just enough room for Neal and me. Tara sat on Neal's lap and somehow Danika squeezed herself into the car by lying on top of the boxes of t-shirts.

After dropping them off we drove to the rental car place to change cars. The PT Cruiser was killing me for gas (22 mpg), and it didn't have seat warmers like the Cobalt had. We got to the counter and the guy could not have been any more enthusiastic, even though it was 3 a.m.

We could swap the PT Cruiser for a Chevrolet HHR, which is slightly bigger and, like the PT Cruiser, looks like a hearse, but more crucially has a better mpg (27 mpg). It also has bum warmers on the seats, which I know Steph would love, as she hates being cold. "But does it have an auxiliary so I can play my iPod?" Neal asked the chipper worker. He knew the car's horsepower, the engine size, and who designed the windshield wipers, but now he was stumped. "I'm not driving 1,000 miles all night without my music," Neal protested. "We are getting this car!" I snapped back. This was our first conflict. Neal and I had have never spent this much time with each other and thankfully we laughed about the situation afterwards because our new car had a full working auxiliary . . . phew!

We made it to Orlando, our first 1,000-mile trip, without stopping in a hotel. Once there, I met Emily and Lauren, Neal's friends who kindly let us stay with them.

Come Saturday, Neal and I headed farther south to Miami. Mike B. was already there visiting a friend, and Justin had just come in from NYC. We all met up and hit a club. It was great that I was able to see so many of my friends, and if it weren't for them and for Neal, I would have gotten extremely lonely between the games.

Game 25. NFL Week 12, New England Patriots at Miami Dolphins, Dolphins Stadium

Final Score: 48-28. Home-win record: 17-8. Capacity: 75,450. Attendance: 67,176. Ticket face value: $80—I paid $80 via Ticketmaster. Picture on ticket: E-ticket. Mascot: "T.D.," a dolphin character. Merchandise: Dolphin headband. Local dish: Cuban sandwich and alligator.

I always knew I was going to take Justin to the Dolphins game, and it was pretty handy that his cousins live just 10 minutes from the stadium. Neal had a "day off."

Justin and I first made our way to see the Finatics tailgating group, whom Hans had recommended. Because the Dolphins were playing the Pats, they decided to cook up Boston food and I tried their clam chowder. I am not a big seafood person, but it was actually very nice.

We then made our way through the great Dolphins fan zone, which is on par with the Falcons fan zone. Maybe it was the heat, maybe it was the big game rivalry, but either way excitement was in the air. We stumbled on a lovely extreme Dolphins fan who goes by the name of Dolphin Fan Rosie. Rosie is a loud, smiling Hispanic lady, and she has not missed a Dolphins game in several years. She made us stay and try her salsa and nachos. Her bench in front of her car was a homage to the team, with bobbleheads, framed pictures of her with past Dolphins players, and hard-to-find Dolphins goodies. I have my own personal Bears collection at home, but I wouldn't think to bring all my prized and cherished pieces to a game and display them. She even had a Dolphins Wheaties cereal box signed by various players.

I had two tickets for this game that I had bought in the summer in section #417, which is up high on the five-yard line. Both teams had 6-4 records, making this game vital for both to qualify for the playoffs. The Dolphins had shocked the football world by beating the Pats in New England at the start of the season, with their new and controversial "wildcat" formation. They were clearly beating teams using a system, as opposed to relying on their talent. The Patriots and their defensive genius head coach, Bill Belichick, wanted revenge. There were plenty of away Patriots fans in our section, which didn't please Justin.

Although I had seen several flyovers from planes just as the national anthems ended, this was the first time I had seen it done with helicopters. The Dolphins also had a unique halftime show. First, hundreds of children and cheerleaders performed an organised dance. Then two trampolines and trampoliners with their amazing spinning acrobatic moves came onto the field. I also noticed that jumbotrons here are extra "jumbo."

Rudy moment: Patriots wide receiver Randy Moss won this for his over-the-head, one-handed catch. Even though he had a defender breathing down his neck, he made it look effortless. The ball floated down like manna from the footballing heavens, and Moss caressed the ball down to earth like he was cradling a newborn baby.

Orange play of the game: Late in the game, the Dolphins needed a score, but their QB, Chad Pennington, threw an interception, only his sixth of the season thus far.

Extreme fan: I saw one Dolphins fan dressed completely in playing gear except for the helmet, as well as a great Pats fan whose body was covered in white paint, while his shaved head was covered in red, white, and blue stripes of the

Pats logo. His body paint was peeling off in the heat, and it just looked freakish. The winner was Dolphin Fan Rosie from the tailgate.

After the game, the tailgaters were still full force post-game, but I had to hit the road. I dropped Justin back with his family and picked up Neal. Justin's family gave us plenty of snacks for the road ahead as Neal and I headed west to New Orleans.

Game 26. NFL Week 12, Green Bay Packers at New Orleans Saints, Louisiana Superdome

Final Score: 29-51. Home-win record: 18-8. Capacity: 72,003. Attendance: 70,668. Ticket face value: Unknown (it was given to me by Dave from Canalstreetchronicles.com). Picture on my ticket: Physically this was the largest of all the tickets. It had two pictures of Saints player, Will Smith. Mascot: "Gumbo" and "Sir Saint." Merchandise: Saints headband. Local dish: Gumbo, jambalaya, and boudin.

We got to the "Big Easy" around 5 p.m. the next day and parked near Bourbon Street. There was a fair amount of Packers fans in town filling up the bars. This party road reminded me of Soho back in London—it was a small busy street and a little bit seedy and I was half expecting Baron Samedi to pop out from somewhere.

Since I only had one ticket for the game, I left Neal to explore the downtown area as I walked to the stadium.

I made my way to the Superdome and saw two guys painting a fleur-de-lis on a child's face. I wanted one and got in line. But just my luck, the police busted them as the face painter was halfway through my face. He packed up his paints and tried to leave. I had to beg the policeman to allow the painter time to finish off the job. I would have looked like a right plonker with just half a Saints logo on my face.

I easily found the Chef Who Dat team right by the Superdome. The area is enclosed, and I could see a band setting up by the fan zone. I could not, however, smell barbecued food like I had at other tailgates because tailgaters are not allowed to use open flames right by the stadium.

Chef Who Dat is tall, lean, and bubbling with energy. He had on a chef's outfit and a fake moustache. Apparently it was "moustache Monday" and I forgot mine. Chef was excited that I was finally at the Superdome, and he became ecstatic when he saw my trainers (sneakers), which were black and gold. It was more a fluke if anything.

Since the Packers were in town, cheese had found itself on the menu. Chef had a cheese voodoo doll with pictures on it from the Packers team. He took great pleasure in chewing and prodding the doll.

I then had some gumbo that had a warm Cajun kick to it. I told Chef about meeting the Saintsations, Chrissy and Randi, in London. He told me that he actually teaches Chrissy at the nearby university. I nearly choked on my gumbo! This wacky, energetic man behind this tailgate party is a university lecturer?! It made me want to enroll. I would love to have been taught by someone as inspiring and humorous as Chef; plus, being in class with cheerleaders wouldn't be so bad either. Chef's humorous game-day menu was titled "A Favre-Free Fromage Tasting Menu . . . Who Dat Say Dey Gonna Cut Dat Cheese," and it had various witty and anti-Packer delights, such as "Aaron Rodgers Cheez Whiz (a semi-soft replacement cheese product)," "Ryan Grant Gorgonzola (moldy & easily crumbled)," and for dessert "Deuce up-side-your-cheesehead cake."

It was time to find my next tailgater. I called Chet, who was an afro-wearing Saints fan at the London game. Chet and his friend, still wearing afros, walked me under several bridges and highways to their tailgate. The rain started and the ground was getting muddy. We kept walking and walking, and I was getting concerned as to how I would find the stadium again, or if perhaps they were kidney thieves.

Under the passageways lay an abandoned patch of grass that was filled with cars and Saints minivans all awkwardly parked. The comfortable surroundings of Chef Who Dat's party felt as if it were miles away. This was more like the Bills' tailgate—rugged, congested, and somewhat insecure. It felt borderline illegal.

Chet and his family had the deep-fried turkey already under way. Night fell quickly and 40 of us huddled around a fire pit. I spotted an elderly gentleman with what looked like a black-and-gold lampshade not on his head, but over his head. He (and his lampshade) had Saints memorabilia all over him. I'm not sure how he was able to see anything but he clearly did as he steered clear of the growing fire, where we all sang the Saints chant: "Who dat, Who dat, Who dat say dey gonna beat dem Saints, Who dat! Who dat!" Once the tune was over I realised this was a culmination of several parties coming together, and only then did everyone introduce themselves to each other. It just goes to show how a nice big fire and some good old-fashioned group cheering can really bring new people together. Bless the tailgate!

I had one more tailgate team to meet, and I finally managed to find my way out of the underpasses towards the "Korner Krewe." Krewe's are organisations mainly in the South that are involved with the carnival season, and no city takes more pride in their carnival than New Orleans for Mardi Gras in February. This band of merry tailgaters is good friends with Tom and Diane from the BirdWatchers in Atlanta.

Alan and Linnea welcomed me with full open arms and they gave me a big hug. They had a great spread going, fit for about 30 people, including several Packers fans.

Then I then met up with Dave from Canalstreetchronicles.com by the band and we headed into the stadium. The Saints had the comfiest seats, which was good because I witnessed probably the longest build up to the players' entrance. First there was an actor dressed like a Packers fan holding a huge piece of cheese, walking around midfield. The two Saints mascots, both ran at the "Packers fan," then they tackled him to the floor, stole his cheese, and took it to a massive cheese grater.

The Packers came straight out onto the field and the whole crowd booed. Perhaps the "mascot mugging" we had just witnessed gave the home fans the licence to boo, because it was unusual to hear boos for the away team at the other NFL stadiums. After the singing of the national anthem a woman named "The Motor Queen" came speeding out of the tunnel on a Harley Davidson. Dave's friend then went and bought a Bloody Mary. Not only do they serve Bloody Marys at this stadium, but they serve them up with a huge olive and green runner beans.

The dome was packed and the atmosphere was electric. The following season Brett Favre came here as a Viking, and he had to wear earplugs because it was so loud. The Packers fans in front of us were very friendly but went a bit quiet once the Who Dat onslaught began.

In the fourth quarter I made my way up to section 641 where "Chef Who Dat" was with his crew. Climbing those stairs to the top of the dome really knocked the wind out of me, but there was a party taking place, so I had to get my breath back quickly.

Chef was adamant that I was made part of their entourage, via an initiation. Before I knew it, I was lifted up by my legs with my arms balancing gingerly on the back of someone's seat. Here Chef and a friend took turns in spanking my arse with a wooden spoon! I was laughing so hard at the ridiculousness of it all and wondered who was getting spanked harder, me or the Packers, as the Saints had just then scored their 51st point, equalling their highest ever score.

Rudy moment: There were plenty of nominees, but the winner is Saints wide receiver Lance Moore, who dived and stretched out to break the touchdown plane as a defender was tackling him in mid air.

Orange play of the game: Saints cornerback Jason David seemed to be asleep in the first half, allowing the Packers to open up their passing game. But he rectified his mistakes in the second half and dodged the orange award by plucking two crucial interceptions. Ironically, it was Moore who won the orange play when he lined up as QB and threw a hospital pass that got intercepted.

Extreme fan: There were plenty here—lampshade hat man, several Mexican wrestlers, fans who donned elegant frilly umbrellas that they kept open throughout the game, a Red Indian character who dressed in black and gold, PFUFA member Da Pope, who wore a huge hat and a long white gown. But my favourite was "The Whistle Man." Dressed in full kit, he also brought his Saints helmet along, which he had turned into a giant whistle. His face is painted black and gold and he spent the game whistling loudly. He was incredibly friendly and even let me try on his custom-made hat, which was incredibly heavy.

After the game I met Neal by the French Quarter, and soon we got onto the highway, heading north for St. Louis. We noticed a lot of traffic and 20 minutes later saw the blue flashes of police cars—two cars had crashed into the side concrete wall. The highway was reduced down to one lane, and most people simply slowed down to see what was going on.

Once we were back in the two-lane world there was no traffic for a good 10 minutes, with most cars going above the speed limit. Then oddly and suddenly, a handful of cars in front of me were all suddenly moving at a snail's pace. This was because the SUV at the front of the pack was dangerously swerving from lane to lane. Cars from behind were catching up to us and then hitting the brakes suddenly. The cars in front of me had slowed so as not to hit the swerving driver, until they "went for it" and raced past. In this two-lane road with no hard shoulder as such, just concrete walls about four feet high, I was not confident to overtake this drunk driver. He then swerved to the left and hit the concrete wall with his front bumper, but instead of realising that he may kill himself he just veered back into the road. He must have pinballed himself from wall to wall about five times, each one with more speed and velocity. The last three times his back wheels caught air.

Neal was on the phone to the police telling them what highway we were on. The police told us they knew of the driver and had sent a car. Apparently this driver was the reason for the earlier crash. It sounds terrible, but finally he crashed hard enough into the wall to stop the car. Either that or the driver came to his senses and must have realised he was likely to kill himself, if not others.

Hours into the night, we were running perilously low on gas. I wanted to trust Gippy by heading off the highway into a small town where he was adamant there was a gas station. Neal wasn't as trusting and wanted us to stay on the highway, where there were likely to be gas stations open all night. He also felt that if we did break down, then help would be easier to find on the highway. This was our second conflict.

For some reason I listened to Gippy. He took us through a pretty, small town full of Christmas lights and decorations that looked like something from *Home Alone*. But as quaint as that was, the gas station was very much closed. Shit! So with just three miles left in the tank I was getting concerned; we were driving aimlessly but there in the distance was a flickering light of hope and it was in fact an all-night gas station. We were saved.

Once we arrived in St. Louis the next day, I noticed the huge arch that represents this fair city. Apparently you can walk up the inside of it, which I would have done if we had more time. I knew nothing of this city prior to this trip and I liked what I saw. Parts of the city were rustic but the downtown looked really modern. I met Neal's friends Amy and Gabby, and they let us stay for the night.

We all went out for sushi and in the morning Gabby and Amy made us a wonderful breakfast including wholemeal blueberry pancakes, scrambled eggs, and bacon. This rivalled Emily and Lauren's Orlando breakfast when they made us a salsa omelette. Neal and I were getting spoiled.

The next day we continued north to Chicago. Here I dropped Neal back home to his mother's apartment for his high school's 10-year reunion the next night. I had to miss mine, which was a few weeks prior in Essex.

Karen had asked both Steph and me to get involved with the November "holiday season" edition of *Tailgater Monthly*. Seeing as my Mum is a great cook, she put in one of her recipes. Though of course in the U.K. we do not celebrate

Thanksgiving, Chanukah was coming up and my Mum makes some bad-ass po-tato latkes. Meanwhile Steph's Mum does her own style Christmas Tree Roast Potatoes, and both mothers were proud to see their recipes printed. They even shared the page with famous chef Guy Fieri and his recipe for pepperoni stuff-ing, as well as Poonster's creamy guacamole dip.[15] Steph and I also jointly wrote an article about the London game, which made the final page for that edition.[16] Steph's involvement got her excited for her leg of the trip.

Game 27. NFL Week 13, Tennessee Titans at Detroit Lions, Ford Field

Final Score: 47-10. Home-win record: 18-9. Capacity: 65,000. Attendance: 60,112. Ticket face value: $95—I paid $95 via Ticketmaster. Picture on my ticket: E-ticket. Mascot: "Roary," a lion. Merchandise: Huge fleece-style Lions gloves. Local dish: Detroit-style Coney dogs (made with beef heart), chili, and burgers.

Because of holiday commitments Hans couldn't make this game, so I went to Ford Field on my own, with a spare ticket. Once parked I called Donnie, other-wise known by his PFUFA name, the Yooper Man. He tried to explain where he was parked, but I struggled to hear him and couldn't find him. Frustrated, I quickly ran around the tailgate taking snaps of the wonders that I did find. It was a freezing cold morning but that didn't stop the hard-core Thanksgiving tailgaters at Eastern Market, a secluded concrete square surrounded by warehouses that sell meat, fish, and fruit during the week. On game days, however, the square is packed with Lions-themed buses, vans, cars, and RVs galore.

The Lions had lost every game of the 2008 season, and so the day's real competition was always going to be at Eastern Market, where the tailgaters tried to out-do each other. I had found tailgaters who brought their own hot tub "ap-proved" by Joe Cahn and go by the name of the Tubgaters. The owner was an older chap, and I was fascinated that someone would bring a hot tub, especially in subzero conditions, to the tailgate. Surely having a hot tub in a parking lot of a football stadium can't be the world's most practical idea. I wondered if it is even legal to have an outdoor hot tub in a parking lot? But I was told that you can ap-parently take a mobile hot tub anywhere.

Sadly, few of my questions were answered and all the owner could tell me was that I was "too late to see the strippers" who were apparently in the hot tub just before. Where did he get strippers at 9 a.m. on Thanksgiving morning, I thought.

I was still looking for Donnie, so I hopped into a taxi. My cab driver, a rather vocal woman in her thirties, told me before I got in the taxi that she knew where the street name that Donnie had given me was. Twenty minutes later, she finally admitted to not knowing where she was going. We got back to the spot where she picked me up and then fortunately I spotted Donnie's Lions jersey. She then charged me 10 bucks, my most pointless cab ride ever. I was happy to see Donnie but I had missed PFUFA Titan fan "Lady Titan," who had already gone into the stadium. Donnie went inside for the pre-game, so I raced back to Eastern Market to look for Kevin who runs "Detroit Tailgaters," a tailgate so popular they usually have bands playing on a stage and they are sponsored by a local beer company.

Kevin was cooking up a deep-fried turkey, while most of his party had gone to the game, but there were still about 20 people outside and watching the game on the TV. Like Club 49, they had a bar set up with beer taps and liquor spigots. They were a friendly bunch and the food was great, especially the "All American pumpkin pie." This tailgate party had one thing I had not seen throughout my travels—a foosball table. Kevin had put a little costume on every foosball man: one was dressed as Big Bird and one as a member of the band Kiss.

I knew I wanted to go and see the Lions play on Thanksgiving, a tradition that had been in the league since 1934. In that year, the Lions moved a home Sunday game to Thanksgiving to get more fans to the stadium. It worked so well that they continue to do so. Since 1966 the Cowboys have also hosted a Thanksgiving game every year, and there is also a third game on this day, after the Cowboys, but the host of that gets picked by the NFL each year. I had been to the Lion's old stadium, the Silverdome, back in 2000 for a pre-season game. That stadium, which still exists, is actually larger than the new Ford Field. Most teams in the NFL get larger when they move into new homes, but not the Lions. They scaled down with this move, so that it would be easier for them to sell out and therefore not get blacked out on TV. Once inside I noticed that Ford Field was incredibly plush, with no bad sight lines, and it had a very shallow gradient.

I had two tickets in section #120 that cost $95 each. Even though the Lions had lost every game of the season it was still a sell out. I ended up giving my ticket to Dave, a semidrunk guy whom I met at the tailgate. I would rather give the ticket away than see it go to waste. As we headed to the stadium, and closer to Ford Field, a policeman asked us to dispose of our alcohol. I had not noticed any police at any other tailgates before, and this copper was mainly there to prevent us taking open alcohol from the tailgate area to the stadium. With no trash cans around the cop asked everyone to leave all of our red cups full of alcohol on the hood of his police vehicle, which any minor could have taken. Though God help any of those Lions fans if they were caught by the cop drinking straight from a bottle of beer.

Our seats were in the lower section by the corner of the end zone, and by sheer coincidence Donnie (aka Yooper Man) happened to be sitting just three rows in front of me and had two empty seats next to him, so I spent the rest of the game watching the game with him. I know what you are thinking. All these "sold-out" stadiums and why was I finding empty seats? That would not happen in the Premiership, but as mentioned many fans buy tickets to spend a lot of the time watching the games from several concourses over looking the field.

Donnie has been coming to the Lions so often that he and the beer vendor are on first-name terms.

In front of Donnie sat a chap named Dick. Donnie and Dick used to play for the same high school football team many years ago. They had not seen each other for over 20 years but then in 1975 saw each other at the Silverdome and have been sitting near each other at every home game ever since.

The game might have been one-sided, but the halftime show was one of the best I had seen and certainly the most unique. Hundreds of young ladies from children to adults swarmed the field with huge coloured balls, and sheets of cloth. They performed choreographed moves that really woke up the crowd. The coloured sheets formed huge multicoloured tents from which fireballs came flying out.

During another break there was a Dunkin Donuts race where three donut mascots raced across the field. I had seen this done before using animation on the jumbotrons but never live. This got more cheers than any Lions play in the game.

The Lions played in their throwback uniforms of blue and silver, with a plain silver helmet, but they got crushed by the unbeaten Titans. It was as if the Lions fans wanted to lose every game this season, so at least they could claim to have broken some kind of record (albeit a losing one) this season.

There were some funny fan signs at this game, my favourite being, "Do me a favor and kick me out!" Donnie was sitting near some young fans who spent the whole game in the stadium wearing brown paper bags over their heads.

Rudy moment: The Lions QB, veteran Daunte Culpepper, threw a weak pass to no one, or so he thought, but Titans defensive end Dave Ball was there in a flash, and four strides later was in the end zone for the TD. This is unusual for a lineman, so he celebrated with a big leap.

Orange play of the game: With his team up 27-10 and minutes left, Titans head coach Jeff Fisher threw the red challenge flag. Many fans booed the call and shouted, "We want to go home!" They just couldn't wait until that final whistle.

Extreme fan: Yooper Man's friend Ron, otherwise known as Crackman, wears a hard hat, long socks, and the shorts version of dungarees. In front of us was another PFUFA member who goes by the name of "The Pilgrim" and dresses all in black, much like a Quaker, who tries to bring good luck to the team. There was a man whose face was painted blue, was wearing his Lions shoulder pads over his jersey, and also had chain mail, a crown on, and a stuffed turkey toy on top of his head. He goes by the name the Detroit Lions King. Now he has added not one but two Lions logo tattoos drawn onto his skull! The award, however, goes to Donnie. He lives 350 miles away and has never missed a home game since Thanksgiving 1993.

After the game I saw a bus called the Booty Lounge, which had blacked out windows. I was told that is this where the strippers were, now that it was too cold for them in the hot tub. The man in charge of the bus explained that people come on to "party" but would not tell me any more. He had a seedy look in his eye."It's 20 bucks to get on the bus, but it's Thanksgiving so you can go on for 10 bucks," the man continued. I gave him a naive look suggesting I didn't know what he was talking about. Every other tailgate bus I had seen across the land had let me on for free. I was about to question if this was a tailgate bus at all, even though it clearly wasn't. He told me to pop my head in and if I liked what I saw I could stay for longer. My head peered in and there were several women actually dancing on stripper poles. I was shocked.

Because of the family-like atmosphere at other tailgates I couldn't believe other tailgaters would let this happen, let alone the authorities. Roger Goodell has often expressed his passion to make the game day experience more family friendly.

He even takes young members of his family to games "incognito" several times a year, just to make sure things are all in check. Yet fans like Tunison dislike Goodell's "Disneyfying" of the league. As he explains, "Some of us want cringe-worthy violence, unprintable language, and nudity for miles."[17] I wanted to ask the owner about *his* contribution to the tailgating world and whether he thought his bus was polluting the good family ethos of tailgating, or if he feels like Tunison, whose vision of football "is something cathartic and restorative for people forced to be polite and civilized against their will for 340 days a year," who Tunison feels "need an outlet for low grade anarchy."[18]

Me: So you guys put several stripper poles on this bus, is it well received? Do you ever get in trouble? Where do you get strippers on Thanksgiving day?

Lounge guy: Okay, okay, I'll let you on for eight bucks.

Me: Look, I'm writing about tailgating and I have never seen a stripper bus before at a tailgate. Is this something you see as a good thing? Something for people to get involved with before a game? Or after? Is tailgating more for "adults" in your opinion? Can "party" busses coexist right next to family tailgate buses? And finally, where does your "Booty Lounge" fit within the meaning of life?

Lounge guy: Okay, okay, five bucks and you can stay for twenty minutes.

Me: Ahh, forget it.

The following year while travelling on Jay's tailgating bus, our rule was that everything on the bus had to be donated. When we visited Poonster to see his hat collection, he actually had a spare stripper pole (seriously, who has a spare?) that he donated to the bus. Jay told me that the "stripper pole" is part of the "party" culture, and at tailgates they are mainly used by overweight, drunk middle-aged men. But here in Detroit the stripper poles were used by strippers, and it seems the fans were unfazed by this bus and the talk of strippers. Even Hans, a morally upstanding man who I respect a great deal, later on said nonchalantly, "Oh, that's just the booty bus." Which suggests the environment around Detroit is very laid back about this sort of thing. I would have expected such debauchery at a tailgate in Las Vegas, not Detroit.

After I found my car, I drove to Crystal's father's house for my first-ever Thanksgiving meal. I wasn't able to pick up a nice gift like chocolates or flowers for my hosts, so I gave them a bunch of my trip t-shirts, which I was starting to use as a form of currency.

There was turkey of course, as well as an assortment of vegetables and Hans's own stuffing. They had sweet potato topped with baked marshmallow and something called "monkey bread," which involved dollops of bread, caramel, and cinnamon, and it was excellent. Plus, they had the Cowboys game on.

The family revelled in having me as a guest and were interested in English food and English culture. It was around dessert time when, out of the corner of my eye, I spotted Crystal's father walk into the living room wielding a shotgun. I was a little shocked to see the huge gun. Flashes of bad American stereotyping came racing into my mind.

I was not sure what to say or do, so I just blurted out, "Wow, *all* Americans really *do* have guns, my Mum was right!" Then I put on my Mum's East London cockney accent and said, "Don't go to America, they will SHOOT ya!"

This got a laugh from everyone, which was a big relief for me, and the shotgun was put away. It turns out that Crystal's Dad is a deer hunter, though, with no deer in the front garden I was still confused as to why was he bringing it out.

Her father had several guns and I was asked if I wanted to hold his .44 Magnum, the same gun that Dirty Harry uses. I'm not really into guns, but when in Rome . . . A heavy chunk of metal that can kill instantly was in my right hand while I still had my dessert spoon in the other—a good combo if I wanted to rob a cake shop. I felt more like a rapper than Dirty Harry. No one at the table, even the children, seemed fazed by the gun. My poor Mum jumps under the table watching the series *24* on TV.

The next day, Hans and I took some great pictures by his questmobile, holding each other's signs. Hans told me that I make an extreme face in all of the pictures when at the football games, which I never did consciously. Hans coined it the "Adam Smile."

We worked up our appetite by throwing around the pigskin on Hans's street, just avoiding the neighbours' cars. It was a shame no one was there to see us play and take some snaps. Nothing fills me with more glee than simply throwing and catching a football. Years ago my good friend Rob used to go out with a sporty girl from Ohio. She could zip a football 40 yards with a great tight spiral. It was oddly very sexy. I told my Dad about it. "Maybe you should be looking for guys," he suggested. Thanks, Dad.

Hans threw the ball with the accuracy of a hot Ohio chick, and that's a compliment. He caught every pass, while I was the one apologising for overthrown balls and dropped catches. Having seen 27 games, I had improved some of my skills, such as reverse parking and finding ridiculous NFL merchandise, but improving my football skills at least one inch was not one of them.

I said my good-byes to Hans and his family and hit the road. It was here that I really began to miss Steph more than ever. Maybe it was because I was used to being with Neal on the road and now I was back on my own. Or maybe it's because after so much time with Hans's family I felt a little homesick. I know that Steph and Crystal would really get along. They would have plenty of stories to share about how both Hans and I have put football first instead of our personal relationships.

I picked up Neal in Chicago, and we ventured south through Illinois to St. Louis for our next game. We stopped off in Springfield to meet Neal's friend Ronnie for lunch at Hooters, which is like any other American sports restaurant/bar—it had plenty of TV screens, wings, and "lite" beer. But in Hooters all the waitresses dress in skimpy white t-shirts, little orange shorts, and have "hooters."

Ronnie usually lives out West, but he had moved back home to help his father, who was sadly dying of cancer. Ronnie's Dad is a big football fan, so I gave Ronnie a t-shirt to give to him. "My Dad would love this, it will really cheer him up . . . He might even like to be buried in it." As much as that was a compliment, it took me by complete surprise and I suddenly felt an immense pressure to make all those games printed on the shirt.

Game 28. Week 13, Miami Dolphins at St. Louis Rams, Edward Jones Dome

Final Score: 16-12. Home-win record: 18-10. Capacity: 66,000. Attendance: 61,046. Ticket face value: $45—I paid $45 via Ticketmaster. Picture on my ticket: Picture of Tye Hill, the Rams cornerback. Mascot: None. Merchandise: Rams baseball cap. Local dish: Toasted ravioli, Cajun food, and gumbo.

It was a 9 a.m. start for a 1 p.m. kickoff, and we could already see many away Miami Dolphins fans shocked by the St. Louis cold. I got my game face "airbrushed" on, which was a bad idea. The freezing conditions meant that the paint was also freezing. Plus, the girls doing the spraying had got the colours wrong; they had put turquoise on my face instead of royal blue so now I just looked like an idiot, because as we all know, having air-brushed logos in the correct team colour on one's face is not idiotic but awesome.

We found our way to Tag-A-Long-Toni's tailgate, the wife of PFUFA fan Ram Man. Unfortunately, Ram Man was ill and this was the first Rams game that he had missed in 15 years. He usually wears shoulder pads, jersey, blue-and-yellow makeup (sorry, war paint), and a large custom-made foam Rams hat. Toni's tailgate was tucked behind some old industrial buildings. Inside the large tents it was warm and cozy and filled with 30 of her friends. Toni, a short woman with a permanent smile, is a bundle of energy. She was wearing a pink Rams jersey with "Tag-A-Long-Toni" emblazoned across the back.

Smokey warm BBQ glazed pork steaks were for lunch and I have never even heard of pork being made as a steak. This slab of meat thundered down onto my plate and made my wrist buckle with the weight. Neal and I had to share one piece. It was already almost 10 a.m., and yet knocking back steak and beer was still unusual for my body so early in the morning, despite being to so many tailgates.

Tag-A-Long-Toni then took us to the Bud Light zone, which is the large tent by the stadium that had a live stage and, more importantly, warmth. The radio station 103.3 KLOU was pumping with life. Ram Man had already informed the presenter and DJ, a chap named Smash, about my journey. I was taken to the front and hoisted up on stage. Smash introduced me to 400 Rams fans. I told the crowd that I was 18-9 for home wins, so hopefully I would bring them a home win, and it was cheers all around.

I thought my moment of fame was over, so I stepped down from the stage, but one of the live musicians placed a tambourine in my hand. The band started back up, and I found myself as part of the band while they rocked out. I only took three trumpet lessons when I was younger and certainly never practiced in front of over 400 people. I did a little dance and slammed the tambourine to the beat of the musicians, as the audience egged me on.

After my music career as a tambourine player came to an abrupt end, we headed inside the stadium. The lower section was pretty full but the upper tier still had some empty seats. The greatest show on turf was clearly no longer, despite the efforts made by workhorse running back, Steven Jackson. There were plenty of banners of their Super Bowl–winning players, Kurt Warner and Marshall Faulk, but the team was a shadow of its former self.

The season was already over for the Rams, but because it was a must-win for the Dolphins they had plenty of fans with them. At halftime I went upstairs to meet Tag-A-Long-Toni, who was sitting next to an empty chair. I sat in Ram Man's seat, and Toni actually gave me his PFUFA fan card and his game-day ticket as a souvenir, this was a hardcopy season ticket, which looks much nicer than my plain Ticketmaster print-out ticket. I looked around, and I really would love to have seen what this venue was like in the Kurt Warner and Marshall Faulk days.

Rudy moment: Dolphins RB Ronnie Brown went in for the close-range TD after bouncing off several Rams linemen.

Orange play of the game: The Rams could have won the game with a late TD, but their QB, Mark Bulger, threw a desperate ball that was intercepted, and the game was over.

Extreme fan: I'm sure it would have been Ram Man had he have been well enough, yet this award goes to his wife, Tag-A-Long-Toni.

That evening Neal and I drove a thousand miles without a hotel stop, all night, all the way to Houston. We only stopped twice. First, to watch the Bears play the Vikings on Sunday night football in a bar, but the Bears were sadly beaten, mainly because of a 99-yard TD that was caught by guess who? Pesky Bernard Berrian. Second was to find a hotel just to have a shower in. The man behind the desk at the hotel looked a little concerned with us two men demanding a room for just an hour in the middle of the day.

Game 29. NFL Week 13, Jacksonville Jaguars at Houston Texans, Reliant Stadium

Final Score: 17-30. Home-win record: 19-10. Capacity: 71,054. Attendance: 70,809. Ticket face value: $60—I paid $60 from Joe Texan. Picture on my ticket: Picture of Mario Williams. Mascot: "Toro," a dark blue bull. Merchandise: Red Texan towel, which was the free giveaway, but in their shop there was an abundance of ridiculous items, such as huge Texans slippers. Local dish: All BBQ, pork brisket, and fowl.

As soon as we stepped into the Platinum Tailgate at the Reliant Stadium lot, you could see why they called it platinum. This is the prime spot for Texas tailgating, where they like to do things on the large scale. To our left was the Raging Bull tailgate party. This party takes up a massive space, with a huge metal grill that can accommodate four chefs. Around 200 people were dancing and cheering as they watched Glenn "Sweet" Miller stand with a microphone on the roof of the Raging Bull tailgate bus. In this frenzy Glenn read out my sign and the crowd cheered.

For Glenn, "every game day is like Christmas morning." Glenn doesn't don the Santa suit, but his Texans red jersey is good enough, and just like Santa Claus he dishes out presents, but these are all in the form of mouth-watering delights for anyone who comes by. "Come one, come all" is his motto. His monstrous tailgate takes up to 36 parking spaces and is like an NFL-themed Santa's grotto. He and his team cook "no less than 600 pounds of meat each game: wild game, such as deer, elk, alligator, as well as fish, shrimp, lobster, filets, rib eyes, pork loin, briskets, ribs, chicken, boudain, kabobs, and bacon wrapped and stuffed with everything. The list is endless." He creates a massive quadrangle for fans to mingle in the space where 36 cars should be parked. He also has my favourite tailgating definition: "The Five Fs. Family, Friends, Football, Food, and Fun," and rather modestly he has some great respect for the Packers fans who he says are "second to no one. [They are] passionate, generous people who live and die for that team. They are a very unique situation that will *never* be duplicated ever again in any sport, anywhere." Well, these Texans fans were right up with the Packers fans.

I then turned around, and a woman with striking red hair called Stephanie (Texans chick) grabbed me and pulled me towards her tailgate. Stephanie and her "lone spot tailgater" crew sprayed my hair red in seconds. I was then given a whole lobster that they brought in all the way from Maine, just for me. The crowd was fun and the party atmosphere was as good as I have experienced anywhere else. Then I went for the steak, which was delicious, and everyone's cameras never stopped snapping.

Stephanie then took us over to the Blue Crew tailgate. I met up with PFUFA fans Texas Ted and Joe Texan, and I had sadly missed them breaking their piñata, but my old friend Jeff, who drove in from Austin just to see me, had seen it and he was buzzing with excitement. Although Jeff isn't a football fan, he couldn't believe the energy at the Texans tailgate.

We tucked into the delicious and huge spread from the Blue Crew, and by the time dessert was being served, Jeff was bowled over and understood instantly why I was doing this trip. He said, "With football (gridiron) as one of America's national pastimes, it's a true tragedy that a Brit had to bring me to my first NFL game. I was impressed with the amount of fanfare that went into just a normal game. All joking aside, everything about the Texans experience seemed, well, professional. Bright lights, huge crowd, and the infamous NFL tailgating. I'd certainly go back, even if I just sat in the parking lot cheering on the team with the awesome and extremely friendly fans who welcomed us to their tents and RVs with open arms, simply because we showed up to support their team."

I was surprised that no one had told me just how great the Texan tailgate is. Maybe it is because they are the newest team in the NFL. The Houston Oilers played here until 1997 when they moved to Tennessee, and the Houston faithful had to wait until 2002 to get a pro team back. Either way, this Texan's tailgate has to be in the top three tailgates across the league, and their fans have been continually supportive, bending over backwards for me to return there. Joe Texan has offered to put up in his house, get me tickets, and pick me up from the airport anytime I want to join him there for a game!

Joe Texan and Texas Ted sold me two tickets in their famous "Bull Pen" section where all the hard-core Texan fans sit behind one of the end zones. Yeee-Haaa!

The atmosphere inside the stadium was powerful. The Texans fans were up for a good time, as this was their first MNF game in 14 years and it didn't matter that they or their opponents, the Jaguars, were both out of the playoff hunt. Reliant Stadium is magnificent, and similar in shape and style to the Cardinals' stadium. I wasn't sure what to expect from this expansion team, but I was blown away by the passion of the fans who did not stop chanting throughout. Though I wasn't too sure about the Texan's decision to play in red pants (I can't ever use the word "pants" because in the U.K. it means underwear) and jerseys, they looked like they were playing in their pyjamas. The Texans were winning easily but stayed loud and proud. With the hairs on the back of my neck continually standing on end and my heart pumping, this was the kind of experience that makes me want to go back to more and more NFL games.

Rudy moment: Texans receiver Andre "The Giant" Johnson caught the ball with his back facing the goal, spun around his defender, and raced to the corner.

His body went out of bounds, but he kept his outstretched arm holding onto the ball in bounds for a TD score.

Orange play of the game: Jags QB David Garrard's pass was deflected back off someone's helmet, which he then caught himself. Then he got tackled, making it a loss of 6 yards. That was orange-worthy enough on its own, yet he topped this play when he was in the opponent's red zone. After the snap he lost his balance, clumsily fell to the ground, got up, and, while getting tackled, threw a bad pass.

Extreme fan: There was an abundance of extreme fans, but in the end it was a tie between Joe Texan, with his huge voodoo-like red-and-blue top hat and his friend Ted, aka Bull Pen Hardhat, with his signed hard hat and painted red beard.

After I stayed with Jeff for the night, he and his wife took us out for fish tacos for breakfast and gourmet sandwiches for lunch, before we headed back east.

After a long drive we were getting close to Charlotte. Risalyn had told us that she and her star NFL boyfriend, DeAngelo Williams, were going to a basketball game that night. Neal loves a bit of basketball so we checked out the NBA schedule and saw that the Charlotte Bobcats were playing at home.

We went to the game, but it turned out that Risalyn and DeAngelo were not at this game at all but a high school basketball game. I was surprised they picked high school over the pro league. That's like David Beckham turning up to watch me play tennis for my school when he has box seats at Wimbledon.

The next morning we drove to the Charlotte airport, leaving the car there for a few days while we flew up to Toronto. I stayed with my old friend Livy who now works in PR. Before we could catch up on old stories, she was e-mailing a press release to half of Canada about my trip. The next day I had something like three or four radio interviews, plus two TV interviews.

Game 30. NFL Week 14, Miami Dolphins at Buffalo Bills, Rogers Skydome, Toronto

Final Score: 16-3. Home-win record: 20-10. Capacity: 54,000. Attendance: 52,134. Ticket face value: $70—I paid $85 (Canadian dollars) via StubHub. Photo on my ticket: Animated drawing of Rogers Stadium, the CN tower, a maple leaf, and the Bills logo. Local dish: Poutine (fries topped with cheese curd and gravy).

My first stop on game day was to meet the wonderful guys from The Ultimate Sports road trip, Peter Farrell and Andrew Kulyk from Buffalo, who have seen a live game at every stadium across all four of the major American sports. Their quest has taken them years to complete. They rate everything from each franchise, including the stadiums, the food, and the fans. They continue their sports trips, checking out newly built stadiums.

They were also with their longtime friend, Gary, who goes to an alarming amount of sporting events in the year, around the 300 mark. I could have chatted with these guys for hours. Peter and Andrew have passion for the sport on the field but, like myself, realise that the fan's experience percolates through the whole franchise, from the management and stadium all the way to the dress code of the staff, and not just the play on the field. Andrew wrote in his blog about the day:

> Sorry if this sounds arrogant or snooty, but we road trippers are a special fraternity, and we applaud Adam for making the sacrifice and taking the trouble to do such an ambitious project. We know what it's like, the good and the bad, and once finished, he will have made new friends and contacts and great memories which will sustain him for the rest of his life.[19]

We said our good-byes and I walked down the cold downtown Toronto street. I passed a George Foreman stand giving out free burgers, which warmed me up quickly. I passed Kenny from Buffalo on the street, though sadly he was not going to do his famous ketchup tailgate show today.

Like London, there was no real tailgating. Canada, like the U.K., does not allow open BBQ flames, plus there is little parking around Rogers Skydome. The fan zone was open to all who were over age 19 and no "tailgate" or game-day ticket was needed. Physically it was probably about the same size as the London fan zone. There were two stages, one for a band and giveaways, the other for interviews. Sure there was a little bit of a line up for food, but it was not as nearly congested and frustrating as London, partly because this tailgate was downtown where there were lots of local bars for people to stay warm in.

The tailgate was about 60 percent Bills fans, 30 percent Dolphins fans, and the rest were just NFL fans, plus a few army people, several of whom were sitting on Ski-doos. NFL games in London has police on horseback, Toronto has the army on Ski-doos.

On the stage they had a small competition to see who had come the furthest to be here today. I kept calling out my home city of London, but it was falling on deaf ears and I was not picked. Maybe he thought I meant London, Ontario, which is only a couple of hours away. I screamed "England" but it was too late. They had their winner from Venezuela, and he won a signed Bills helmet.

I took Livy to the game while Neal checked out the Toronto Raptors basketball game with a friend. I left the ticket buying until the last minute via StubHub. Many of the tailgaters I met in Buffalo were not coming up to Canada for this game. Some felt the ticket prices were far too expensive, while others stayed behind for more political reasons. If the game becomes a success up in Toronto, then the worry for Bills fans in Buffalo is that the team may move up to Canada. The Bills would be Canada's team, giving them a massive fan base, but inevitably pissing off their loyal fans in Western New York.

I had seen a Toronto Blue Jays baseball game at Skydome in 2000 and at the time would have laughed at you if you told me I would be returning eight years later to see an NFL regular-season game there. The Bills fans wanted the roof open so they could take advantage of their famous "cold-weather" advantage against the warm-weather Dolphins, but after braving the snow in Buffalo, I really wanted the roof to remain closed, which thankfully it was.

Inside the stadium, I noticed it was a steep gradient down to the field. We sat with a mixture of Dolphins and Bills fans, but the noise did not quite feel like a Bills home game, and maybe that was in part because the football being played was not great by either team.

In the stadium they sold poutine, which is a great Canadian dish, consisting of fries, cheese curds, and gravy. At the halftime break the Syracuse University marching band came onto the field and strutted their stuff.

Rudy moment: The Bills were down 13-3 and needed to score. The Bills QB, J. P. Losman, sent up a high, looping ball. The Dolphin's CB read it beautifully, turned, and jumped first, intercepting the ball.

Orange play of the game: The Bills QB backpeddled back so much while under pressure from blitzers that when he was sacked he was lucky not to give away a safety.

Extreme fan: One person was dressed like an ape. Several Bills fans came without shirts. Kenny's friend dressed up like a Bills super hero, with shorts, socks, a belt with a B on it, and a massive Bills-type furry hat. One fan dressed like an actual Dolphin mascot—he even brought the furry suit and a dolphin mask that covered his whole head. The award, however, goes to Short Michelle of the 2Michelles, whom I saw at the tailgate. Tall Michelle wasn't at this game, otherwise they would have shared the award.

The next morning Neal flew back to Chicago to spend some time with his mother, while I flew back to Charlotte and awaited Steph's arrival for the fourth quarter.

8

Fourth Quarter:
The Adam and Steph Trip

The day I landed in Charlotte was my two-year anniversary with Steph. For our first-year anniversary, I took her to Milan. This time I stepped up the romantic stakes by taking her to the mouth-watering battle between the Carolina Panthers and the Tampa Bay Buccaneers on Monday Night Football. I tried to get an anniversary message on the jumbotron, but sadly the Panthers wanted over a week's notice in order to do it, and I was too late.

I could not find a nice hotel downtown for the big Monday night game, but I managed to get a room at a Days Inn a few miles away. I know how much Steph loves her hot tubs, so I got a room with a jacuzzi. There is no end to my romantic charms! When I got to the room I was expecting the jacuzzi to be in the bathroom—nope, not in this classy establishment. They plonked it right next to the bed.

Steph's domestic flight from NYC was delayed getting into Charlotte, which was frustrating. Waiting for her to land at the airport was eating into precious tailgating time. When I saw Steph, she looked great, and I had far less nerves than when I came back for the London game. I probably didn't show much love, because I so was focused on rushing her to the car and the tailgate. I really wanted Steph to enjoy her first real American tailgate, and I was getting angry that we were missing it.

Game 31. NFL Week 14, Tampa Bay Buccaneers at Carolina Panthers, Bank of America Stadium
Final Score: 23-38. Home-win record: 21-10. Capacity: 73,504. Attendance: 74,113. Ticket face value: $58—I paid $58 via Ticketmaster. Picture

on my ticket: E-ticket. Merchandise: Panthers fuzzy dice. Local dish: BBQ ribs and brisket with a sop sauce.

We only had an hour to tailgate before kickoff. We struggled to find tailgater Panther Dano and his Panther Fanz tailgating party, which once hosted a tailgate for over 250 away Ravens fans. Apparently they tailgate in Lot B, but none of the police were being very informative and guiding us in their direction.

Yet I was still committed to finding us a tailgater. I felt like I was starting my trip all over again when I was going up to tailgaters cold turkey. Because I had seen so many fan-owned, NFL-themed vehicles at all the games, I had become desensitized to the extremity of the tailgating rigs. Steph, however, was experiencing all of it for the first time and was amazed at the themed buses and grills on display.

We found some TV tailgaters, which was perfect considering it was nearing kickoff. Bryana and her family could not have been more welcoming. They even apologised that they were running out of food, even though they had no clue who we were. Bryana and her husband cooked us up tri-tip steak that was succulent and rich in taste. She also made ribs that were equally as good. Not a bad anniversary meal. Steph was amazed and shocked by the size of their grill and their hospitality.

En route to the stadium we passed a band playing in a tent nearby. Unlike other tailgates I had passed, this one had a hanging chandelier and carpets, making it more like someone's living room. There was a Panthers logo that shone brightly via projector onto a huge wall behind one of the car parks, and the large statue of a panther outside was decorated in Christmas attire.

We made our way into the stadium. The tickets were on the 20-yard line but right at the very top. The game was a sell out due to the magnitude of the MNF game. Both the Bucs and the Panthers were sitting pretty atop of the NFC South division, both with a 9-3 record. The game had just kicked off as we climbed up high to our seats. Once I got my breath back I asked my neighbour if he was a season ticketholder. He said they were sitting in his friend's seats as he can only take the high stairs one game per year. What a game to choose!

Steph began noticing a few stadium oddities. Inside the concession area the fridge that stored cold drinks had a sign that read, "wet your whistle," which made us giggle. Sir Purr, the Panther's mascot, was wearing a white jacket that read, "victory shag dance." Steph and I had no clue what else "shag" meant other than a British term for sex or a deep, plush 1970s carpet. We laughed that the mascot might perform a "victory sex dance." Later I found out that "shag" is a dance native to the Carolinas. We also noticed the sounds of a wild jungle cat attacking someone, every time the Panthers got a first down.

This game was the most important game of the trip for two reasons. First, of all the games on the trip, this one turned out to have the most playoff implications. The winning NFL team would secure a playoff position and have a better chance to bypass the wildcard round. Second, it had relationship implications. It was Steph's first NFL game in the States and our second anniversary, and I needed her to have a good time. If the tailgate, game, or atmosphere could win her over, she would understand the trip and me much more. I hoped that if she enjoyed the experience, then it would be Steph and me securing our own "playoff" positions afterwards, and hopefully, I could perform for her my own "victory shag dance."

NFLUK pundits Neil Reynolds and Keith Webster have used similar football tests to prove if their partners were the loves of their lives. Reynolds wrote that NFL games "formed a crucial and integral part of my honeymoon in Florida. A week later, my wife and I drove about eight hours in one day for a round trip to Dolphin Stadium."[1] Webster wrote, "The first American football game I ever saw in the flesh and it also confirmed I would one day marry my girlfriend. If she came out with me then on the sort of night Noah built the Ark for, she was in it for the long haul."[2]

Thankfully it turned out to be one of the best games of the season. The lead changed hands with nearly every possession, and the game went right down to the wire. DeAngelo Williams broke the Panthers' franchise record for the most TDs scored in a single season, and he still had not fumbled all season long. With 301 combined rushing yards, the "smash and dash" pairing of Williams and Jonathan Stewart set a new Panthers franchise rushing record, with both players going over the 100-yard mark and both scoring two TDs each.

But did Steph enjoy it? She found the game a little confusing and hard to follow at times, probably not helped by how high up our seats were, or how cold the temperature was. Thankfully the halftime show had a multitude of massive fuzzy mascots taking to the field to play a game of tackle football, which sent Steph into a flurry of giggles for the rest of the night. I know the Panthers and Bucs players worked extremely hard to impress Steph with their athletic ability, high-octane running, and passion, but in the end it was the mascots that truly saved my relationship and the trip.

Rudy moment: Bucs receiver Antonio Bryant found a way to grab an ambitious pass. It looked too low and too wide, but Bryant was fully outstretched and somehow got to the ball. I was too far away to even believe he caught the ball. It didn't look possible and I was shocked, as were the fans around me, that he had made the one-handed catch. All Steph remembers about the game is the mascots.

Orange play of the game: Although veteran defensive back Ronde Barber of the Bucs got an interception, he simply got smacked around on two separate plays by Williams and Stewart, who both slammed him to the ground with their stiff arms.

Extreme fan: We found PFUFA member Cat Man. He wears a bright blue wig like that of those old troll dolls, dyes his beard blue, and has a mini helmet for every NFL team around his neck. He wears a cloak, and to top it off, he has his very *own* bobblehead doll. Despite this, the award has to go to Risalyn, DeAngelo Williams's girlfriend who "hooked us up" big time!

After the game Risalyn asked us to come and meet her by one of the concessions. She was easy to spot because she had a sign that read, "We love DeAngelo." Risalyn is energetic, humorous, and a pure fan. In fact I have seen TV sports anchors see her in the crowd and tell the audience what a great DeAngelo fan she is, not knowing that she is the record-setting running back's girlfriend.

Risalyn walked us into the plush player's lounge, where several people were congregating. I did not know what to expect. I didn't really know what to do with myself. I saw large men in casual clothes coming in through another door, and I couldn't tell who was who, as none of them had their jerseys or numbers on. Risalyn grabbed my arm and told me to have my picture with two large strangers. She was getting excited for me, but I felt slightly embarrassed because I did not know who these guys were. As it turns out, I was sandwiched between two great linebackers: Panthers' captain Jon "The Beast" Beason and Thomas Davis, leaving me in the middle to form a triple-headed ferocious linebacking core.

I then spotted the huge Maake Kemoeatu, and while he signed my hoodie I asked him to thank his brother for the Pittsburgh tickets he gave me. Risalyn was still excited for me and wanted me to meet everyone. There were only a few other "fans" in the room as it was mostly family and friends and I didn't want to tread on peoples' toes. The players were meeting their families, and the last thing they probably wanted was a star-struck Brit asking for autographs.

"I'm pretty sure *he* is English," Risalyn tugged my arm and pushed me towards a smartly dressed man. Normally I don't like it when Americans try to find me other English people to talk to, assuming that we English people all like each other. In fact I rather self-indulgently like being the only Brit in a room full of Americans; however, in this case I'm pleased she did.

Rhys Lloyd was dressed like an Italian soccer player, decked out to the nines in a fine-tailored grey suit with slicked back hair. Nearly every other player was wearing casual attire and Rhys looked like a movie star. "He is definitely *not* American," Risalyn added. It turns out Rhys is the Panthers' kicker and hails from Dover in South England. He told me of his love for soccer and talked to me about his favourite soccer team, Chelsea FC. I couldn't believe I was talking with an NFL starter, especially one who was more interested in soccer than football.

Rhys told me that he mainly only does the kickoffs. He can really belt the hell out of the ball, and he was really proud that five of his kickoffs that season had gone through the uprights. That's an 80-yard kick! He told me he had to make a tackle in the game that night, something he doesn't particularly like doing. Other than having to make the odd football tackle, to me his life sounds perfect.

I asked Rhys how the sporting life differs in the U.S. Amongst the many things he expressed, one was that as a player he has the power to get security to remove an offensive fan, no questions asked. Granted, the fans in the NFL are usually physically further from the players on the sidelines than at soccer games, but it is good to see that the NFL gives that power to the players. Rhys told me he can do this even when he is playing at an away game.

I couldn't believe how open and interested Rhys was. Surely he had family and friends to see, but we kept chatting away for at least 20 minutes. I missed a whole handful of Panthers players in the meantime, but it didn't matter because I had moved from a wide-eyed fan to actually having an adult conversation with an NFL player. I would like to think that Rhys enjoyed talking to me as much as I enjoyed talking to him.

I then felt a tap on my shoulder. I turned around and instantly recognised the record-breaking man himself by his iconic dreadlocks and cheeky smile. Although small in height, DeAngelo Williams has a large presence, especially when you have just seen the man power for nearly 200 yards, making the usual ferocious Tampa D look like a flag football team.

"My girlfriend told me about your trip, these are for you," DeAngelo said looking up at me. All of that hard work moving from boy to man had snapped back and I was a giggling child again. I was at a loss for words as DeAngelo handed me his game-day boots, already signed! Not a new pair of boots, but his actual game-day boots! I was speechless and stunned that he had signed them and given them to *me*! The boots that he broke an NFL record in. Now they belong to me! It was a magical moment that I will never forget. They now live in a clear plastic box, protecting the hallowed boots, the Bank of America stadium soil, and his signature in silver.

After 30 minutes, many of the players and families had left and I was still in a state of shock. I wasn't sure what to do or where to go. Just like at Soldier Field in the summer, I could have just remained there all night in awe.

Up to this point the only anniversary "sweet nothings" Steph had received were: "I have DeAngelo's game-day boots, signed! He signed them, his game-day boots! Signed!" She had to pat me on the arm to calm me down, as if I were an overexcited small dog. To top it off, someone asked us if we wanted a ride out of the stadium on the golf cart—a journey that is as magical as riding a gondola in the canals of Venice, or in a horse-drawn carriage in Central Park, though I'm pretty sure Steph didn't feel quite the same.

After the amazing game we got lost looking for the car, which was happening more frequently than I'd like to admit. We had walked past a brick building called the Dog House, where there was a huge tailgate party before the game and where a local radio station beams out game-day information on the Panthers. Steph, a dog lover, was intrigued. She suddenly got excited because she found her prized piece of merchandise in the nearby bushes: a larger-than-life cardboard cutout of a Jack Russell dog. Steph has two Jack Russells at home and she simply was over the moon with this find. This was our best anniversary yet!

So at 1 a.m., we were meandering through the derelict streets and buildings looking for our car. I was holding an NFL star's game-day boots, while Steph clasped her larger-than-life cardboard cutout of a dog. That's when we found a man named Eric, who was still tailgating outside his RV, and he asked us to join him inside. It was the first time Steph had been on an RV, and she was impressed at how comfortable they are. I was thinking that perhaps Steph would like to live on an RV like Joe Cahn, and maybe go and see more football year after year? I know, it's wishful thinking.

Eric gave us some late-night snacks (venison sausage peppered with cream cheese), and we stayed there for another hour before he drove us to the abandoned buildings where we found our car. He was so impressed by DeAngelo's boots that he said he would swap me anything on his RV for them. Of course, I declined.

In the first half of the trip I did little other than go to games and write. With Neal we met up with plenty of his friends, but on the whole I focused on travelling and football. But because Steph had not seen much of the States and because she took a whole month off work to be here, I really wanted her to have a good time and for us make more of a holiday of the rest of trip, even though there were still plenty of games, travelling, and some brutal winter weather ahead of us.

Because Neal is over 25, it only cost me $2 per day for him to be insured to drive my rental car. But as Steph was only 21 at the time, the rental car folks wanted $40 per day for her to drive the car. So I was back to driving full time, and that was a bit of a shock to my system.

That night Steph was very impressed with the jacuzzi, and that's when we had our very own "wildcard" round. The next day we spent some time in the quaint city of Charlotte, before heading north to Chicago.

The day before my first home Bears game we stopped somewhere in Tennessee for lunch. I had a phone interview with Chicago-based radio station, 670 The Score. I blurted out the details of my trip and I was quickly off the air, but I could still hear the live feed through the phone. They told their viewers they did not believe I was a Bears fan. I was a little disgruntled. Of all the media outlets in all the NFL cities, I would have thought the Chicago-based ones would be on my side.

That night we stayed with Neal's mother, Stellie, and although Steph was now with me on the trip, I simply had to take Neal to the Bears game. I was extremely excited to be going to my first home Bears game in Chicago. Steph went shopping with the 20 percent discount Macy's card that Traci had given her, and trust me—she had a great time.

Game 32. NFL Week 15, New Orleans Saints at Chicago Bears, Soldier Field

Final Score: 24-27. Home-win record: 22-10. Capacity: 61,500. Attendance: 61,692. Ticket face value: $68—I paid $150 for two via "Bearman." Picture *on my ticket: Picture of Devin Hester. Mascot: "Staley Da Bear," a Bear named after the Chicago Bears' original name, Decatur Staleys. Merchandise: Bears wristband, earwarmers, cushion, scarf, and gloves. The freebie was a Bears mouse mat. Local dish: Italian beef sandwich, polish sausage, and deep-dish pizza.*

In Chicago, 31st Street is where much of the great Bears tailgating takes place. We got down there early, and our first stop was with PFUFA fan Don the Bear-man. He had two tickets for Neal and me at $150 for the pair in the north end zone, which was great as StubHub was coming in at $100 for one nosebleed seat. He was with his friends, who had some great Bears goodies for Neal and me, including Bears scarves and gloves.

Don took us over to another tailgate where everyone takes a shot of "whatever" from a full bar attached to the back of a Bear van. One fan on the van had actually taped together a tower of beer cans. This is his "wizard staff." For every can of beer you drink, you tape each can on top of the last. When the staff reaches your actual height, you stop adding cans because the "wizard staff" has now reached your "wizard height." The drinking doesn't stop there, however, as you just create another staff.

Back at Don's tailgating tent, we warmed ourselves up with their gas heaters, which made the tent feel like we were in Florida. They cooked us up some great ribs, though before we knew it, it was time to make our way to "Da Bus," where Timmy was waiting for us.

Timmy is a really nice, energetic guy, who has only missed three home games in the last 26 seasons, which is quite the feat considering he lives in Texas! Timmy is superbly passionate about his bus and he gave me a great tour. Da Bus is a converted 1974 school bus, painted navy and orange, which has been totally gutted. There is green astro turf on the floor and 10-yard markers on the ceiling from goal line to goal line. At the 30-yard line there is Walter Payton's number, 34. Several windows have ex-Bears names and numbers on the window panel, all of which are Hall of Fame Bears players. "You need to get in [the hall of fame] to get on," Timmy proudly told me. Although Da Bus has no flat-screen TV or satellite, it has something better—a plethora of ex-Bears who have signed it. Over 40 Bears players spanning seven decades have come onto Da Bus and left their signature. On the front of the bus is the Bears hall of fame "end zone" section, including Bears legends such as Dick Butkus and Mike Ditka. Towards the back are the more contemporary signatures, which include Brian Urlacher, Charles Tillman, Lance Briggs, and Robbie Gould. It was like my dream bedroom!

Timmy told me many Bears players "come on board a lot of times, their families will come here, instead of being all stuffed up in the suites, they come out here because they enjoy the food and the camaraderie that goes along with tailgating . . . It's not about us, but about tailgating."

"Rumor has it," Timmy continues, "that the bus was in a junkyard in the '80s when someone from the Chicago police won it in a card game and then turned it into 'Da Bus' in 1990." Ten years later they passed the keys over to Timmy because of his passion for tailgating and for the team, and they knew it would be in good hands. In its 20 years, Da Bus has served over 5,000 tailgaters!

Timmy was honoured to be solely responsible for this Chicago icon and feels it is his duty to continue its legacy. Da Bus rolls out at other events too, like the St. Patrick's Day Parade, and it has become *the* tailgate icon of Chicago. On game day Timmy is up at 5 a.m. He spends the day before preparing all the food. He doesn't stop cooking, and ironically, he barely eats anything at all. He usually winds up having a sandwich in the stadium.

Like Dog Nut Dan, Timmy has won one of Jay and Karen's competitions, and his "Da Bears Bus Beef" recipe sits proudly in their book. Karen had told me that many of the tailgaters she knows have a "seven-year itch" before burning out. Timmy has broken well through that barrier and doesn't look like slowing down, though some of his crew have come and gone over the years.

The following year, Timmy and his tailgating team took on Buffalo's tailgating team, "Conklin's Tailgate bar and grill" and their bus "Illegal motion," in the pilot episode of *Tailgate Warriors*. In two hours both groups had to create an appetizer, two mains, two side dishes, and a dessert. Timmy, with his custom-built grills made by Bob the Bus Doctor, was victorious.

Timmy used to be able to take his bus right near Soldier Field, which is situated in a beautiful park between Michigan Avenue and the lakefront, just south of downtown. The area is stunning, with numerous galleries and museums, but now Da Bus and other tailgaters have been forced further south into a derelict car park (31st Street), and now Bears tailgaters are not allowed to be in the lots during the game at Soldier Field. This has angered the Chicago tailgate nation, and other teams have been dealt a similar blow.

Tailgating is such a tradition now and so synonymous with football that if NFL teams did charge for food and drink in the lots or push away the tailgaters, then they could end up losing their fans, and the tailgaters would just park further and further away anyways. Timmy makes the point that although his tailgate has been curbed, ironically where he sits in club level of Soldier Field, the bars are open two hours before each game and two hours after it. "That is seven hours or so of total access to any kind of drink you want."[3]

Pushing the "drinking" fan away from the stadiums was used in the U.K. to push away soccer hooligans. Alan, the infamous Chelsea hooligan, rather philosophically asked that "if football violence doesn't take place in the stadium, is it even football violence?"[4] My worry is that tailgaters will be pushed so far away that it ceases to be tailgating. Lamm is of the opinion that "grilling and socializing in a parking lot two miles away from the stadium is not true tailgating." Proximity to the stadium is crucial for Lamm and many other tailgaters. Otherwise, it is just urban camping.

To create real change, Lamm told me he feels it is up to the "tailgaters to police themselves and reel in those tailgaters that get out of hand." Timmy told the *Chicago Tribune* newspaper that he usually "stops at fourteen other tailgate parties to ask them to clean up after themselves."[5]

Back to the tailgate, and right on time a lovely chap named Jesper arrived as planned with a black London Taxi, exactly like the one my Dad drives. Seeing this made me feel right at home. Some months prior to the trip, Jesper, whose old firm at the time owned several London black taxis, found out about my trip because he read my interview on Canalstreetchronicles.com, where I had told Dave that I would love to do the trip in a London black taxi. Jesper initially wanted to give me a taxi for the whole trip, but the vehicle would not have been able to handle the long distances on the highways, plus if I had broken down, getting parts would have been really difficult. So we decided that the taxi would simply come along to the Chicago tailgate.

This taxi was even more special because it was literally the same vehicle that British writer (and non-gridiron fan) Stephen Fry had used when driving across America for his book and TV show. He broke down three times, but unlike myself he didn't have a tight football schedule to adhere to. I was impressed that even the steering wheel was on the American side.

Jesper threw me the keys, and with Neal in the back I drove this bad boy all the way round the tailgate lot. The Chicago fans came by and loved it. If I ever move to America, I will buy myself one of these and use it as my tailgating vehicle!

When we got back to Timmy, a journalist named Sarah Spain, from Mouthpiece Sports, had just arrived. MPS is a Chicago-based sports website whose main focus is showing the fans "athletes like you've never seen them before—off the field, off the court, when they're just like you and me."[6] Sarah Spain is their wisecracking, Bears-loving reporter who arrived wearing a Walter Payton jersey. We conducted most of the interview in the back of the taxi, which instantly became my favourite interview. I did not know of Sarah's dry sense of humour and sarcastic interviewing style beforehand, but her sexual puns and quick-fire wit quickly turned the interview into something unique and fun. I later found an online clip of her interviewing then Bears safety Chris Harris, when she was trying out to be a Bears wide receiver: "You cover me . . . and I can just juke you silly out of your pants, don't read into that."[7]

Sarah had read my blog (it was nice to hear that *someone* was reading it), and her questions about my trip were very specific. When she asked me about Steph, I naturally said that Steph is a "keeper." Sarah's response was, "Well it's pretty obvious *she's* a keeper . . . the question whether you're a keeper after leaving her behind after months at a time is a little bit more important, I think." Errr, thanks, Sarah.

Sarah too has done something drastic in the art of seeing her beloved team. Sarah wanted a Super Bowl ticket when the Bears made it there in 2006. So she put herself online as a "date for the Super Bowl." Turns out, not only did she get to go but she managed to take three friends with her. Being a guy, I wasn't sure I'd get the same kind of response if I tried the same tactic.

While Sarah was interviewing Timmy on Da Bus, Steph joined us, having caught a taxi from downtown. In Steph's words:

It didn't take long for the cab driver (who was female and of a similar nature to Queen Latifah) to realise that I was English and her excitement for me as a young girl let loose in Chicago was immediate. Barely stopping for breath, she planned my day: "Where am I taking you? Oh girl, you gonna love this city . . . I'll just drop you right at the Michigan Mile and you gonna love it . . ." It was much to her dismay that I had to interrupt her with the location that I read from my piece of crumpled paper: 31st Street McCormick Place Lot B. A screech on the breaks and a swift head movement to the back passenger seat ensued. "Girrrrl? You be trippin?" "Erm. No, ma'am, I am not 'tripping.' Well you see I'm in Chicago 'cos my boyfriend's doing this trip and . . ." "Oh, your boyfriend. Uh-huh, is that so? Well, he better be worth it honey 'cos I ain't dropping you at some *parking* lot in the freezing cold for no time waster." Even a Chicagoan questioned why on earth anyone would want to hang out in a car park on a freezing cold night in the windy city.

Steph, Neal, and myself visited a few other tailgates before it was nearing game time. Jesper insisted on dropping Neal and me off at Soldier Field before driving Steph to the shops. Being driven in a black London taxi to Soldier Field while looking out onto Lake Michigan was magical and life felt very good.

We hopped out of the cab, and as I was fiddling with the long lens on my camera, I slipped on some ice. The lens shot up and smacked me square into the lip. Blood came out and Neal cackled with laughter before randomly spotting his cousin, who was working outside the stadium helping people sign into the corporate club. I must have looked like a fool as I spoke to her with my swollen and bloody lip. She then gave Neal and me each $10 worth of "Bear vouchers." I thanked her and then we rushed into one of the greatest rooms on the planet, the Bears gift shop. Although I could have spent a small fortune, I had to hold back. In the end I bought a Bears seat cushion (so no more cold bum for me), as well as a game-day programme and the Bears 2008 yearbook.

Before the trip had started, Chicagobears.com had an online competition looking for the five biggest Bears fans. I submitted my trip story and was told I had made the top five. Like an actor looking for his first review, I hurriedly flicked through the thick magazine. Bang, there I was on page 35. I was so proud to actually be in the Chicago Bears Yearbook. The strains of the trip all started to look worth it. I wanted to call up the sportscasters on 670 The Score right then and there and prove to them what a huge Bears fan I am.

Soldier Field has the smallest capacity of the NFL stadiums, but with its rocking noise, it didn't feel the smallest. We got to our perfect seats in the lower bowl, just behind the end zone in the loudest part of the stadium. I was merely feet away from the inflatable Bears head as I saw my team run out to a flurry of flashbulbs and fireworks.

That night I saw many people walk into the stadium with a yard or so of carpet tucked under their arms, which I thought was odd. "It's for your feet," the woman near me said. I was still confused. Perhaps she feels more at home with the comfort of carpet under her heels? "It stops the cold concrete floor from conducting through your shoes," she explained. Ahh. She moved over and I gave it a try. Wow! What a difference the carpet made!

Like Seattle's Twelfth Man, the Bears fans have a nickname. They call themselves the 4th Phase, as offense, defense, and special teams make up the other three phases. The 4th Phase enjoyed the weather report that was put up on the jumbotron several times. They also displayed the "Bear down" Bears fight song chant, "You're the pride and joy of Illinois, Chicago Bears. Bear down," on the dot matrix screens around the tiers of the stadium. At the concessions they serve a cracking polish sausage—a Chicago staple—and in the main hallway on the west stand is a Bears gallery and shrine to Bears greatness, with glass cabinets displaying some great Bears memorabilia from their history.

It was an electric game with the Bears starting off with a TD from the kickoff. We were winning 7-21 at one point, but somehow the Saints got back in it with 17 unanswered points. With seconds to go, Robbie "as good as" Gould chipped in a field goal to send the game into overtime. Mr. Gould then kicked the winning sudden-death field goal sending me, Neal, and 62,000 Bears fans into hysterics, taking our record to 8-6, and keeping our playoff chances very much alive.

Rudy moment: The nominees are Daniel Manning's TD kick return in the very first play; Mike Brown intercepting the ball; Adewale Ogunleye's interception just as he was blitzing Drew Brees; Orton's scramble and dive for a Bears TD; Pierre Thomas's 42-yard slicing run through the Bears secondary for an exquisite TD; Brandon Lloyd's diving catch after the ball hit him square in the helmet (it bounced off and he had to spin and react); Marques Colston's perfectly timed run for his TD from Brees's inch-perfect pass; and the Saints two interceptions. And the winner is . . . Daniel Manning for his kickoff return. I was behind the end zone, and it was like Manning was running right at me.

Orange play of the game: It was going to be Bears centre Olin Kreutz for his fumbled and overturned snap on his own 1-yard line. But the winner was Saints defensive tackle Sedrick Ellis. The Bears were down 24-21, and they had 10 yards to go and just seconds left on the clock. Orton was scrambling around looking for an open receiver, and Ellis then cut him down for a sack. This stopped the play, giving Orton the chance to call a timeout to stop the clock and score a field goal to send the game into overtime. Had Ellis not have sacked him, the clock would have run out and the Saints would have actually won the game. It's a tough orange because Ellis did what he was paid to do, sack the QB, but ironically its knock-on effect lost them the game.

Extreme fan: Neal had found the fan who claims to have created a Bears chant. When there is a penalty flag, in Chicago the announcer says, "There is a penalty flag." This fan then always answered loudly, "Where?" as in, where is the flag—*on* the field or *off* the field? This caught on and now the whole stadium says "where" before the announcer tells them the answer. Though my extreme fan of the game award has to go to Don the Bearman. He was dressed in full bear fur and has a real actual bear head that he turned into a hat. He paints his face navy and orange and has a wooden sign around his neck that reads, "Beware of the Bears."

The next day Steph and I took in some classic Chicago-style deep-dish pizza, a show at Second City Theatre, and of course more shopping, and then we headed to Traci's to pick up my mail. At nearly every game I had managed to sign up for a new credit card with Visa so I could obtain one of their free gifts (an NFL team towel or blanket), and now, because I gave Traci's address, I was staring at dozens of credit card applications. I'm sure it didn't do my credit rating any good, but I got free NFL blankets, so it was worth it. Though what I was really waiting for was the large box in the corner.

I ripped it open to find my wonderful custom-made styrofoam Bears hat. It has two bear foam arms on the side and a Bears head on top. He is clutching a football in one hand and an "Adam's Football Trip" sign in the other, and he is kickass! We named him Staley (the name of the Bears mascot), of course. The hat was handmade by Jeff Kahlow, a Packers season ticket holder from Wisconsin, and his custom-made foam hats are the best thing if you want to be an NFL super fan.

Game 33. NFL Week 15, Pittsburgh Steelers at Baltimore Ravens, M & T Bank Stadium

Final Score: 13-9. Home-win record: 22-11. Capacity: 71,008. Attendance: 71,502. Ticket face value: $50—I paid $100 via a scalper. Picture on my ticket: E-ticket. Mascot: "Edgar," "Allan," and "Poe," named after the *poet who wrote "The Raven" and lived and worked in Baltimore. Merchandise: A great Ravens balaclava, shaped like a football helmet. Local dish: Blue crabs and lump crab cakes.*

Steph was excited about heading to Baltimore because this is where the musical *Hairspray* was set, and talking of music, the very first thing we saw by M & T Bank stadium was the Ravens marching band—the largest NFL band with 250 musicians. I too was excited, not just because the Ravens were 8-5 and the Steelers 10-3, making it a must win for the Ravens over their divisional rivals, but because this is where the original Colts had played with their legendary QB Johnny Unitas. Those Colts were also the first NFL team to have cheerleaders, so that's certainly a reason to give thanks to the city of Baltimore.

In 1984 the Baltimore Colts moved to Indianapolis. The city was without a team until 1996 when the owner of the Cleveland Browns relocated his team to Baltimore, renaming it the Ravens.

Steph and I took a stroll down "Ravens Walk," their fan zone. We took our picture by the Johnny Unitas statue and had the pleasure of seeing two Ravens cheerleaders who picked up a smiling older gentleman and took him for a ride on their custom-built golf cart.

It was then straight to Lot F where we saw plenty of Ravens-themed vehicles, including a Ravens VW Beetle. I found John from "Gametime" tailgate party and he was really pleased to see us. His truck was easy to spot because he was flying the Union Jack just for us. I have to say having a flag is essential. So many tailgaters simply told me, "I'm the one with the themed bus" or "I'm the one wearing the NFL jersey!"

Gametime had a friendly tailgate party, but Steph felt oddly uncomfortable. Maybe it was the large size of the crowd, or that she knew little about football, or that we could have been perceived as possible "moochers," which is even worse, even though John was incredibly welcoming and generous.

Since Steph didn't feel out of place in Carolina or Chicago, I couldn't understand why she was feeling that way here. It soon dawned on Steph that these folks were not talking about football but were merely drinking, eating, and having a good time. Steph thought that only football fans come to tailgate parties. I had to explain to her that many tailgaters are here as much for the tailgate as they are for the game. Although, Tunison wrote that "we [NFL fans] generally want to be around people who are into the game."[8] The tailgate gives people who may not be that into the game the opportunity to have a great day out. Tunison feels that "tailgating has transformed into something of a sub culture . . . [where] . . . many [tailgaters] don't attend . . . these games . . . and have no interest in their outcomes." He believes that this is "bizarre and borderline parasitic . . . they are roving partiers and nothing more."[9] Yes, I would be concerned for the NFL if all the tailgaters were just there to party, and none of them went in to the game or liked football, but what I was experiencing was that while many were there for the game, the tailgate opens up an experience for the wider community, where NFL fans, friends of NFL fans, partiers, chefs, and food lovers can congregate. Basically, would Steph come with me to a soccer game? No, she doesn't like soccer. Would she come with me to an NFL game? Yes. Even if she didn't go into the game, she likes the tailgate enough for us to at least share that.

John had a great bus decked out with Ravens gear galore. The winning kick was that he not only had an outdoor beer pump attached to the back of the bus, but he had an authentic-looking wooden sign written in "Ye olde English" font, saying "Gametime Pub."

At one point a truck from the famous "Scores" strip club came by, and their ladies gave out cards. As was the case in Detroit, no one really seemed to be fazed by the strippers and their impact on the family-friendliness of the tailgate.

We moved through the lots and found a Tiki tailgate bus that had a wooden bamboo bar filled with alcohol and mixers outside. On the inside, the roof was all bamboo and there were Christmas lights all around. There was distressed beach wood painted in several colours, giving it that laid-back vibe.

Although Steph loved the Tiki tailgate, something suddenly made her disgruntled and she wanted to leave that party instantly. I still needed a ticket for the game, so we left the Tiki tailgate, looking for a scalper. Only then did she tell me that while in the Tiki tailgate one of the guys on the bus flashed her his penis! At the time I was talking to the other chap about where they bought all their bamboo sticks and I missed the "flashing." Steph was rather upset and certainly felt this was not the sort of tailgating experience that I had described to her over the phone after every game. She was angry, and rightly so.

With the two best defenses in the league locking horns and both teams gunning for a playoff spot, tickets were hard to come by. We found a scalper. He had no sign with him; he was just unsubtly waving tickets in his hand, shouting, "Tickets, who needs 'em?" Steph knew I was practically running on credit card money and told me not to get her a ticket, and that she would be happy to go and check out the famous Baltimore Marina while I was at the game. Luckily for her, she had not seen the TV show *The Wire*, highlighting Baltimore as one of the most dangerous cities in North America. She skipped off singing tunes from *Hairspray*.

I did the walk away move from my scalper twice. Then, oddly, he asked, "How much do you want to pay?" "Well, nothing." What else was he expecting me to say? We settled on $100 for the ticket. I looked down. It was worth $50 plus taxes.

I got to my seat in the upper deck on the corner of the end zone. Like a bird's nest, it almost perched itself over the lower sections. I was just in time for the pre-game player introductions. The food stands were called the "Craven" zone and my ticket was near something called "The Flight Deck," which is an opening between two stands on the upper deck where people can stand and watch the game.

The Ravens had their own "spirit squad" made up of one guy for every cheerleader, and they held those long, old-fashioned megaphone cones. The guys would assist in helping to throw the cheerleaders into the air. These cheerleaders were more acrobatic and ambitious than any other cheerleading team I had seen, constantly doing flips and aerial manoeuvres.

There was something dark, edgy, and mysterious about this stadium. Maybe it was the deep purple and black colours, their rather creepy logo, or just simply their scary yet powerful leader, Ray Lewis. The Grecian concrete pillars around the ultra-wide jumbotron gave the stadium a medieval feel. The fan code stated to "have fun, root hard, show respect for the fans around you." Then it changed tack and went with the informal "and don't be a jerk!" Perhaps they were advising on overall life skills?

Then came the famous Ravens pre-game show. Being a defensive team, they introduce their defensive players only, whereas most other teams only introduce their offensive players. The New Zealand national rugby team performs a war dance called the Haka before kickoffs, to intimidate their opposition. In Baltimore the players perform strange individual bird dances. The last name mentioned was Ray Lewis, who lapped up all the attention with a strange bird-like jagged dance manoeuvre that is part ridiculous and part scary. I'm sure *Dancing with the Stars* will be signing him up soon.

It was a low scoring yet intense game. A sack, interception, or fumble got a louder cheer here than scoring a touchdown or field goal. It was the second loudest stadium on my tour.

On the contrary, in soccer, defensive teams do not usually inspire the crowd to be loud. A defensive soccer team will likely get boos from their own fans for being a "boring" team. There is not too much to show on a highlight reel for good defenders in soccer. For teams like Baltimore and Pittsburgh, however, their "attacking" defense can be very entertaining.

The atmosphere was so tense that any mistake might just cost that team the game. A Steelers fan behind me told me that his team are a "4th quarter" team. (Including this game, they had outscored their opponents 37-0 in the fourth quarter of their last three games.)

It was getting cold and dark and I did not want to leave Steph too long to wander Baltimore in the night sky, so with four minutes to go I left with the Ravens up 6-9. The Steelers had the ball but had struggled all day. I thought they would punt it and the game would be over. I found out afterward that the Steelers offense did wait for the last quarter to score a TD. Santonio Holmes, the Steelers' wide receiver, caught the ball with his feet inside the end zone, but his body and more importantly his hands and ball were outside the end zone. The ball has to "cross the plane" to count as a score. Yet after a coach's challenge it was controversially counted as a TD.

Rudy moment: Ed Reed's stunning swift delayed blitz of the Ravens got big cheers when sacking Roethlisberger. But later, Steelers safety Troy Polamalu hit a Ravens receiver, knocking the ball out, and Steeler Ryan Clark made a spectacular diving finger-tip catch just before it would have kissed the turf.

Orange play of the game: Santonio Holmes made a quick-fire slant catch, then leapt over a defender, only to fumble, and the ball was scooped up by the fleet footed Ed Reed.

Extreme fan: We briefly met PFUFA fan Sports Steve, who had hundreds of purple-and-black beads on, with a long fleece Ravens poncho and rather scary black makeup. We then met another fan, this time an older man with slightly fewer beads and not quite as scary makeup who had a great flat hat with lots of Ravens badges. The winner, however, was a man who was at least 70 years old. He was climbing up the stairs to the nosebleeds. He was dressed in full playing gear, not just the socks, the boots, and the pants, but the thigh- and kneepads, shoulder pads, and an old-school leather helmet.

After the game I found Steph in a bar, where the bartender had taken a shine to her and given her free drinks. We had dinner at the Cheesecake Factory where the portions are famously large. With energy to burn I suggested we go into the ESPN Zone sports bar. Steph was reluctant to go into a sports bar because I wanted to watch yet another football game, as the Cowboys were hosting the New York Giants in the night game.

Steph did not know that the upstairs of an ESPN Zone has all-sports-based arcade games. Twenty dollars on the ESPN card gave us plenty of game time. We played the football throwing game, which I was useless at, as well as horse riding (which was a killer), plus skiing, canoeing, and driving.

There was Baltimore Ravens and Baltimore Colts memorabilia peppered throughout the bar, including Johnny Unitas's kit in a glass container. After one too many pink lemonades, Steph went to the toilet. She came back excited that I should go and check them out because they have TVs in the toilets so you don't miss the game. And when I did go, that's when I saw today's controversial Steelers TD, which I would have seen had I not left the game early.

Game 34. NFL Week 15, Cleveland Browns at Philadelphia Eagles, Lincoln Financial Stadium

Final Score: 10-30. Home-win record: 23-11. Capacity: 67,594. Attendance: 69,144. Ticket face value: $65—I paid $65 via the box office. Picture on my ticket: Text on plain background. Mascot: "Swoop," an eagle. Merchandise: Eagles Christmas hat. Local dish: Philly cheesesteak, brisket, and pulled pork.

Steph was excited getting to Philadelphia because of the TV show, *The Fresh Prince of Bel Air*, whose main character came from "West Philadelphia, born and raised." We got to Lot K, where PFUFA Eagles fan Stephanie and her friends welcomed us with open arms at their tent. We had 40 minutes before dinner was served, so we sprinted over to the Wachovia car park to find the tailgater named One Crazy Fan. As we were walking through this great lot we noticed fireworks being lit at several tailgate parties, which I had never seen before. Several parties used Christmas lights to dress up their tailgates, giving them a warm holiday feel.

Two people were handing out freebies. This had happened at other tailgates too, but it was usually football-related items, maybe stickers or magnets, but not in Philly. They handed out mini bottles of Pepcid AC, which I thought was odd at the time.

We found Mike (One Crazy Fan) and his awesome Eagles Ambulance, the Tailgate Rescue Bus. This ambulance had players' signatures in the ceiling and Eagles stickers and badges throughout, though the real highlight of this bus was the amount of technical wizardry Mike had pumped in. The back of the bus was all subwoofers and speakers belting out rock tunes with stadium sound.

Mike was incredibly hospitable. We had boiled brats, pulled pork, chicken breast, potatoes, black and white cookies, plus more that I simply couldn't eat because I wanted to leave some room for Stephanie's tailgate.

Mike told us that every week he cooks up the local favourite, a Philly cheesesteak, but sadly this week he decided on homemade clam chowder. We told Mike we had a Philly cheesesteak that morning at Subway. He was disgusted that we went there and gave us two "quality" places to hit after the game where we must buy ourselves one of these famous sandwiches.

As we were about to leave Mike's party, a gentleman came around giving out free waffles and ice cream to simply anyone in the area, and that's when those Pepcid AC bottles came in handy.

That night was actually 103 days since my first game back in September. Peter Baroody, the world-record holder, had completed 32 NFL games at 31 NFL stadiums in 107 days. Because of the extra Steeler game with Neal, this night in Philly was my 32nd NFL game in 30 different NFL stadiums (I include the Toronto and London games as NFL stadiums, but not Fawcett Stadium in Canton), and I had done it four days quicker than Baroody. Granted I had still yet to see games in Jacksonville, Kansas City, and Tampa Bay, but in my heart I knew I had broken his record.

When Emmitt Smith broke Walter Payton's all-time rushing record he said, "Once I got it, I just wanted to extend that out and create another level."[10] I wanted to do the same.

We made it back to Stephanie's tailgate, which was in a more subdued car park. She had laid out a table for Steph and me with cutlery, Eagles salt and pepper pots, and an Eagles tablecloth. She plated us up pork chops, potatoes, and applesauce. It looked like Steph and I were on our own romantic dinner date at a tailgate party as we had our own table, chairs, and service in the middle of a car park. Stephanie has not missed a home game in 21 years and at the time was just three stadiums short of having seen a game at every NFL stadium.

It is clear the Eagles have brought a lot of joy to Stephanie's life. She loves her team, loves meeting new NFL fans, and, more importantly, loves what she calls her "Eagles family," who supported her when she was diagnosed with breast cancer in 2004. *Tailgater Monthly* interviewed her, and she said that her Eagle friends "lifted me and stood by me through it all, and I continued to tailgate with them, scheduling my surgeries and chemotherapy treatments for when the Eagles played their games away."[11] Most of the people at her party were people she simply had met in the parking lots at either home or away Philly games.

I mentioned to Stephanie and other PFUFA fans over e-mail that I would love to go the NFL Enshrinement/PFUFA gathering the following August. Foolishly I had not explained any of this to my Steph. So when Stephanie rather innocently told me she hopes to see me in Canton in August, my Steph shot me a look that Vernon Kay would clearly have described as "pissed off."

Steph thought that come the end of this season, my football odyssey would be over. She was annoyed I hadn't told her about an Ohio trip that I had not actually planned yet. She was upset that I was planning yet more football trips. We got mad at each other. Although this trip had started as being a "one-off" trip, it was becoming much more. I was living and breathing football, and I was thoroughly enjoying it. Not only was I loving the culture surrounding football, but I was also getting more and more involved, meeting new friends everywhere I went. Steph was naturally scared that if I did not put an official "end" to the football trip, then I would end up doing this sort of thing every year and never putting "us" first. I snapped at her: "Well, if I had enough money for the rest of my life, of course I would go to as many football games as I possibly could." I must have sounded like a drug addict. Steph clearly wasn't excited about spending the rest of her life going to football matches. It's just as well as the season is only a few months long.

Although we were arguing we came to the conclusion that we were going to enjoy the game, even though I was still without tickets. We bypassed the scalpers and optimistically headed to the ticket window, and what d'ya know, they actually had tickets left. Steph did not want me to spend more money than I had to on this trip, so she was happy either going into Philly or hanging out at the tailgate during the game. The local surrounding folks around us piped up and said, "A pretty blonde like you alone at night in downtown Philly, it's not a good idea." Point taken. "Two tickets, please."

"Would you like to sit or stand?" For so many games I had stood for the duration of the games even though I had seats, so I figured a standing ticket would be fine. Steph shot me another pissed-off look. The man showed us choices of where to sit.

There were two local gentlemen behind us in the ticket line, and they were somewhat brotherly after reading the back of my shirt. I asked them to pose for a picture, and in true Philly style they posed with their middle fingers up. I asked them if the Philly fans were as rude as everyone had told me they were. I recalled an infamous incident when the Eagles fans had pelted Santa Claus with more than a hundred snowballs during the halftime show of a game in 1968. I expected them to be apologetic or try to wriggle out of it by saying something like, "The media took it out of context," but they didn't. They proudly said, "Santa had it coming. He never brought gifts. What kinda Santa is that?" Wow.

Inside the stadium we could only find one narrow escalator to transport thousands of Eagles fans to their seats. The players were about to come out and we could hear the *Rocky* theme tune being pumped out. Steph is too young to pick up on that Philadelphia reference, and she was hoping to hear the *Fresh Prince* rap. It was at this point that I began to hear the famous Philly four-lettered foul words. I was a little shocked, but like Tunison suggests, "have a thick skin or stay at home."[12]

We got to the upper deck but realised that we were in the wrong section entirely. Unlike most other NFL stadiums, Lincoln Financial Stadium, otherwise known as the Link, ironically doesn't "link" up, so we had to go back downstairs, around the stadium, and back up again.

We got to our seats up high, behind the end zone. They were a carbon copy of the seats I had when I saw the Eagles play at the Dallas Cowboys in week 2. Inside the stadium the Eagles have their own "Phlite Deck," which is much like the Ravens version, only much larger. It has a sports-turf-like floor, and it hosts a band on the roof of the concession hut. The band played as the audience entered the building, and this was where they played during the halftime show, not on the field.

During the game the Eagles mascot jumped into the crowd. Steph got jealous and told me she would have preferred lower bowl seats. I tried to explain to her that being up high you can watch the whole game play out in front of you and therefore you can further admire the receiver's routes and the defensive schemes. She wasn't convinced.

At other games I had seen cars or trucks roll onto the turf to be given away, but in Philly they went further. They wheeled out an actual small wooden house as a prize.

The Browns got booed and I noticed the distinct lack of away fans. There were three loud mouths behind us who swore at early nearly every play. They even booed their star player, Donovan McNabb, who was actually having a great game. The Eagles fans even booed him when the Eagles picked him in the draft. Though by comparison to Red Star Belgrade FC, these Eagle fans were angels. On one occasion the Belgrade fans "had burst into the team's training session with bats, bars, and other bludgeons, [where] they beat up three of their own players . . . because they could no longer tolerate lack of commitment on the pitch."[13]

The Philly foul language and boos shocked me, but if this were a soccer game in the U.K., these three chaps would have been outsworn by seven-year-olds in the first minute. Culpepper was shocked and somewhat impressed, while on his soccer tour in the U.K., at hearing what the Americans' call the "F-bomb" at stadiums. He says, "I had never— *never*—heard the English word 'f---' used in so many creative forms . . . I heard it as a noun, verb, adjective, and maybe even a gerund. I heard it hollered without compunction within earshot of children, which would be taboo in the United States."[14] I guess I was shocked because I was simply judging these Philly fans by the same family sports standards of American sports culture. Tunison, however, disagrees with me and his message for the NFL: "Don't try to impose your rigid morals on football fans."[15] Culpepper also discovered that "some English fathers teach their children that there's football-ground language and there's language for everywhere else."[16] Well, hearing the chaps behind me in Philly there seems to be football language for 31 teams, and then there is Eagles language.

Soccer fans use their own made-up chants to bully a particular target and rile up the opposing fans. Some of which are witty but are often filled with swearing, which would be curbed quickly in the 31 NFL teams, but not at the Eagles. It is common at U.K. soccer games to hear whole stands chant, "Let him die, let him die, let him die," when an opposing player goes down injured. Tick off which chants would be accepted at the Eagles or at your local NFL franchise:

"Sol, Sol, wherever you may be, You're on the verge of lunacy, And we don't give a f*** when you're hanging from a tree, Judas c**t with HIV."

Aimed towards Sol Campbell because of his alleged mental frailties, rumoured homosexuality, and because he left Tottenham for arch rivals Arsenal.

"He'll shoot, he'll score, he'll eat your Labrador, Ji Sung Park!"
This was sung towards Ji Sung Park, Manchester Utd.'s Korean player.

"Van Persie, If the girl says, 'No,' molest her."
This was sung towards the Arsenal player whose rape charges were dropped and was sung to the tune of "Rewind" by Craig David.

"Posh takes it up the arse!"
This is actually sung by Manchester Utd. fans towards their own player, David Beckham, who is famously married to Posh Spice.

"Always Look on the Runway for Ice."
A sickening chant towards Manchester Utd., a team that tragically lost eight players in the 1958 Munich runway aeroplane crash.

Culpepper said that such chants "would seldom fly in the United States," where they are "more cautious [with] humor."[17] I turned to the loud mouths behind us in Philly, and to be honest they were actually nice guys; Steph even called them "loveable rogues." They told us that to experience a true Philly experience we would need to shout out a little bit more, and they soon had Steph shouting: "Down in front." She specifically picked a nonswearing chant.

The guys behind us were impressed with Steph's hollering and told us we were nearly fully initiated into being "true Eagles fans," but there was one more challenge. "You are not really Eagle fans until you get kicked out of a stadium at an away Philly game." Thankfully I had no more Philly away games to get myself kicked out of. The fellas were able to laugh at themselves for being so foul-mouthed. During a break, as one young boy appeared on the jumbotron, they began hollering, "You suck!" almost parodying their own image.

In 2008, NFL commissioner Goodell instilled a fan "code of conduct" that was present on billboards and the jumbotrons at every stadium. I have to say it was a tad patronizing, but if it stops antisocial behaviour, then that's just the way it's got to be.

Later I discovered that "the league keeps an extensive list of banned words that can't be put on a jersey ordered from an NFL shop."[18] This became slightly embarrassing for the league when in 2005 fans could not purchase a Randall Gay jersey because the word "Gay" was one of those banned words.

High-fives continued throughout the game as the Eagles dominated in nearly every aspect of the game, keeping their slim playoff chances alive. On the way out we noticed one more unusual thing, an actual ice sculpture of the Eagles logo, which was two feet wide, just sitting there on a plinth near the exit.

Rudy moment: Browns defensive back, Brandon McDonald, intercepted the ball, juked out would-be tacklers, and ran for 24 yards before completing a diving forward somersault into the end zone.

Orange play of the game: DeSean Jackson won his second orange of my trip. Stroking his own ego, he lined up as a QB in the red zone. He looked to run but as the defense was homing in on him, he panicked and threw an interception.

Extreme fan: One fan was having an identity crisis. He was wearing a Bears Christmas hat while his jersey was two jerseys stuck together down the half. On one side was an Eagles top and on the other a Browns one. He got some abuse from the Eagles fans. The award was a tie between our two great tailgaters that night, Stephanie, and One Crazy Fan.

After the game we took a stroll to the car amidst celebratory fireworks. At this point I thought "I had seen it all" in terms of extreme buses and NFL-themed tailgating machines, until Steph asked, "Is that a *London* bus?" We made our way over to the double-decker bus, which had its own three-man security. We asked the gentleman if we could have a look on the bus seeing as we are from London. He replied that it was a private party, but a woman onboard heard our accents, hopped off the bus, and asked us if we'd like a tour. With more speed than a DeSean Jackson touchdown celebration, we hopped on.

The bus used to be an open-top double-decker London tour bus that was shipped over by Laurie, our host, who owns it with her husband. The whole bus is now black with floor lights, leather interiors, two huge flat-screens, and Laurie's favourite, a Star Trek–style electronic sliding door. This was the deluxe of deluxe as far as football buses go. Laurie took us up to the upper deck, where they have catered hot and cold food. The whole cost to get the bus customised and shipped was in the region of $400,000, plus they pay for their own security.

We found our car, though foolishly I had parked front first into the space, meaning I had to reverse out to exit into the stream of traffic, which was proving difficult. The Philly fans honked and berated me every time I tried to get out. Ahh, there's that Philly spirit. Then I heard,"London! Hey, London!" It was the two guys who were behind us in the ticket line before the game. "I can't get out, I'm blocked in," I hollered back with a sprinkling of some colourful, Philly language that I picked up at the game. "That's okay because I'm gonna f****ng block him out." If it weren't for the two Philly fans, who knows how long we would have been stuck there!

Sadly, as it was already so late, we headed straight back to NYC instead of getting a local Philly cheesesteak, which we both kicked ourselves for missing. Though the following year at the NFL Enshrinement (I managed to persuade Steph to let me go back for more football in 2009), I did try one of Stephanie's home-cooked Philly cheesesteaks and it was delicious.

Once back in NYC, Steph finally got to meet the 2 Michelles. I let the three ladies talk before I pitched in with some good football talk. The 2 Michelles then interviewed us both and Steph enjoyed meeting such great female football fans.

Game 35. NFL Week 16, Indianapolis Colts at Jacksonville Jaguars, Alltel Stadium

Final Score: 31-24. Home-win record: 23-12. Capacity: 67,164. Attendance: 65,648. Ticket face value: $160—I paid $160 via Ticketmaster. Steph got a free ticket. Picture on my ticket: Mine was an e-ticket, Steph's was a Ticketmaster hard-yet-plain ticket. Mascot: "Jaxson DeVille," a dancing Jaguar. Merchandise: Jaguar ears. Local dish: Seafood.

My friend Ryan, whom I know through my London flag team, invited us to stay at his girlfriend Emily's house in Jacksonville as they were going to the game. We arrived there in the middle of the day for this Thursday night game, and both of them took the whole day off in preparation for the tailgate. Although Ryan is a Jags season ticket holder, both are more ardent fans of the Florida Gators, as shown by their matching Gator towels in the bathroom.

I guess I had never seen just how much work goes into a tailgate. We jumped into Ryan's huge new pick-up truck and went to various places, picking up essential tailgating items including beer, propane, ice, and food. It was the first time on the trip I was going to be involved in the tailgating process right from the start, rather than just turning up post-setup. Ryan parked up on the grass, as his friends had saved him a good spot. Everyone brought something to the tailgate, which housed about 50 people, all very friendly and many of whom were Colts fans who had come down from Indianapolis that day. Steph and I were welcomed as part of the crew, and just like real tailgaters, we mucked in as much as we could.

Deep-fried turkey was on the menu, with chicken wings and sauces. Steph had never even heard of the concept of deep frying a turkey before and until a few weeks prior neither had I.

Ryan told me that in October this stadium hosts a tailgate named the "largest cocktail party in the world," where the great college rivalry between the University of Georgia Bulldogs and the University of Florida Gators takes place. The stadium capacity for such games then expands from 67,164 to 84,000.

Earlier in the day, the Jaguars mascot, Jaxson DeVille, had called me to arrange a private show. He told me not to tell anyone his real name as only a few people know his true identity. On cue at 6:15, Jaxson came racing over to our tailgate on a golf cart alongside four Jaguar cheerleaders who had their own funky army-style golf cart. Steph was ecstatic. Jaxson did a little dance show just for her and she turned into a giggling kid. Jaxson also gave Steph a signed t-shirt before he got mauled by other fans. He then made his way up onto the bandstand and played the electric guitar very well considering his costume hands were massive. He tries to enter the stadium in an elaborate fashion. In the past he has even entered the stadium on a zip wire. Steph was bubbling with excitement, and after getting her "mascot fix" she became an instant Jags fan.

I had bought only one ticket for this game and it was another expensive club one, via Ticketmaster. I was going to buy Steph a ticket from a scalper, but one of Ryan's friends kindly gave Steph his spare ticket for one of my trip t-shirts. If only I could have gotten all my tickets that way.

We all made our way into the stadium. I could have walked in through the "Crown Royal" club section, but I did not want to leave Steph, so we headed to the "Bud zone," which is a huge bar that stretches across one of the end zones. The bar was packed as the crowd was chatting, eating, drinking, and occasionally looking up at the TV.

Inside the stadium for Jaguar games, the team erects huge banners at the top of the stadium covering thousands of seats so they can "sell out" and not get "blacked out." This stadium replaced the old Gator Bowl Stadium, and there are still parts of the old stadium remaining. This is where the college Gator Bowl game takes place. From the vibe I was getting, and the Florida Gator tents and merchandise on peoples' cars, these fans were stronger college fans than NFL fans.

This Thursday night game between the Jags and the Colts was the place to be seen that night in Jacksonville. Steph noticed that many Jacksonville women were wearing summer dresses in the colours of their team: teal green, gold, and black. The women walked with a flirtatious swagger looking to scope out a partner, while drinking beer from plastic cups and consuming popcorn by the bucket load.

The Jags had a young party crowd and it felt very social. One extreme fan even lent me his Jags foam hat to walk around in. Some of the fans were a little too "randy," and Steph got hit on right in front of me. "I'd bang her," said a juvenile fan within my and Steph's earshot. *I* took this as a compliment, but Steph wasn't pleased.

I briefly checked out the "Crown Royal" club, just to see where my extra few bucks went. As expected it was nice and plush, but I didn't stay there long and preferred the high-fiving atmosphere by the Bud zone. It was nearing halftime and the Jags were surprising us all as they were actually beating their AFC rivals 7-17, despite the fact the Jags were awful all season long and the Colts really needed the win to secure a playoff spot.

In the third quarter I asked security if I could go into the lower bowl so I could meet PFUFA Jags fan "Jags Arrowman." He nodded and gave me 15 minutes. I walked down to the front row, where I waited on the aisle steps until a play was over, then I politely asked the man at the end of the aisle to let me pass, but he surprisingly shook his head no. Before I knew it he was up on his feet, towering over me. I explained to him that I just wanted to say hi to Arrowman who was waving for me to come down the row. "You are being ridiculous," I told him in a posh English accent, hoping that for some reason this would make me sound tougher. It didn't, and he retorted by swearing at me and adding something about his arse and me kissing it. He then had the audacity to beckon over to security, claiming that *I* should be ejected from his "expensive section." I told the angry wannabe football hooligan that my ticket was actually in club, a far more expensive seat than his. (I didn't want to sound snobby but I was merely trying to make a point. It didn't go down well.) Everyone around us got to their feet (people love a good fight, don't they?). They all told him to sit down and let me pass.

He looked around confused and frustrated, yet he wouldn't sit. His own Jaguars peers hurled profanities at him.

"Listen," I told him, "you see the back of this shirt? I am going to every single NFL stadium this season and you are the first arsehole I have encountered. I hope your children are proud." I said this to him calmly, but I was really frightened on the inside. He continued with his tirade. I really thought he was going to punch me, so I changed tactics. "Look, I am doing this trip so that more people go to NFL games. Look at those empty seats and banners up there. Your own team can't sell out a Monday Night Football game, and you are not helping!" Sure it was a little egotistical of me to think that my trip would single-handedly save the ticket crisis in Jacksonville, but hey, you never know. In the end Jags Arrowman came out to meet me. When I left, the angry man snarled more swear words at me. "Oh, how very mature," I said to him sarcastically. I may have seemed "cool" at the time, but as I rushed back to Steph, my heart was pumping. My worry was that I would be punched in the face and kicked out of the stadium, something that would fill the Eagles fans with pride.

I got back to Steph, shaking. She had made friends with two ladies in their mid-forties, one of whom plays softball with the wife of Jags QB David Garrard. All of their football talk was about local sports sensation Tim Tebow, the Christian heartthrob quarterback. Not only was he the first sophomore to win the coveted Heisman Trophy in 2007, the trophy given to the best college player each year, but he was being coined as the greatest college player of all time. Steph began flicking through the game-day programme to find him, especially once the ladies had discussed his good looks. Our new friends had to tell her that he was not playing that night. "Oh, is he injured?" Steph asked. She then got told that Tebow wasn't even in the pros, he was still at university as the QB for the Florida Gators. Steph was dumbstruck. He was being talked about with such sporting prowess and he wasn't even at the professional level. He was the "star" player inspiring discussions and debate when over our shoulders the pro players of the Jaguars were facing NFL legend Peyton Manning.

In 2006, when Tebow was a freshman and only a mere back-up QB, Clay Travis saw him play and realised that "in the eyes of Gators across the country. Tebow can do no wrong. . . . Tebow has managed to make the quarterback sneak an art form . . . [and is] the most difficult white man to tackle,"[19] thus creating Tebow-mania.

The Jags have struggled selling out their stadium, and in January 2010 they announced they would be slashing their ticket prices for three years. Webster felt this is an attempt to "to re-establish a connection with a large section of the support and to safeguard the franchise's future in Jacksonville. [But] will it do enough to head off a hostile approach from another city to steal the team for themselves?"[20] College teams cannot just up sticks and move—they are very much grounded in the campus. Likewise in the U.K., sports teams never move. When Wimbledon FC did move, just 56 miles, there was a public outcry. NFL franchises cannot simply just "wait for the good times" to roll back. The pressure is always on to keep the fans coming back. Because of the shared revenue in TV and tickets, if a team does not do well, then the other 31 teams lose out. The hoopla and doing things like installing a whole bar across the end zone, or air conditioning in Arizona, or comfy seats in New Orleans, or the best sound system in Baltimore, will all help to keep the fans coming back. But in every NFL season there is just one Super Bowl winner and 31 losers, meaning 31 teams need to find other ways of keeping the fans happy.

The college system, with all their bowl games (around 30 per season), allows for many teams and fans to have that "winning feeling." Likewise, in soccer there are many ways to get that winning feeling other winning the Premier league: promotion to a higher league, two knockout cups, champions league, and the Europa league. Some teams consider qualification into the European leagues, or having a decent "cup run," or simply not being relegated as a "winning" season. One domestic soccer team could actually win as many as four major trophies per year.

Webster says that the Jaguar franchise needs "the community to save the franchise for the community."[21] The NFL does not have relegation, so a failing team on all fronts may have to move elsewhere, though they get the first pick of the next year's draft, which ensures teams do not stay terrible teams for too long.

Tim Tebow was projected to go in the third round of the 2010 draft, because of his unorthodox passing style and lust for running. Quite low down considering he was the youngest Heisman trophy winner (he came third and fifth in the Heisman after that) and helped Florida win two national championships and the Sugar Bowl in his glittering college career. The Denver Broncos traded up and picked him in the first round with the 25th pick overall in the 2010 draft, shocking the football world. Ryan, who was on the track team at the University of Florida, told me later that "the Jags broke my heart when they didn't draft Tebow, along with every other heart in Jacksonville. For a team that can barely fill the stadium to pass on a player that would have guaranteed to sell out every game, it makes you wonder what they are thinking."

Towards the end of this game we all turned to see the action on the field where Peyton Manning engineered a great comeback. The winning Colts were ecstatic and flooded the field at the final whistle, keeping their playoff chances alive, while the remaining home fans were left dumbstruck that their team lost after having a comfortable lead.

After the game no one forced us to actually leave. Take note, Wembley Stadium! We were allowed to watch the band playing on the concourse. One musician even had a hairstyle with black round spots on his bleached blonde hair that looked very Jaguar-like.

Rudy moment: Colts cornerback Keiwan Ratliff intercepted Jags QB Garrard and scored a touchdown while the score was tied at 24-24. This really stabbed at the heart of the Jags as they had been leading the whole game.

Orange play of the game: Colts kicker Adam Vinatieri missed a field goal from just 30 yards out.

Extreme fan: I found two guys with pineapple-like wigs on and three guys doing the naked-torso body-paint thing, but it was PFUFA member "Jags Arrowman" who stood out. His face is painted green with black arrows on it. His custom-built foam hat is in the shape of a paw print, which also has arrows on it, with the idea that he will throw off the away team's kicker.

Despite the loss, plenty of fans told us they were to still going to continue the party spirit and asked us to go clubbing with them, but we declined as we had a long drive the next day.

In the morning I received a call from a software specialist. Since the Arizona game I had been in and out of an electronics store trying to get them to get the footage off the internal hard drive from my broken HD camcorder. They shipped my camera to a specialist, and although he could retrieve the data, it was going to cost me $1,400. "Hang on," said the specialist, after viewing some of my football footage, "are you the guy going to all those football games?" He had heard me on 670 The Score in Chicago, and being a football fan himself, he was so impressed with my trip, that he extracted the data for free and posted the DVD for me. Turns out my "little plug" on the radio really helped me out quite a bit.

Steph was enjoying the Florida sun and was reluctant to head north that day where we heard it was going to be cold. We were on our way to Kansas. Again I noticed a large amount of adult shops on the highway, many of which were next to pro-life billboards, which I thought was a tad ironic.

In the middle of the night we stopped at a Waffle House for a late-night snack before finding a motel. Steph had never been to a Waffle House before and these little trips to American fast food chains had become charming, somewhat beautiful, and incredibly American.

As we were eating, an elderly bearded man came over to us, mumbling. We nodded and wished him a good night, thinking he was possibly homeless. Once outside the restaurant we began taking a few random pictures before the man asked me if we were taking pictures of the meteor shower. I shook my head thinking he was crazy. He told us that a meteor shower was passing that part of America and that five minutes prior he had spotted several meteors. Granted, I do not have the best eyesight, but I would like to think I could spot a meteor shower if one was hovering above my head. His language became suddenly more technical and far more believable. He knew the names of the stars and the constellations. Though for all I knew he could well have been making it up.

"Wow," said Steph, as she looked up at the sky and began to perk up. "That is really cool." I thought she was just going along with it to make the man feel better. He told us he had a PhD in astrophysics, which he may well have done but maybe by now he had gone a bit senile? I walked back to the car with my head in the sky just to please him. Then pow, I saw it. "Holy crap, what the hell?!" I blurted out as I actually saw a star in the night sky suddenly burn into a red colour and then disappear. It was mad. The man then helped us spot up to twenty more meteors.

On Saturday evening we were already 40 miles from Kansas City for our next game. I gave Steph the choice of bars: Buffalo Wild Wings or Hooters, to watch the Cowboys play their big Saturday night football game, their last game to be played in Texas Stadium before they knocked it down. Unsurprisingly, she chose Buffalo Wild Wings. Steph was initially reticent about watching a football game in a bar, because at home pubs are usually quite small and when there is a big soccer game on, the place gets rammed and you spend most of the 90 minutes standing and getting bustled about. However, here the atmosphere was far more sophisticated, with lots of seating, waitress service, tasty wings, and plenty of TVs.

The next morning Steph didn't want to exchange the warmth of the bed for the -18 degrees Celsius (that's -0.4 degrees Fahrenheit) of the outside chill. When I finally dragged her outside her hair was still slightly wet, which then instantly froze and snapped off! She cried. Her tears then froze to her own face, and she cried some more. I laughed.

On the drive to Arrowhead Stadium, the radio host told his listeners how he admired anyone going to the Chiefs game as the temperature outside just clocked in at -1 degree Fahrenheit. I was up for being admired. Steph wasn't.

Game 36. NFL Week 16, Miami Dolphins at Kansas City Chiefs, Arrowhead Stadium

Final Score: 38-31. Home-win record: 23-13. Capacity: 77,000. Attendance: 73,869. Ticket face value: $125 (club level)—I paid $125. Picture on ticket: E-ticket. Mascot: "KC Wolf," a grey wolf. Merchandise: Chiefs fleece hat and gloves. Local dish: BBQ—pork ribs, brisket, chicken.

At Arrowhead Stadium we easily found a parking spot on the deathly cold concrete. I finally persuaded Steph to get out of the car, and although the sun was shining, it was colder than I have ever known, and hope to know. I thought I was prepared for the cold. I wore thermal underwear, long johns, two thick winter socks, pyjamas over the long johns, jeans, and winter boots with hand warmers under my toes. On top I had a t-shirt, a fleece, a hoodie, my ski jacket, gloves with hand warmers inside, then my football trip hoodie. There was no point spending money on "ridiculous" merchandise; we needed warm merchandise, so I bought a fleece-style Chiefs hat and gloves. Steph had brought a blanket along, and I got a free Visa one, but I had to take my glove off to fill out the form. My hand struggled to write in the cold, and after that we made sure that no piece of skin was left exposed for fear it would simply fall off.

I had heard so many good things about the Chiefs tailgate, but because of the cold, there was little cooking going on. We found a bus named "Die Hard, Pirates of Arrowhead" and the warm fans inside invited us in. We got on board and the heat hit us in the face, it was like walking into a sauna. The gentleman running this bus goes by the name of Helmet Head and over the years he has only missed only one or two Chiefs games. His family showed us pictures of their tailgate parties spanning decades. They normally cook up food and have a stuffed Pirate outside on display. One member of their group was still asleep, slouched, and hungover from the night before. Helmet Head gave us some hot chocolate to warm us up. We took a sip and our insides burnt. We soon figured out that the hot chocolate was spiked with some kind of fiery alcohol. Helmet Head told us that today's game was going to be the second-coldest game in Chiefs history and the coldest game the Miami Dolphins will have ever played (-12 degrees Fahrenheit with wind chill!). Steph didn't want to get off the bus.

We braved the cold and found one of the original PFUFA members, Arrowman. He looked at our tickets and told us we were in club section, #220. As you know club section is not my favourite place to watch the game, but when it's -12 degrees Fahrenheit outside, I'm taking it. It was the best bit of news Steph heard all day, because she had seen pictures of club sections from other stadiums and heard about me rattle on the about how luxurious, plush, and more importantly warm they are, and she wanted to race into the stadium.

I, however, was keen to find the "Tepee" tailgating crew. We asked a member of staff who was driving a golf cart if he knew where they were and he told us to hop on. Like royalty he drove us around the tailgate, but sadly he couldn't find them either. He then began apologising that there was not much tailgating going on, and we would have to come back another time. Steph explained she was not willing to risk a return trip. Although it was fun riding on the golf cart, the wind cut through our skin with even more velocity.

We made our way up to the stadium and up the ramp to the middle level. We showed our tickets to a woman behind a metal gate and took one step forward. I looked behind. The section was as exposed as everywhere else. This club section was *not* enclosed! Sure there was a roof over our head from the tier above, but the cold wind was cutting us in half. A staff member told us that only the luxury boxes are fully covered and enclosed, and more importantly warm, but our tickets were not valid there. Any blood that was left in Steph's face drained. I couldn't believe that this was the club section, there wasn't even carpet! Just so you know, nonclub tickets on StubHub were going for as little as five bucks!

We found our seats, but they were in the shade. The stadium was maybe only 60 percent full, if that, so we moved right round to be in the sun. Most of the fans had the same idea and kept following the sun around the stadium. I was amazed that some Dolphin players were not even wearing long sleeves.

This was no longer about watching a football game but about sheer survival. On the concourse we spotted a gas lamp and squeezed our way near it. A Dolphins fan's beer had completely frozen solid, so we stood next to him, waiting our turn to be warm. Our priority was trying to keep our body organs warm enough so we didn't die, while his priority was to drink his beer without the annoying icy bits.

The blue light of joy in the lamp was short-lived and faded. Steph groaned and ran to the toilet. After 20 minutes I asked a steward to go in and get her. "I'm sorry, sir, but your girlfriend will not come out, she seems rather attached to the heater." I knew it! She had found a working heater and would not leave. She finally came out, took the car keys, and huddled off. I'm not sure how the "official" attendance count was 73,869. There were huge gaps in every section. Could 20,000 people all be hiding in the toilets too?

I moved up to the top tier where I knew "Helmet Head" and his crew would be. Up top it was even colder. They wrapped me up in a blanket and put blankets under my feet and across my body. My camera was starting to drain in the cold. While I took my gloves off to change the batteries the lady next to me gave me rubber gloves to wear as undergloves, this made my hands sweat quickly and they felt instantly warmer. Like I said, it was all about survival.

After halftime, I made my way down to the lower bowl behind one of the end zones where I knew Arrowman would be. Here I found another PFUFA member, "Weirdwolf." He was alarmingly only wearing a fleece top. I guess he really must be a wolf? He called himself after the Chiefs nickname which was created by a commentator when he broadcasted once that the Chief fans were howling like wolves. Since then it has stuck.

Arrowman personally knows the cameraman by the end zone as he is often filmed after TDs and such for the jumbotron. Before I knew it the cameraman was filming us and we got instantly beamed onto the big screen. I felt so American!

Although it was warmer down by the field, I felt bad for the players. Still it did not faze the Dolphins as they came out victorious from what was a "shootout" of a game. It was a shame I was too busy trying to stay alive most of the time to pay much attention. It was as if it were too cold for both defenses because this was an amazing matchup where touchdowns came from everywhere and the Chiefs played the best game of their season despite losing.

Steph missed the Chiefs mascot, a wolf named KC, who I thought was playing things a bit too sarcastically when he strutted out in Bermuda shorts and sunglasses. Sure it might be warm for him—he is a huge grey wolf with fur, but for us humans in the stadium it was colder than death.

Rudy moment: Dolphin QB Chad Pennington wriggled free of two blitzes and made a short throw to Ronnie Brown. Brown juked a defender, got a good downfield block, the referee accidently got thrown to the ground, before Brown then hurdled a player Walter Payton–style before getting tackled.

Orange play of the game: Instead of winding down the clock, the Dolphins looked for more points and their running back, Ricky Williams, fumbled, giving the Chiefs one more try, which luckily for him, the opposition didn't score from.

Extreme fan: Arrowman, Weirdwolf, or Helmet Head? It has to be Arrowman because he had one of the best outfits of all the extreme fans. He wears the away team's jersey (he has one for every NFL team), and he sticks broken arrowheads into himself all over the jersey, as if he has been shot at by his very own Chiefs team.

I got back to the car, and poor Steph was practically frozen. I'm just really glad that I changed the car for one with seatwarmers. We warmed up and then drove north to Chicago.

The next day we checked into a fancy downtown hotel. My friend Dionna got us a voucher for a free night there, and it had a fantastic view of the city. Our room had its very own goldfish and was only a 10-minute walk from Soldier Field. Perfect.

Game 37. NFL Week 16, Green Bay Packers at Chicago Bears, Soldier Field

Final Score: 17-20 (OT). Home-win record: 24-13. Capacity: 61,500. Attendance: 62,151. Ticket face value: $245—I paid $200 via Craigslist. Picture on my ticket: Picture of Brian Urlacher. Mascot: "Staley Da Bear," this time he was in Christmas outfit. Merchandise: Two foam Bear claws.

This is the big rival game I had waited my whole life to see. To make it extra special, this was a must-win game to keep our playoff chances alive. Because the Vikings lost the day before to the Falcons, the Bears could win the division if they won against the Packers and then won the following week at the Texans, but they would also need the Vikings to lose their next game against the Giants.

I searched Craigslist for a ticket but finding a single was tough. I saw a posting asking $200 for a club seat. It seemed steep but the seller was willing to sell me just one of his four tickets. Two e-mails later, I was meeting the seller Tony by his workplace, where we made the exchange.

This time at the 31st Street tailgate lot I was sporting my custom-made Staley hat. I was becoming a super fan! Everyone loved my hat, and thankfully it was not quite as cold as the day before, but it was still cold enough to warrant that game being the coldest ever to be played in Chicago. My excitement for the big game was keeping me warm, while Steph was tucked up in bed, defrosting from the day before.

I visited "Fork You Tailgating Club," where their leader, Dennis, had an inflatable Homer Simpson dressed as Santa mounted to his truck, lots of food and drink, and candies in the colours of both teams. Then someone invited me into their tent, which was connected to a series of other tents. Once inside I felt like I was in the trenches like in World War I movies. It was warm inside and like an underworld secret bunker—you could move from one Bears tent to another.

After swinging by Da Bus and seeing Timmy, I walked to the stadium from the 31st Street car park. Once inside the tunnel the noise was electric with hungry Bears ready to feed on some cheese. Thankfully the club-level concourse had both warmth and carpet. Tony was already there with his friends to greet me with high-fives.

I had to actually sit in someone else's seat because my seat was frozen solid and wouldn't open. There was a leak from above and the water dripping down turned a perfect plastic seat into a block of ice. Tony told me that "during the football season it is a two paper Sunday; one paper you keep under your feet and the other under your ass!" He dished out the different sections of the Sunday paper for all of us.

I was way too excited for this game and I was studying every Bears player on the field, making sure there were no lopsided matchups that the Packers could exploit. I spotted the Bear's mascot, Staley, in a Christmas outfit, and due to the fact we were playing the Packers he was walking around with a sign saying, "Free cheese sandwiches," and he began throwing cheese sandwiches into the crowd instead of t-shirts.

In the first quarter we traded punts with the Packers. My heart was thumping throughout every play. Despite the 0-0 score in the first quarter, I was having the time of my life. I had to pinch myself that I was really at a Packers-Bears game. I was more into this game than any of the others and my throat was already getting sore from screaming. Sadly we were losing 14-3 at the half, but I wasn't going to walk out on my Bears again. This time I had faith!

At the break Tony's friend bought me a pizza and initially a beer. To prevent drunkenness at this stadium, fans can only buy two beers at a time. I asked for my drink to be in a Bears souvenir cup (I'm such a tourist), but I wasn't allowed to drink beer from a souvenir cup. "Where are we? In England with these stupid petty rules?" The manager didn't seem to understand my cross-cultural comparison. My choices were a beer in a Miller cup or Coke in a Bears cup; of course I picked the latter, which then froze solid by the time I got back to my seat.

I heard fireworks going off above my head, but I couldn't see them, so I went through the crowded club-level concourse, to find a door leading to an outside rooftop. In front of me were the beautiful Doric pillars that have been part of the fabric of Soldier Field since it was first built. When they rebuilt the stadium in 2002, they kept the pillars but moved them slightly further away from the field. I had driven past the stadium several times on the trip and always saw the pillars from the outside, but I did not know the fans could actually zigzag through them on the upper outdoor concourse. It was beautiful, with a great view of the city.

When I came back from the break, Tony and his friends had gone to meet other friends, and my neighbours farther to the left were not too friendly. The main guy took one look at my bag, with all of my merchandise and freebies that the tailgaters had given me and muttered, "This isn't da beach, ya know, it's football!" He motioned to his friends who then proceeded to laugh at me. None of the Packers fans teased me about my bag or my great Bears hat. In fact, at the start of the game, the Packers fan in front of me gave me two of his disposable hand warmers.

The Packers then muffed their punt return and the home team cheered. My eye caught the eye from my unfriendly neighbour. After such a play he instinctively was about to high-five me but then realised he had mocked me just moments before and so he pulled away. Oh, the shame of it . . . To not be high-fived, to be "left hanging" after a great play by a neighbouring and fellow fan was a low blow that gave me a deeply hollow feeling. He was clearly ashamed of my being there. I was uncomfortable and upset. No one had pulled their high-fives away from me in the previous 36 football games—you just don't do it. Tunison says that the high-five "is a manoeuvre steeped in tradition, reeking of valour, and one that should not be overused or executed improperly."[22]

I felt alone and uncomfortable. This was not a feeling I was expecting to experience at my own personal Mecca. I felt ugly and disconnected. Thankfully a while later these unfriendly guys to my left started to read the back of my hoodie. One of them (though it took him a while) figured out that I had actually been to *all* those games in the 2008 season. He was impressed—could I give them another chance? I told him I was from London and it was my dream to see the Bears play the Packers, implying that their hostility towards me was ruining that very dream. With no further discussion he then did something that surprised the crap out of me. In front of thousands of fans and midway through a play, without any hesitation he simply hugged me. This is apparently an unusual action in American sports. Culpepper said that "in America, we'll chat with a stranger all game long, but we'd never hug them after a favorable play,"[23] but here I was getting hugged, not because of the play on the field but because of my dream.

Later on, this fan went to the toilet. On his return from the bathroom he looked really mad. He was muttering about a guy (a Bears fan) who he had just got into an angry slagging match with about something or other. I chipped in, "I guess this other guy must have had a *really* big beach bag then?" He laughed (phew) and slapped me on the back saying, "You're okay." (Double phew.)

Minutes later Matt Forte broke through for a delightful 30-yard burst, sending us crazy. The guys to my left all turned to me and I got the hearty high-fives I was craving. Did a tear roll down my face? Perhaps.

We clawed our way back into the game, and when Forte helped the Bears get a first down when it was fourth-and-one on the Packers' 4-yard line, which lead to a TD, there was almost a stampede in the stands. Our season was still safe. It was a tie game but the Packers crept down the field. The Bears D prevented a Packers TD, forcing the yellow and green of Wisconsin into a 4th down and 6 on our 20-yard line with just seconds left.

Sixty-two thousand eyes were on the Packers' kicker as he lined up to write himself into Green Bay folklore. A win would mean nothing to the Packers, other than the joy of beating their oldest rivals and spitefully stopping our playoff hopes.

I saw the ball placed. I saw the snap. I saw the kicker strike the ball, though I didn't see the ball in the air. Instinctively my head and eyes focused on where the ball normally would have been, i.e., heading towards the goal posts. I was confused, the ball had vanished. The Bears punched their arms in the air, and there was a quick-fire scramble of bodies diving all over the icy turf. They began jumping up and down. Where was the ball? What was going on? And why were they all jumping? Why was everyone around *me* jumping? Why was I being hugged? The vibrations from the stampede sent my frozen Coke flying out of its souvenir cup. The field goal was blocked! Bears defensive end Alex Brown had got his mighty Bear claw in the way of the kicked ball, which then squirted out and another Bear landed on it. We were heading into overtime and we had the momentum.

We won the coin toss, and Greg Olsen, our tight end, caught the first play, but he was horse-collared by a Packers player, which gave us a further 15 yards. "Thank you very much, unprofessional Packers player. You have just given us a huge chance to win," I shouted out. Even after 37 football games I still didn't have the trash talking down, but I didn't want to just sound like everyone else who were all chanting the uncreative "Packers Suck!" which was ironic because for most of the game they were very much the better team.

Robbie "as good as" Gould came on the field to win the game from the 20-yard line. I couldn't bear to watch, but I couldn't look away. The snap was good and Gould connected. I followed the ball in flight as I saw the brown pigskin spinning forwards, and it was glorious. Time stood still. The ball sliced through the uprights. Boom! Boom! Boom! We beat the Packers! We could not stop jumping and hugging. I felt like a part of history.

To watch the Bears defeat the Packers at Soldier Field to keep us in the playoff hunt was a dream come true and worth every penny. After the game, the atmosphere was carnivalesque. The Chicago Bears drumline band, which had majestically played throughout the game, was now jamming down on the concourse. The fans didn't actually leave but formed a massive crowd and everyone was dancing and cheering them on. I could have danced all night and not one steward asked us to leave. It was beautiful.

Rudy moment: Three words: Alex, Brown, block.

Orange play of the game: During a kickoff return, the Packers' punt returner waved his arms to shoo his teammates away from the bouncing ball, but it accidently hit his teammate's leg. The Bears pounced on the ball, resulting in a TD from that possession.

Extreme fan: I watched Lorenzo "Grizzly Bear" transform on Timmy's Da Bus. He put on real Chicago Bears game socks, old-school game-day football pants and top, shoulder pads, an old-school, 1930s-style Bears jersey, topped with a huge bear mask and then added furry bear-like arms. He even had a foam piece of cheese that he put in the bear's teeth.

As I walked through the snow after the game I felt spiritually connected to everyone present at such a wonderful game, even the away Packers fans. Their team had turned up, played well, and we had all experienced the same wonderful game. At home a fight could have broken out, especially after such a dramatic outcome but everyone was walking together, talking together, and touched by the magic of the game.

I got back to the hotel where Steph was waiting for me. My face was dirty and my throat sore. I took off my gloves. My hands were black from the debris of the hand warmers. I took off my boots. My feet were bruised from the debris of the other hand warmers that I put in my boots. My teeth were chattering and my mouth was dry. My body was shattered. I was tired and drained, but excited and adulated. My Mum wasn't there to ask if I "had a good time" and "who won?" but Steph was. She opened the door, and this time I knew exactly who won as I belted out, "We *beat* the Packers! *We* beat the Packers! We beat the *Packerssssssssssss*!"

The next day I felt as if the world was just that little bit better, so Steph and I did some touristy things, such as museums, sight-seeing, and of course more shopping. That evening we met Traci for dinner. We used the valet parking service. Don't ask, but somehow and rather foolishly I somehow locked the car with the keys still in the ignition. Shit!

The valet guys told me to relax and enjoy my meal, while they made some calls to find someone who could jimmy the lock. I was nervous that someone could come by, break the window, and drive off with my hire car and all of my stuff.

Twenty minutes after our meal a shifty-looking fellow came by in a beaten-up car as requested by the valet guys. The man got out of his car, gave me a nod, and shook the hands of the two valet guys, and then walked to his boot. Rather ironically he struggled in opening his own boot, which didn't fill me with confidence. He finally got out a briefcase and went to work like a skilled surgeon. He slid a Slim Jim (the metal thing, not the brand of jerky) into the side of the door; with another device he pumped air into a bag, much like a whoopee cushion, which pried open the door about an inch. With a trusty piece of wire he got a good grip around the lock on the door and pop, he unlocked the car! Phew!

The next day was Christmas Eve and we headed south towards Tampa Bay for our next game, but we had the whole week to make it down there, so we decided to spend Christmas in the lovely city of Nashville. Steph was really surprised that so many things were open in the States on Christmas Day because in England everything is closed. We not only had a fantastic lunch at a nice hotel, but we went to the cinema and then to an arcade, where we played enough skeeball to win some tacky presents for our families, including a Tennessee Titans teddy bear and playing cards.

The next day, however, was pretty bleak. Our only highlight was a KFC stop. We were heading to Orlando for a college bowl game between Florida State and Wisconsin taking place the next day. I was addicted to seeing more and more football and Steph was happy going wherever as long as it was warm. After 200 miles we hit traffic on the highway, a jam so bad that cars had fully stopped.

After 10 minutes cars around me turned their engines off.

After 20 minutes people got out of their cars and stretched a little.

After 30 minutes people began walking their dogs and letting them relieve themselves on the grass verge to the left.

Many people had taken the emergency lane to head to the next exit, which was blocked by the accident. Those cars were then blocking the emergency vehicles getting to the injured people. We were there for two hours. A darkness came over all of us when the coroner's car drove past. People were very patient and no one honked their horns, knowing that something very bad had happened.

We drove past the tragic scene and saw the remains of a crunched car, the blood-stained asphalt, and a zipped-up black body bag. We didn't say anything for a while. I felt bleak and miserable. I didn't want to rush to the game the following day and I didn't feel like driving much more. We found a hotel in Byron, Georgia, and went to sleep.

The next day we didn't go to that college bowl game, but we got to Florida and found a road named St. Augustine. We turned down looking for food, and for about a three-mile stretch it was all food chains. Poor Mr. Gorman would have had a heart attack down this street. We made a count—it was well over 20.

We got to Tampa Bay the night before the final game of the regular season and found a nearby hotel within walking distance to Raymond James Stadium. The only problem was that this hotel was situated between a rough-looking bar and a rough-looking strip joint.

Game 38. NFL Week 17, Oakland Raiders at Tampa Bay Buccaneers, Raymond James Stadium

Final Score: 31-24. Home-win record: 24-14. Capacity: 65,647. Attendance: 64,847. Ticket face value: $100—I paid $100 via Ticketmaster. Picture on ticket: Tickets were e-tickets, but we also got four laminated Pirate ship tickets, which were placed around our necks at the ship; they had a picture of the skull from the pirate ship. Mascot: "Captain Fear," a pirate. Merchandise: Bucs visor like then Buc's coach Jon Gruden wore. Local dish: Cuban sandwich.

On game day, Steph and I walked from the stadium up a main street to find the Pillage Inn crew. We passed several houses that had huge BBQs, with people selling chicken and pork sticks from their front lawns. Music was coming from every direction: bands, cars, and houses.

We took a right on Webb Street and passed a TV station. We continued to walk another 100 yards and the street suddenly became residential. Detached houses with big lawns stretched down the road with white picket fences. I didn't see any tailgaters or tents. I had a street address, but I was confused. Could this party be *in* the house? Could it still be a tailgating party if it was? There was a man sunbathing in the front garden of the house. "Excuse me I'm looking for Greg or Brian?" I asked. "Who?" the man replied, looking at me strangely. "Um, the Pillage Inn guys, they are a tailgating group . . . they are having a BBQ? Apparently," I answered. "Oh right, I dunno the names of those guys in the backyard, but it might be them." His answer took me by surprise. Either he doesn't actually know who is in his own backyard, or he is just randomly sunbathing in someone's front garden.

We walked down the side of the house, where the garden opened out. There was an SUV, a trailer, a large Bucs tent, and about 20 people. It was exactly what a decent tailgate looks like, only it was in someone's back garden. We were instantly welcomed by Greg. It turns out it is not his garden or even his house. The Pillage Inn gives the lady who owns the house a little money each week to secure their tailgating spot in her back garden, which felt very intimate.

Greg introduced us to his friends. We had a quick shot to celebrate the last game of the season. It was only 9:30 a.m. and scorching hot. The liquor went straight to the pit of my stomach and almost congealed there. I felt like I had been kidney punched. Surely I wasn't going to be sick from one shot? Luckily they had some food already on the go, and rather rudely I had to tuck in before being offered as I was starting to get giddy. Greg, Brian, and the effervescent Hardy were really hospitable. Greg gave us a copy of *Southern Tailgater* magazine, in which they were proudly featured.

Their tailgate had several hanging pirate skulls. Steph was having a good time with these folks, she also liked the fact they were playing a lot of hip hop, because she likes shaking her bum to those beats. Before we moved on, the Pillage Inn guys invited us to come back after the game for a little post-game tailgating.

Our next stop was to visit Derek "Old School" Fournier, who is a key member of the "What the Buc?" tailgating group and he had invited me over to his massive party, which took up a whole corner of the parking lot, with easily over 50 people enjoying their food and drink. When we arrived, Derek was involved in the final round of their prestigious cornhole battle. They had pirate and Bucs gear galore, with a Super Bowl–painted trailer, several tents, masses of food, liquor, and a blowup pirate boat.

We then rushed to meet our third tailgater of the day. Afro Man and his three extreme buddies were just locking up their Bucs-themed short bus. Afro Man has a huge orange afro and his friends were just as loud.

Steph and I then found my friends, Adam and Nick, whom I knew through my flag football group and who both live close by. They had brought some drinking buddies along and prepared a "shotgun" beer for me. Basically you cut an opening of the beer can with something sharp, say a pen, big enough for the beer to leave. Then in one swift movement, you place that new hole over your mouth and open the can from the top. This makes the beer flow in one gush, and you have to drink the can of beer in perhaps three huge gulps. I didn't quite get it all and plenty went down my shirt as the others laughed at me.

I had bought tickets for what was supposed to be my last game of the trip at $100 each in the summer. The Bucs PR team called me the day before the game and offered me four tickets on their famous pirate ship. I would still need my purchased tickets to get into the stadium. It was a massive last game for the Bucs who needed to win, which would knock out the Eagles' chances of making the playoffs. Then the Bucs would have needed the then knocked out Eagles to do them a huge favour by beating the Cowboys in the 4 p.m. game in order for the Bucs to make the playoffs.

We went inside the stadium and walked past the ship and got to our paid seats first, which were in the lower section on the 5-yard line. I wanted to see the ship's cannons blast off, which I knew they fired off when the Bucs score. We waited the whole first quarter but there was no scoring action. Steph had gone to get some much-needed water as we were getting scorched, and just as the Bucs finally made it into the red zone, there was a "Boom! Boom!" sound. The loud cannons took me by surprise. I thought it was only going to go off after the Bucs scored. I couldn't believe how loud the sound was. We were at the complete opposite end to where the ship was and it was still so loud. The Bucs soon scored a TD and by that time I was more prepared.

Steph came back alarmed by the cannons. I didn't tell her to expect them, and she thought the stadium was under some kind of attack. We then made our way to the pirate ship that sits on the north stand as part of the "Buccaneer Cove," which runs the entire length of the end zone. It features a weathered two-story fishing village façade hosting beach hut kiosks. The food stand is aptly named the Captains Grill. The 103-foot-long ship is "an authentic replica of an early 1800s pirate ship. The most menacing aspect of the pirate ship is its massive 9'x7' skull and crossed swords facing the playing field which features huge, glowing red eyes and a mouth that breathes smoke. Additionally, eight cannons celebrate Buccaneer touchdowns by releasing thundering cannon fire, smoke, confetti, mini-footballs, and a variety of Bucs merchandise into the stands. The rigging crew raise and lower its huge 32'x 50' foot sails." Of course no pirate ship would be complete without "a larger-than-life interactive talking parrot that sits perched at the ship's stern. "[24]

It's as if the Bucs got a theme-park architect in on the stadium's design. It was big, fun, and surreal. I thought the ship was a public space, like the Bud Zone in Jacksonville, but even an expensive club ticket would not get you aboard this bad boy. I did not realise just how elite being on the pirate ship was. I had chatted with several hard-core fans who have never missed a Bucs game in thirty years and none of them have been invited on the pirate ship. I felt very honoured.

We had to show our IDs just to get on board. There was a list, and it felt like being a VIP at a nightclub. I was surprised at how few people were there. It was mainly "crew" who were all dressed in black and red and torn shirts and shorts like pirates. I looked down to my "Pirate ship" pass and it said, "Proper attire is required." The ship has three floors and would be a great place for a kid to have a party, which the team allows but not on game days. It certainly beats the local Scouts hut where we had our parties growing up.

The view from the pirate ship was great. The floor is flat though, so if you do not perch yourself at the very front then you will not be able to see much of the game, while just below us were the mighty cannons.

Prior to this game I had merely just watched the hoopla, but at this game we were fully involved with it. On the ship we got to talking to the married couple who are the captains of the ship. The man was in charge of hitting the button to set off the cannons. He had to concentrate on the game, and apparently he had made the mistake of firing off a canon when the Bucs went into the red zone when it should only go off when the Bucs' score. His wife is responsible for firing out t-shirts to the crowd. She was really friendly and she even kept two t-shirts back for Steph and me. During the timeouts, the rest of the pirates on the ship threw out beads to the crowd. On the captain's call we all threw out the red, black, and silver beads to the screaming fans below, and the jumbotron cameras zoomed in on Steph and me as we flung out the beads.

It was halftime very quickly, and the Raiders were playing very well against a better team and were winning 14-7. After the break, the Bucs scored and the cannons fired, nearly knocking me off my feet. Steph noticed a female fan below us who continually propelled her body in front of the cannons, every time they blasted off. The Captain told me that she does this to keep cool, because the "smoke" that fires out of the cannon is pressurized carbon dioxide and has to be kept cold. Next to this fan was a woman holding her baby. Not a good place to stand for her child's delicate ears, I thought. But instead of moving to another part of the stadium, the mother simply put sound protecting headphones on the baby, the kind that construction workers use, straight after a home score. The mother had to keep an eye on the game at all times, because one missed Bucs TD and the baby's ears would surely get blown off. Apparently it's not just the babies that don't like the cannons. The then Bucs head coach, Jon Gruden, didn't like them either, but his team lost this game and the Bucs did not make the playoffs. Like the cannons, he was fired.

I love the dying moments of an all-action game. The Bucs needed a magic quick touchdown to tie, but sadly they couldn't manage it. By then with so much action in the second half my ears were ringing from the cannons and the bells that followed. Sadly, that day my Bears also lost to the Texans, meaning no playoffs for them.

Rudy moment: Bucs receiver Michael Clayton was ridiculously wide open and after catching the ball calmly plodded home 58 yards for a TD.

Orange play of the game: Down 31-24 with 15 seconds to go. All eyes were on Bucs QB Jeff Garcia. He stepped back and waited for the open man. He pump-faked and then saw the open man down field. He pulled back his arm but didn't see the low Raiders defender from behind. He got smacked to the ground. The clock ran out. This was the last play of the game and the last play of the Bucs season.

Extreme fan: It was the battle of the pirates and there were plenty to choose from both teams. "Big Nasty" is a Bucs fan with a hard hat with a horn sticking out, with red-and-black face paint and lots of beads. But my fan of the game was Afro Man. His huge red afro is ridiculous, and he spent the whole game being the ringmaster for the cheering fans.

After the game most of the Bucs fans were quiet and desolate. Steph and I headed back to the Pillage Inn. Often the post-game tailgates aren't quite as much fun when the home team loses but the Pillage Inn crew were still out enjoying themselves, and these fans were remarkably upbeat. I would have thought they would be desperate to get to the Super Bowl that year because this is where it was going to be hosted, and they would have had such a huge home field advantage. So far not one NFL team has ever played in the Super Bowl when their stadium has hosted the game. Greg and Brian explained why they were so upbeat—this way they could get rid of Coach Gruden. They felt if they got to the playoffs, they would only lose in the next round and Gruden would have stayed. They had the Eagles game on, which they sparingly watched, and the Eagles crushed the Cowboys. The result now made no difference to the Bucs, but it put the Eagles into the playoffs, when just weeks ago the playoffs seemed very unlikely for Philly.

The Pillage Inn crew cooked up some great peppered burgers, chicken drumsticks, apple sauerkraut, and then they brought out the Cheez Whiz (cheese in a can). Steph was rather sceptical. I took a shot of it straight from the can and wriggled with disgust. Steph tried some on a cracker, she smiled politely to our hosts, but I knew she didn't much like it. Then again, who actually does?

That evening Steph and I met up with Adam and his friends for some sushi and drinks. I got to watch the last regular-season game, the late night Sunday game between the Broncos and the Chargers on TV in the bar, while Steph played pool and got to dance to some more hip hop. I was happy to see that the Dolphins had beaten the Jets, which meant they would be hosting a wildcard game in the playoffs, meaning that Steph and I could hit an NFL playoff game in Miami without having to travel too far before heading home via NYC in just a couple of days.

9

Post Season

The only playoff game I would be able to see before flying home would be the Miami wildcard matchup the following week, so we stayed in Florida for a week, which meant I could call yet another audible and catch a college bowl game too.

Game 39. Capital One Bowl, University of Georgia Bulldogs vs. Michigan State Spartans, Citrus Bowl Stadium, Orlando

Final Score: 24-12 (neutral ground). Home-win record: 24-14-1 (1 is for neutral). Capacity: 74,365. Attendance: 69,748. Ticket face value: $80—I paid $60 via scalper. Picture on my ticket: Animated picture of the Capital One logo with the conference helmets pointing towards each other. It was the nicest-looking ticket of all them. Georgia Mascots: "Uga," a real bull-dog, and "Hairy," a caricature of a bulldog. Michigan State: "Sparty," a comic Spartan. Merchandise: The programme. Local dish: Boiled peanuts from Georgia and chili from Michigan.

It was New Year's Day and what better way to ring in the New Year than with football. We drove to the parking grounds, two miles away from the stadium. I did not know any specific tailgaters for each of these two schools. Some people had small tailgates out of the back of their cars, but it wasn't like an NFL game and yet it wasn't like the college tailgates I had heard about, which some fans believe outweigh their professional brothers. We hopped on an old yellow school bus that took us to the game, and Steph was pleased to ride the iconic vehicle because it reminded her of her favourite show, *The Simpsons*.

The Bowl games are on neutral turf, so we had to pick a team. Steph picked the Bulldogs because she loves dogs and so it was set—we were Georgia fans. The grass lawn surrounding the stadium was filled with the biggest fan zone I had experienced so far and it had activities for both teams. Like a school kid I ran straight in there taking pictures of as much as I could. Of course there were all the usual inflatable games like at other fan zones, but here there were just a lot more of them.

I was beaming when I had my picture taken with the Heisman Trophy. Two of these trophies get made each year. The winner gets one and his school gets the other. With the sun shining and fun in the air, Steph was having a great day and it was her idea to try on the helmets of the day's two teams. We had our picture taken going helmet to helmet. As for wacky merchandise, we spotted a Georgia-themed wedding girdle and a Michigan State t-shirt that read, "Lose carbs. Eat Wolverine."

The Citrus Bowl Stadium was bleak and grey, but the division and its sponsors plastered it with colourful banners. Here we saw an old-school Budweiser horse and carriage, and on top of the wooden cases of beer lay a wilting Dalmatian. I'm not sure what the Dalmatian has to do with the beer, but Steph wanted to save him from the sweltering heat.

The teams picked for bowl games varies from bowl to bowl and is dependent upon factors like divisional records, what divisions the teams play in, rankings, and apparently on how well the teams' fans travel. The Capital One Bowl always features teams from the Southeastern Conference and the Big Ten conference. Clay Travis says that "no two conferences in America hate each other more than the Southeastern Conference and the Big 10."[1] Elizabeth, my editor for this book, studied at Michigan State University. She told me that MSU is "popular with bowl organizers because we are such great fans, tailgating, spending money, and willing to go anywhere to see our team." Of course, being an editor, she is fully objective.

There were still tickets available and every ticket (no matter the section) costs $80 each. A scalper told me he had great seats on the 50-yard line at the front of the second tier and he wanted $80 a piece. With the game not being sold out, why would I risk buying from him if I could still buy tickets at the door for the same price. I gave him "the walk away." He then asked me the same question that the Baltimore scalper asked: "Well what do you want to pay?" Did these two guys go to the same school of ticket scalping?

We took them off him for $60 each, and luckily they were on the UGA side. In college games the fans sit on different sides of the field, like a cup final at Wembley, only here there were no fans behind either end zone.

We got to our seats and the scalper was right on. Bang on the 50-yard line and the front row of the second tier, perfect seats. The Citrus Bowl stadium was rather bleak, but the teams' spirit squads soon added plenty of colour.

It was still sometime before kickoff, but most of the crowd was already seated, awaiting the pre-show. The Bulldog marching band and cheerleading squad came out and circled the field. They had a whole synchronised setup. The music was loud and every one of those college students was in time. It was mesmerizing watching them move about the field.

The Spartan cheerleading team then followed them and slightly outdid their competitors. Steph and I were amazed at the sheer amount of people involved. There must have been over 200 people on the field and the teams had not even come out yet. It was breathtaking.

Capital One sponsors the annual "College Mascot of the Year" contest, and so several mascots from across the league came running onto the field, which made Steph's day. The winning mascot for the season gets $10,000 towards their school's mascot programme. I pretended to Steph that I knew all of this and that's why I suggested this game. The mascot that really caught Steph's attention was Uga, the actual live white British bulldog who was sporting a spikey black collar. He is the sixth bulldog as the Georgia mascot, all from the same lineage, and all named Uga (University of Georgia). Each dog mascot even has its own stats, as in which has the most amount of home victories and bowl games. The gentleman next to me told us that you can actually watch the funeral of the last mascot (UgaV) online, whom they buried (along with the other Ugas) in a mausoleum by Georgia's Sanford Stadium. At Sanford, Uga has his own air-conditioned doghouse.

The one thing I noticed from kickoff was the sheer amount of spirit from everyone attached to the teams. The cheerleaders were actually excited and jumping up and down at seeing their teams take to the field, the players high-fived each other, and the fans were really passionate.

The game kicked off to a roar. The two bands were now in the stands and took on a secondary battle trying to be louder than their opponents. I also noticed there were far more players on the sidelines than in an NFL team, all of whom never sat down once. Their spirit was incredibly high, and this was not even the national championship.

I knew little about these college players, but our neighbour pointed out that we should keep an eye on two Georgia players: QB Matt Stafford and running back Knowshon Moreno. Both were not playing well in the first half, and both were juniors. He told us that both of these players may not go back into college the following year and go straight into the draft.

Maybe Stafford heard us talking about him and got nervous because he then threw two feeble passes that had no weight on them whatsoever. I shot a glance at my neighbour, suggesting Stafford needs another year in college. With one more Bulldog drive before the break, Stafford threw three consecutive bricks that didn't go anywhere near the receivers, leaving the Spartans up 6-3 at the half.

After the break Stafford realised he was going to need to play a bit better if he wanted that NFL contract the following season. He zipped the ball around with much more confidence and engineered an impressive comeback win to become the game's MVP. Even Steph was surprised by the turnaround in Stafford's arm and accuracy. Months later he was selected first in the 2009 draft by the Detroit Lions and signed a $71.1 million contract, $46.5 of that guaranteed. Lucky thing he wasn't benched at halftime during the game.

Rudy moment: Moreno timed his route to perfection, as he stepped inside to come away from his defender, he turned, and the ball from Stafford hit him right in his stride, he ran on to score the game-winning TD. It was poetic.

Orange play of the game: Pretty much any of the plays by Matt Stafford in the first half.

Extreme fan: Below us in the midst of the Georgia section was an extreme Spartan fan. He was only wearing green-and-white-striped boxer shorts, while the rest of his body (torso, legs, arms, neck, and face) were covered in green paint. On his back he had a big white S, and on his arms the Spartan logo. He also wore an inflatable Spartan football helmet. I'd like to see him try that at a soccer game and survive. I was told later that he goes by the name of John Spartan, and that his own mother does his body paint. He attends every Michigan State event possible, even graduations.

Game 40. Wild card playoffs, Baltimore Ravens at Miami Dolphins, Dolphins Stadium

Final Score: 27-9. Home-win record: 24-15-1. Capacity: 75,450. Attendance: 74,240. Ticket face value: $51—I paid $51 via box office. Picture on my ticket: Text on football watermark. Merchandise: A white towel similar to Pittsburgh's Terrible Towel.

Three days later and it was time to focus back on the NFL. At the Dolphins tailgate, our first stop was to meet with Bill. He was tailgating with his extended family of about 15 people. They gave us hot dogs and coleslaw and Steph got her corn-on-the-cob fix. They pumped as much Dolphins merchandise into their tailgate as possible. They had *everything* Dolphins including napkins, paper plates, plastic cutlery, camping chairs, cups, bowls, and many of the tailgaters were sporting Dolphins trainers and Dolphins socks. One of Bill's friends was wearing an authentic Channing Crowder game jersey, and when I say authentic I mean "authentic." You could still see bloodstains.

After going to every stadium I knew that the Dolphins had one of the best fan zones in the country. There were jugglers dressed as referees on stilts, Dolphins rickshaws, a fan photo section, cheerleaders signing pictures of their cheerleading squad, large inflated mascots walking around, a super fan was riding on a Segway dressed like a Miami super hero, a human-sized Dan Marino bobble-head being paraded, sculptures of Dolphins legends, a giant Dolphins muscle man made from foam, a mini Dolphins car, tents that had free crafts and sign making, a whole area with lounge seating in the shade, headless mannequins with Dolphins jerseys to put your head in, and extremely kitschy female Dolphin fans on roller skates. To top it off, the stadium is on Dan Marino Boulevard. We saw the Budweiser horse and carriage again, with the same melting Dalmatian on top. Steph now refuses to drink Budweiser.

We then found Dolphin Fan Rosie, in exactly the same car spot as before. She recognised me instantly and gave me a big hug. Steph loved her energy and Rosie took great pride in explaining to Steph all of her prized Dolphins trinkets.

Before we knew it, the fans were heading into the stadium. I had called the Dolphins box office as soon as tickets went on sale a few days before, and I was pleased I got a ticket for $51. I said good-bye to Steph as she was going to hang at the tailgate or sunbathe on the straw-like Miami grass. I got to my seat just in time before kickoff, and the noise was immense, much louder than the regular-season game. I was sitting behind one of the end zones up nice and high so I could see everything.

I was actually sitting in the family zone, which meant alcohol was not allowed in that section. Maybe that's how I was able to get a ticket so easily. I felt bad for the steward in my section because every five minutes a fan not knowing the rules would come up the stairs with a beer and be told to go and drink it elsewhere.

The Dolphins were making plenty of mistakes in the first half and by halftime were down 13-3, when really it should have been a lot more. The Miami faithful only had so much patience as they watched their quarterback, Chad Pennington, throw for an alarming four interceptions when he had only thrown seven the whole year. Superstar safety Ed Reed of the Ravens picked up two interceptions, one of which he returned for a touchdown. On top of the four interceptions, the Dolphins also fumbled the ball twice, and no team can win with those kinds of stats.

The Dolphins fans had seen their team fall on their own sword once too often in the game, and with two minutes to go in the 3rd quarter they began departing.

Rudy moment: The Dolphins' only touchdown was a wonderful one-handed catch by their running back, Ronnie Brown. But it was the Ravens' Ed Reed's day, and his over-the-head graceful interception and majestic return for a TD was the Rudy moment.

Orange play of the game: Dolphins QB Chad Pennington and his four interceptions clearly won the orange award overall. Though his teammate Ted Ginn Jr. must get a segment of that orange too. His fumble, which lost the Dolphins 18 yards, took them out of field-goal range and killed off any potential comeback for the home team.

Extreme fan: A Dolphins fan below me was wearing smart trousers and a white dress shirt. His tie was orange with a Dolphin logo on it. He had aqua-green sunglasses on and a mohawk that was dyed Dolphin green. Then there was the Miami Finatic, who had some great posters that he held up in the stadium, like "No Saven the Raven." He told us that he came to London when the Dolphins played there in the '80s. Back then he simply turned up in London with nowhere to stay, no ticket, and no money. He got to the game, stayed at someone's house, and managed to somehow get transport back to the airport for his return flight.

The winners were three chaps who call themselves the Dolphin Bandits. They only wear orange shorts but cover themselves in body paint with massive Dolphins logos on their chest and back. Their faces are painted white around their lips, making them look like skeletons with exposed teeth. Although scary looking, they were very friendly and were really fired up for the game.

After the game we managed to get out of the stadium traffic and race the 1,300 miles back to NYC in just two days to make our flight home. The night of this wildcard game I had a slew of e-mails. Sky Sports had aired the segment with Steph and me from the London game during their broadcast of the Dolphins game that day. Many of the comments were not about the content of the interview but about one of the pundits' comments afterwards. Apparently, Jeff Reinebold, who was on the panel for Sky Sports that night, had a message for Steph along the lines of, "If things don't go well with Adam, I have a son about your age that I'm sure would love to take you out." Steph was flattered that she had just been asked out on national TV.

After our 1,300-mile journey I barely had enough time to say good-bye to Justin before we took our night flight back to London. When we landed, Baz proudly came to pick us up in his XXL "Adam's Football Trip" hoodie. At this point I thought the trip was well and truly over.

I spent the next couple of weeks watching the playoffs at home on TV, and like many NFL players not involved, I was gutted I wasn't at those games. That's when I got a lifeline. Jay and Karen asked me to be part of their four-day Super Bowl party team in Tampa Bay called Super Gate II. They told me if I could fly out to meet them and be an extra pair of hands and take plenty of pictures, then I would not have to spend another penny. Another flight got booked, spending more money I didn't have as I made my third flight to the States, heading to the Super Bowl tailgate. Sadly Steph had to go back to work.

After seeing 40 games, I was inspired to get out on the field and play some flag football before going out for the Super Bowl. Being in the car for about four months had left me rather unfit, despite the 10-mile charity run that nearly killed me.

My friend Johnny, with whom I play flag football, got in touch with the BBC and their sports presenter Mike Bushell. The BBC wanted to do a piece on my story for their Super Bowl build up and air it the Friday before the big game.

In the morning of my flag game, a BBC cameraman came round to my parents' house and he did some shots of me with lots of my merchandise from the trip. He even got my Mum in on the action: coming into the lounge bringing in a nice cuppa tea. He then drove Steph and me to Hyde Park where they filmed me playing flag, which is probably not the best way to sell the game to newcomers.

The cameraman had taken lots of footage of the game, but my highlight reel certainly wasn't going to make it in to Deion Sanders's top 10 plays of the week. I did a sideline interview with Mike Bushell, just like they do at the Pro Bowl. Towards the end of the game, the cameraman and Mike were packing up their things. The game was tied so Tariq, our QB, called for the cameraman to film the last play. Tariq designed an easy play for me to at *least* catch the ball. I was worried about catching the ball because I had dropped every pass so far.

Then it came, my "Rudy" moment. Not only did I catch the ball, but I found myself with a lot of space, which surprised me because clearly the other team knew I was going to get the ball after Tariq made it blatantly obvious by calling out at the cameraman to keep filming. Instinctively I turned towards the end zone and put my head down. I dodged one tackler and I was surprised that I did not hear the "pop" of the flag coming off. I don't usually have the pace to beat people one on one, but I just kept going.

I side juked another would-be tackler, and I then saw Sagar (a Bears fan as well) who is pretty speedy, coming straight for me to make the tackle, yet he acrobatically dived right past me, so I could head straight for the end zone to win us the game!

I was excited to see how the final edit would come out. It was aired on breakfast TV the Friday before the Super Bowl. E-mails came flooding in from people I had not heard from since primary school. The BBC edit made me look just a tad crazy but thankfully they got my touchdown on film, which I sent to Deion. It has been four years, and I'm still waiting for his response.

Just a couple of days before flying out for the Super Bowl, Neil Reynolds asked to interview me on his weekly show on NFLUK.com. It was my second time at the NFLUK HQ and I felt very honoured that he had asked me to come by. Neil asked earnest questions and was genuinely thrilled by my trip and wished me luck in obtaining a Super Bowl ticket. Then two other NFLUK pundits, Mike Carlson (whom I had met only as a cardboard cutout at Wembley) and Nick Halling, both came into the room. They were genuinely pleased to meet me, nearly as much as I was pleased to meet them.

Neil interviewed both pundits for his weekly "in the huddle" show. They discussed the upcoming Super Bowl. Halling, who is a huge Steelers fan, was excited to have his team in the big game. He even waved his Terrible Towel during the show. Nick was still in shock that the Cardinals had made it to the Super Bowl, especially as they had the worst running game in the league.

Just days later I was saying good-bye yet again to Steph at the airport. This time I knew it would just be for a few days and Steph knew I just *had* to go out there. Although most of the time that Steph had spent during the trip was either in the car or at football games, we had shared so many experiences, some great and some freezing cold, but they were our stories and that made us closer. Steph understood the power of the tailgate, and when we said good-bye, neither of us was nervous about the strength of our relationship upon my return.

At the airport, Staley's big head got caught in the x-ray machine and received some strange looks. The usual stone-faced security people couldn't resist and gave him a little try on just to make sure he wasn't a bomb.

Throughout the whole season I had been focused on getting tickets. However, the opportunity to tailgate at the Super Gate for four days with Karen and Jay was such a great offer that getting a ticket for the game would only be an added bonus. If a ticket landed in my hands for a good price, then great, but I wasn't going to spend the four days killing myself trying to get my hands on one. The cheapest seat in the house at Raymond James Stadium for the Super Bowl at face value was $800, but getting face value was nigh on impossible. I heard possible leads around the $3,000 mark!

San Diego tailgater Dog Nut Dan had been to a Super Bowl, and he told me not to waste my money as very few real fans are able to go, since it is so commercial. He told me that playoff games have much more atmosphere, and he would much rather go to an NFC or AFC championship game than a Super Bowl. Joe Cahn gave me similar words of wisdom, but he knew it was just one of those things every football fan would love to experience, more so if it is your own team. I was certainly willing to borrow a lot more on my credit cards if it were the Bears in the final.

When I landed in Orlando I called Jay to pick me up. He pulled up in a sweet yellow Jeep Wrangler, and we had one of those handshakes that turns into an awkward semi-hug. We got to their hotel and I gave Karen a big hug. Before I knew it we were already at the RV rental place and I was signing the insurance papers to drive it.

Although I had racked up plenty of driving miles during the season, I had never got behind the wheel of a vehicle this big before and I was rather nervous. Jay was driving the other RV they had hired, and Karen was driving the Wrangler.

I gingerly made my way out of the car park and headed straight onto the main road. The RV steering was surprisingly light. The power steering must have been souped up to the max, which is not what I can say for the brakes, as I had to slam my foot all the way down to come to a stop. An hour and thirty minutes later, and I was pulling the RV into a huge car park for the ultimate in Super Bowl tailgating!

Super Gate II

Since 9/11, the Super Bowl does not allow tailgating at the stadium for safety reasons, though some cynics say that now the NFL can charge people for their week-long "Super Bowl Experience," the ultimate fan zone. Tunison was miffed and asks, "Why has the NFL turned on something [tailgating] that has always been an integral part of its lifeblood?"[2]

Because of the no stadium tailgating policy, Jay and Karen created Super Gate: "In response to the limited access and ability for most fans to attend and tailgate at the Super Bowl, Super Gate seeks to secure ample parking to allow tailgate enthusiasts the opportunity to take their game day traditions all the way to the Super Bowl."[3]

They had hired a huge empty parking lot just a couple of miles from the Raymond James Stadium, asking fans from across the country to tailgate with them for four days. The focus of the tailgate is for people to have a good time and bring together all tailgaters, whether their team is in the big game or not. They had created a "tailgating decathlon" where points are collated across 10 tailgating events, culminating in the Grand Champion of Tailgaters.

The events were: Poker, Beer Pong, Ladder Golf, Washer Toss, Corn Hole, BBQ Cook-off, Bloody Mary Mix-off, Wing Bowl, Blacktop Babe/Super Fan, and Radical Rig/Site Setup.

On Thursday afternoon I entered the vast blank canvas of the concrete car park, and in just a matter of hours the space was filled with an abundance of RVs, becoming a tailgating paradise. Chuck Culpepper said that that the tailgate is "an extraordinary invention, and it's among the top five reasons for the United States to exist . . . if there's a heaven then, it looks something like this."[4] I had made it to Tailgaters' Heaven.

Jay's 2008 tour bus was already parked in the corner. His monster RV that his sponsors gave him for the year is sheer beauty. It is called the UTV (Ultimate Tailgating Vehicle) and is specifically made for tailgating.

This 43-foot monster vehicle has four flat-screen TVs, an amazing sound system for inside and out, a pull-out grill, and a massive atrium-like kitchen that takes up the back half of the RV. It has two sinks, a fridge, freezer, icemaker, and the whole kitchen wall is a roll-up door with a counter in the middle so your guests outside can see what you are up to. The outside TV is a whopping 52 inches. Karen told me the best thing about this super RV is that it has not one but two bathrooms. Apparently separating the boys from the girls at a tailgate is a luxury. It only has one sleeping area, hence Jay and Karen hired two sleeping RVs—one for them and another for their team, including me.

Last year's Super Gate winners, Kirk and his BBQ Raider tailgate, already had their Grillzilla fired up. Kirk had brought with them two trailers and hired a local RV to sleep in. They had made the drive all the way across the country, bringing all of their food with them from Oakland. Now they had added a Nintendo Wii with Guitar Hero to their flat screen, a popcorn machine, a margarita maker, and a portable hot tub.

Kirk and his team had spent over $5,000 on this Super Gate trip alone, and I got the sense that the competition was going to be fierce. People gathered at Kirk's tent, as Barbecue Bob cooked for everyone. Tri-tip steaks, red-skin potatoes, and salad were passed around, enough for the 40 of us that were there.

At 1 a.m., I got back to my RV and climbed up onto the double bed that was on a shelf above the steering wheel, covered by a massive mattress. It was my first night ever sleeping in an RV and in a car park.

At breakfast I found myself back at the Raider Nation crew, where they were cooking up scrambled eggs and bacon. Do these guys ever stop cooking? Just as I was about to make my way to see Jay and Karen, a stunning vehicle parked itself right by me. It was a huge monstrous SUV that had its whole body sprayed in homage to the Oakland Raiders, with Raider helmets, logos, and players, including a great image of Raider coaching legend John Madden in his slimmer days.

More and more RVs and tailgating groups were showing up all day and getting "plugged in." Jay's huge generators and shower block meant that he had created a huge concrete campsite that met all our needs. Unless someone was going to the actual game on Sunday there was no reason to leave the lot. Karen then introduced me to a Chicago tailgate crew known as the Area 4 gun club, so called because their team captain, Darryl, is a South Side Chicago cop.

They steamed me up a Chicago-style Polish loose meat sandwich that was delightful, and after an hour of debating the public schooling system in Chicago and whether Kyle Orton should be our starting QB next season, I realised that I had found my "crew." They told me to come by anytime.

Then I saw a flicker of rival Packers pass the window. I knew there wouldn't be a fight over this rivalry, because NFL fans don't behave like that, but I was prepared for some kind of trash talk. The door opened. My new crew stood up and charged towards the Packers fans. Both sets of "rival" fans embraced each other with long hugs. They had not seen each other since the last Super Gate, where these rival fans became instant friends. Awwwww.

Next, I visited the Green Bay guys, who had some wonderful cheeses on their table. Their tailgate forecourt was filled with taxidermy animals, including a deer, a raccoon, and a bear! Then they popped out a huge piece of ham on the bone, which Jay carved and it was devoured quickly. The sheer amount of red meat I had already consumed in two days was what I would normally have in a week!

The famous Food Network chef Guy Fieri turned up later with a camera crew. The energetic Guy, with his trademark spikey hair and Dickies shorts, swung by everyone's tailgate, trying out all the food. The tailgaters were ready to show the world their stuff. The Grillzilla was firing up giant prawns, tuna, salmon, and steak. The "Iron Lot Tailgaters" from Dallas had steaks grilling before they busted out massive whole lobsters that were around two feet in length. Apparently they had an even bigger lobster stored on ice for the cooking competition the next day. The Packers guys cooked up raccoon and bear meat, while Jay, over at his UTV, was cooking fish.

When it started to get dark, the first of the 10 challenges kicked off with poker and I played as the dealer. While we were all playing, at least five or six tailgaters were cooking up a storm and kept bringing us more and more food. Once the poker was over it was back to the Raider Nation crew who cooked for everyone . . . again. This time we had giant shrimp, chicken teriyaki, and pork, and there were around 70 people enjoying the late-night food. I just couldn't figure out where they were storing all of it. Unbelievable!

The next day was when the real competition started. I stood alongside Jay, Darryl from "the "Area 4 gun club," AM830 KLAA's hilarious, loud-mouthed radio presenter Gordon "Lug Nutzz" Stewart, and football writer Chris Warner, as we made up the food judging panel. What an honour that was.

We all hopped on board the UTV as the tailgaters brought over their four dishes on red plastic plates. We scored each dish in terms of "presentation," "originality," and "taste." Jay starts everyone with a score of seven. If something is good, it gets extra points, and if it is bad, it loses points. Each tailgating group had to make a cocktail, a starter, a main, and a dessert. There were only four contestants. Of course there were far more tailgaters out in the lot, but not everyone wanted to compete in the BBQ cook-off.

All four of the cocktails were tasty, which was a good start. Then the starters came out: The lamb chops on a bed of lettuce were remarkably succulent and sweet. There was a cheese platter, with crackers and venison (I figured that was from the Packers guys); then came some giant prawns; and finally my favourite of the starters, potato chips that had caramel and chocolate drizzled all over. They would have gotten a full 10 points from me had they have used what Jay called my "orange crack": Cheetos.

The main dishes came up, and some teams put in two or three plates. There was not one hot dog or hamburger in sight. I tried BBQ raccoon, duck breast, wild boar taco, venison cubes, lobster, teriyaki salmon, pork, chicken, beef, steak, crabsticks, and finally I even ate bear! It was rich in taste, but I can't say I enjoyed eating it. Damn those pesky Packers fans.

For dessert there were gold and black cupcakes (Pittsburgh Steelers style), upside-down pineapple cake, folded pancakes with cream, and my favourite, a kind of cream roll fondant with strawberries inside—my first piece of fruit in three days. I had eaten some pretty good food on the tour, but being a food taster at Super Gate blew me away.

The Packers teased Darryl and me for having eaten bear, but I still had a gift for them: Branston Pickle. In the States, if you ask for a pickle you get pickled cucumber, otherwise known as a gherkin, but at home, pickle is tough to describe: "It is black stuff, with vinegar, and chunky pieces of pickled vegetables, and you put it on cheese!" I told my new friends, but I wasn't winning them over with my description.

They were naturally scared that my so-called black shit was going to contaminate and destroy their famous Wisconsin cheese. They nervously spread the black gooey goodness onto the cheese and took a small bite. They winced with the vinegar kick, which is expected for a pickle rookie, but then as they munched on the crunchy vegetable, I saw them break into a satisfactory smile, even though they were trying to hold back their compliments. Soon they all gave me the nod of approval, saying, "I could get used to that."

I was surprised at just how much I cared, and wanted them to like my addition. Not because I needed approval, but I think it was because I felt that I could "give something back," I *could* contribute and add to the tailgating spectrum. Could it be this moment where I would begin to turn from tailgatee to tailgater?

For the whole season people told me why they love tailgating, but until I gave something of myself and of my culture, I couldn't fully digest the buzz that so many tailgaters get when they're cooking for others. I was thrilled that I had broadened someone else's palate.

The rest of the day was all about the rest of the decathlon games. In the afternoon, from nowhere three mighty super Raiders fans, dressed up to the max with black-and-silver face paint, spikes, skulls, and leather trousers, met up with the audience. Violator, Raider Jerry, and Toozak all took to the stage. They looked amazing and their intensity was just shy of menacing.

Two nights before, I had met the Violator, who is a Raiders fan named Wayne and is particularly articulate and intelligent. He was so passionate about his tailgate team competing for the Super Gate decathlon that he crossed the country, even though he had to fly back to Oakland on Super Bowl Sunday, missing the big game. I had discussed with Wayne at great length how so many Americans that I met at games seemed to "dumb" themselves down when a camera was in front of them. For two nights over huge plates of tailgate food we covered a full range of philosophical theories to understand the NFL, the phenomenal fans, and the power of TV within the sport.

On that Saturday evening when the extreme Raiders fans took to the stage, I noticed who the Violator really was and I was shocked by Wayne's playfully menacing alter ego. This was the superbly intelligent, thoughtful man, who was now sporting a manic smile, black leather trousers and boots, black-and-silver face paint, a black leather bandana, silver spikes coming out of his shoulders, a custom Raiders jersey, silver metal studs on his arms, black wide-receiver gloves, a silver sword, and finally a black leather fanny pack (bumbag for us Brits) that normally would receive some mocking, but alongside the outfit, it actually pretty looked good. The Violator snarled right down the barrel of my camera with "I'm going to kill someone" menacing eyes. It boggled my mind because as Wayne he was so calm and pensive. It wasn't even a football game day so I was surprised at his focused "game face."

Later that night the Violator was slowly morphing back into his everyday Wayne persona. While he had on regular clothes, he still had on the black-and-silver face paint, and there was a real sense of his double personality. He told me that as soon as the face paint goes on, "that's it" and "The Violator" has been formed and is ready for football. There was a blur between the real person and the alter ego. In the end it was the Violator who dominated, snarling at me that it is he who tries to keep Wayne at bay, at least during football season.

While the beer pong event was taking place, a local band got up on stage and played an array of classic rock tunes. That's when Lisa from the Iron Lot Tailgaters asked me to come and see her tailgate. Each team gets 10 points if they win the "radical rig," and she had a new addition to show me, which had only just arrived.

Sitting there in all its glory under the Tampa Bay moonlight was an enormous ice sculpture. You've got to give credit to someone for bringing an ice sculpture to Tampa Bay. It was a square piece of ice with two football helmets facing each other, both with the Super Bowl teams' logos. Above that was another chuck of ice in the shape of a football. But that was not the best part. The sculpture had a full working ice luge with a small funnel at the top. Bart, Lisa's husband, poured some drink down the tube. I watched as the bright green liquid moved around the inside of the ice and then dribbled out of the spout on the side. I knocked back the shot, which was perfectly chilled. I was flabbergasted.

"Tailgateville" from Florida was now having a small party by its stripper pole, which included its own disco lights. I thought maybe an overweight drunk man might be stripping, but instead they were doing something called a keg stand which was causing everyone to shout out in wonder and merriment. Before I could figure out the actual exercise, I was hoisted upside down with my mouth on the spout of the keg and told to not stop drinking. Beer rushed in at full speed into my mouth and all I could do was drink. 1-2-3-4, I heard someone count. It really was drink or drown. 5-6-7-8. The beer was fizzing at the back of my throat and dribbling out. 9-10-11-12. I simply could not swallow quick enough and my lungs were running out of air. 13-14. I spurted beer all over myself and I got a hefty pat on the back as I was turned back onto my feet, woozy and shell-shocked.

Personally I thought I did pretty well—until the next person drank upside down for 34 seconds, that is.

The evening become a little sparse, and then I realised it was the Saturday night before the Super Bowl, when there are lots of Super Bowl parties going on all over the city. Allen St. John says that "tickets to the Playboy party are even more in demand than Super Bowl game tickets, and often commanding more on the black market."[5]

I got to my bed, excited about Super Bowl Sunday the next day. The morning was kicked off with the Bloody Mary mix contest, and lucky for me I was not judging that one as I was nursing a slight hangover. Kirk's Raiders team won the Bloody Mary contest.

The Iron Lot Tailgaters ice luge had sadly already begun to melt. I had whizzed around the entire site, and there were tailgaters here representing nearly every NFL team. I could only find two Cardinal tailgate groups—not a large amount, considering they were playing in the Super Bowl. The majority of the tailgaters were supporting Pittsburgh.

Next on the agenda was the 100-yard shot stick, where 85 people all took a shot of alcohol at the same time as the "shot sticks" clicked together. I got myself up on top of the UTV and started to snap away. The 100-yard shot was one of those things in life, that take forever to set up and get right, and then it is over in a matter of seconds. Still it looked awesome from where I was standing.

We then gathered around the stage for the decathlon prizes. Predictably, Kirk's team won the radical rig award. As he went up to collect the award, his teammates colluded, and peeled towards him with a bin full of ice and water giving him the famous "Gatorade dunk," just like the players do to their coach when they win a big game.

The most prestigious award, "The Blacktops Best BBQ," was up next and this award gives the tailgate team 30 points instead of the usual 10. The crowd was nervous for the four teams involved, and by just half a point, the Iron Lot Tailgaters were victorious.

I turned to Kirk and saw that he had one large tear in his eye. The winning team hugged him and they walked up to collect their prize. The 30 points had pushed this Dallas team over the edge, giving them a victory in the overall decathlon, making them the tailgating team of the year and the Super Gate II champions.

I felt gutted for Kirk. The Iron Lot Tailgaters had some great food and probably deserved to win, but it was just that Kirk and his team had fed so many of us day after day, night after night, and I had come to know his team more than any other tailgating team in the league. No one apart from my mother has cooked this much for me in my entire life.

Kirk and his crew were magnanimous in defeat. Kirk said, "It is good for the competition to have a new winner." This is in direct reflection of the socialism in the NFL, where the league is stronger because of the equality in the teams when the NFL wants a different winner each season. Would tailgate groups still try in the future if the Raider Nation won every year? Would fans of all 32 NFL teams be drawn to the league if they knew the Patriots would win every year?

For Kirk and his crew there was only one way to take such defeat. With the Super Bowl just 30 minutes away, the Raiders crew brought out their game-day feast—an actual pig lying flat out on the Grillzilla. All were welcome to make their own pulled pork sandwiches for a Super Bowl snack. Barbecue Bob and Uncle Stan were waiting for me, and they filled my plate with pork, salad, chicken teriyaki, and popcorn and put a margarita in my hand. I found a comfy chair and I was all set for Super Bowl XL.

"Just out of curiosity, just to humour me," I said to Brian, the ticket broker who was selling tickets for the Super Bowl at the Super Gate, "how much have you got a ticket for?" He called his people down at the game. They were asking $1,800 for a nosebleed ticket! "Ahh, nevermind," I sighed.

I wasn't upset that it was beyond my price range, because I got to sit amongst 600 tailgaters, three miles from Raymond James Stadium ready to watch the big game on an inflated jumbo screen. Jay had told me that he and the others at the tailgate had done a whip round for me to be at the game, but the ticket was still too expensive. Still it was a lovely gesture.

It was a superb game, and towards the end the underdog Cardinals were up by three points. Yet with just 40 seconds to go, the trailing Steelers QB, Roethlisberger, fired to Santonio Holmes in the end zone. He leapt high, and despite being covered by three defenders, he caught the ball while on his tiptoes and fell to the floor, keeping himself inbounds. It was the stuff of beauty. With little time left Cardinals QB Kurt Warner tried for one last hurrah, but as he was throwing he was hit and the refs called it a fumble, while many others thought it was just an incomplete pass. We will never know if just one more play would have changed the outcome. But it stood as a fumble to end the game, giving the Steelers their record-setting sixth Super Bowl trophy.

Santonio Holmes was the game's MVP for his nine catches and 131 receiving yards, but mainly for the ultimate in Rudy plays—the game-winning, iconic catch at the end. The season's MVP was Peyton Manning, the offensive player of the year was Drew Brees, and the defensive player was linebacker James Harrison of the Steelers.

I thought I would dish out a few awards based on the games that I saw. My two best offensive players that I saw were Drew Brees, who I saw throw nine TDs and a combined 894 passing yards in three games, and DeAngelo Williams, who in the two games that I saw scored three TDs and rushed for a combined whopping 326 yards.

On defense I picked the best two safeties in the league. I saw Troy Polamalu in five games, and he played like a man possessed in all of them, picking off two interceptions. The other safety was Ed Reed, who I saw grab two interceptions, one TD, one sack in three games. If Polamalu is the rabid dog, then Reed is the opposite; he is smooth, precise, calm, and majestic. If only the two could play on the same team.

Warren St. John feels that "the end of the season is unnervingly abrupt,"[6] and I couldn't agree more, because in the following calm crisp morning, I woke up in the RV and realised that my football odyssey was all over.

It was my first post-game morning with the RV crowd, and I didn't know that amongst the RV faithful "everyone wakes early and blows out of the lot, fearful for being the last out,"[7] wrote Warren St. John. It was very early, surprisingly cold and nearly everyone had packed up their grills and began driving home, leaving a frosty, empty car park, peppered with full black bin bags. The DiEugenio family and I were practically the last to leave. Even the Raiders tailgate crew, who had been cooking solidly for five days, finally had packed up their stuff. They even apologised that they didn't have any breakfast for me. It's never good to be the last one to leave a party. And in that instant, just like that, my trip and the 2008–2009 football season had ended.

When I got back home Karen had asked me to write a "best of" article for *Tailgater Monthly*. I did so in collaboration with Hans. In Karen's editorial note for that month's edition, she mainly wrote about the Super Gate and had some lovely words for me:

> The best part was finally getting to meet Adam from England, whom I've spoken with all season long as he attempted—and achieved—his epic feat, attending forty football games in eighteen weeks! Seeing him reconnect with all the friends that he has made along the way, spoke to the magnitude of his tailgate experience.[8]

Three months later it was May 2009, and I was suffering from football separation anxiety, a widespread condition that attacks NFL fans between the months of February to August. There is no natural cure, apart from more football. Warren St. John says that "our drug is doled out according to a strict schedule, our highs carefully rationed. Try as might, we're rarely given enough to overdose."[9] Well if an average NFL season ticket holder only sees 8 games a year, then I think we can all agree that by seeing 40, I somewhat overdosed on my choice of drug, and now I was paying the price by having a terrible comedown.

Yes, of course all 32 teams start reevaluating their squads—there is the Pro Bowl, free agency begins, players are moved to other teams, and other such activities that take place between February and August—but it isn't real football action, or at least not on the field. Sure I was teased with the NFL draft in April '09, but then nothing until the summer when the teams go into training camp and pre-season starts. For those lucky enough to actually work in the NFL, there apparently is no "off-season." The only "real" holiday the NFL takes is two weeks in July, which Rich Eisen says has become the "wedding season in the NFL."[10]

Keith Webster pointed out that "in the violent world of the NFL, six months a year of down time, free from the heavy hitting, is the greatest health protection and benefit the warriors of the gridiron have."[11] This is all very good for the players, but what about the fans? Where's our health protection plan? Where's our counselling? When's our next football game?

I felt like a drug addict going cold turkey, sniffling out stories on football blogs and watching the past season highlights on NFL.com to give me some kind of a kick. But it wasn't enough. I needed new, fresh football.

Steph had thought it was just a one-season adventure, but I had been bitten by the football bug far deeper than I thought, and it probably didn't help matters when the NFL commissioner himself, Roger Goodell, personally wrote to me:

Dear Adam:

British fans have shown tremendous enthusiasm for NFL football for many years. However, we are not aware of anyone that has made the kind of football pilgrimage to the United States that you did in 2008.

You couldn't have picked a better time for your trip. Our game has never been stronger. From your first game at Giants Stadium for NFL Kickoff 2008 to your last at Dolphin Stadium in the Wild Card playoffs, I hope you enjoyed the compelling action you witnessed during your coast-to-coast trip.

Now that your whirlwind NFL tour has ended, I trust you will continue to follow the league with the same passion in the future.

Thank you for your tremendous support of the National Football League.

Sincerely,
ROGER GOODELL

10

From Tailgatee to Tailgater and from Fan to Super Fan

The automobile, and ultimately the motor home,
opened the floodgates for fans.[1]

Roger Goodell's comment in his letter to me—"*I trust you will continue to follow the league with the same passion in the future*"—was calling out to me, and so when the 2009 schedule came out, as a matter of habit I got my stadium-to-stadium mile matrix out and began mapping which games I would go to if I could do it all over again. Only this time I was picking the matchups based on possible tailgating scenarios, rather than the teams and their style of play.

NFL.com writer Steve Wyche posted up a "fictitious" wonder trip that would take in a game at all 32 franchises. That's when I knew I wasn't the only NFL fan doing the same thing. I wrote to him saying that he should give his trip a try. He wrote back saying, "I remember your journey and I was beyond impressed by your will, determination, and stamina!"

America is a country in love with vehicles and the open road, so it was no wonder that vehicles and food were the main ingredients needed to conceive tailgating. In the seventies, tailgaters started to bring RVs and motor homes to the tailgate. They could use their own bathrooms, cook, and take lots of friends in one vehicle. Warren St. John said that "the RVs blew open the experience," and because the RVers were taking up lots of space they started to arrive earlier and earlier, where he says "it is not unheard of for fans to arrive in their motor homes a full week before kickoff." He continues to say that for a "typical Alabama game, between 250–800 motor homes show up . . . the RV offered the possibility of total immersion."[2] I had been pretty immersed in football the year before, but how do I go even deeper?

So I thought why not do a similar trip, but with more focus on my being the tailgater instead of the tailgatee? I could give something back to the tailgating world, other than just a pickle. How about full-on British food? Steph was taken with the tailgating spirit by now, and she was excited about the prospect of *us* doing this trip together. We wanted to be called the "Great British Tailgaters," and we wanted to drive from stadium to stadium in a black London taxi cooking British food along the way. But, despite our efforts, we couldn't find a sponsor, and I didn't have another apartment to sell, so this became another pipe dream.

That's when Jay and Karen threw me yet another lifeline. They asked us to join them on their 2009 tour, which would involve living on their new tiki tailgate tour bus that they had personally converted from a classic yellow school bus. I instantly said yes and headed straight to Joe Cahn's informative site to understand what I needed to be a true tailgater. He wrote:

> Dress in team colors. Plan your menu. Make a list of the items. Plan to arrive three to four hours early and stay one to two hours after the game. Find a good spot to park, fly a flag, decorate your tailgate site, have jumper cables, toilet paper, plastic trash bags, extra ice, rain gear, first aid kit, sun block, a friend, comfortable shoes, antacid, meet your tailgate neighbors, food should be ready, leave the area clean.[3]

I was really eager to see Jay's final schedule. When he published it, I was really happy because he was throwing in several college games too, something that I wanted to explore and experience. Our schedule was to start at the Hall of Fame game in August, which was a perfect start because it meant I could actually meet all the PFUFA members. I sent my new schedule to Steve Wyche and his all-American response was simply, "Adam. This is awesome!"

Because of work commitments, Steph was only going to join me for the second half of the season after the mid-season London game. Unfortunately, I didn't go back on the tour after the London game for various reasons. Steph was disappointed, but I couldn't complain, because in that half-season I went to 15 football games in 8 weeks, including games at the Hall of Fame, Buffalo Bills pre-season, the Seattle Mist (Lingerie Football League), Washington Huskies,

Seattle Seahawks, Oakland Raiders (twice), UCLA, San Diego Chargers, Stanford University, Arizona State University, Denver Broncos, Notre Dame University, Atlanta Falcons, and the game between the New England Patriots and the Tampa Bay Buccaneers in London, which Steph joined me for. The London game was a chance for me to see the great Tom Brady finally play a game, as the year before he was out with a season-long injury.

My first adventure as a Great British tailgater was at the Hall of Fame game with Jay on his new bus nicknamed the Mullet. The Mullet has an upper deck on the back part of the roof, a tiki bar inside, a sink, toilet, two couches that flip down into a sofabed, a satellite, and a flat-screen TV (of course). But the real kicker is that one of the side walls flips down to make a large lower deck, exposing the whole tiki bar. Jay had littered his bus with NFL merchandise galore, all of which had been donated to him over the years.

I brought over a suitcase full of Great British sauces, dips, and cooking ingredients to start my culinary adventure. Jay and Karen gave me my blacktop/super fan name, "The Tailgate Knight," in homage of their favourite film, *Monty Python's Holy Grail*. With a nickname I felt like I was really moving towards being a super fan.

I arrived in Canton, Ohio, in August 2009 just days before the NFL Hall of Fame enshrinement ceremony. "We are here!" I told my upbeat taxi driver, as soon as I saw the plethora of tailgaters on the lawn beside a hotel with grills and NFL-themed tents. A large man came up to me with his arms open. He knew my name and shook my hand with all the friendliness akin to us being very good friends, but I was thinking, Who is this guy? He then proudly stated, "I am Ram Man, man!"

I had only seen pictures of this great NFL super fan when he was in full NFL garb, including his blue-and-gold face paint, a huge foam ram hat, and a Rams football uniform. Many of the PFUFA members had arrived for their reunion alongside several PFUFA nominees. They were all "tailgating" outside the hotel, cooking on their grills. None of them were in character, which meant I could barely recognise any of them, though nearly everyone recognised me and I felt a little embarrassed asking who they all were. I came face to face with fans that I had missed on the 2008 tour. Hans and his bride, Crystal, arrived with their daughter. It felt like it was a not only a reunion for the PFUFA members but also a reunion for my 2008 trip.

The next morning we all met at 5:30 a.m., in full character and costume for the community parade that was going to through downtown Canton. Luckily, I didn't have a full character outfit and face paint to put on, just my trip t-shirt and my Staley hat. The night before, Sergeant Colt told me I could get involved with everything the PFUFA guys were doing that weekend. This meant I was actually allowed to be on their float, called the 12th Man, with all the super fans!

On our float I could sense just how much respect all the fans have for each other regardless of what team they support. This 2.2-mile parade is the third-largest street parade in the United States, and it included the NFL enshrinees! Sandwiched between us were huge inflatable cartoon characters, clowns, classic cars, and several high school cheerleading groups alongside their marching bands.

I stood proudly on the float as it weaved through Canton. It was like *we* were the superstars of the NFL.

In the afternoon we were back at the Hall of Fame and all the PFUFA members sat in a large tent, where for two hours they proceeded to sign their own cards, as if they were pro football player cards. Lots of young fans passed through and I was wowed by all the colour and positive energy. The PFUFA fans brought lots of team trinkets, such as posters and player cards that they gave to the younger fans.

Soon after, Hans, his family, and I went into the Hall. The staff remembered me and although I'm not usually a fan of museums, I could go back to this place over and over again. Hans and I both had visited before but we still ogled at the classic artefacts and listened to the guides like transfixed children. Even after going to 37 NFL games the previous year I still wasn't desensitized to the magic of the game.

The "Adam's Football Trip" informal reunion continued when Hans and I bumped into the Ultimate Sports Trip guys, Peter and Andrew. We were all magically together under one roof, the Hall's famous and instantly recognisable rotunda.

Later, we entered Fawcett Stadium for the NFL's Hall of Fame enshrinement ceremony. The many Bills fans were excited about seeing their franchise owner, Ralph Wilson Jr., and legendary ex-Bills player and sack machine, Bruce Smith, get enshrined.

I was unsure of what to expect as I had never seen the event on TV. We were momentarily halted getting into the stadium to allow the Tennessee Titans players, who were scheduled to play there the following day against the Bills in the first pre-season game, to pass. Lady Titan shrieked and bellowed at her favourite players. Several came over to sign autographs and they all knew her by her super fan name.

Once the audience was settled, everyone got very excited when they introduced the current Hall of Famers, who graced the stage wearing their proud yellow Hall of Fame jackets. My new friend, Michael Irvin, was up there as was John Madden, just a few months after announcing his retirement.

The always charming face of the NFL network, Rich Eisen, was our host, and he shouted out to the hungry NFL fans that "Football is back!" resulting in a huge cheer. The drug of football was being zapped straight back into my blood cells and my withdrawal symptoms instantly vanished. "Let's do some enshrining," Eisen added. The fans got excited but I thought that comment sounded frankly bizarre, something that a cult leader might say. I was half-expecting the players to have their heads doused in water and for Mr. Goodell to come by and actually bless them.

The evening however was far more tame and straightforward. In fact, for an American show there was little performance. Just a few fireworks and not even one single free t-shirt was fired out to the crowd. The night was simply listening to speech after speech after speech, which although I was happy with, for a non NFL fan it would have been a bit of drag. It was just as well that Steph wasn't there.

The NFL's equivalent of the Academy Awards brought a series of heartfelt and proud speeches before "Bruuuce" Smith, the last of the six enshrinees, made his speech. This beast of a man who spent a career ripping through line men and pouncing on QBs suddenly brought the water works, and many a Bills fan around me shed a tear or two. If the Sack Machine, who claimed 201 sacks in an illustrious career, can cry in public, than any of us can.

It was pretty incredible that over 25,000 people came to see these six men receive their Hall of Fame status, which is basically a statement from the league saying, "You had a very good career, well done."

With my new PFUFA buddies I got a lift back to the hotel, where Jay and his Mullet bus were waiting for me. I was really excited that this vehicle was going to be my new home for the next eight weeks. When I saw the bus, I was more than impressed and was looking forward to the season ahead.

The next morning I was invited to be part of PFUFA's breakfast enshrinement ceremony. This was held in the main theatre at the Hall of Fame. Sergeant

Colt made a speech before we all tucked into a French toast casserole, sausages, fresh fruit, and a delicious quiche-like tartlet. Before long it was time for the 14 nominees to make their speeches.

Sergeant Colt was asked in *Tailgater Monthly* the season before, "What makes PFUFA so special to you?" His answer was,

> You will be very hard pressed to find a better, kinder, more passionate group of fans under one roof. Here, we have Brownies drinking with Bengals fans. We have Packers, Vikings, Bears, and Lions fans standing shoulder to shoulder grilling, laughing, breaking bread. We have too many examples to list. In short, PFUFA is a family.[4]

There was something surreal about seeing each nominee in his or her full fan costumes on a formal podium, being articulate, pensive, and melancholic. "Gorilla 'Rilla" had nearly passed out during the procession the day before because he was in his character suit for so long that he got dehydrated. This morning he recited his whole speech while still wearing his full gorilla mask and outfit. One would normally see such fans riled up and shouting at the top of their lungs in their natural habitat of an NFL stadium. HawkFiend of the Seahawks wears a scary mask with large green horns, a bright green goatee beard and rubber gloves with long green talons, yet his speech was as touching as that of the NFL enshrinees the night before.

Dave Motts, the head of marketing and operations at the Hall of Fame, made a speech about the importance of this very unique group. Purple Dame of the Ravens ironically became speechless during her speech because of the sheer honour to even be nominated. She tried to refer to her notes but they had been confiscated and she had to speak from the heart (PFUFA does not allow notes at the speeches, which makes for an interesting rule).

All 14 nominees were drafted and I have to say the speeches were far more entertaining than that of the NFL enshrinees the night before. These wonderful guys and gals live for their clubs and use their characters/alter egos to bond with their communities and to raise plenty of money for charity.

At the end of the colourful speeches and unique tales of football fandom, it was time for all 14 new members to receive their gold coins and pose for a group picture. It was a fascinating and emotional few hours—I felt drained yet inspired.

There were a series of tales of how PFUFA members representing different teams help each other in the off-season, especially with older members who couldn't make the trip to Canton that weekend because of illness.

Ram Man had asked me to come back the following year, and the hairs on the back of my neck stood up, thinking about one day being on that podium being enshrined into this unique group and how proud I would feel if I simply got nominated.

Many of the PFUFA members who were not going to the game later that night began heading home and everyone began saying their emotional good-byes and looking through the NFL schedules to plan when they would see each other next. I motioned over to Sergeant Colt to thank him once again for allowing me to be so involved with the reunion, and that's when he took something out of his bag. It was a PFUFA draft card. I was speechless. Even if I never actually get drafted to stand alongside these legends of fandom, it still made me incredibly proud just to be nominated. Plus I was the first "international" fan to obtain a draft card. The Sergeant has only actually nominated three people since he was drafted five years prior.

Sergeant Colt told me, "I see in you the qualities that we want to promote in this organization. I see a great fan, great character, and great dedication. You, to me, is exactly what this group is looking for," which sent a tingle down my spine, and it put all the strains of the trip into perspective. It was indeed worth it. I was thankful that when I was a boy I held onto my John Elway American football in primary school in the face of adversity . . . Soccer.

An hour later there was an impromptu and odd informal marriage ceremony between Darth Packer (Sergeant Colt's brother) and "Go Go," his real-life wife, who is a Saints fan. Both of them are PFUFA members. Da Pope, in front of the Hall, married this couple as NFL "Super Fans." The usual marriage vows were said but Da Pope added "respecting his or her team" at the end and finished off with "we hope you live a happy and competitive football life together!"

Before the Hall of Fame game we tailgated on someone's front garden by Fawcett Stadium. Of course Joe Cahn was there, as were Scott and his dog bus from Cleveland, Kenny with his "Pinto Ron" car from Buffalo, and Hans with a new "QuestMobile," for the first tailgate of the 2009 season.

That night in Fawcett Stadium watching the first pre-season game of the 2009 season, I sat with Hans (I wore his spare Bills jersey) and the rest of the remaining PFUFA crew. Although I had been welcomed as a "guest" for the Hall of Fame weekend, I had originally felt a little uneasy being in the group pictures, because at the time I didn't even have a draft card and I didn't want to come across as overstepping my welcome. These fans had earned the right to be there and I didn't want to devalue the PFUFA name. During the third quarter of this game, the announcer asked *all* of the PFUFA fans to stand up. This time I proudly stood as my draft card was securely in my wallet, and the crowd cheered us all on.

A week later, I was in Buffalo for the pre-season game against the Bears. The 2008 trip was about being a home fan, but I couldn't root against my Bears again, so I grabbed my Staley hat, put on my Walter Payton jersey, and headed to gate seven as a clear "away" fan. As I got closer to the stadium something strange started to happen, something that took me by complete surprise, and it didn't happen once but several times.

"F**k da Bears" was hollered at me from Bills fans as I waited to go into the historic stadium. There were other people wearing Bears jerseys, who got the odd "Bears suck," but none of them got the verbal tirade that I was under. I was shocked and intimidated. My big Bears foam hat was making me a target for abuse. Of course I expected a little horseplay, but I was alarmed to have 10 people surround me who then repeatedly swore at me. It was really quite scary. "What are you a bunch of soccer hooligans?!" I belted back, but it didn't work. One moron got in my face repeating, "Payton's dead." I replied calmly, saying, "I know that sadly Walter Payton has passed away, but by all means please show me exactly where it states in this stadium that I'm not allowed to wear a jersey from a deceased NFL player, especially one that happens to be an NFL legend?" The moron looked confused and was shaken by my accent and my calm sarcastic response. I think he is only programmed to hear "Bills suck" from away fans.

All the loving and warmth of the PFUFA reunion the week before about how they respect each others' teams and looked after each other, was not quite working out for me in the reality of this game. All I had on was my hat and my Bears jersey. So how much abuse would I have got if I had my face painted, donned shoulder pads, beads, and further Bears trinkets? I figured this might be why some PFUFA and extreme super fans don't go to some away games, or certainly not in full character.

I took my hat off as I was getting annoyed with the abuse, until I found Scott in the front row at the corner of the end zone—he is the chap who paints Bills logos on either side of his mohawk. He demanded that I put my hat back on, vowing that no one would tease me while I sat next to him, and indeed no one did.

I had heard similar stories the week before about PFUFA members who have hosted away PFUFA members in the Dawg Pound or the Black Hole and the away fans have been "protected." Sergeant Colt told me that "you would expect to be hounded and booed, maybe even have something thrown at you. But that is not what I have experienced. In fact, just the opposite. I have been to Denver twice, Cincinnati, and Oakland. Each time, I was welcomed with warmth and friendship. Of course, there is always the 10 percent exception out there, but they are not the majority. I have also hosted around ten PFUFA members in Indianapolis. Same. They were greeted with a smile and a beverage. And should someone trundle up to start something, the hosting PFUFA member will always say, 'Back off, they're with me.'" At half-time, I was talking to Scott, when I realised I was on the jumbotron. I spun round in a tizzy, flailing my arms to find the camera, but I was soon off-screen. At the post-game tailgate, my Bears brethren congratulated me on the Jumbotron performance, saying that I looked menacing. Yet Jay and Karen knew why I was really flapping about, and they gave me a new nickname: Jumbotron.

Several weeks later I went to several games as a "neutral" fan at both the college and NFL levels, and plenty of people were enjoying the British food. There was no Bears game on Jay's schedule, so for his weekend off I hired a car in Chicago and drove down to Atlanta where the Bears were playing the Falcons on Sunday night. I donned my Payton jersey again, but because of what I had experienced with the Buffalo Bills fans, I had lost some of my confidence and simply held onto my hat while walking around the fan zone and the tailgate. This time, however, Bears fans were everywhere and their presence gave me the confidence to proudly wear my Staley.

I tailgated with Tom, Diane (the BirdWatchers), and their son. They kindly gave me their extra ticket, even though I was an away fan. Once inside the stadium I kept my hat on and this time everyone, including Atlanta fans and Falcons staff members, were very friendly. This took me by complete surprise, but not Diane, who is from Tennessee, and told me that southerners are famously friendly.

The year before at the Atlanta game I was stuck in the club section, where the atmosphere was rather weak. Yet for this game, just one year later, it was a total turnaround. Despite the Bears losing, the atmosphere was amazing. Maybe it's because I was right down near the front, sitting just behind the parents of Falcons duo QB Matt Ryan and left tackle Sam Baker. Their families, whom I met, all got really into the game. Or maybe because it was my team playing, plus it was a great game of football and I was watching it with great fans—the BirdWatchers.

Behind us a woman wanted a picture with me as she said, "I have always wanted to have my picture taken with an extreme fan." Despite selling my flat, leaving my job, and nearly losing my girlfriend for my football odyssey the year before, it was literally at *that* moment when I honestly felt consciously "extreme."

Months later, during the off-season, I was suffering football separation anxiety again, when I received a letter from Ram Man, the chairman of PFUFA. I ripped open the letter. Sadly I didn't make the cut from the 37 PFUFA draftees because I did not get at least 80 percent of the vote. Only 16 made it to the nomination stage. (My draft card, luckily, is good for three seasons.) Ram Man wrote, "It is now 2nd and goal from the 1-yard line. It's time to call a timeout, regroup, then score!"

Right, Steph, let's go hit some more football games and a lot more tailgates!

APPENDIX A
My Original 35-Game Schedule

The 35-game schedule was nearly perfect. I say "nearly" because there were two things that prevented such perfection. Firstly, I could not figure the schedule so that I could see every team play away at least once. The Bengals and the Cowboys eluded me. Though with my "extra" game in Pittsburgh, I did see the Bengals play away, which left me seeing the Cowboys play just once at home in Dallas.

Secondly, I saw games at every time slot apart from one: I managed to work the schedule to see games on Thursday nights, Sundays at 1 p.m., 4 p.m., and 8 p.m., and Monday nights, but the sole Saturday night football game in Dallas was not possible. If only the Chiefs and the Dolphins could have had a better season. If only . . .

Appendix A

Game No./ Week No.	Date	Home Team	Away Team	Stadium	Kickoff Time (local)	Miles to next destination
Game 1 Week 1	Thursday, September 4	New York Giants *	Washington Redskins	Giants Stadium, East Rutherford, New Jersey	7:00 p.m.	Drive to Indianapolis, Indiana–730 miles
Game 2 Week1	Sunday, September 7	Indianapolis Colts	Chicago Bears	Lucas Oil Stadium, Indianapolis, Indiana	8:15 p.m.	Drive to Green Bay, Wisconsin–400 miles
Game 3 Week 1	Monday, September 8	Green Bay Packers *	Minnesota Vikings	Lambeau Field, Green Bay, Wisconsin	7:00 p.m.	Drive to Seattle, Washington–1,950 miles Fly on Friday, September 12, from Seattle to Chicago Saturday, September 13 Participate in the Walter Payton Run for charity Fly on Sunday, September 14, from Chicago to Seattle
Game 4 Week 2	Sunday, September 14	Seattle Seahawks *	San Francisco 49ers	Qwest Field, Seattle, Washington	1:00 p.m.	Fly on Monday, September 15, from Seattle to Dallas
Game 5 Week 2	Monday, September 15	Dallas Cowboys*	Philadelphia Eagles	Texas Stadium, Irving, Texas	7:30 p.m.	Fly on Tuesday, September 16, from Dallas back to Seattle Drive from Seattle to San Francisco–800 miles

* indicates a divisional rivalry

Game No./ Week No.	Date	Home Team	Away Team	Stadium	Kickoff Time (local)	Miles to next destination
Game 6 Week 3	Sunday, September 21	San Francisco 49ers	Detroit Lions	Monster Park, San Francisco, California	1:00 p.m.	Drive to San Diego–500 miles
Game 7 Week 3	Monday, September 22	San Diego Chargers	New York Jets	Qualcomm Stadium, San Diego, California	5:30 p.m.	Drive to New York–2800 miles
Game 8 Week 4	Sunday, September 28	New York Jets	Arizona Cardinals	Giants Stadium, East Rutherford, New Jersey	1:00 p.m.	Drive to Pittsburgh–400 miles
Game 9 Week 4	Monday, September 29	Pittsburgh Steelers*	Baltimore Ravens	Heinz Field, Pittsburgh, Pennsylvania	8:30 p.m.	Drive to Denver–1,250 miles
Game 10 Week 5	Sunday, October 5	Denver Broncos	Tampa Bay Buccaneers	Invesco Field at Mile High, Denver, Colorado	3:00 p.m.	Drive to Minnesota–1,000 miles
Game 11 Week 6	Sunday, October 12	Minnesota Vikings*	Detroit Lions	Hubert H. Humphrey Metrodome, Minneapolis, Minnesota	1:00 p.m.	Drive to Cleveland–700 miles
Game 12 Week 6	Monday, October 13	Cleveland Browns	New York Giants	Cleveland Browns Stadium, Cleveland, Ohio	8:30 p.m.	Drive to Canton, Ohio (Hall of Fame)–60 miles Drive to Cincinnati–230 miles

(continues)

Appendix A (continued)

Game No./ Week No.	Date	Home Team	Away Team	Stadium	Kickoff Time (local)	Miles to next destination
Game 13 Week 7	Sunday, October 19	Cincinnati Bengals*	Pittsburgh Steelers	Paul Brown Stadium, Cincinnati, Ohio	1:00 p.m.	Foxborough, Massachusetts–1,000 miles
Game 14 Week 7	Monday, October 20	New England Patriots	Denver Broncos	Gillette Stadium, Foxborough, Massachusetts	8:30 p.m.	Drive to New York City–200 miles Fly on Thursday to London
Game 15 Week 8	Sunday, October 26	New Orleans Saints	San Diego Chargers	Wembley Arena, London	6:00 p.m.	Fly on Monday to New York City Drive to Nashville–900 miles
Game 16 Week 9	Sunday, November 2	Tennessee Titans	Green Bay Packers	LP Field, Nashville, Tennessee	12:00 p.m.	Drive to Washington, D.C.–700 miles
Game 17 Week 9	Monday, November 3	Washington Redskins	Pittsburgh Steelers	FedEx Field, Landover, Maryland	8:30 p.m.	Drive to Oakland–2,900 miles
Game 18 Week 10	Sunday, November 9	Oakland Raiders	Carolina Panthers	Network Associates Coliseum, Oakland, California	1:00 p.m.	Drive to Glendale, Arizona–750 miles
Game 19 Week 10	Monday, November 10	Arizona Cardinals*	San Francisco 49ers	University of Phoenix Stadium, Glendale, Arizona	6:30 p.m.	Drive to Atlanta–1,900 miles
Game 20 Week 11	Sunday, November 16	Atlanta Falcons	Denver Broncos	Georgia Dome, Atlanta, Georgia	1:00 p.m.	Drive to Buffalo–900 miles

Game No./ Week No.	Date	Home Team	Away Team	Stadium	Kickoff Time (local)	Miles to next destination
Game 21 Week 11	Monday, November 17	Buffalo Bills	Cleveland Browns	Ralph Wilson Stadium, Orchard Park, New York	8:30 p.m.	Drive to Miami–900 miles
Game 22 Week 12	Sunday, November 23	Miami Dolphins*	New England Patriots	Pro Player Stadium, Miami Gardens, Florida	1:00 p.m.	Drive to New Orleans–900 miles
Game 23 Week 12	Monday, November 24	New Orleans Saints	Green Bay Packers	Louisiana Super-dome, New Orleans, Louisiana	8:30 p.m.	Drive to Detroit–1,100 miles
Game 24 Week 13	Thursday, November 27	Detroit Lions	Tennessee Titans	Ford Field, Detroit, Michigan	12:30 p.m.	Drive to St. Louis–550 miles
Game 25 Week 13	Sunday, November 30	St. Louis Rams	Miami Dolphins	Edward Jones Dome, St. Louis, Missouri	1:00 p.m.	Drive to Houston–1,000 miles
Game 26 Week 13	Monday, December 1	Houston Texans*	Jacksonville Jaguars	Reliant Stadium, Houston, Texas	8:30 p.m.	Drive to Charlotte, North Carolina–1,000 miles Fly on Thursday to Toronto
Game 27 Week 14	Sunday, December 7	Buffalo Bills*	Miami Dolphins	Rogers SkyDome, Toronto, Canada	4:00 p.m.	Fly on Monday to Charlotte
Game 28 Week 14	Monday, December 8	Carolina Panthers*	Tampa Bay Buccaneers	Bank of America Stadium, Charlotte, North Carolina	8:30 p.m.	Chicago–800 miles

(continues)

Appendix A (*continued*)

Game No./ Week No.	Date	Home Team	Away Team	Stadium	Kickoff Time (local)	Miles to next destination
Game 29 Week 15	Thursday, December 11	Chicago-Bears	New Orleans Saints	Soldier Field, Chicago, Illinois	8:15 p.m.	Baltimore–700 miles
Game 30 Week 15	Sunday, December 14	Baltimore Ravens*	Pittsburgh Steelers	M & T Bank Stadium, Baltimore, Maryland	1:00 p.m.	Philadelphia–100 miles
Game 31 Week 15	Monday, December 15	Philadelphia Eagles	Cleveland Browns	Lincoln Financial Field, Philadelphia, Pennsylvania	8:30 p.m.	Jacksonville–900 miles
Game 32 Week 16	Thursday, December 18	Jacksonville Jaguars*	Indianapolis Colts	Alltel Stadium, Jacksonville, Florida	8:15 p.m.	Drive to Kansas City–1,200 miles
Game 33 Week 16	Sunday, December 21	Kansas City Chiefs	Miami Dolphins	Arrowhead Stadium, Kansas City, Missouri	1:00 p.m.	Drive to Chicago–530 miles
Game 34 Week 16	Monday, December 22	Chicago Bears*	Green Bay Packers	Soldier Field, Chicago, Illinois	8:30 p.m.	Drive to Tampa Bay–1,200 miles
Game 35 Week 17	Sunday, December 28	Tampa Bay Buccaneers	Oakland Raiders	Raymond James Stadium, Tampa, Florida	1:00 p.m.	Drive to New York City–1,200 miles Fly home to London

APPENDIX B
Stadium Ratings

E veryone has asked me about rating the stadiums, the games, and so on. In the end I buckled and in the presence of hindsight some months after the trip, I made my own system. Please bear in mind that I tried to be objective, but more often than not the figures only reflect *my* experiences on *that* day.

The System

I used the same method that Jay DiEugenio uses when he judges tailgate food. He has three criteria: presentation, originality, and taste. So I decided to use a similar three-pronged system myself. I swapped presentation with stadium, originality for stadium "loudness," and taste for "atmosphere." I would have liked to have included tailgating, fan-friendliness, number of hard-core fans, and fan support.

Volume, or loudness, is pretty easy to judge, but I was looking for consistent support—not just screaming when your team scores, although at some games there was not as much to cheer about than at others. Atmosphere included the fan zones outside the stadium, which I really like. The building rating takes into consideration how impressive the stadium was—including how easy it was for me to find my seat, and the view. I like both old and new stadiums, so I tried to remain objective here. Only those three areas count in the "total" column, but I did also include a score for the "enjoyability" of the football game on the field itself, just to show that the game does not always drive the atmosphere or vice versa. The following is in trip order.

Appendix B

Home team	Loudness (Average score: 7.6)	Atmosphere (Average score: 8.5)	Building (Average score: 7.9)	Total (Average score: 23.7)	Game Enjoyability (Average score: 8.4)	Notes
New York Giants	6	6	6.5	18.5	6	Everything was slightly below average—not a great start on the trip.
Indianapolis Colts	8	8	9	23	10 (I am biased, of course, because the Bears won at an away game).	The building would have gotten a score of 10 if they didn't have that concrete plinth above my head, and if the TVs were showing the game—instead they showed baseball. I moved downstairs, and it was much better.
Green Bay Packers	8.5	10	10	28.5	8	I loved everything, especially the modern atrium.
Seattle Seahawks	10	8	8	26	7.5	How do they get so loud?
Dallas Cowboys	8	9	6	23	10	An amazing game—one of the best ever.
San Francisco 49ers	6	6	7	19	7	I had a great view of the mountains.
San Diego Chargers	7.5	8	8	23.5	9	L.T. vs. Brett Favre—enough said.

Home team	Loudness (Average score: 7.6)	Atmosphere (Average score: 8.5)	Building (Average score: 7.9)	Total (Average score: 23.7)	Game Enjoyability (Average score: 8.4)	Notes
New York Jets	8	8.5	6.5	23	10	Favre vs. Warner—and a 56-35 final score.
Pittsburgh Steelers, Game 1	9	9.5	10	29	8.5	An amazing place to watch football, especially if you like defensive football.
Denver Broncos	7	8	8	23	7.5	A decent game, despite the low score.
Minnesota Vikings	7	7	7	21	6.5	A poor game. The Vikings were only loud after the brief moments of quality football.
Cleveland Browns	8.5	9	8.5	26	9.5	Both the crowd and players fed off each other as the Browns gave the Super Bowl champs a knockout blow.
Hoover Vikings (high school)	8	8.5	4	20.5	8	For a high school stadium it was amazing, but to include it on this list I had to compare it fairly with the NFL. They still scored higher than three NFL games.
Malone (college) at Fawcett Stadium	4	5.5	7	17	8.5	A good game, but an empty stadium, sadly.

(continues)

Appendix B (*continued*)

Home team	Loudness (Average score: 7.6)	Atmosphere (Average score: 8.5)	Building (Average score: 7.9)	Total (Average score: 23.7)	Game Enjoyability (Average score: 8.4)	Notes
Cincinnati Bengals	7	8	8	23	8	The crowd noise and atmosphere came mostly from the huge number of away Steelers fans.
New England Patriots	8	8	9	25	8	A one-sided game, but it had lots of great TDs and featured a Randy Moss Lambeau–style leap.
New Orleans Saints (Wembley Arena)	7	8.5	8.5	24	9	The neutral NFL fans may have diluted the loud noise and atmosphere initially, but it was special enough and a great game.
Tennessee Titans	7	8.5	8.5	24	9	They get an extra half point because they beat the Packers!
Washington Redskins	7.5	7.5	7	22	7	A poor game that didn't live up to the political hype.
Oakland Raiders	7.5	8	8	23.5	7.5	Perhaps if I was down in the "black hole" things might have changed for me. Plus, I am not including the amazing tailgate or the fact that I got to go on the field in the pre-game in my score.
Arizona Cardinals	8	9.5	10	27.5	9.5	Great game, great stadium, lovely fans.

Home team	Loudness (Average score: 7.6)	Atmosphere (Average score: 8.5)	Building (Average score: 7.9)	Total (Average score: 23.7)	Game Enjoyability (Average score: 8.4)	Notes
Atlanta Falcons	4	6	7	17	7.5	A pretty good game, but the fans never got behind their team. They had a great fan zone though.
Buffalo Bills	8	9	7.5	24.5	8	There were plenty of hard-core Bills fans despite the snow, and they had a great fan zone.
Pittsburgh Steelers, Game 2	8.5	9	10	27.5	8	Another good show from Steeler Nation.
Miami Dolphins	7.5	9	8	24.5	8.5	A good game and a very good fan zone from the Dolphins.
New Orleans Saints	8	8.5	8	24.5	10	A 51-29 Saints defeat against the Packers was wonderful. Plus, the seats were very comfy.
Detroit Lions	7	7.5	8.5	23	7.5	This was a one-sided game as the Lions got thrashed, but the worst team in the league had a sell out for Thanksgiving and got their one cheer when they finally scored a TD.
St. Louis Rams	5.5	6	7	18.5	7	A shadow of the greatest show on turf, but they had a great fan zone.

(continues)

Appendix B (*continued*)

Home team	Loudness (Average score: 7.6)	Atmosphere (Average score: 8.5)	Building (Average score: 7.9)	Total (Average score: 23.7)	Game Enjoyability (Average score: 8.4)	Notes
Houston Texans	9	9.5	10	28.5	8.5	My experience was amazing, which took me completely by surprise. Their fan zone is inside, but it is decent.
Buffalo Bills (Rogers Skydome)	7.5	8	7	22.5	7	Wembley beat them in the battle of the International series, as the game and atmosphere were better, but there were more "home" fans here in Toronto than Saints fans in London.
Carolina Panthers	8	9	7	24	9.5	My two-year anniversary with Steph and her first game stateside was perfect. A great MNF game.
Chicago Bears, Game 1	8.5	9.5	9	27	10	A great overtime win. I couldn't find the fan zone but did find a Bears shrine in the stadium.
Baltimore Ravens	9.5	8	7.5	25	7.5	A damn loud stadium, and I was foolish to miss the controversial ending.

Home team	Loudness (Average score: 7.6)	Atmosphere (Average score: 8.5)	Building (Average score: 7.9)	Total (Average score: 23.7)	Game Enjoyability (Average score: 8.4)	Notes
Philadelphia Eagles	8	9	8.5	25.5	8.5	A good win for the Eagles, though I did struggle to navigate around the stadium.
Jacksonville Jaguars	7	8	8	23	8	The Colts made a great comeback!
Kansas City Chiefs	6	7.5	6.5	20.5	9	I'm sorry, Chief fans—I'm sure the scores would be different if there were more fans. Staying alive became the priority despite the great game.
Chicago Bears, Game 2	8	10	9.5	27	10	Club seats kept me warm, but lacked noise. But then I gave a bonus point for being able to walk out on the concourse by the famous pillars. Oh, and we beat the Packers! This game had it all—divisional rivals, playoff possibilities, *and* an overtime win!
Tampa Bay Buccaneers	8	9.5	9.5	27	9	I didn't count the cannons towards the noise, but maybe I should have? It was amazing to watch the game from a pirate ship!

(continues)

Appendix B (*continued*)

Home team	Loudness (Average score: 7.6)	Atmosphere (Average score: 8.5)	Building (Average score: 7.9)	Total (Average score: 23.7)	Game Enjoyability (Average score: 8.4)	Notes
Capital One Bowl (Citrus Bowl Stadium)	8.5	9.5	6	24	8.5	I could see why the stadium was about to be knocked down. But that did not stop the great atmosphere and game.
Miami Dolphins, Game 2 (playoffs)	8	8.5	8	24.5	8	A hard one to judge. The loud volume and atmosphere was monstrous at the start, but fizzled as the Dolphins just kept giving the ball away. Deciding the score for the game portion of this review was tricky. Raven fans loved it, Dolphin fans hated it. I too enjoyed parts but got frustrated by the Dolphins at other times.
40 games	302	338.5	317	948	334	Totals

APPENDIX C
NFL Players featured on
Dancing with the Stars

Jerry Rice, Season 2—Runner-up
Emmitt Smith, Season 3—Champion
Jason Taylor, Season 6—Runner-up
Warren Sapp, Season 7—Runner-up
Lawrence Taylor, Season 8—7th place
Michael Irvin, Season 9—7th place
Chad Ochocinco, Season 10—4th place
Kurt Warner, Season 11—5th place
Hines Ward, Season 12—Champion
Donald Driver, Season 14—Champion

ACKNOWLEDGMENTS

Some fans love the expectation more than the match itself. Others revel in the spectacle and the sense of theatre. To many supporters, sport is about belonging to a team, a club or a community of fans. A different type is more detached, imagining himself as the manager or captain, looking down on the melee and searching for the right strategy. More common I expect, is the fan who watches a match gripped by the narrative of a novel, simply wondering what will happen next.[1]

Coming back to the U.K. having digested football from every angle, from TV production, to gambling, to stadium shapes, to fans, and more, something strange happened. I couldn't help it, but despite all my "soccer bashing" or rather "hooligan bashing," and yes, I see the irony there, I actually became a lot more interested in soccer. I had taken soccer for granted. In the past I thought because the fan culture is different that I couldn't like both, or rather that I would always defend the NFL over soccer. When in fact it took going to 37 NFL games to appreciate that I could actually enjoy both.

I was now intrigued by soccer's TV exposure, the interesting stadiums, the funny chants, and the strategy—all of which I never saw before. I was taking a fresh look at soccer, which has been on my doorstep for years, but this time with the same wide eyes as I had recently just done with the NFL. If I looked at soccer from a foreigner's point of view like I had done with the NFL, I realised that I liked it more than I thought. Looking at Ed Smith's model from the beginning of this chapter, I used to support my team but did not feel a sense of belonging with the soccer fans; hence I became frustrated and distant.

By looking at the NFL through several different lenses, it rubbed off on my soccer-watching eyes. I appreciate soccer now by being a different type of fan. Yes, I enjoy now "the spectacle and the sense of theatre," but for me, like Smith writes, I had also become more detached (in a good way) because now I was "imagining [myself] as the manager . . . looking down on the melee and searching for the right strategy," which I had mostly done for the NFL once I knew the rules, and now I was doing it for soccer and found that I could like both.

Without a doubt, the trip threw me into the wonders of the NFL—I had made new friends and have great memories of every NFL franchise—but I didn't think it would make me more intrigued about the characteristics and culture surrounding other sports too. Upon my return to the U.K. I went to soccer games, Rugby League games, and boxing matches—and long may that continue.

I have so many people to thank for the support before, during, and after my trip. I want to say a big thank you to my parents and my sister for supporting me when I was just getting into the NFL at such an early age and throughout my life. Steph stood by me while I spanked all my money away to chase my dream. Thank you—I love you all.

I would like to give a huge thanks to my editor, Elizabeth Sherburn Demers from Potomac Books, who, despite being a Lions fan, saw faith in my project when 167 other publishers, editors, and agents did not! Thanks to all the staff at Potomac Books who have been supportive and helpful.

I have to thank Channel 4 for beaming the sport in the U.K. in the first place. The 1985 Super Bowl–winning Bears team, led by Walter Payton. John Madden and his video games, my flag football and Aber teammates. My U.K.-based friends, with a special mention to the "Redbridge Massive." My international friends who were all very supportive and willing to help me in any way they could. There are so many other people to thank including bloggers, journalists, players, fans, media, NFL franchises, the NFL, and the NFLUK, who were all very helpful, and everyone else who gave me support, be it in terms of just giving me a simple high-five or giving me a place to stay.

And lastly, the mighty Tailgaters. I never asked them for food or drinks, just a few moments of their time, which sometimes magically turned into hours. I was incredibly grateful to them for inspiring me and being so welcoming.

When explaining the "tailgate" to English people, I have been asked by many if people go out freebie hunting, looking to exploit the good will of tailgaters, since you are not allowed to sell anything at a tailgate. I'm sure there are "moochers" out there, but I rarely saw them. The tailgate was like an organic street festival. Like any strong community or neighbourhood, there is a give and take, and for the most part everyone mucks in for a good time.

The Internet was obviously a big help, especially blog sites and fan-based forums, where many fans gave me some great information about their team and stadium setup.

Although the trip was very hard physically and psychologically at times, I do not regret it. Sure, with hindsight I can see where I made mistakes, and probably could have spent less money on a few things, but I am proud that I was able to go to all the games I set out to, and more. I am proud that I have a wonderful girlfriend and very supportive family and friends.

The real aim of the trip was not just to live out a dream and connect with other NFL fans, but to open up the world of American football to those possibly not fully aware of its fascinating culture and friendly community. I was genuinely overwhelmed by the generosity of everyone who helped me along my quest. It certainly concreted my faith in humanity.

I started out on my journey as an English NFL-loving boy looking for his sporting home. Thanks to the friends I have met at each franchise, I can now call any of the 32 NFL franchises my home.

My relationship with both Stephalicious and football is now stronger than ever. Like two friendly opposing NFL fans at an NFL stadium, both of these loves can sit integrated, in my heart, high-fiving all the way from the tailgate party to the Super Bowl.

While I was running on empty, getting frustrated, burning out, and on the brink of psychological turmoil, I continually turned to the great man himself, Walter Payton:

It's okay to lose, to die, but don't die without trying, without giving it your best.[2]

Go Bears!

NOTES

1. WHY?

1. Franklin Foer, *How Football Explains The World: An Unlikely Theory of Globalization* (London: Arrow Books, 2005), 13.
2. Nick Richards, *Touchdown UK: American Football Before, During, and After Britain's Golden Decade* (Central Milton Keynes: AuthorHouse, 2009), 22.
3. Ibid., 29.
4. Walter Payton, *Never Die Easy: The Autobiography of Walter Payton*, with Don Yaeger (New York: Villard, 2000), 29.
5. Ibid., 137.
6. Michael Tunison, *The Football Fan's Manifesto* (New York: It Books, 2009), 17.
7. Payton, *Never Die Easy*, 127.
8. Ibid.
9. Michael Oriard, *Brand NFL: Making and Selling America's Favorite Sport* (Chapel Hill: University of North Carolina Press, 2007), Kindle location 2726.
10. Payton, *Never Die Easy*, 122.
11. Ibid., 54.
12. Clay Travis, *Dixieland Delight: A Football Season on the Road in the Southeastern Conference* (New York: It Books, 2007) 301.
13. Richards, *Touchdown UK*, 31.
14. Rich Eisen, *Total Access: A Journey to the Center of the NFL Universe* (New York: St. Martin's Press, 2007), 26.
15. Tunison, *Football Fan's Manifesto,* 46.

2. FROM SOCCER TO RUGBY TO AMERICAN FOOTBALL: A SHORT, PERSONAL HISTORY

1. Dave Gorman, *America Unchained* (Ebury Press, 2008), 16.
2. Sal Paolantonio, *How Football Explains America* (Chicago: Triumph Books, 2008), xiv.

3. Ibid., xiv–xv.
4. Ibid., 7.
5. Ibid., 9.
6. Ibid., 7.
7. Michael MacCambridge, *America's Game: The Epic Story of How Pro Football Captured a Nation* (New York: Anchor Books, 2005), 25.
8. Keith Webster, "Webster's World," November 24, 2009, http://www.nfluk.com/features/websters-world_241109.html.
9. Ibid.
10. Ed Smith, *What Sport Tells Us About Life: Bradman's Average, Zidane's Kiss and Other Sporting Lessons* (London: Viking, 2009), 121.
11. Paolantonio, *How Football Explains America*, 77.
12. H. G. Bissinger, *Friday Night Lights: A Town, a Team, and a Dream* (London: Yellow Jersey Press, 2005), 45.
13. Oriard, *Brand NFL*, Kindle location 735.
14. Richards, *Touchdown UK*, 88.
15. Oriard, *Brand NFL*, Kindle location 556.
16. *Real sports with Bryant Gumbel*, HBO.com, January 22, 2008, http://www.hbo.com/real-sports-with-bryant-gumbel/episodes/index.html#/real-sports-with-bryant-gumbel/episodes/0/130-january-22-2008/synopsis.html.
17. Stephen Fry, *Stephen Fry in America* (New York: William Morrow, 2008), 124.
18. MacCambridge, *America's Game*, 61.
19. Paolantonio, *How Football Explains*, 36.
20. Ibid., 41.
21. Ibid., 45.
22. Eisen, *Total Access*, 144.
23. Ryan McGee, "What Goes Up . . .," *ESPN Magazine*, August 2009, 44.
24. Michael Lewis, *The Blind Side: Evolution of a Game* (New York: Norton, 2007), 109.
25. Oriard, *Brand NFL*, Kindle location 2705.
26. MacCambridge, *America's Game*, xvi.
27. Oriard, *Brand NFL*, Kindle location 3246.
28. Ibid., Kindle location 242–53.
29. Ibid., Kindle location 2169.
30. Ibid., Kindle location 459.

3. The Trip's Creation

1. Jay DiEugenio, "Steel Away to the Iron City," *Tailgater Monthly*, September/October 2008, 32, http://www.tailgatermonthly-digital.com/tailgatermonthly/20080910/?sub_id=D2ERDUKlGKdA4#pg32.

2. Eisen, *Total Access*, 47.
3. Allen St. John, *The Billion Dollar Game: Behind the Scenes of the Greatest Day in American Sport Super Bowl Sunday* (New York: Doubleday, 2009), 11.
4. Ibid., 143.
5. Oriard, *Brand NFL*, Kindle location 3012.
6. St. John, *Billion Dollar Game*, 21–22.
7. Ibid., 120.
8. Ibid., 31.
9. Arizona Cardinals game day programme, October 16, 2006, 5.
10. Richards, *Touchdown UK*, 124.
11. NFL.com, "NFL schedule chat with Howard Katz," April 20, 2010, http://chat.nfl.com/front/archived_chat/877.
12. Gorman, *America Unchained*, 22.
13. Neil Reynolds, *Pain Gang: Pro Football's Fifty Toughest Players* (Washington, DC: Potomac Books, 2007), 38.
14. Lewis, *Blind Side*, 13.
15. Ray Lampe, *The NFL Gameday Cookbook: 150 Recipes to Feed the Hungriest Fan from Preseason to the Super Bowl* (San Francisco: Chronicle Books, 2008), 7.
16. Eisen, *Total Access*, 13.
17. Keith Webster, "Webster's World," November 4, 2009, http://www.nfluk.com/features/websters-world_041109.html.
18. Eisen, *Total Access*, 144.
19. MacCambridge, *America's Game*, 24.

4. FIRST QUARTER
1. Paolantonio, *How Football Explains America*, 193.
2. Eisen, *Total Access*, 332.
3. They made a film of their trips, which had a home on miamidolphins.com.
4. Chuck Culpepper, *Up Pompey* (London: Weidenfeld and Nicolson, 2007), 112.
5. Travis, *Dixieland Delight*, 63.
6. Culpepper, *Up Pompey*, 199.
7. MacCambridge, *America's Game*, 193.
8. Warren St. John, *Rammer Jammer Yellow Hammer: A Journey into the Heart of Fan Mania* (New York: Crown, 2004), 131.
9. Eisen, *Total Access*, 7.
10. Ibid., 187.
11. Paolantonio, *How Football Explains America*, 139.
12. Culpepper, *Up Pompey*, 27.
13. Travis, *Dixieland Delight*, 332.

14. Eric Schlosser, *Fast Food Nation: What The All-American Meal is Doing to the World* (London: Penguin, 2002), 3.
15. Gorman, *America Unchained*, 19.
16. Karen DiEugenio, *I Got Your Tailgate Party Right Here!* (Yorba Linda, CA: Camp Chef, 2006), 10.
17. Travis, *Dixieland Delight*, 11.
18. Ibid.
19. Augusto Boal, *Theatre of the Oppressed* (New York: Theatre Communications Group, 1979), 155.
20. Culpepper, *Up Pompey*, 82.
21. Tunison, *Football Fan's Manifesto*, 116.
22. Dave Lamm, "Tailgating Etiquette: Don't Be the 'Moocher,'" Tailgatingideas .com, August 17, 2007, http://www.tailgatingideas.com/tailgating-etiquette.
23. "Chargers' Tolbert Plans To Dance for the Patriots," NFL.com, September 15, 2011, http://blogs.nfl.com/2011/09/15/chargers-tolbert-plans-to-dance-for -patriots/.
24. Foer, *How Football Explains the World*, 102.

5. SECOND QUARTER

1. Keith Webster, February 25, 2009, http://www.nfluk.com/features/websters world_250209.html.
2. Paolantonio, *How Football Explains America*, 178.
3. Reynolds, *Pain Gang*, 121.
4. The following year Brett Favre was playing for the Vikings. NFL column-ist Pat Kirwan said that the Metrodome was then the loudest stadium in the league. Well, maybe it is when you have Favre on your team and you are not playing the winless Lions.
5. Joe Cahn, "Tales of a Tailgater," *USA Today*, November 2005, http://find articles.com/p/articles/mi_m1272/is_2726_134/ai_n15875739/pg_2/?tag =content;col1.
6. Ibid.
7. Paolantonio, *How Football Explains America*, 149.
8. Tunison, *Football Fan's Manifesto*, 116.
9. Paolantonio, *How Football Explains America*, 165.
10. "Boom! Madden suddenly retires from broadcasting; Collinsworth takes over," NFL.com, http://www.nfl.com/news/story?id=09000d5d80fcedbe&te mplate=without-video-with-comments&confirm=true.
11. John Madden, "Talkin' Trash Tailgate Bash," Tailgater Monthly, July/August 2008, 18, http://www.tailgatermonthly-digital.com/tailgatermonthly/20080708 #pg18.

12. "History of PFUFA," http://www.pfufa.org/index.php?option=com_content&view=article&id=54&Itemid=76.
13. Ibid.
14. Ibid.
15. Payton, *Never Die Easy*, 40.
16. "Bombs Away," *Tailgater Monthly*, September/October 2008, http://www.tailgatermonthly-digital.com/tailgatermonthly/20080910#pg25; Karen DiEugenio, "British Invasion" *Tailgater Monthly*, September/October 2008, http://www.tailgatermonthly-digital.com/tailgatermonthly/20080910#pg63.
17. Travis, *Dixieland Delight*, 253.

6. HALFTIME (BYE WEEK)
1. Tunison, *Football Fan's Manifesto*, 124.
2. Smith, *What Sport Tells Us About Life*, 53.
3. Keith Webster, April 28, 2009, NFLUK.com.
4. Keith Webster, November 4, 2009, NFLUK.com.
5. In 2010 I was at a London sports bar watching the Bears. Jay Cutler was the Bears QB, who has diabetes, when I heard a British Bears fan chant in tune: "Oh Jay Cutler, you're the love of my life. Oh Jay Cutler, I'd let you shag my wife. Oh Jay Cutler, I want diabetes too."

7. THIRD QUARTER: THE ADAM AND NEAL TRIP
1. Eisen, *Total Access*, 300.
2. "Exclusive Interview with the Mayor of FedEx Field," *Tailgaiting Digest*, August 3, 2008, http://www.tailgatingideas.com/interview-mayor-of-fedex-field/.
3. Jay DiEugenio, "NFL: No Fun League," *Tailgater Monthly*, September/October 2008, 30.
4. Culpepper, *Up Pompey*, 15.
5. Keith Webster, February 25, 2009, NFLUK.com.
6. *Real Sports with Bryant Gumbel*, HBO.com.
7. Dave Lamm, "Tailgating Etiquette: Don't Be 'The Moocher,'" http://www.tailgatingideas.com/tailgating-etiquette/.
8. Eisen, *Total Access*, 297.
9. Randy Earick, "The Whole Lot," *Tailgater Monthly*, September/October 2008, 36.
10. Ibid.
11. The Quest for 31, Hans Steiniger, "Stadium Review—The Proposal," http://www.nflfootballstadiums.com/University-of-Phoenix.htm.
12. Travis, *Dixieland Delight*, 346.

13. Oriard, *Brand NFL*, Kindle location 385.
14. Tunison, *Football Fan's Manifesto*, 124.
15. "On the Menu," *Tailgater Monthly*, December 2008, http://www.tailgater monthly-digital.com/tailgatermonthly/200812#pg34.
16. "Wembley Stadium" *Tailgater Monthly*, December 2008, http://www.tailgater monthly-digital.com/tailgatermonthly/200812#pg66.
17. Tunison, *Football Fan's Manifesto*, 114.
18. Ibid.
19. Andrew Kulyk, accessed October 2008, http://wnymedia.net/thesportsroad trip/2008/12/meet-football-road-tripper-extraordinaire-adam-goldstein-from -the-uk/.

8. FOURTH QUARTER: THE ADAM AND STEPH TRIP

1. Neil Reynolds, http://www.nfluk.com/features/football-firsts_200709.html.
2. Keith Webster, May 17, 2009. NFUK.com.
3. Tim Shanley, "NFL: No Fun League," *Tailgater Monthly*, September/October 2008, 31.
4. Foer, *How Football Explains the World*, 98.
5. Zak Stambor. "Tim Shanley, Bears Tailgater," *Chicago Tribune*, December 20, 2009, http://articles.chicagotribune.com/2009-12-20/features/0912170545_1_ tailgating-pork-loin-tim-shanley.
6. "About Us: Sports Buzz," http://www.sportsbuzz.com/pages/about-us.
7. Sarah Spain, "The Newest Chicago Bears Wide Receiver?," http://www. youtube.com/watch?v=mPmh4njOrsI.
8. Tunison, *Football Fan's Manifesto*, 126.
9. Ibid., 125.
10. Eisen, *Total Access*, 46.
11. Stephanie Phillips, "Phillips is her last name," *Tailgater Monthly*, September/ October 2008, 68, http://www.tailgatermonthly-digital.com/tailgatermonthly /20080910#pg36.
12. Tunison, *Football Fan's Manifesto*, 264.
13. Foer, *How Football Explains the World*, 7–8.
14. Culpepper, *Up Pompey*, 21.
15. Tunison, *Football Fan's Manifesto*, 264.
16. Culpepper, *Up Pompey*, 21.
17. Ibid., 37.
18. Tunison, *Football Fan's Manifesto*, 258.
19. Travis, *Dixieland Delight*, 257–58.
20. Keith Webster, "Webster's World," January 12, 2010, www.nfluk.com/features /websters-world_+120110.html.

21. Ibid.

22. Tunison, *Football Fan's Manifesto*, 131.

23. Culpepper, *Up Pompey*, 18.

24. "Buccaneer Cove," http://www.buccaneers.com/rjs/cove.aspx.

9. POST SEASON

1. Travis, *Dixieland Delight*, 234.

2. Tunison, *Football Fan's Manifesto*, 125.

3. "About Us," accessed January 2009, http://www.supergateii.com/about-us/.

4. Culpepper, *Up Pompey*, 26.

5. St. John, *Billion Dollar Game*, 62.

6. St. John, *Rammer Jammer*, 265.

7. Ibid.

8. Karen DiEugenio, "Tailgate Away," *Tailgater Monthly*, January/February 2009, 10.

9. St. John, *Rammer Jammer*, 169.

10. Eisen, *Total Access*, 4.

11. Keith Webster, NFLUK.com, November 24, 2009.

10. FROM TAILGATEE TO TAILGATER AND FROM FAN TO SUPER FAN

1. St. John, *Rammer Jammer*, 76.

2. St. John, *Rammer Jammer*, 7–8.

3. "Tailgating," Joe Cahn, http://www.tailgating.com/index.php/tailgating-institute/tailgating-101.

4. Sergeant Colt, "True Colors," *Tailgater Monthly*, September/October 2008, 28.

ACKNOWLEDGMENTS

1. Smith, *What Sport Tells Us About Life*, xii.

2. Payton, *Never Die Easy*, 54.

BIBLIOGRAPHY

Arizona Cardinals Game Day programme. October 16, 2006.

Bissinger, H. G. *Friday Night Lights: A Town, a Team, and a Dream*. London: Yellow Jersey Press, 2005.

Boal, Augusto. *Theatre of the Oppressed*. New York: Theatre Communications Group, 1979.

Culpepper, Chuck. *Up Pompey*. London: Weidenfeld and Nicolson, 2007.

DiEugenio, Karen. *I Got Your Tailgate Party Right Here!* Yorba Linda, CA: Camp Chef, 2005.

Eisen, Rich. *Total Access: A Journey to the Center of the NFL Universe*. New York: St. Martin's Press, 2007.

Foer, Franklin. *How Football Explains The World: An Unlikely Theory of Globalization*. London: Arrow Books, 2005.

Fry, Stephen. *Stephen Fry In America*. New York: William Morrow, 2008.

Gorman, Dave. *America Unchained*. Ebury Press, 2008.

King, Peter. *Monday Morning Quarterback: A Fully Caffeinated Guide to Everything You Need to Know About the NFL*, New York: Sports Illustrated Books, 2010.

Lempe, Ray (Dr. BBQ). *The NFL Gameday Cookbook: 150 Recipes to Feed the Hungriest Fan from Preseason to the Super Bowl*. San Francisco: Chronicle Books, 2008.

Lewis, Michael. *The Blind Side: Evolution of a Game*. New York: Norton, 2007.

MacCambridge, Michael. *America's Game: The Epic Story of How Pro Football Captured a Nation*. New York: Anchor Books, 2005.

Oriard, Michael. *Brand NFL: Making and Selling America's Favorite Sport*. Chapel Hill: University of North Carolina Press, 2007.

Paolantonio, Sal. *How Football Explains America*. Chicago: Triumph Books, 2008.

Payton, Walter. *Never Die Easy: The Autobiography of Walter Payton*. With Don Yaeger. New York: Villard, 2000.

Richards, Nick. *Touchdown UK: American Football Before, During, and After Britain's Golden Decade*. Central Milton Keynes: AuthorHouse, 2009.

Reynolds, Neil. *Pain Gang: Pro Football's Fifty Toughest Players*. Washington, DC: Potomac Books, 2007.

Schlosser, Eric. *Fast Food Nation: What The All-American Meal is Doing to the World*. London: Penguin, 2002.

Smith, Ed. *What Sport Tells Us About Life: Bradman's Average, Zidane's Kiss and Other Sporting Lessons*. London: Viking, 2009.

St. John, Allen. *The Billion Dollar Game: Behind the Scenes of the Greatest Day in American Sport Super Bowl Sunday*. New York: Doubleday, 2009.

St. John, Warren. *Rammer Jammer Yellow Hammer: A Journey into the Heart of Fan Mania*. New York: Crown, 2004.

Travis, Clay. *Dixieland Delight: A Football Season on the Road in the Southeastern Conference*. New York: It Books, 2007.

Tunison, Michael. *The Football Fan's Manifesto*. New York: It Books, 2009.

ADDITIONAL RESOURCES

For more pictures from my trip, go to www.adamsfootballtrip.com.

For my "Tailgate Knight" road trip blog, go to www.thetailgateknight.com.

For book tour information, go to www.tailgatetoheaven.com.

If anyone fancies doing a similar trip to mine, or just wants to know more about the NFL and tailgating, here are some great websites:

www.nfl.com
www.pfufa.org
www.nfluk.com
www.profootballhof.com
www.coldhardfootballfacts.com
www.payton34.com
www.questfor31.com
www.dblcoverage.com
www.tailgatingideas.com
www.yourtailgateparty.com
www.usfootball.dk
www.canalstreetchronicles.com
www.tailgatermonthly.com

www.bleacherreport.com
www.espn.com
www.skysports.com
www.footballdiner.com
www.deadspin.com
www.kissingsuzykolber.com
www.profootballweekly.com
www.mouthpiecesports.com
www.2michelles.com
www.tailgating.com
www.si.com
www.thesportsroadtrip.com

ABOUT THE AUTHOR

Adam Goldstein was born and raised in London. Since he was five, he has been a Chicago Bears and NFL fan. He dreamed of doing nothing more than playing quarterback for his beloved team. However, Adam played and got injured in both kitted football and flag football in the United Kingdom, so he now prefers to watch, cheer, eat BBQ food, and write about American football and tailgating for various websites. Adam is also a drama tutor based in London, which he has found causes him less injuries than playing the game he loves.